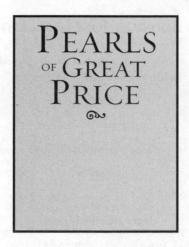

PEARLS
OF GREAT
PRICE

OTHERS BOOKS BY JONI EARECKSON TADA

How to Be a Christian in a Brave New World
(with Nigel M. de S. Cameron)

The God I Love

Diamonds in the Dust

More Precious Than Silver

Heaven

When God Weeps (with Steve Estes)

Joni (with Joe Musser)

A Step Further (with Steve Estes)

All God's Children (with Gene Newman)

Barrier-Free Friendships (with Steve Jensen)

The Life and Death Dilemma

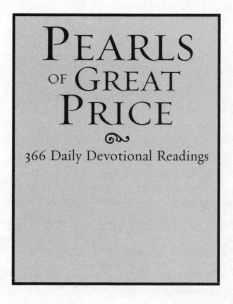

PEARLS
OF GREAT
PRICE

366 Daily Devotional Readings

Joni Eareckson Tada

ZONDERVAN®

ZONDERVAN®

Pearls of Great Price
Copyright © 2006 by Joni Eareckson Tada

Requests for information should be addressed to:
Zondervan, *Grand Rapids, Michigan 49530*

ISBN-10: 0-310-26298-4
ISBN-13: 978-0-310-26298-5

Published in association with the literary agency of Wolgemuth and Associates, Inc.

Interior design by Pamela J. L. Eicher
Illustrations by Joni Eareckson Tada
Printed in the United States of America

For my husband

KEN TADA

*who has journeyed alongside my wheelchair
these many years, giving love and support
every step of the way.*

೮ಌ

For

STEVE ESTES

*whose teaching from God's Word
has enriched my life these many years.
If anyone gleans something precious from this book,
I probably learned it first from him.*

Before You Begin ...

> Again, the kingdom of heaven is like a merchant looking
> for fine pearls. When he found one of great value, he went
> away and sold everything he had and bought it.
>
> —Matthew 13:45–46

One day my father-in-law presented me with a family heirloom, a string of genuine pearls. He told me they had been harvested in Japan, not far from where he lived much of his life. I was captivated by the milky, soft glow of each perfect pearl. My husband, Ken, draped them around my neck, and I wheeled to a mirror.

Dad Tada explained how a pearl is produced. A tiny bit of sand lodges in the flesh of an oyster and becomes an irritating intrusion. Unable to expel it, the oyster covers the particle with layer after layer of a milky secretion until the irritation has become smooth, round, and acceptable. It also, inadvertently, becomes a precious gem.

Some jewels may be made from rocks and crystals; other jewels might be mined out of the earth, but not so pearls. Unlike other gems, pearls are drawn from something that's *alive*. Pearls are produced by a life that has overcome affliction, that has overcome suffering. Little wonder they are so valuable!

Jesus is the Pearl of Great Price. He is unlike any other. Our Savior is the precious gem set apart from the rest. He lived in such a way that he overcame suffering and affliction ... Jesus overcame the working of death. He is superior because his love poured forth from a life wounded by pain. He has become our example. And he has bound us with other believers who value his priceless friendship.

I have experienced more than a few irritants in my life, not the least of which is four decades of quadriplegia. The twelve months during which I wrote *Pearls of Great Price* was a year of pain and hardship like none other. My bones are getting old, tired, thin, and frail ... and lately, it's not been easy. But God continues to give layer after layer of life-transforming grace;

he has made each irritation smooth and acceptable. All because of his help and hope. What was once an intrusion—debilitating pain—has become a precious gem. I wouldn't trade this pearlescent experience for *anything*.

Many friends have helped me collect the pearls of wisdom you will enjoy in this book. People like my dear friend and secretary, Francie Lorey, who served as my hands, sitting next to me at the computer. And friends like Larry Libby who fashioned beautiful vignettes from much of my raw material—he is a writer extraordinaire. I thank Scott Bolinder, John Sloan, and especially Bob Hudson at Zondervan. And Dr. Robert Wolgemuth and Andrew Wolgemuth at Wolgemuth & Associates. I appreciate the prayers of the staff and volunteers at the Joni and Friends International Disability Center. Most of all, I thank my dear husband, Ken, and my friend and spiritual mentor of many years, Steve Estes. His ideas and insights are reflected on virtually every page, and I owe much to him for "seeing me through" many a difficult time over these last decades.

Like my other devotional books, *Diamonds in the Dust* and *More Precious Than Silver,* each vignette on the following pages has been tested and tried through affliction. As we move forward together into this new year, it's my prayer you'll discover insights that will stir your soul and strengthen your faith ... you'll see the warm, translucent glow of Jesus Christ ... and as you do, you'll encounter the precious Pearl of Great Price in a fresh, new way.

It is worth everything—absolutely *everything*—to be his friend.

—JONI EARECKSON TADA, FALL 2006

January

An Eternity of Discovery

Eye has not seen, nor ear heard, nor have entered into the
heart of man the things which God has prepared for those
who love Him.

—1 CORINTHIANS 2:9 NKJV

It's a new year, a time for the adventure of discovery. And I love it.
I'm the first to take a side road to explore a different part of the
countryside. There is something about wheeling along a path I've never
traveled or driving down a highway for the first time that stirs my excitement and curiosity. What's around that next corner? What's over that next
hill? That's what the thrill of discovery will do for you. You feel truly *alive*,
with all senses fully engaged.

Now … just think of heaven! Think of all there will be to learn and
explore. And because God himself is eternal, the discovery will never, never
end. We will delve into unknown worlds and perhaps even second and third
universes. All of these discoveries will magnify the greatness of our Creator.

On this earth explorers and scientists will continue to make new discoveries, and for those who honor God, we will marvel again and again
at his character, his handiwork, and his creative genius. But just imagine
what God is saving for us to discover about himself and his creative might
throughout all eternity! Understanding his glory—and responding in
worship—will be a never-ending adventure.

Commit to entering this New Year fully alive with all your senses
engaged! You are about to learn and explore God's perfect plan
for you for the next 365 days. And one more thing: If you find
yourself in a drab, humdrum moment today—perhaps standing
at the gas pump—turn your thoughts toward your future home.
Do you have loved ones on the other side? Imagine the awe and
joy they are experiencing right now! Let your visions of a radiant
heaven awaken your sense of adventure for this year ahead.

*Lord of all eternity, give me a sense of adventure about the new year. Help me
to see that this year brings me closer to my Eternal Home where I will enjoy
your presence forever!*

ல

What's Up Ahead

Commit your way to the Lord; trust in him and he will do this: He will make your righteousness shine like the dawn, the justice of your cause like the noonday sun.

—PSALM 37:5–6

I sit so tall in my wheelchair that I need a van with a raised roof. The trouble is, I can't see the road. My friend Careen and I once drove from Chicago to Urbana and I didn't see a single cornfield or farmhouse for three and a half hours! She kept describing lovely country landscapes, but it only frustrated me. I wanted to *see*. I'm the sort of person who likes to know what lies ahead. If I can't see the whole road, then at least a few feet?!

We are like that spiritually. We say to God, "If you don't mind, please show me where I am going. I don't need to see the whole road, but at least a little bit." We think our faith *has* to be supported by a bit of evidence. A hint, a signpost, a whisper ... *something* to give us a clue as to what God is doing. We wrongly assume that faith is the ability to take a couple of puzzle pieces and be able to envision the entire picture. Not so. Faith that must be supported by the five senses is not genuine. Jesus said to doubting Thomas, "You have believed me because you have seen me, but *blessed are those who have not seen and yet believe.*"

Our insistence upon discerning what's up ahead is natural, but it is a hindrance to real faith. It's why God constantly encourages us to trust him in the dark (Isaiah 50:10). True faith means resting in who God is. He has charged himself with full responsibility for your eternal happiness, and he stands ready to take over the management of your life. He is wise and good. Trust him with what's ahead.

No ifs, ands, or buts, dear God. I trust you with the road ahead!

၆ာ

The Bread of Tears

You are from God, little children, and have overcome them; because greater is He who is in you than he who is in the world.

— 1 JOHN 4:4 NASB

*Y*ears ago my missionary friend Gesina was thrown into a communist prison in the Balkans because they caught her with Christian literature in the trunk of her car. Sitting in that pitch-black cell, surrounded by a sickening stench with filth and trash on the floor that she couldn't even see, she suddenly thought of a verse of Scripture. That very morning, she had read Psalm 80:5 in her quiet time: "You have fed them with the bread of tears."

The verse came back strongly to her heart in that dark moment, but—it wasn't particularly comforting in her present circumstances! Frightened and overwhelmed, she had no idea if her friends would realize what had happened to her. Just then, the jailer opened the small food door and shoved through a stick of salami and a chunk of bread. Frustrated that she couldn't even set the meat down on the dirty floor in order to tear off a piece of bread, she began to cry. Without thinking, she wiped her tears with the chunk of bread. And suddenly the verse she had read that morning flashed before her. She laughed out loud. *God knew!* He hadn't forgotten her! She could eat her tear-soaked bread knowing that he had specifically given it to her. She didn't mind being fed the bread of tears if it had come straight from his hand.

Today, Gesina has a marvelous ministry among the disabled in Albania. And to the end of her days, she will remember how—in the worst and darkest of circumstances—God came near and reminded her of his constant presence and care.

Whatever your circumstances, difficult as they may be, remember: God knows precisely where you are and how to care for you.

Oh Lord Jesus, what joy this brings! Because you live within my very spirit, nothing but nothing in life can truly defeat me.

ᘒᘒ

Be a Blessing

I will surely bless you and make your descendants as numer-
ous as the stars in the sky and as the sand on the seashore. . . .
Through your offspring all nations on earth will be blessed,
because you have obeyed me.

—GENESIS 22:17–18

ould you like to know for sure that God's favor rests upon you?
The clue is in today's verse. The angel the Lord was saying to
Abraham, "The reason I am blessing you is so that you, in turn, can pass on
the blessing to all nations. They will receive something through you, and it
is in this way you shall know my hand of favor is upon you."

Few of us are called to bless entire nations. But everyone has a circle of
family and friends. The surest evidence that the Lord's hand of blessing is
upon you is when *others get blessed through you.* When you encourage fainthearted believers, wounded friends, discouraged saints, curious pagans, or
questioning onlookers, you can be sure you have God's blessing. It happens
when you point people to the Lord through your unwavering example,
perseverance through trials, or spirit of gentleness or gratitude.

The greatest blessing God can ever bestow upon us is Jesus. Get to
know him, and the blessing that results will be something you just have
to pass on.

Is the joy of your relationship with Jesus overflowing to those
around you? Is their prayer life deepening because of time spent
with you in prayer? Has their boldness in witnessing ratcheted up
a notch because your witness rubs off on them? If so, God's hand
of blessing is upon you. To be blessed is to be pushed deeper,
higher, and further into the heart of the Savior, so that his comfort and encouragement can be passed on to others.

*I covet your favor and approval in my life, dear Lord. Keep prodding me to pass
on your joy and encouragement to others, and I will have the assurance of your
pleasure and blessing upon me.*

JANUARY 5

Heart Exam

If you have run with footmen and they have tired you out,
then how can you compete with horses? If you fall down
in a land of peace, how will you do in the thicket of the
Jordan?

—JEREMIAH 12:5 NASB

Would you like to know what you really believe about God? I'm
not talking about what you *say* you believe, or what you *ought*
to believe, but what you truly do believe. Would you like to see the truth
about you that God sees?

Well, you can. You can actually know what's way down deep in your
heart. And here is how: The next time you suffer, watch how you react.
Watch what happens in your head and heart. Take an attitude check.
Because nothing reveals the stuff of which your Christian beliefs are made
than tough times. Maybe that's why the Bible says, "Rejoice in suffering"
and "Welcome trials as friends." Maybe it's because then we can know
what we're really made of.

It's what happened to the Israelites when they were in the desert. It
says in Deuteronomy chapter 8 that God caused the tough times to test
them … to see what was in their hearts. Well, the fact is, God already
knows what's in your heart. He just wants *you* to know what's in your
heart. You may be facing some keen disappointments today: loneliness,
a bad medical report, financial worries, chronic pain, or an important
relationship on the rocks. It's *hard*. But it's also strangely helpful. Because
when you find out who you are and what you really believe, you're facing
the truth. And remember, the truth always sets you free.

What have your recent trials or setbacks revealed to you about
your faith and trust in the Father? That insight wasn't meant to
crush or discourage you. It's an encouragement to set aside distractions and seek him with fresh urgency.

*Dear Lord, I'm so far from where I want to be in my walk of faith. Draw me
closer to your heart this day, and help me to release my anxieties and fears into
your loving hands.*

෨

God Means *It*

> You intended to harm me, but God intended it for good
> to accomplish what is now being done, the saving of many
> lives.
>
> —GENESIS 50:20

I draw a lot of inspiration from the story of Joseph. Although he was never paralyzed, a lot of things happened to him that could be construed as accidents. There were plenty of unfortunate mishaps in Joseph's life, like being tossed by his envious brothers into a pit and left to die. But later on — after more mishaps — Joseph told his brothers, "You intended to harm me, but God intended it for good so that others might be saved."

I like that word *intended*. He is a God of intention — he has a purpose, a target, a goal, and a plan. God was a giant step ahead of Joseph's brothers, aborting their evil intentions to suit his own purposes. Joseph's problems did not catch God off guard, presenting him with situations he wished would never have happened. From the beginning, God calculated for Joseph to experience all these things. Why? *For the salvation of others.*

God is not a sweep-up boy who follows you with a dustpan and brush, second-guessing how everything will fit into a divine pattern for good. He does not put on a hazmat suit so that an evil situation doesn't contaminate his holy reputation.

Think of disappointing or bad things that have happened to you. God's hands stay on the wheel of your life from start to finish so that everything follows his intention for your life. This means your trials have more meaning — *much* more — than you realize. Your problems have more purpose than you can imagine. Not because God merely used bad things, but because God intended them so that *others* might be brought to Jesus through your example.

Lord God, I praise you that your intentions in my life are always good. Every "accident" happens so that somehow, someway, others might be introduced to the Savior through me.

A Right Resolution

Therefore we do not lose heart. Though outwardly we are wasting away, yet inwardly we are being renewed day by day.

—2 CORINTHIANS 4:16

My first week of New Year's resolutions is behind me. Truth is I am *not* big on making them (it's probably because I never keep them). Give up desserts for a year? I blow that at the first sight of a chocolate éclair. A few years ago I made a resolution to answer all my mail within a week of receiving it—I'm still catching up on November's letters. The list goes on: do not bite nails ... give up sugar ... quit being a slave to email ... put smaller portions on your plate ... turn off the TV ... organize your ATM receipts.

There is, however, one resolution worth considering. Second Corinthians 4:16 states that the inner man—your inner being, the new creation—must be renewed "day by day." It's a necessity. The inner man has to be daily nourished, whether it's January seventh, eighth, ninth, February, March, summer, or fall. Too often we feed our inner being only on Sunday mornings or when we hear a good sermon or during a monthly Christian luncheon or a seasonal Bible retreat. Many of us allow the year to wear us down because we ignore this simple fact— our fellowship with God must be renewed day by day. Our inner being metabolizes quickly and just one day of neglect will bring on spiritual malnutrition.

I pray "that he would grant you, according to the riches of his glory, to be strengthened with might by his Spirit in the inner man" (Ephesians 3:16 KJV). Covenant with God today to invite his Spirit to replenish you as you spend time in his Word and in prayer. It's a must. It's one resolution you can't afford not to keep. It'll make this year *happy*.

Lord Jesus, show me fresh insights every day in your Word. Reveal your heart to me in prayer ... and in so doing, renew my inner being, day by day.

ରେ

JANUARY 8
Advancing the Gospel

Now I want you to know, brothers, that what has happened to me has really served to advance the gospel. As a result, it has become clear throughout the whole palace guard and to everyone else that I am in chains for Christ. Because of my chains, most of the brothers in the Lord have been encouraged to speak the word of God more courageously and fearlessly.

—PHILIPPIANS 1:12–14

My wheelchair is the cause of many crazy circumstances, as well as conversations. Especially in elevators. The other week a man standing next to me remarked, "Now what's a nice looking girl like you doing in that thing?" I looked up in surprise and replied, "Well, sir, I'm serving the Lord in this thing." I went on to describe how we were giving wheelchairs and Bibles to disabled people around the world.

After we parted company, I thought of today's verse. What has happened to me really *has* served to advance the good news. I may not be "in chains for Christ" like Paul, but I am in this wheelchair for Christ. My quadriplegia isn't a hindrance or a barrier; rather, like Paul's prison, my circumstances have created new and unusual opportunities for the gospel. The jailer might never have heard about Jesus had it not been for Paul's imprisonment; that man in the elevator might never have heard about him either, had it not been for this wheelchair kick-starting an unusual conversation.

Your problems and difficult life circumstances, your health challenges, struggling marriage, or financial problems—your prison, your suffering—is not a hindrance to the gospel. God has allowed these hardships in order to create exceptional occasions to talk about the power and the reality of the Lord in your life. How have your hardships given you an unusual platform from which to share the gospel?

Lord God, I give you the "chains" in my life that seem so limiting. Help me to understand that my circumstances do not limit the power of your gospel in my life.

January 9

The Prodigal's Brother

"My son," the father said, "you are always with me, and everything I have is yours."

—Luke 15:31

Read the story of the prodigal son, and you get the idea that hardship never seemed to touch the life of the older brother. After the prodigal headed for "Hollywood," the older son kept faithfully managing the father's farm and paying the bills. He kept his nose clean and never suffered consequences of disobedience. Then one day, when his younger brother showed up, the father went crazy with excitement. Steaks on the barbecue. Crepe paper strung on the tent posts. "Welcome home" banners over the doorway. It wasn't the cost of confetti and fatted calves that irked the older brother; it was the gushing favor his father showered on his sibling.

Just when the older brother thought he was missing out, he heard these words of tender reassurance: "My son," the father said, "you are always with me and *everything* I have is yours." The prodigal son only had a portion of the inheritance. The older son possessed everything. He simply forgot that.

> This is an important lesson for those whose lives have not been touched or scarred by deep suffering. Christians who do not regularly taste pain and hardship must live more circumspectly and carefully. Without suffering, one could become like the prodigal's older brother who, in his trouble-free circumstances, *forgot how much he had.* But God has blessed every believer "in the heavenly realms with every spiritual blessing in Christ" (Ephesians 1:3). God has nothing more beyond Christ to give those who suffer ... or those who do not.

Father, thank you for giving me all things in Christ. If my days are blessed with ease and comfort, help me not to forget the rich and many spiritual blessings you have bestowed upon me. Help me to desperately and urgently cleave to you, even when my circumstances are pleasant. May I never forget what I have. May I always be grateful.

Christian Exiles

> Dear friends, I urge you, as aliens and strangers in the world
> to … live such good lives among the pagans that, though
> they accuse you of doing wrong, they may see your good
> deeds and glorify God on the day he visits us.
>
> —1 PETER 2:11–12

As we move deeper into the new year, today's verse serves as a faithful guide. It seems the days are more dangerous than ever with "wars and rumors of wars" crowding the nightly news programs. It appears as though the entire world is spiraling toward Sodom for "the whole world lies in the power of the evil one" (1 John 5:19 NASB).

But as Christians, we should not smirk at the misery or the merrymaking of our immoral culture. This is no time for smug self-righteousness. This is no time to get cranky that our country has been hijacked by the "radical left." This is a season, perhaps like none other, to truly *influence* the world, to showcase the love of Christ through ministries of mercy. Others may whine about the triumphs of evil, but not followers of Jesus Christ. We know better. We know that ultimately good will triumph. So we showcase what that will look like by rolling up our sleeves and feeding the poor, telling about Jesus, helping the elderly and disabled, bridging racial distances, and raising the bar of common civility. "For we are … created in Christ Jesus *to do good works*, which God prepared in advance for us to do" (Ephesians 2:10, italics mine).

Dr. John Piper has said, "The greatness of Christian exiles is not success, but service. Whether we win or lose, we witness to the way of truth, beauty and joy. We don't own culture, and we don't rule it. We serve it with joy and mercy, for the good of man and the glory of Jesus Christ."[1]

Take a quick attitude check. If you find you are pessimistic about our culture, then commit today to serve it in practical ways that showcase the love of Christ.

Lord, make me an instrument of your peace today in my community.

೧೨

Jon Campbell ... Servant

This is the one I esteem: he who is humble and contrite in
spirit, and trembles at my word.

—ISAIAH 66:2

A good friend of mine went home to be with Jesus this year. His name was Jon Campbell, and he was quite a servant. Whenever we were together, Jon would somehow, someway hunt down the keys to my van and take it to the car wash. I tried to hide my keys several times, but to no avail. An hour or so later, I'd look out the window and there he'd be wiping the hubcaps. I never kept my van clean, but he sure did.

You may not think Jon's service was all that unusual. But up until he went to heaven, Jon served as president of one of the most prominent media organizations in the United States. He served on the board of trustees of colleges, and he helped lead a prestigious national association with thousands of members. Jon was a busy man with many ministry priorities, and cleaning my van should not have been one of them. But it was.

That's because Jon was not only a servant, but a humble one. He delighted in finding lowly, menial tasks with which most people never bothered. He enjoyed doing things quietly and discreetly, and he never drew attention to himself. Jon was truly "humble and contrite in spirit." All of us who knew him are absolutely certain it's because he trembled at God's Word.

Cultivate a spirit of humility today by doing a simple act of service and doing it anonymously. Folding towels for your roommate ... cutting roses for the desk of a new employee ... baking cookies for your coworkers ... taking out trashcans for an elderly neighbor ... scholarshiping a disabled kid to camp ... giving a gift certificate to a working single mom ... washing a car for a friend.

Lord Jesus, may I follow your example of humble service today. Give me the resolve to delight in doing things quietly without drawing attention to myself.

White-Water Rafting

I saw the glory of the God of Israel coming from the east.
His voice was like the roar of rushing waters, and the land
was radiant with his glory.

—EZEKIEL 43:2

His voice was like the sound of rushing waters.

—REVELATION 1:15

When I got out of the hospital, my Eagle Scout cousin, Eddie, took me canoeing down the Gunpowder River in Maryland—he wedged a foldable beach chair in the front of his canoe and sat me in it. At first, I was frightened when we hit white water. Our canoe slapped up and down in the river, and I yelled, "Is everything under control back there?" Eddie called out, "No problem." That's all I needed to know. I was still scared, yet relaxed. Frightened, yet thrilled. And I had the ride of my life.

Embracing God is something like rafting through white water. David Swartz wrote, "God resonates throughout his being with a fiery love. All those who long to embrace God should expect boulders and white water. Sometimes God is better found in turbulence than in security; calm may be a stagnant backwater for the faithless. Others may hold back, stick a toe in the water, or splash around to test the temperature. But let us plunge into God's love and be swept away in life abundant and eternal."[2]

My cousin Eddie told me that no one ever really beats white water. You learn to respect it and move with it. Under a deep roar lies wild power that nothing can tame, and it graciously rewards those who esteem it. There is something about God that's a little like rafting through white water. There are times we are—and should be—scared; yet because we rest in his control, we can feel safe. How would you describe your relationship with God? Safe and predictable? Watch out! You could be in for the ride of your life this year!

Lord, I cling to you in the tumult of my life. Take me over the rough waters and land me safely on the other side.

Silence

Let all the earth be silent before him,

—HABAKKUK 2:20

he Sierra Mountains of California rise abruptly from the flat floor of the Mojave Desert. It's a place of dramatic vistas, and I love traveling there this time of year. Right now the Sierras are covered in snow. And so is the desert, which stretches all the way to the eastern horizon. It's one long, high, wide, breathtaking panorama of endless white.

It's an infinite, colorless world; it's also a quiet world. Not a stirring in the air, not the sound of a car in the distance, not the trickling of a brook or the rush of a river. You can hear—no, *feel*—the quiet. It's heavy and profound. On this crisp January day, the Sierras, and the desert lying at its feet, are a perfect illustration of Habakkuk 2:20. The awesome display of God's creative power seems much more powerful when it is silent in its splendor.

Charles Wesley wrote,

> *Let all mortal flesh keep silence,*
> *And with fear and trembling stand;*
> *Ponder nothing earthly minded,*
> *For with blessing in His hand,*
> *Christ our God to earth descendeth,*
> *Our full homage to demand.*[3]

Find time today to get outside, even if you have to wrap up warmly. You may not be near a desert or the mountains, but locate a place of quiet, a scene of icicle silence. A park covered in snow. A bird feeder all frosty. A tree wearing icy diamonds in the sunlight. A distant woods across a field. Or perhaps watch the cool, pink winter sunset from your back porch. Take in the beauty around you ... then join in with the landscape and be still before God in wordless worship.

Lord of creation, I want to learn from the motionless, stark landscape of winter. Help me not to rush into your presence today, but praise you with a quiet heart rather than in a tumble of words. May I find long moments to be silent before you.

The Bible Trunk

> But his delight is in the law of the Lord, and on his law
> he meditates day and night. He is like a tree planted by
> streams of water, which yields its fruit in season and whose
> leaf does not wither. Whatever he does prospers.
>
> —PSALM 1:2–3

*T*he Ten Commandments have been hand carried out of courtrooms, and in some places, school children cannot pledge allegiance to "one nation under God." Even Christian pastors cannot pray in the name of Jesus at public events. I know this breaks your heart as it does mine. Especially when we consider the Bible is the source of western culture.

Dr. Vishal Mangalwadi of L'Abri Fellowship describes how the Bible is like a trunk on a large tree. Its branch of truth has given rise to liberty, education, and science. The Bible's branch of law has sprouted smaller branches of justice, democracy, rights, and equality. Grace has brought forth the blessings of family, community, righteousness, and forgiveness. Wisdom has sprouted health, peace, technology, and prosperity. Finally, the branch of faith from the Bible has resulted in character, morality, sacrifice, and heroism. These characteristics of western civilization all find their root in the Word of God. To debunk the Bible in western culture is to push the self-destruct button![4]

For almost a century the American church has reacted to the secular agenda without significant advancements. Rather than knee-jerk responses to secularism, we must now mount a positive effort that reintroduces the Bible into western culture. Pray for Dr. Vishal Mangalwadi of *The Book of the Millennium* Project—as well as Dr. Ravi Zacharias, his fellow journeyman, as they labor in the media, the corporate world, and in universities to cast the vision of the unique importance and unmatched value of the Bible to *all* culture.

Lord God, I pray for great Christian philosophers who are working hard to show the world the power of God's Word to shape nations and cultures. May the nations of the world cleave to the Bible as the source for truth, law, grace, wisdom, and faith.

January 15

A Borrowed Smile

For You have been my help, and in the shadow of Your
wings I sing for joy.

— Psalm 63:7 NASB

In a crowded ladies restroom during a break at a Christian conference, a well-dressed woman putting on lipstick turned to me and said, "Oh Joni, you always look so together, so happy in your wheelchair. I wish I had your joy! How *do* you do it?" Several around her nodded.

"I *don't* do it," I said. "In fact, may I tell you honestly how I woke up this morning?" Several women leaned against the counter to listen. "This is an average day. After Ken leaves for work at six, I'm alone until I hear the front door open at seven. It's a friend coming to get me up. While she makes coffee, I usually pray, 'Lord, my friend is about to give me a bath, get me dressed, sit me up in my chair, brush my hair and teeth, and send me out the door. I don't have the strength to face this routine one more time. I have no resources. I don't have a smile for the day, but you do. May I borrow yours? I urgently need you, God.'

"So when my friend walks into the bedroom, I turn my head on my pillow and give her a smile sent straight from heaven. It's not mine, it's God's. Whatever joy you see today" — I gestured at my paralyzed legs — "was hard won this morning."

I have learned, as I hope those women learn, that the weaker we are, the harder we must lean on God. And the harder we lean on him, the stronger we discover him to be.

Where do you feel weak today? When you borrow from God the strength, courage, and joy you don't have, people can't help but notice. Just make sure they know where it came from!

Lord, be my strength today — not only in the areas where I know I am weak but also in the areas where I think I am strong. And may all the credit, all the glory be yours.

ᘓᓂ

God's Longings

Yet the Lord longs to be gracious to you; he rises to show you compassion.

—ISAIAH 30:18

I have longed for many things over the years. When I was a child, I longed for my daddy's approval and praise. In high school I longed for a date on Friday night, good grades, and graduation day with a college acceptance letter. After my accident, I longed to be on my feet. My longings nowadays are often pretty mundane, such as hankering for a slice of something sweet and chocolaty after dinner.

Today's verse tells us what God longs for: "The Lord longs to be *gracious to you.*" The word *longing* is only used this way twice in Scripture—the other time is when Jesus *longed* to gather the people of Jerusalem under his wings. Notice something about God's longings? They are focused not on things but on people. His yearnings are never directed inward or self-focused; they are outward. Never does he express a longing to benefit himself. His heart's desire is to benefit his people that they might glorify him.

Oh, how different my yearnings are from God's! Too often my desires are about what *I* want rather than what I desire to see happen in others. How often do I actually yearn for God to be glorified and his kingdom advanced?

The journey of the Christian is to strive to be more and more like God. Take a giant step in that direction today by asking the Lord to cleanse and refine your longings. A good place to begin is with James 4:8 (KJV) where it says, "Draw nigh to God, and he will draw nigh to you. Cleanse your hands, ye sinners; and purify your hearts, ye double minded."

Purify my heart, O God, and place within me a passionate longing to know you better and to look out for the interests of others before my own. I long for you to be glorified in my life. I desire for your gospel to go forth into the world. I long for your soon return!

JANUARY 17

Growing Churches God's Way

God has ... given greater honor to the parts [of the body]
that lacked it, so that there should be no division in the
body. If one part suffers, every part suffers with it.
— 1 CORINTHIANS 12:24–26

*T*picked up the sports page in a newspaper last week and was intrigued by a comment from a world-champion boxer: "People listen to winners ... so I'm going to keep winning!" I put the paper down and sighed. The boxer is right.

Society idolizes the power and prestige of a winner. But God's different. He loves losers. His divine favor rests upon people who die to self, defer to others, serve in humility, and sacrifice comfort — all for the glory of God. This rubs against human nature. We hate losing.

This intoxication with strength has even dulled the church. We're bent on building bigger, better, and more beautiful churches. We even gravitate to churches that are "winning," whether it's an on-the-go youth group or a burgeoning building campaign. If we were God, most of us would "grow a church" by picking the smartest people to be on our team. Our strategic planning sessions would include Madison Avenue types. We'd have our best public relations people doing focus groups. Weak people need not apply. Our gospel team would be smooth in speech and skilled in technique. We would accept only the cream of the crop.

Thank God we're not calling the shots. He is. And although there are aspects of "winning" that are good, God builds churches a different way. Jesus says, "go out into the streets and alleys ... find [the weak] ... make them come in ... so that my Father's house may be full" (Luke 14). God wants his house filled with inadequate and weak people. That way, *everyone* focuses on the strength of the Lord rather than the skill and wisdom of man.

Lord Jesus, cultivate in me a Bible-blessed spirit of losing. And help me today to reach out to the weakest people I can find.

༄

For the Love of Football

Now that you have purified yourselves by obeying the truth so that you have sincere love for your brothers, love one another deeply, from the heart.

—1 PETER 1:22

My husband, Ken, loves this time of year. It's almost time for the Super Bowl. Ken loves football—he has played and coached it, he appreciates the physical demands it makes on the body, he loves the tackles, plays, strategy, *everything*. He doesn't even care who is playing. On the other hand, I'm a football snob. If it isn't "my" team on the field, I'd just as soon watch paint dry. The difference between Ken and me? He's not so selective—Ken delights in the game, even one between two last-place teams. But me? If it isn't a team I can relate to, then I don't care to be involved.

Ken loves the game because it's, well . . . football. Wouldn't it be wonderful if we could love the church because . . . it's the church, the bride of Jesus, his body?! Most of us, though, are far too selective. We prefer a church we can relate to: a group of other Christians we like and can identify with.

God calls us to love his people because they are, well . . . his people. And we are to love our brothers and sisters deeply, as from the heart. True, there will be people in the body of Christ with whom you can identify better than most. But the church that God calls us to honor and cherish is bigger than your denomination or mine. We can't be denominational snobs. The same Holy Spirit who lives in me also lives in certain Christians I'm not prone to cheer for or fellowship with. This year, widen your circle of Christian fellowship to include brothers and sisters in other denominations.

Lord Jesus, I confess that I do not love my Christian brothers and sisters with a sincere affection and deeply from the heart. Help me to fervently love all those who claim you as Savior.

JANUARY 19

The Littlest Things

> That night the king could not sleep; so he ordered the book
> of the chronicles, the record of his reign, to be brought in
> and read to him.
>
> —ESTHER 6:1

One night King Xerxes, the emperor of Persia, can't get to sleep—even with servants to fan away the heat, musicians to serenade him, a harem full of companions, and endless wine to drink himself into oblivion. Who knows why he tosses and turns on his pillow? But instead of calling for the fanners, musicians, wine stewards, and concubines, he calls for someone to read him the chronicles of his reign (guaranteed to make anyone nod off).

As the reader drones on, an obscure passage gets Xerxes thinking (read about it in chapter 6 of Esther). What he learns that night in the pages of those chronicles precisely prepares Xerxes for an empire-altering request that his wife, Queen Esther, will make of him the next day. The little-known passage tips his mental scales—he will grant the request. And his granting it will end up saving the Jewish race from annihilation. A great people will be spared. And centuries later, this people will produce a young boy who will grow up to die for the sins of the world. All because an emperor could not sleep.

Your life is no exception to God's delight in arranging coincidences. God uses the most innocuous, everyday, bland circumstances to engineer the most earth-shattering and significant moments in your life. How he does it is one of the great mysteries. But he does it. Totally natural. But mind-bogglingly complicated.

Father God, thank you for the story of Queen Esther and how you used a minor thing to circumvent a major holocaust. It all resulted in the preservation of your people, as well as the birth of Jesus. I praise you for the small things you arrange in my life ... and how they are a part of your marvelous plan for my good!

Thought Patrol

> When anyone hears the message about the kingdom and does not understand it, the evil one comes and snatches away what was sown in his heart.
>
> —MATTHEW 13:19

he devil can invade our mental privacy?! The very thought sends shivers. And it should. Satan tries to tap into our brains all the time. He's a regular soul-hacker—like the techno-geeks on their computers at home, breaking security codes and logging onto sensitive government systems. Scripture calls him "the spirit who is now at work in those who are disobedient," and today's verse describes his access to the human soul.

People joke about this and say, "The devil made me do it." They laugh because they don't think he exists. And if there is a devil, he's their ex-spouse. Meanwhile their minds are as soaked with his suggestions as a pickle in vinegar. They don't see him—he's a spirit. They don't hear him—he has tiptoed in sock-footed. If they do catch some small noise at their mind's door, they assume it's just opportunity knocking.

But Christians know better; they understand the power of their invisible tempter. We are aware, as well as wary. The wonderful thing for the Christian is, 1 John 4:4 says, "The one who is in you is greater than the one who is in the world." His Spirit helps you stand guard over your mind with the power of God's Word.

Put a barbwire fence around your thinking. Make your will "stand guard" over your mind with the ammunition of God's Word. Learn to recognize the devil's tactics so that you can shoot down every suggestion—every temptation—of the Enemy today. And take courage knowing that if Satan can be stealthy for evil's sake, God is *much* more at work for goodness' sake.

Spirit of Christ, please help me stand guard over my thoughts today. Help me resist any suggestion from the devil that I offend you, hurt my brother, or tarnish my own testimony through sin or selfishness.

෨

Don't Let Me Doe

But now, this is what the Lord says ..., "Fear not, for I have redeemed you; I have summoned you by name; you are mine. When you pass through the waters, I will be with you; and when you pass through the rivers, they will not sweep over you.... For I am the Lord, your God, the Holy One of Israel, your Savior."

—Isaiah 43:1–3

Abbey Muzio is a three-year-old little girl with blonde hair and the biggest smile ever. Although a fun-loving child, she has a fear of water. If she dares stick her foot in a pool, she only does so wearing water wings, clutching her mommy's neck and whimpering, "You won't let me doe? Please, don't let me doe." Though her mother struggles to breathe in Abbey's vise grip, she assures, "Sweetie, I won't let you go."

Life situations that have a potential for danger or disappointment can easily foster fear in our hearts. We are so like Abbey, attempting to grab God in an armlock and insisting, "Don't let me doe!" Rather than fear, we need to have faith; Isaiah 43 is a beautiful picture of God's provision in the midst of trouble. Jesus himself said in John 10:28, "I give them eternal life, and they shall never perish; no one can snatch them out of my hand." God has a vise grip on us ... he has the eternal security of our souls in an armlock. He will never, *ever* let you go!

Abbey's mother told me, "I wish Abbey would simply relax and trust me. I don't want her to be afraid; I want her to have fun in the water. She needs to realize that my hold on her is more secure than any grip she has on me." It's a lesson about God we all need to learn.

Lord Jesus, thank you for the promises in your Word, which chase away fears that overwhelm. I trust you with scary life situations. Thank you for holding me tight.

Divine Singing

When they had sung a hymn, they went out to the Mount
of Olives.

—MATTHEW 26:30

hether I'm wheeling through the office, driving down the
freeway, or puttering in the backyard, I *love* to sing. My heart
wants to sing whenever I'm enjoying the routines of life. But have you ever
wondered if Jesus sang? It's easy to picture him humming a melody as he
walked up the road from Jericho to Jerusalem. We know they sang in the
synagogues. During the holy feast days, Jesus' family probably sang. There
must have been *many* times that Jesus' heart filled with joy and he let loose
with a song. So ... where in the Bible does it say that he sang?

The only place it records such a time is in Matthew 26:30. The scene
for the song is not on a sunny hillside ... it's not as he sailed with his
disciples in the boat ... and it's not as he walked along the beach with his
friends. It was in the upper room the night that Jesus was betrayed. After
he broke the bread and offered wine, they sang a hymn and then went out
to the Mount of Olives. Of all the times and places, the Lord Jesus chose
to have us remember him singing as he was led off to his death.

This speaks to me in my wheelchair. It shows me how to follow the
Lord in song when my heart is heavy, when I'm facing disappointment, or
when my back aches. As we follow his steps up to the Mount of Olives,
into the garden of Gethsemane, and down the road to Calvary, we take up
our cross and *sing*.

Our natural inclination is not to sing when we are sad or hurting.
Yet think of the apostle Paul who sang, despite his chains in jail
(Acts 16:25). No matter if your emotions are up or down, follow
the Lord's lead today and ask God to put a song in your heart.

*In my heart there rings a melody of love, dear Jesus. You are my song today and
every day. Please keep tuning my heart to sing your praises.*

☙

Religious Spirits

In the synagogue there was a man possessed by a demon, an evil spirit. He cried out at the top of his voice, "Ha! What do you want with us, Jesus of Nazareth? Have you come to destroy us? I know who you are—the Holy One of God!" "Be quiet!" Jesus said sternly.

—LUKE 4:33–35

Once when I visited an old, large cathedral, a choir was practicing at the front of the sanctuary. Beautiful music echoed everywhere. Even though I was in the back near the narthex, I could tell they were singing a hymn in Latin. I recognized the tune as one of my favorite hymns, "All Creatures of Our God and King." There weren't many people around, so I began singing along. A church worker approached and in no uncertain terms told me I was being a disturbance. I looked around at the high arches and lovely stained-glass windows, the tables of candles and statues—wasn't this a place to praise God?

I'm not about to pass judgment on any cleric at that cathedral. But I have to admit, the church felt "religious," a grand display of formality and ritualism. I was reminded of today's verse. Evil spirits—that is, religious spirits—feel very at home in some churches and synagogues. They feel very comfortable in church buildings, or even congregations, where the focus is on rituals and traditions, rather than the vibrant life of the Spirit of Christ.

That particular church building was not the only place in which I've sung impromptu praises to God. There were great cathedrals in Europe, as well as in Notre Dame (the cornerstone for this cathedral was laid in 1163). Should you ever visit one of these church buildings in cities around the world, softly fill it with prayers and hymns. Let's remind those old arched ceilings that they were built for the glory of God.

Father God, thank you that your Word has been preached from ancient pulpits for over two thousand years. I pray against every religious spirit that wars against the Spirit of life.

ॐ

JANUARY 24

Questionable Motives

Jacob made a vow, saying, "If God will be with me ...
and will give me food to eat and clothes to wear so that
I return safely to my father's house, then the Lord will be
my God."

—GENESIS 28:20–21

When I was a little girl, I knew that whenever my older teenaged sister, Linda, would sidle up to my daddy and ask him if he "wanted or needed anything," she was just buttering him up to ask for extra cash beyond her allowance. I was just a little kid, but I knew what sweet talk sounded like. And what drove me up the wall was that it worked. I knew that Daddy knew she didn't have the best of motives.

When I recall family incidents like that, I can't help but cringe. It always makes me feel like the older brother in the story of the prodigal son. Let's face it, that wild-living younger brother didn't have the best of motives when he came crawling back home to Dad. He was hungry! And he needed a job. He really only wanted what his father could give him. But did the father care? When he saw his lost son coming at a distance, he didn't pause even for a moment to measure the reasons or motives behind his boy's homecoming. He just ran to meet him with open arms. It's a lesson for me. Sometimes I'll catch myself almost sweet-talking the Lord in prayer, as though I could dress up my petitions to make them look more respectable. Listen, God knows me and you inside out. He is not charmed by us. And the miracle is he invites us to come to him—even if for all the wrong reasons. You'll find he'll purify those motives of yours, once you are in his embrace.

How would you describe your motives for drawing close to God? As with mine, they're probably not always the best. But our Father says, "Come anyway. Come home. I'll welcome you with open arms."

O God, you know my motives. Yet you welcome my prayers and invite me into intimacy. What a gracious Father!

JANUARY 25
Choices

Choose for yourselves this day whom you will serve.... But
as for me and my household, we will serve the Lord.

—JOSHUA 24:15

After living with quadriplegia for a short time, I finally got tired
of being fed at our dinner table. But as I tried to feed myself
with paralyzed arms, I felt like giving up. I wanted my arms back! Wasn't
there an easier way than having a bent spoon inserted into the pocket on
my leather armsplint, then straining my weak shoulder muscles to scoop
food on the spoon, and finally balancing and lifting it to my mouth? It
was humiliating to have my food land more times on my lap than in my
mouth.

I could have surrendered—it would have been easy and many
wouldn't have blamed me. But I had to make a choice. Was I going to let
disappointing failures overwhelm me? I decided the awkwardness of feeding myself outweighed the fleeting satisfaction of self-pity. It pushed me to
pray, *O God, help me with this spoon!* Today I can easily feed myself. No, I
didn't recover the use of my hands, but I was able to leave self-pity behind,
as well as cultivate a little bit of humility. It meant making the hard choice
many, many times.

My growth in Christ can probably be boiled down to one word: *choose.*
Choosing the right path is hard. Often we have to keep pushing through
failures. Sometimes it seems easier just to ignore God's instructions. But
Proverbs 8:10 says, "Choose my instruction instead of silver, knowledge
rather than choice gold."

What a difference you can make for the kingdom if you will follow the lead of the Savior and "choose life, so that you and your
children may live and that you may love the Lord your God,
listen to his voice, and hold fast to him. For the Lord is your life"
(Deuteronomy 30:19–20).

*Father, every day is filled with so many choices. Touch my awareness, open
my eyes, quicken my understanding to the eternal implications of seeking your
heart and choosing your path.*

Valley of Vision

Blessed are those whose strength is in you, who have set
their hearts on pilgrimage. As they pass through the Valley
of Baca, they make it a place of springs; the autumn rains
also cover it with pools.

—PSALM 84:5–6

In the days of the conquest of Canaan, the Valley of Baca was
known as a dry, waterless place where only balsam trees could
grow. Some have called it "a place of weeping." However, when we trust
God during dry, parched times, we can turn our valley of weeping into a
refreshing "place of springs."

My favorite Puritan prayer about valleys has seen me through many a
dry place in my spiritual journey: "Lord, high and holy, meek and lowly,
Thou hast brought me to the valley of vision.... Let me learn by paradox
that the way down is the way up, that to be low is to be high, that the
broken heart is the healed heart, that the contrite spirit is the rejoicing
spirit, that the repenting soul is the victorious soul, that to have nothing
is to possess all, that to bear the cross is to wear the crown, that to give is
to receive, that the valley is the place of vision. Lord, in the daytime stars
can be seen from deepest wells, and the deeper the wells the brighter thy
stars shine; Let me find thy light in my darkness, thy life in my death, thy
joy in my sorrow, thy grace in my sin, thy riches in my poverty, thy glory
in my valley."[5]

Psalm 23:4 says, "Though I walk through the valley of the shadow
of death, I will fear no evil." We fear no harm in the valley because
death can only cast its shadow on us. Evil has no grip on us. Truly,
we find God's brightest glory in our darkest valleys.

*Lord, you are the Great Shepherd who leads me through every dark valley. I
trust you to turn my valley of weeping into a place of refreshment and encouragement.*

ഡ

JANUARY 27

Wonder

As soon as all the people saw Jesus, they were overwhelmed
with wonder and ran to greet him.

— MARK 9:15

The first time I saw the Grand Canyon, I stood in silent wonder.
When I felt the spray of Niagara Falls against my face, I did the
same. I will never forget that crystal clear night in the Sierras when the stars
looked like powdered sugar. I was breathless with wonder. Today's verse
describes wonder well — it's a powerful emotional response, which literally
overwhelms us with amazement and delight.

It's a fine line between wonder at God and worship of God. That he
would bless us with eternal pleasures when he could easily char us like
burnt toast is a *wonderful* thing. His grace and goodness make us stand
breathless. It's why Isaiah 9:6 calls him "wonderful."

Charles Spurgeon wrote, "Holy wonder will lead you to *grateful worship* and *heartfelt thanksgiving*. It will cause within you *godly watchfulness*;
you will be afraid to sin against such a love as this. Feeling the presence
of the mighty God in the gift of His dear Son, you will put off your shoes
from your feet, because the place whereon you stand is holy ground. You
will be moved at the same time to *glorious hope*. If Jesus has done such
marvelous things on your behalf, you will feel that heaven itself is not too
great for your expectation. Who can be astonished at anything, when he
has once been astonished at the manger and the cross? What is there wonderful left after one has seen the Savior?"[6]

It is the desire of the Holy Spirit to show you how full of wonder
Jesus truly is. In preparation for Sunday worship this week, ask
the Spirit to reveal fresh, new insights into the gracious character
of Christ. Ask him to overwhelm you with a sense of wonder
so that your adoration of God overflows with amazement and
delight.

Jesus, you are the Wonderful Counselor, the Prince of Peace. I love you!

Inspiring Examples

For none of us lives to himself alone and none of us dies to
himself alone.

—ROMANS 14:7

No man is an island. We are all connected. Our lives are always influencing others, whether for good or for bad. When people who
face lesser conflicts—like a bruised ankle or sow bugs in the shower—observe
someone gracefully handling *greater* conflicts, it speaks volumes. Liz Hupp
knew a godly saint like that in her church. And Liz wrote:

> *I saw the woman in the chair; she was in church again today.*
> *Someone said they've sold their house; they're going to move away.*
> *No! I cried, they cannot go; they cannot move away.*
> *I didn't get to know her; there's something I need to say:*
> *Please tell me your secret; I want to sit at your feet,*
> *I need to know how you handle the pain that is your daily meat.*
> *How do you keep on smiling when each day your health grows worse?*
> *How do you keep depending on God when you're living with a curse?*
> *Every time I see her, her smile comes from deep within.*
> *I know her fellowship with God isn't scarred by the chair she's in.*
> *She admits her health is failing; she knows she's fading away.*
> *How can she remain so calm when I'd be running away?*
> *My friend, can you tell me how you can trust the Lord?*
> *How can you stay so gentle and sweet when He seems to wield a sword?*
> *You are to me a promise that even in the midst of pain*
> *God is near and faithful if I will turn to Him again.*

Who are your role models of inspiration? Who are the godly
examples of perseverance? Who do you think of when you need
an example of the sufficiency of Christ in hardship? Pray for that
person—or persons—whom the Lord has placed around you.
These Christian men and women struggle with doubts and discouragement too.

*Lord Jesus, I pray for _____ today. Give grace and encour-
agement, divine help, comfort, and the inspiration of your precious Holy Spirit
in the life of this dear saint.*

January 29

Send Them Away?

> As evening approached, the disciples came to him and said,
> "This is a remote place, and it's already getting late. Send
> the crowds away, so they can go to the villages and buy
> themselves some food." Jesus replied, "They do not need
> to go away. You give them something to eat."
>
> —MATTHEW 14:15–16

*P*icture what happened before Jesus fed the five thousand. The hour was getting late, yet the crowd just sat there with their tummies growling. They came all the way out to the countryside to hear Jesus preach, but they didn't think to bring a bag lunch. The disciples probably thought: *Where were these people's heads when they left home this morning? Didn't they know they'd get hungry?* I can identify with the disciples: "Send them away, Lord. They got themselves into this mess. Sure, they're hungry, but it shouldn't be *our* problem. If they're hungry, it serves them right; they made their own bed, now let them lie in it—it'll teach them a lesson!"

Have you ever thought that? We reason that if people got themselves into a jam, they should get themselves out. Like the mother who has five children, and three of them are mentally handicapped because of her own addictions. Or the guy who broke his neck from driving drunk. Or the teenager who thought he knew better than his coach and ended up paralyzed. They all should have known better.

Let's learn a lesson from Jesus' response. The Bible says that when he saw these people, his heart went out to them. And you know the story from there. Jesus appealed to the disciples out of his own compassion.

Yes, the five thousand should have known better. Nevertheless, the heart of Jesus went out to the people. There are individuals in your community who "should have known better" but now are in sad straits. Jesus has compassion for them and he is appealing to you to help them. Will you?

Lord, make my heart more compassionate toward those who need my help. May I make a difference in their lives for your name's sake.

෨

Exposing Hidden Idols

All who worship images are put to shame, those who boast
in idols.

—PSALM 97:7

A verse like this makes me think of wooden figurines who
squat on shelves with fat lips, bloated stomachs, and who
hold bowls on tops of their heads. I saw one the other day when I passed by
the open door of a Vietnamese nail parlor. A little Buddha sat on an altar
behind the receptionist's desk. It was draped in flowers and surrounded by
candles and incense.

We think we are too "contemporary" to take an idol like that seriously.
But today's verse is *not* out of date. Idols put us to shame ... whenever we
feel ashamed.

Shame is what *exposes* the things you idolize. Imagine having coffee
with a new friend. As the conversation flows, you feel witty and interesting.
Your friend seems fascinated, which only makes you pleased as punch with
yourself. But then you knock your cup and spill coffee all over your white
shirt. Everyone turns their heads, and instead of laughing it off, you feel
stupid and silly. *What a jerk I am! I want to crawl into a hole.*

What idol did the feeling of shame and embarrassment expose? Pride
in appearance? Smug self-confidence in conversational skills? An inflated
idea of importance? You were hoping to come across as clever and winsome, but a little spilled coffee washed away your self-confidence, exposing a hidden idol. God has engineered our sense of shame to reveal those
things, people, or vocations we idolize. But once our idols are unearthed,
we can more easily do away with them.

The next time your cheeks turn red with shame, ask yourself,
"What idol is my embarrassment revealing?" Once it's knocked
off the shelf of your heart, toss it. Keep your heart clean of idols.
And then pray ...

*Father, forgive me for worshiping anything or anyone—especially
myself—above you. Teach me to recognize shame as your way of exposing the
idols in my life.*

෨

JANUARY 31

Overwhelmed

No temptation has seized you except what is common to man. And God is faithful; he will not let you be tempted beyond what you can bear. But when you are tempted, he will also provide a way out so that you can stand up under it.

— 1 CORINTHIANS 10:13

h, Joni, isn't it wonderful that God will never test us beyond what we can endure? That's a promise from God!"

I knew my friend Sue was looking for an affirmation, a confirmation that God would never "bend the bruised reed." As I nodded slowly, relief flooded her features. Sue had never faced the kind of mind-bending, soul-obliterating pain that now loomed on her horizon. But with the recent medical report and the looming prospect of a morphine-drip pump in her future, she was scared. *Surely the Lord won't give me more than I can bear,* she was thinking.

First Corinthians 10:13 is certainly a promise—but it isn't talking about trials. It's talking about temptation. The promise is that God will always, always give you the power to say no to sin. But when it comes to heartaches, physical problems, and disappointments—things out of your control, difficult circumstances suddenly thrust upon you—*you may very well be overwhelmed beyond what you can bear.* There is a kind of suffering that rips your world apart and leaves you bewildered and wounded. There *are* trials that overwhelm.

I drew a deep breath, showing my friend the context of the promise—and her brow furrowed. "But take heart," I told her. "It's when we are at the end of our strength ... *that's* when we fall helplessly into the everlasting arms of God. That's when God floods our hearts with sustaining grace."

You and I may indeed find ourselves overwhelmed at times—at the end of our rope and beyond. But we will never fall farther than the palm of his hand. And where he has called us, his grace will sustain us.

Gracious Redeemer, I want to trust in you fully now, so that when the waves of trials come, I will trust in you then.

February

FEBRUARY 1

When Life's Not Fair

For our light and momentary troubles are achieving for us
an eternal weight of glory that far outweighs them all.

—2 CORINTHIANS 4:17

When Vicky's husband abandoned her and her two-year-old son, she needed to find work. On one fateful day of job hunting, she was brutally attacked—and shot through the neck—by a man pretending to hire her. Later that day, lying in an emergency room, she knew she would live … but as a quadriplegic in a wheelchair for the rest of her life.

In the years that followed, Vicky's anguish and bitterness finally began to melt under her friends' prayers, warming to the Word of God and its promises. "But sometimes I wonder," she once told me, "about the fairness of it all." I explained to her that it took the most unfair act in history, the execution of Jesus, to satisfy divine justice in a world full of injustice. That event made it possible for the least deserving of all—a convicted thief on a cross next to his—to gain an eternity of undeserved happiness. One day the scales of justice will not only balance, but they will be weighted in our favor, all for our good and God's glory.

Vicky now understands that, even in her wheelchair, she is no better than that thief on the cross. By all that's "fair," she knows she should be on her way to hell and that there was nothing "fair" about Christ paying the penalty for her sins. She doesn't deserve such mercy. And neither do we.

This present life of ours is infinitely shorter than the blink of an eye compared with the eternal beauty, purpose, and joy we will experience in the Father's house. Let your thoughts linger on heaven for a while, and then give thanks to the One who made it possible—by the great injustice of dying on a cross to pay the penalty for our sins.

Lord Jesus, I praise you for enduring the humiliation, the injustice, and the unspeakable agony of your crucifixion to win an eternity of light and hope for me.

Stand Firm, Ladies

Therefore, my brothers, you whom I love and long for, my joy and crown, that is how you should stand firm in the Lord, dear friends! I plead with Euodia and I plead with Syntyche to agree with each other in the Lord. Yes, and I ask you, loyal yokefellow, help these women who have contended at my side in the cause of the gospel, along with Clement and the rest of my fellow workers, whose names are in the book of life.

—PHILIPPIANS 4:1–3

Oh, to have labored alongside Paul! To listen to his preaching, share his passion, pray beside him, and follow him high and low, always contending for the faith. In this rare celestial air of apostolic fellowship, surely the esprit de corps was strong, unswerving, and sweet. Euodia and Syntyche were in that exceptional circle of intimate Christian friends. These two women were dear companions of Paul, and they fought valiantly beside him for the cause of the gospel. They faced the same opposition and risks to their lives, the same hardships and struggles. Like Paul, they spread the gospel everywhere they went.

Somehow they lost their focus. Things degenerated between them, and these two sisters in Christ started knocking heads. News of their haranguing and berating of each other even reached the ears of Paul who was in prison. They forgot their purpose. They didn't consider how their shenanigans would wound not only those around them, but the apostle. Their disagreement terribly deflated others. Most of all, the gospel took a backseat—their dispute was more important to them!

Paul first addresses these two women with the command, "Stand firm." Recapture your passion, reclaim the vision, recall your focus! No one is above becoming disagreeable and argumentative—not even Euodia and Syntyche. Today, remember Philippians 2:14 says, "Do everything without complaining or arguing."

Thank you, Father, that you included the story of these two women in Scripture. I take it as a warning to me today. Help me to agree with others "in the Lord."

☙

Righteousness

> If you love me, you will obey what I command.... He who
> does not love me will not obey my teaching. These words
> you hear are not my own; they belong to the Father who
> sent me.
>
> —JOHN 14:15, 24

"He's a righteous man!" I once commented about a pastor friend. Immediately the group I was with gave a funny look. "Is that supposed to be a compliment?" one of them laughed. They assumed I meant he was stiff and rigid, legalistic, and not at all spiritual. In other words, self-righteous. Nothing could have been further from the truth. My pastor friend has a buoyant, happy love for the Lord Jesus; because of this, his goal in life is to pursue *righteousness*.

God expects evidence of the love we profess to have for him. Jesus tells us in Matthew 6:33, "Seek first his kingdom and his righteousness, and all these things will be given to you as well." To pursue his righteousness is to *live rightly*. It is to obey his commands. Love the Lord God with all your heart, soul, and mind ... honor your father and your mother ... look out for the interests of others ... love your enemies ... rejoice always ... do not lie ... don't grumble or complain. If our lives reflect no significant difference from our old ways, we should seriously ask, "Do I *really* know Jesus?"

We call Christians "spiritual" or "committed," but we rarely speak of believers as "righteous." We've become influenced by our culture, which hates true righteousness. Why such an aversion to the biblical word *righteousness*? John 3:19 – 20 explains, "This is the verdict: Light has come into the world, but men loved darkness instead of light because their deeds were evil." Seek first his kingdom and his righteousness—*first* means in order of priority. As you live *right* today, you will shine his light into the world's darkness.

Lord of Righteousness, I take delight in obeying your commands. Today and always, I want to live differently than the world lives. May my life be an evidence of my faith.

❧

FEBRUARY 4

Scattered Saints

> Peter ... writing to exiles scattered to the four winds. Not one is missing, not one forgotten.
>
> —1 PETER 1:1 THE MESSAGE

In the very first verse of 1 Peter, the apostle says he is writing to God's elect, strangers in the world and scattered. I've met sisters and brothers in Christ like that as I've traveled around the world. *Scattered.* They feel forgotten at times because they live so far from "the action," so removed from everything that seems to be happening. One brother I met in Peru who had traveled far from the Andes Mountains to attend one of our meetings told me that he was a nobody ... no one of real importance. My heart went out to him, but he isn't alone.

You don't have to live in the mountains to feel as he does. You could be in a small apartment in a big city. You feel like a stranger in your own community—perhaps even distanced from other believers. You're out of the flow, jobless, single, maybe divorced, and isolated. You feel like one of those "scattered" believers. If this is you, please remember the rest of those words in 1 Peter. You may be a stranger, and you may be "scattered," but you are God's elect, chosen according to the foreknowledge of God the Father, through the sanctifying work of the Spirit, for obedience to Jesus Christ. Did you get that? The entire Trinity—Father, Spirit, Son—is actively involved in your life. And *that*, my friend, puts you right in the center of the *real* action, the divine action of God's universe. No matter where you live, no matter how humble your circumstances, you are God's chosen. And you are deeply loved and treasured by your Creator.

Get in the flow, my friend. You're in the mainstream of mainstreams! Praise the Father, agree with the Spirit, and obey the Son ... and you'll never feel like an isolated stranger again.

Wonderful Savior, I don't know why you would ever choose me—let alone lay down your life to save me! I offer you this day the praise and gratitude of my heart.

A Comforting Verse

And we know that in all things God works for the good of those who love him, who have been called according to his purpose. For those God foreknew he also predestined to be conformed to the likeness of his Son.

—ROMANS 8:28–29

*I*t's a promise we've staked our lives on for years. The idea of God being in control can sound alarming, but once we settle into the promise, it begins to feel immensely comfortable. If God did not restrain evil, then headaches and hardships would come barreling at us, uncontrolled. His decrees and ordinances shape good and evil in such a way as to warn us of hell, woo us toward heaven, and fit us for life here and in the hereafter—all inspired by his love, pure and passionate.

You can't ignore love like this. You can't sit on a fence or put it off until later. The love of Romans 8 begs a daily response. God is working all things together for your good today. Will you not participate with him through your obedience? Today you may be forced to make tough decisions, as well as choices in hardship. Today you may be tempted in a new area—a part of you that you thought was safe. God is working for your good. Will you not obey him and work for his glory?

When we say yes to following God, and when we say no to worrying or fears of the future, walls collapse, sashes are thrown open, and windows in your life are raised to let in the fresh air of change and transformation. One day heaven will arrive and we will embrace each other, free of pain, and marvel how God worked it all, everything, lock, stock, and barrel, for our good. Until that day, until God drops the curtain on suffering, let's commit to work for *his* glory.

Thank you, Father, for working everything in my life into a pattern for good. I want to participate with you and work today for your glory!

৵

FEBRUARY 6

Believe the Lord

Abram believed the Lord, and he credited it to him as righteousness.

—GENESIS 15:6

*S*andy had just returned from Cuba where she served as leader on our Wheels for the World distribution of wheelchairs and Bibles. She shared some pretty amazing stories. I knew she wasn't exaggerating facts. She's not like that. When Sandy says something, I accept it as true. I believe her. Interestingly, I did not say, "I believe *in* Sandy," but "I *believe* her." There's a significant but subtle difference between the two. When I say that I believed Sandy, I was basically saying, "I trust her; her word is good. I know her and have confidence in her character . . . I believe her!"

Abram in our verse today understood the same thing. To believe someone is to have complete confidence in the very fiber of their being—it means they are utterly reliable and truthful when they say something. Abram took the Lord at his word; he had complete confidence that God was as good as his word. Conversely, if Abram had merely believed *in* God, it wouldn't have meant nearly as much. Believing in God does nothing more than qualify you to be a demon, for even the demons believe that (James 2:19).

> Many people believe in God. They believe in a Supreme Being out there—in fact, lots of pagans believe a God exists. Some even believe that the God of the Bible is real, but they still don't place their trust in him. In John chapter 1, Jesus is called "the Word." To believe Jesus is to *trust* in who he is. Do you believe in God for your needs today?

Lord and Savior, I have every confidence in your character. You are utterly reliable and truthful. Today I am going to take you at your word even if doubts or fears arise. You have the words of life, and I am happy to say, I believe the Lord!

☙

FEBRUARY 7

God's Gladness

I have told you this so that my joy may be in you and that
your joy may be complete.

—JOHN 15:11

*T*he other night at 2:00 a.m. I panicked. A bad flu on top of paralysis had my mind playing weird games. *If the Father loves me so
much, then why overload my circuits with all this hardship?!* I did a split
screen in my head; since I couldn't emotionally go to the Father with my
panicky feelings, I found myself running to the Son. I realize the Father
and the Son are one, but at 2:00 a.m., with the flu, paralysis, and a pounding headache, I seemed to identify best with Jesus who also suffered.

The next morning after I felt better, I re-anchored my soul deep into
the biblical truth that, yes, the Father *is* full of love. He is joy and happiness spilling over. He swims in elation. And because the Son is the exact
representation of the Father, both persons of the Trinity are driven to share
that joy with us (Hebrews 1:3). But God is nobody's water boy. As the solemn king of the universe, he shares his gladness on his own terms. Those
terms call for us to suffer, in some measure, as did his beloved Son while
on earth.

Should we never taste pain when our Savior had to swallow it
whole? Jesus is the Man of Sorrows acquainted with grief. How
can we say we know him if we don't experience at least some of
that grief? We may not understand his reasons, but we are insane
to fight him on this issue. He is ecstasy beyond words, and it is
worth *anything* to be his friend—even at 2:00 a.m. with paralysis
and a pounding headache.

*Father God and precious Son, thank you that you invite me into your joy in the
fellowship of the Holy Spirit. May my afflictions this day draw me deeper into
your fellowship, and may I experience all the divine joy I can contain!*

ॐ

FEBRUARY 8

Be Engaged!

Therefore, my dear friends, as you have always obeyed—not only in my presence, but now much more in my absence—continue to work out your salvation with fear and trembling, for it is God who works in you to will and to act according to his good purpose. Do everything without complaining or arguing, so that you may become blameless and pure, children of God without fault in a crooked and depraved generation, in which you shine like stars in the universe.

—PHILIPPIANS 2:12–15

f I were to follow the advice to "let go and let God," I'd be letting myself off the hook. A hands-off approach to my walk with Christ has never gotten me anywhere. God played the key role in my justification, and I have the responsibility to play the key role in my sanctification. Today's verse calls me to be actively engaged in my own salvation as I "work it out with fear and trembling." Why the fear and trembling? If I become spiritually lazy—not praying or reading the Bible much, not witnessing or trusting God when I should—I am making light of the blood that Jesus shed for my redemption. I want to have a healthy fear of offending God and a righteous respect of what my salvation cost the Lord Jesus.

You have a responsibility to actively pursue the person God designed you to be. The perfect "you" is that glorious saint you will become in heaven, and you're called to step daily into that image. God has purchased you, and he is asking you today to be actively engaged in your own sanctification—you will have strength to accomplish this because it will be God who will be working in you to act according to his good purpose. Take a bold step toward your sanctification today, and let God take care of the transformation of your character.

Lord, I commit to obey you today, knowing I'm stepping into the person you have saved me to be.

༄

FEBRUARY 9

Treasures in the Darkness

He reveals deep and hidden things; he knows what lies in
darkness, and light dwells with him.

—DANIEL 2:22

y friend David lives on the edge. He's a quadriplegic, his
wife left him after the car accident, he survives on government benefits, and he lives alone in a little apartment downtown. After
getting up in the morning, he more or less fends for himself after his part-
time attendant leaves. Despite all his struggles, David always orders the
public access van on Saturday evening so that he can come to our church
for Sunday services.

"Who helps you with dinner?" I asked him once. David explained that
he usually powers his wheelchair over to the Pizza Hut for dinner. "The
Lord always provides someone to help," he laughed. "Sometimes it's one
of the waiters on break. Or a stranger having dinner who offers to help. I
can feed myself," he said proudly. "I just need someone to place the pizza
in the curve of my hand just so. But Joni, I'll tell you something. All this
helps me to depend on the Lord. I mean ... I *depend* on him."

David inspires me because he's not afraid to live on the edge. Somehow, he finds light in the darkness and hope in the midst of helplessness.
And God has revealed to him the preciousness of Isaiah 45:3, where the
Lord promises, "I will give you the treasures of darkness, riches stored in
secret places so that you may know I am the Lord, the God of Israel, who
summons you by name." Oh, how wealthy are the people who need God
desperately, whose treasure in the darkness is a deeper knowledge of him.

In the midst of your own darkness, there is treasure and riches
that could never be discovered in the light of ease and peace.
Needing God desperately will *always* make you wealthy.

*Lord Jesus, you left the rainbow radiance of heaven to taste darkness and death
for me ... and bring me home to your Father's house. And even now, in the
worst of times and deepest of sorrows, you have become my treasure and my
hope.*

Do What Love Says

> But the fruit of the Spirit is love, joy, peace, patience, kindness, goodness, faithfulness, gentleness and self-control.
>
> —GALATIANS 5:22–23

Valentine's Day is coming up quickly—my neighborhood market has been displaying chocolates and roses for weeks now. All for the sake of love. Or is it? Why should we listen to the greeting card companies? Why should chocolate do the talking? Today's verse says it much better. Many Bible translators place a colon after the word love, indicating that joy, peace, patience, and the rest are actually all characteristics of one thing: love.

I like this paraphrase from The Message of 1 Corinthians 13. It says, "Love never gives up. Love cares more for others than for self. Love doesn't want what it doesn't have, doesn't strut, doesn't have a swelled head, doesn't force itself on others, isn't always 'me first,' doesn't fly off the handle, doesn't keep score of the sins of others, doesn't revel when others grovel, takes pleasure in the flowering of truth, puts up with anything, trusts God always, always looks for the best, never looks back, but keeps going to the end."

Write out 1 Corinthians 13 from The Message and place it where you can glance at it often. Then, "Do not merely listen to the Word. Do what it says" (James 1:22). Who do you say "I love you" to? Do you show this person kindness? Are you faithful with his or her reputation? Do you give, expecting to receive something in return? Do you keep score when this person has wronged you? Can you rejoice as he or she develops strong relationships with others? "And now these three remain: faith, hope and love. But the greatest of these is love" (1 Corinthians 13:13).

Lord God, I pray for those whom I love. Make me a clean vessel through which your selfless love will flow toward others. May I expect nothing in return, only the pleasure of showering your goodness and graciousness on those around me.

❦

Divine Stonework

As you come to him, the living Stone—rejected by men
but chosen by God and precious to him—you also, like
living stones, are being built into a spiritual house to be a
holy priesthood, offering spiritual sacrifices acceptable to
God through Jesus Christ. For in Scripture it says: "See, I
lay a stone in Zion, a chosen and precious cornerstone, and
the one who trusts in him will never be put to shame."

—1 PETER 2:4–6

There wasn't a man in Maryland who could build a stone wall like
my father. Daddy was able to combine his building skills with his
artistic talent to design walls that resembled something out of a Robert
Frost poem. His walls were weathered sentries, balanced and sturdy. When
my father would build a wall, he wouldn't rush. He would unload a big pile
of boulders, then sort through them, putting aside the ones for the wall.
Daddy would pick up a rock, brush off the dirt, turn it over in his hands,
and line it up, this way and that, placing it just right in the wall. Then
Daddy would cement it in with the trowel.

Picture the saints who, through the ages, saw persecution and pes-
tilence, holocaust and heartache—they realized they were living stones
being troweled into the kingdom building. They understood that suffering
was, at times, sickening, but life was worth living if it meant more time
granted for the world to hear the good news.

Like these saints, we experience the biting reality of suffering, but
we also remember the enormously high price Jesus placed on a
soul. Suffering is bad, but a soul lost is worse (Matthew 16:26).
We realize God is permitting something he hates (pain and persecution) so that something he prizes (more souls salvaged) could
be achieved.

*I am happy, dear Lord, to be a living stone that you have troweled into your
kingdom building. I pray that many more living stones will be added today to
your "wall of salvation."*

A Soft Heart

But encourage one another daily, as long as it is called Today, so that none of you may be hardened by sin's deceitfulness.

— HEBREWS 3:13

hen I was first injured, my wheelchair whined and screamed for my undivided attention. Demoralized, I gave in. I justified my giving up with rationalizations like, *Why not be glum-faced? I'm paralyzed! Why not complain? Good grief, I'm a quadriplegic!* I allowed my wheelchair to define who I was, but all it accomplished was a dry and brittle soul. I didn't become a bad person; I just lacked passion and interest in life. With no spiritual energy, I spent my days in tired defeat, the day-to-day routine sucking me down further. Relief was not sought in prayer or in the Bible, but in TV sitcoms and weekends at the mall.

Focusing on suffering is a dead end. Rationalizations and justifications do nothing but harden our hearts, making things worse. However, softness of heart comes when we encourage one another in our suffering — spreading truth, imparting hope, bearing the burden, sharing the load, praying alongside, and offering a comfortable shoulder to cry on. Thank God there were Christian friends who stuck with me, scolding me when I complained, and cheering me on when I chose a brighter outlook. My hardness of heart melted, and I became soft and pliable in the hands of God.

My friends took a risk when they boldly reminded me to obey God and turn away from selfishness. They risked my disapproval, as well as my anger. Thankfully, they cared more for the state of my soul, than my displeasure. Do you know a Christian friend or relative who has become deceived by sinful attitudes and actions? Do they believe in suffering, rather than the God of hope found *in* suffering? Take a risk. Pray, come alongside, and gently help them choose a brighter outlook.

Help me, dear Lord, to recognize when sin is trying to deceive me. Soften my heart, oh God!

FEBRUARY 13

God Is Love

And so we know and rely on the love God has for us. God is love.

—1 JOHN 4:16

The Father, Son, and Holy Spirit are fellowshiping in a waterfall of love and joy. It is nothing short of amazing that the Trinity is driven to share that joy with *us*. It was the Savior's mission: "I have told you this so that my joy may be in you" (John 15:11). What joy the Trinity enjoys! Misery may love company, but joy craves a crowd, and so the Father, Son, and Holy Spirit's plan to rescue humans is not only for man's sake. It is for God's sake. The Father is gathering a crowd—an inheritance, pure and blameless—to worship his Son in the joy of the Holy Spirit. "God is love" and the wish of love is to drench with delight those for whom God has suffered.

Soon believers will step into the waterfall of joy and pleasure that is the Trinity. Better yet, we will become part of a Niagara Falls of thunderous delight as "God is all and in all." In heaven, we will not only know God, we will *know* him in that deep, personal union, that utter euphoria of experiencing him. There in heaven we will "eat of the tree of life" and be filled to overflowing with more joy and pleasure than we can contain (Revelation 22:2).

Amazing grace, how can it be, that God would share his joy for eternity with *me*? Remember, God shares his joy on his terms; and those terms call for us to, in some measure, suffer as his beloved Son did while on earth (1 Peter 2:21). If you and I experience hardship, it is paving the way for a deeper joy for all of eternity!

Father, Son, and Holy Spirit, thank you for inviting me into the fellowship of your joy. Thank you for preparing me for heaven's joy as I trust you in the fellowship of your sufferings while on earth.

ର୍ତ

Get Tough on Technology

> May the God who gives endurance and encouragement
> give you a spirit of unity among yourselves as you follow
> Christ Jesus.
>
> —ROMANS 15:5

The other night Ken and I had a few coworkers to our house for dinner. Long after dessert, we were still gathered around the table having a great time. Lorraine sat back and said, "Isn't this wonderful? Isn't this better than emailing each other? Don't you despise the way computers have disrupted this kind of fellowship?" Her comment kick-started a conversation about technology and the way it has ambushed everyday relationships. We electronically communicate with people who sit less than thirty feet away.

Speaking of technology, my friend sitting next to me asked my opinion on video conferencing. At the other end of the table, Judy pulled out her new cell phone to show its photograph feature to Doug who, at that point, asked her how he could send photos off of his phone. Others were giving each other advice about getting rid of junk mail and, before we knew it, we had become fractured into tiny little groups advising each other on how we could live happier and more meaningfully if we used our cell phones to do this ... emails to do that ... video this ... and voice mail that. Finally Lorraine announced, "People, would you look at us?! Here we go again, allowing ourselves to be splintered apart by technology!" We laughed, but she was right.

If ever there were a culture in which relationships need to be strengthened—especially between Christians—it is *our* culture. Today's reading gives great advice for any believer who uses a cell phone, answering machine, or BlackBerry. Inspire a spirit of unity among your friends today and write a personal note (or Valentine card?). Bless your coworkers with a little encouragement—not by clicking the send button, but by getting up from your desk and going over to the other cubicle. I think it's what Jesus would do.

Lord God, thank you for the relationships with people you've placed in my life. May I never take any friendship or working relationship for granted. Bless my friends this day.

David Wept, but Jesus More

I have loved you with an everlasting love.

—JEREMIAH 31:3

Ever wonder just how much Jesus loves you? Bearing God's wrath on the cross testifies to his immense love, but did Jesus *desire* to come to earth or was it his divine duty? I want to serve the *Lover* of my soul as well as the *Master* of my soul. I cannot bear the thought of one without the other. The story of Jonathan and David illustrates Jesus in this regard. Together, they were held hostage to Saul's murderous motives. Only a clandestine escape by David would save Jonathan and preserve God's plan. At their parting, "David ... fell on his face to the ground... They kissed each other and cried together, but David more" (1 Samuel 20:41 NLV).

First Samuel 18:1 says, "The soul of Jonathan was knit to the soul of David." Their affections and destiny were bound together. Their deep love for one another is displayed with tears. They wept ... but David more. Why? Was he simply more emotional? The story does not say. But we do know that David—the man who would be king—felt great passion. Here is a king who didn't have to love. He wanted to love.

... But Jesus more. Our Savior is the Son of David. As such, his love is deeply fervent; not borne of duty or obligation. And so, I am drawn to him not only because of his sacrifice for my sin but because of his desire for my soul.

Considering the depth of Jesus' love, you can respond with Paul that we have but one purpose in life—to *know* him. Just as Jonathan's life was transformed because of David's love, our intimacy with Jesus will mark us as changed people. To be bound to any less, or with another, would be life's greatest tragedy.

Precious Savior, knit my soul to yours in love and oneness, our spirits so deeply bound together that we breathe the same air. In you alone I live and move and have my being.

Ꮗ

FEBRUARY 16

Through and Through

Wash me throughly from mine iniquity, and cleanse me
from my sin.

—PSALM 51:2 KJV

Because I cannot reach for a Bible and flip open the pages with
my hands, I make it a point to memorize Scripture. It's the only
way I can have the Word of God at my fingertips! For me, memorizing portions of the Bible is very practical. I use the King James Version of the Bible
when I commit God's Word to memory. The words are uncommon—a
little like poetry—and my mind seems to retain it easier.

When I was memorizing Psalm 51, I stopped short at the second verse.
It says, "Wash me *throughly* from mine iniquity." At first I thought it was
a printing error, but after a little research, I learned it was the Elizabethan
English way of saying "through and through." You could paraphrase it,
"Wash me through and through from my iniquity." It's not many times I
prefer English from the sixteenth century, but this time I did. I don't want
God to merely scrub me good on the outside—it's not a matter of cleans-
ing me from my sin—but washing me clean, clear through.

The word *throughly* doesn't exist anymore. When I wrote it on my
computer, my automatic spell check kept trying to change it to *thoroughly*.
But I'm with Shakespeare, Queen Elizabeth, and King James on this one. I
don't want God to do a surface job on my character; I want him to get rid
of every vestige of deep-down hidden sins.

First Thessalonians 5:23 says (in modern English), "May God
himself, the God of peace, sanctify you *through and through*. May
your whole spirit, soul and body be kept blameless at the coming
of our Lord Jesus Christ." From what hidden or secret sins can
you ask God to wash you through and through today?

*Lord, I confess _____. Thank you for forgiving me and
completely cleansing me from all unrighteousness. Safeguard my heart and
mind and keep me pure.*

ॐ

FEBRUARY 17

Hardships That Hang On

Three times I pleaded with the Lord to take it away from me. But he said to me, "My grace is sufficient for you, for my power is made perfect in weakness."

—2 CORINTHIANS 12:8–9

I will never forget the day they moved me from "acute care" to "chronic care" in the hospital. As they wheeled my stretcher under the sign, I got a lump in my throat. It meant "the doctors don't know what else to do, and I won't regain use of my body." My condition was chronic.

Why do some hardships never go away? You pray and plead until your knees are sore; yet the pinched nerve doesn't heal, the multiple sclerosis doesn't halt, the Alzheimer's doesn't regress, the marriage doesn't get better, the job promotion never comes, and the engagement ring never arrives. After decades in a wheelchair, this is my conclusion:

The core of God's plan is to rescue us from sin and self-centeredness. Suffering—especially the chronic kind—is God's choicest tool to accomplish this. It is a *long* process. But it means I can accept my paralysis as a chronic condition. When I broke my neck, it wasn't a jigsaw puzzle I had to solve fast or a quick jolt to get me back on track. My paralyzing accident was the beginning of a lengthy process of becoming like Christ.

May I share with you one of my "chronic" Bible verses that won't go away? James 1:2–4 says: "When all kinds of trials crowd into your lives my brothers, don't resent them as intruders, but welcome them as friends! Realise that they come to test your faith and to produce in you the quality of endurance. But let the process go on until that endurance is fully developed" (Phillips). When that finally happens, the only thing that will be chronic is *joy*!

Lord, help me to embrace the chronic conditions in my life. I want endurance to be fully developed in my life. Help me to hang on.

FEBRUARY 18

Insults

> That is why, for Christ's sake, I delight in weaknesses, in
> insults.... For when I am weak, then I am strong.
>
> —2 CORINTHIANS 12:10

I was at the airport, waiting to board our flight. The gate agent had transferred me onto a narrow chair so I could be wheeled down the aisle of the plane. My two friends had already gone ahead to place their carry-on luggage under their seats. While I was waiting, I mentioned my seat number to the gate agent—he just grunted. When it was okay for me to board, I told him my seat number again. He still refused to take me on board. When I explained that I knew my seat assignment, he said he wanted to double-check with my friends. I knew why he didn't believe me. People see my paralyzed body and assume that my brain must be paralyzed too. I felt insulted.

I also felt indignant. But later on, I thought of Philippians 2:5–7: "Your attitude should be the same as that of Christ Jesus: Who, being in very nature God, did not consider equality with God something to be grasped, but made himself nothing." Other translations say "made himself of no reputation." As I thought about the many insults Jesus endured, I realized that I too could delight in insults. The reproach I experienced was only minor compared to what Jesus suffered, but it gave me a wonderful sense of identification with him. I was able to delight in the insult because I had a far deeper security, a greater confidence, and a sense of eternal worth—all for the sake of Christ.

First Peter 2:23 says, "When they hurled their insults at him, he did not retaliate; when he suffered, he made no threats. Instead, he entrusted himself to him who judges justly." If someone misreads or misrepresents you today, don't retaliate. Rest your confidence in Christ. Who knows? You may find yourself taking pleasure in the reproach.

Oh God, I humble myself before you. I consider myself as "nothing" ... I make myself of no reputation. Help me not to retaliate when others hurt me.

Your Measure of Faith

It is the glory of God to conceal a matter.

—PROVERBS 25:2

received an email from Marjorie who wrote, "I have been house-bound for several years with Parkinson's disease. I cannot get out of bed anymore. Could you help me understand God's purposes?" I started to write back, asking if she would consider a ministry of prayer from her bed, but then I read Marjorie's PS: "I use my time to pray. But still, it's hard." This dear woman is simply trying to understand—or at least, see—the good resulting from her many problems.

We cannot always see the good that results from our heartaches. We may see some good—perhaps we're a bit more patient since arthritis slowed us down or more sympathetic to single parents since our marriage collapsed. But on the whole, the good that we are able to tally in this life does not outweigh the bad that we observe. The lost innocence of Eden opened floodgates of sorrow, deluging this world with sadness deep beyond telling. It will take heaven to dry it all up—to provide the total picture that will ease our hearts forever.

Only heaven will reveal the complete and clear picture of how Marjorie's fainthearted prayers shook the destinies of nations and countless people on her prayer list. Until then, it is the glory of God to conceal a matter; it's the glory of God that she trust him in it.

Great faith believes in God even when he plays his hand close to the vest, never showing all his cards. He has his reasons for doing so. God wants to increase your "measure of faith" (Romans 12:3). He does this whenever he conceals a matter, *and you trust him nevertheless*!

Lord, thank you for granting me faith to believe you. I purpose to trust you this day with the things I don't understand. I long and look forward to the glorious Day when you will reveal that which you now conceal.

ତ

He Loves Me

> I have been crucified with Christ and I no longer live, but Christ lives in me. The life I live in the body, I live by faith in the Son of God, who loved me and gave himself for me.
>
> —GALATIANS 2:20

I love the well-known words of John 3:16, "For God so loved the world ..." It makes the love of God sound so far-sweeping, so big, so ... world-sized. Yet Jesus did not generally die for the general sins of the whole world at large. The early witnesses who suffered most for being Christians were captivated by the fact that Christ "loved me and gave himself for me." They took the act of Christ's sacrifice *very* personally. And so should we. Jesus died specifically for *your* sins and *mine*. This is why I love Galatians 2:20. Jesus doesn't wave his hand over the entire earth, brushstroking everyone with his love. Rather, he "loved *me* and gave himself for *me*."

This is the way we should look at the sufferings and death of Christ. They have to do with *me*. The stripes on Christ's back are about his love for me personally. It is *my* sin that cuts me off from God, not sin in general. It is *my* spiritual laziness that demeans the worth of Christ. And it is *I* as an individual who must plead for mercy. This is why I take great relief and delight in John 15:13, "Greater love has no one than this, that he lay down his life for *his friends*." Is it possible that I can be one of his "friends"? Yes, I am his friend. Jesus paid the highest price possible to give me the greatest gift possible. Oh, joy! Jesus loves even me ... and he calls me his friend!

Ephesians 5:25 says, "Christ loved the *church* and gave himself up for *her*." *You*, as an individual, are part of the church. Allow your heart to be enthralled by the beauty of Christ's love for one single, solitary *you*.

My heart is yours, Savior, and I am overwhelmed by your great love for me.

૭ఌ

Bending Over Backward

They ask me for just decisions and seem eager for God to come near them. "Why have we fasted," they say, "and you have not seen it? Why have we humbled ourselves, and you have not noticed?" ... Is not this the kind of fasting I have chosen: to loose the chains of injustice and untie the cords of the yoke, to set the oppressed free and break every yoke? Is it not to share your food with the hungry and to provide the poor wanderer with shelter—when you see the naked, to clothe him, and not to turn away from your own flesh and blood?

—ISAIAH 58:2–3, 6–7

God's heart intent is to alleviate suffering, and he is bending over backward to do it. He is moving heaven and earth to dry the tear, lighten the load, ease the burden, mend the marriage, give to the poor, care for the widow, stamp out crime, help the elderly, uphold justice, bandage the battered, and much more. God rallies us to his noble cause, but we often fall behind.

God longs to push back the pain through those who serve as his body, his hands and feet on earth. "He is the head of the body, the church" (Colossians 1:18). And "From him the whole body ... builds itself up in love, as each part does its work" (Ephesians 4:16).

God has placed his work in your hands, and "we take our lead from Christ, who is the source of everything we do" (Ephesians 4:15 The Message). God's directions to us couldn't be clearer. But we hem and haw. This is ironic since so many of us fault *him* for allowing suffering to be the world's status quo. (The *quo* wouldn't be so *status* if we got off our duffs and followed his lead.) Let's change that today!

Lord Christ, you are my head, and I take directions from you today. Show me how I can partner with you to alleviate suffering in my world.

ৡ

FEBRUARY 22

Music in the Dark

By day the Lord directs his love, at night his song is with me.
—PSALM 42:8

I was sitting on the stage at a large pastors' conference in the Philippines. Outside a heavy monsoon rain fell, while the crowd inside was being entertained by a small band of blind musicians. Their music was intricate and lively, and the audience was enthralled with their performance. Suddenly there was a rumble and a loud crash of thunder. In the next instant, the entire conference hall went dark. The powerful storm caused the lights to go out. Unfazed, the musicians hardly skipped a beat, even though it was pitch-black. When their song was over, the audience burst into thunderous applause—the darkness gave us all a unique and amazing appreciation for the extraordinary talent God had given these blind musicians.

What really turned up the wattage on the praise that night was the fact that they *played through the dark*. The same is true when we live for God. Sure, our lives resound with praise when he lights our path and we follow him—a disciple *should* follow his master. But when there's no light for your path and you follow him through dark times, the volume and the intensity of praise to God goes up many more decibels.

Do we know the Savior by heart? Have we practiced the presence of God to the point where, if times went dark, if we couldn't see the conductor, we would still make his music? Psalm 89:15, 17 puts it this way: "Blessed are those who have *learned* to acclaim you, who walk in the light of your presence, O Lord.... For you are their glory and strength." Even through the darkness.

Keep playing the music, friend. It may be dark out, but keep playing by heart what you know from years of practice. It's worth the applause of God.

Father, I wait on you. I desire to learn your song so that even in the darkest night, I might declare your praises for all to hear.

෨

Golden Intervals

> For in the day of trouble he will keep me safe in his dwelling; he will hide me in the shelter of his tabernacle and set me high upon a rock.
>
> —PSALM 27:5

Jay was my favorite sister. With her tousle of blonde curls, she looked like Betty, the fair-haired girl with the ponytail in the *Archie* comics. Even though she was older, she didn't treat me like a tagalong. She *liked* me. I tried to copy everything she did. And I could never understand why Bert Parks didn't want her for the Miss America Pageant.

Jay must have known how much I looked up to her. Maybe that's why, many years later in the early seventies, after my accident, she asked me to come live with her. There was lots of room in the old stone house up on the farm. I was still a novice at being a quadriplegic, struggling to adjust to life in a wheelchair. But Jay made the early years of adapting to paralysis bearable. Sometimes, even sweet.

My favorite memory was one late summer evening on the back porch under a full moon when Jay pulled up her rocker. There, with crickets calling under the willow and fireflies floating over the creek, with moonlight on her golden hair, we lifted up our voices on a beloved old hymn: "There is a fountain filled with blood, / drawn from Immanuel's veins, / and sinners plunged beneath that flood, / lose all their guilty stains." We didn't need accompaniment. I slid my harmony beneath her melody as our voices, soft as country down, blended into the night and made our praises to God as sweet as honeysuckle.

Even in the hardest and darkest of times, our loving Father weaves treasured memories and intervals of music and laughter through our lives. And when we sing aloud of his goodness and grace, our pain—even if only for the moment—loses its grip.

Lord, I praise you today, for you are the one who pierces dark and heavy clouds with shafts of sunlight, like purest gold.

Pleasures in Paradise

No eye has seen, no ear has heard, no mind has conceived what God has prepared for those who love him.

—1 CORINTHIANS 2:9

This is hard to believe, but pleasure is not earth's invention. God invented every delight, and each delectable sensual experience. It is natural to wonder whether or not in heaven our cravings will be satisfied. (Earth is the culprit that keeps itching, tickling, and teasing our desires, all the while diminishing the possibilities of fulfillment.) Will the pleasures of heaven really be *that* pleasurable? Consider this unusual but excellent analogy by C. S. Lewis:

> Our present outlook might be like that of a small boy who, on being told that the sexual act was the highest bodily pleasure, should immediately ask whether you ate chocolates at the same time. On receiving the answer "no," he might regard absence of chocolates as the chief characteristic of sexuality. In vain would you tell him that the reasons why lovers in their carnal raptures don't bother about chocolates is that they have something better to think of. The boy knows chocolate: he does not know the positive thing that excludes it. We are in the same position. We know the sexual life; we do not know, except in glimpses, the other thing which, in Heaven, will leave no room for it. Hence where fullness awaits us we anticipate [loss].[1]

Earth has conditioned us to think heaven is a place of less, not more. But enraptured in heaven's joy, we won't think about carnal pleasures because we will have something better, something far more pleasurable to consume us. The delight I experience with my husband, Ken, is merely a hint, a whisper—a bite of chocolate—compared to the resounding joy that, in heaven, will sweep me away in a deluge of ecstasy.

I praise you that every good and perfect gift is from above, coming down from you, the Father of the heavenly lights. I believe what you tell me: heaven will be paradise.

O Love That Won't Let Go

God has said, "Never will I leave you; never will I forsake
you." So we say with confidence, "The Lord is my helper;
I will not be afraid."

—HEBREWS 13:5–6

My friend Melanie and I love to sing the old song, "O love
that wilt not let me go, I rest my weary soul in Thee." We
need to. It's not only because she's holding life together by her fingers and
toes, raising two active little boys and a toddler in diapers, cheering on her
pastor-husband, keeping house, shopping, cooking, and running countless
errands.

On top of that, she is going blind. Her world is blurring over. First it
was labels on soup cans. Then it was the aisles in the store. Soon it will be
her children's faces. In an email Melanie wrote: "The toughest battles in
my life are coming up, and it's as though I'm already losing the war! I feel
as though life is leaving me as my vision fades. I have such a sense that 'in
this world you will have trouble....' Joni, I am waiting for the peace."

I want to stay close on my friend's heels as we journey further into the
fellowship of Jesus' sufferings. It's a road no one should walk alone. Me or
you. Melanie, on this eve of your birthday, I'll tell you what: I'll keep being
your eyes, and you keep being my hands. And Jesus will keep holding us
with his grace ... his love will not let us go.

Jesus has promised never to fail us, never to leave us, never to let
us go. But there are times when we need the warm touch of a fellow traveler along the sometimes difficult path of life. Will you be
our Lord's touch, his smile, his comfort, his word of encouragement and hope to someone in a dark place today?

*Lord, you have comforted me so many times with a word or a hug or a note
from one of your children. I'm asking you this day for the opportunity to pass
that love along.*

❧

Chicken Shelter

> I long to dwell in your tent forever and take refuge in the
> shelter of your wings.
>
> —PSALM 61:4

My coworker at Joni and Friends, Billy Burnett, was raised as one of eleven children in a poor sharecropper's cabin on the corner of the Jimmy Lynch farm in east Texas. When Billy's father scraped together enough money from cutting cotton, he moved his family to Texarkana.

When Billy was a little boy, he'd watch his mother—Mama Teal—throw grain to the chickens in the backyard. He would sit on his haunches and observe how the chicks would flock around the mother hen. Whenever dark clouds of a storm gathered and wind would blow, the hen would lift her wing a certain way and her chicks would come running. Her arched wing was their signal that danger was near. She was indicating they should scurry and find safety by her side.

Oh, that you and I were like one of those chicks. Oh, that we would run without hesitation or question to find refuge in the shelter of God's wing. Even Jesus, when he looked out over the Holy City, said, "O Jerusalem, Jerusalem, thou that killest the prophets, and stonest them which are sent unto thee, how often would I have gathered thy children together, even as a hen gathereth her chickens under her wings, and ye would not!" (Matthew 23:37 KJV).

Don't be one of the "would not's" today. When the dark clouds of trouble start brewing on the horizon, run—don't walk—to find protection near the breast of God. When the Lord gives you the signal, "Come quickly," take it as an indication from the Holy Spirit to find refuge under the shelter of God's wing. There you will be safe from any stormy trial.

Under your wings I am safely abiding, though the night deepens and tempests are wild. Still I can trust you; I know you will keep me. You have redeemed me, and I am your child.

෨෨

Singing in His Shadow

Because you are my help, I sing in the shadow of your wings.

—PSALM 63:7

Under His wings I am safely abiding,
Though the night deepens and tempests are wild,
Still I can trust Him; I know He will keep me,
He has redeemed me, and I am His child.

Under His wings, under His wings,
Who from His love can sever?
Under His wings my soul shall abide,
Safely abide forever.

Yesterday's devotional reminds me of the words to this old gospel song, "Under His Wings." I often sing it as a prayer in the middle of the night when I am unable to sleep. During dark hours when my mind is tired or my thoughts are scattered, I "pray" the safe, reliable words from a time-honored hymn (I'll sing quietly so as to not wake my husband). One of two things usually happens: my worrisome thoughts disappear ... or I fall asleep!

In more than a dozen places in Scripture, God bids us to draw close to him and find shelter—in most places, it says "refuge." Or "in his wings." Psalm 91:4 says, "He will cover you with his feathers, or under his wings you will find refuge; his faithfulness will be your shield and rampart." That God describes himself so often as a powerful and beautiful bird arching his protective wing over us for our refuge, should tell us something. It should assure us that we can always find shelter, refuge, and safety. *That's* reason enough to sing.

Memorize the words to several favorite hymns and tuck them away in your heart for those late-night restless hours in bed when you can't sleep. Let God's Word, as well as a Christ-honoring hymn, remind you of his precious and abiding faithfulness.

Father, you are my shield and barricade against fear and worry. I can sing in the shadow of your wings because your faithfulness never fails. Help me to remember this in the middle of the night!

᠅

FEBRUARY 28

Discipline or Punishment?

Those whom I love I rebuke and discipline. So be earnest,
and repent.

—REVELATION 3:19

ften when I share my testimony, I reflect on how "off-track" I
had become in my Christian life before my diving accident. "You
know," I said recently, "I was involved in some pretty immoral stuff when
I was on my feet. Even though I was a Christian, I was sinning big-time,
heading down a wrong path. Deep in my heart, I know that if my accident
hadn't happened, I would have completely ignored my convictions in college." Someone who was listening asked me, "Joni, are you saying that God
was *punishing* you with a broken neck?"

It was a good question. My mind went to Hebrews 12:6: "The Lord
disciplines those he loves, and he punishes everyone he accepts as a son."
And I had to look that person straight in the eye and say, "Yes, I believe
God was punishing me for doing wrong." But there are two kinds of punishment. One is *retribution*: that's what God does with unbelievers, with
wicked people who shake their fist at him, scorn all his standards, and
walk right into judgment. But the other kind is *restoration*. That is when
the Father sends discipline into the life of one of his own, to bring that son
or daughter back to the path of life. It is restorative suffering intended to
purge sin and rebellion from our hearts.

No, it still isn't easy to take. As Scripture says, "No discipline is enjoy-
able while it is happening—it is painful!" (Hebrews 12:11 NLT). But during my long months in the hospital, I finally admitted and repented from
that disobedience—even to the point that I could thank God for rescuing
me from a wayward life.

God wants to purge us and restore us. He's done it with me (and
keeps on doing it!), and he will do it with you. After all, you're one
of his kids. And he loves you too much to let you ruin your life.

*Thank you Father, that though you discipline, you never reject me, leave me,
or let me go.*

In a Mirror, Dimly

For now we see in a mirror dimly, but then face to face; now I know in part, but then I will know fully just as I also have been fully known.

—1 CORINTHIANS 13:12 NASB

orinth was a famous manufacturing center for mirrors. In Paul's day, state-of-the-art mirrors were made of polished metal, silver, or brass. By gazing intently into the shiny metal, the viewer could have a general—if somewhat vague—impression of reality. But when you compared looking at someone's reflection with seeing them face-to-face ... well, there was no comparison. The reflection was at best a dim shadow of the full-blooded reality.

For now we see in a mirror, dimly. The word Paul used for "dimly" is the Greek term for "puzzle," or "riddle," or "enigma." That's what life is like, Paul was saying. Even for a Christian. It's an inscrutable enigma. Yes, we have a general apprehension of reality for we have the Word of God and the Spirit of God to guide and teach us. We have "eyes of the heart" that are at least partially functional here on earth. But let's face it—we are only catching the merest glimpse of the full, eternal reality in Christ. We find ourselves here on earth peering into an imperfect mirror, trying to make sense of it all. We come with our pain and sorrow and gaze and gaze, wanting so much to see the full picture. It seems that God only allows us enough of a glimpse to bring comfort and encouragement—he has shown us enough of life in the Spirit to embolden us to keep going!

What heart-cries still remain unsatisfied for you? What questions still remain unanswered? What yearnings remain unfulfilled? Remember that this life is only a dim reflection of the true reality yet to be revealed. Bring your heart-cries and questions and yearnings to the feet of Jesus. Let his Word shed light and meaning on your heartbreak ... and leave the rest to faith.

Lord Jesus, help me to gaze and gaze upon you this day, for you hold the answers ... you fulfill each longing ... you are my satisfaction. Help me to see you clearly!

ভ

March

MARCH 1

Mangled Earrings

Therefore, if anyone is in Christ, he is a new creation; the old has gone, the new has come!

—2 CORINTHIANS 5:17

I once was wearing a favorite pair of gold earrings, which were large and square with a smooth, shiny surface. While I was on the telephone, one fell off. When I backed up my wheelchair, it wasn't on the floor. I wheeled into the hallway to look for someone to help me, and immediately I felt a clunk-clunk. The gold earring was impaled on my tire. My friend plucked it off, but it was a mangled mess.

I asked a jeweler, "Sir, could you please make the crumpled earring look like this nice one?" He rubbed his chin and replied, "Lady, forget it. But I *can* make this one" — he pointed to the smooth earring — "look like your smashed one." It was an option I hadn't considered. After a few minutes of hammering, I had a unique designer original: a pair of crinkled gold earrings that reflected even more light than before!

When God allows hammering and hurting, he is purposing to transform us into something new and different. Like those earrings, we are the same, yet poles apart. Best of all, we are better; we are closer to reflecting the light of Christ because of our weakness. The jeweler at the mall could turn a flawless earring into a mangled one, but only God can take a mangled life and change it into a life that reflects the flawless perfection of his Son, Jesus Christ. One day the hammering process will cease and we will perfectly reflect the image of our Savior.

Someone has said, "God ruthlessly perfects whom he royally elects." In what way have your hopes or dreams been smashed? Agree with God to hold on to his wisdom and grace through the hammering. It'll be a change for the better.

Lord Jesus, I believe you are transforming me into someone far more beautiful, more complete than if I had never experienced pain. I trust you with the hammer!

MARCH 2

At Jesus' Feet

As she stood behind him at his feet weeping, she began to
wet his feet with her tears.

—LUKE 7:38

Amazing things happened at the feet of Jesus. Some people fell at his feet, others kissed them, still others sat in reverence. Bowing low before him gives a view of life like no other. And miracles are never very far away.

I experienced this recently with my friends Francie and Judy on a visit to the Johns Hopkins Medical Center. In a grand lobby, a twenty-five-foot statue of Christ towers beneath a four-story glass rotunda. The sculptor fashioned Jesus looking down with his arms outstretched, as if bestowing a blessing. We were awestruck. "It's good to be at his feet," I whispered.

Suddenly an official-looking man approached. "Isn't your name Joni?" he asked, introducing himself as an administrator at Johns Hopkins. "I'm a Christian too," he said. "If there's anything I can ever do to help, let me know." It was a generous offer, but after we flew home to California, I forgot all about it. I forgot, that is, until my friend Melanie—who is rapidly going blind, told me, "My specialist says that the only people who might be able to do anything are back at Johns Hopkins. But I don't know a soul there. How would I ever get an appointment?"

Instantly remembering what happened at the feet of the statue of Jesus, I made a call to the administrator, asking if he would be in touch with Melanie ... and the door opened for her. Before she flew east for her appointment, I emailed her: "Dear Melanie, there's a statue of Jesus you must see when you go to Johns Hopkins next week. Don't miss it. Amazing things happen at his feet."

Spend time at his feet today. Worship, weep, repent, pray ... or just wait for his touch. In all the world, there is no better place to be.

Lord Jesus, wounded on the cross for me, I fall at your feet this day. I quiet my heart in your presence now and treasure these moments of intimacy with you.

MARCH 3

Once Enemies

Whoever believes in the Son has eternal life, but whoever rejects the Son will not see life, for God's wrath remains on him.

—JOHN 3:36

When you think of God's wrath, what comes to mind? When I was little, I saw a painting of Zeus, the Greek god who lived "up there," surrounded by puffy clouds. He threw lightning bolts at people for the silliest reasons. I wondered if the God of the Bible was the same way. Was he the kind of God who would fly off the handle? Was he ill tempered, mean spirited, and—dare I say—flighty?

From today's verse, you can see that the wrath of God is not an emotional outburst of anger. It is the punishment due for disobedience to God (Romans 1:18). God's wrath is nothing like the anger of a mythical god or a vengeful human being. His wrath is sinless. It is his punitive justice and has nothing to do with expressions of cruelty. God is holy—that means he hates sin. God is just—that means he must punish sin. That should give us the shivers. We humans have no idea how offensive our sin is against a holy God.

This is why Jesus Christ's sacrifice is so *astounding*. Knowing his wrath would incinerate us in a nanosecond, God came up with the incredible plan described in John 3:16–17, "For God so loved the world that he gave his one and only Son, that whoever believes in him shall not perish but have eternal life. For God did not send his Son into the world to condemn the world, but to save the world through him."

The doctrine of the wrath of God offends many people—even Christians. Nowadays, the love of God is what most Christians concentrate on. But God's love can *never* be appreciated until we see what we have been saved from!

Lord Jesus, I will never fully know or appreciate the fact that you absorbed God's wrath so that I might know his peace. Thank you for such amazing love.

☙

MARCH 4

Objects of His Wrath

All of us also lived among them at one time, gratifying the cravings of our sinful nature and following its desires and thoughts. Like the rest, we were by nature objects of wrath. But because of his great love for us, God, who is rich in mercy, made us alive with Christ even when we were dead in transgressions—it is by grace you have been saved.

—Ephesians 2:3–5

Read that again. See if something disturbs you. It's talking about nonbelievers as "objects of wrath." This was the verse that came to mind this morning after I drove away from our neighborhood Shell station. The owner, a delightful man from Amman, Jordan, had just finished telling me how much he was enjoying reading the *Joni* book in Arabic. "You're a great gal," he said, slapping the door of my van. I replied, "Oh, but that's only because we have a great God." He shrugged his shoulders. I could tell he didn't get my point. Perhaps through prayer, time, and a few more pages of the *Joni* book where I share the plan of salvation, he will.

Until he does—and this is what came to mind as I drove away—he is an object of God's wrath. But wait! Christ did not die in order to *force* God to love us; God the Father came up with the plan to rescue fallen man. "And so we know and rely on the love God has for us. God is love" (1 John 4:16). Praise the Lord, that's good news for my Arab neighbor!

Galatians 3:13 makes the good news *great*: "Christ redeemed us from the curse of the law by becoming a curse for us, for it is written: 'Cursed is everyone who is hung on a tree.'" Should my Arab neighbor come to Christ, God has no more wrath or anger against him—all his anger was poured out on Jesus. Hallelujah!

Lord Jesus, thank you for bearing the Father's wrath against my sin. Hallelujah, Amen!

MARCH 5

Answering Isaiah

Is not this the kind of fasting I have chosen: ... Is it not to
share your food with the hungry and to provide the poor
wanderer with shelter—when you see the naked, to clothe
him.

—ISAIAH 58:6–7

D iana is a "working" homeless person. She puts in hours at a
local fast-food restaurant and showers every couple of days at a
nearby Methodist church. Sometimes with her earnings, Diana is able to
get a good night's sleep at a Motel 6. She is sixty-two years old and starts
each day with a "Good morning, God!" then tends to her cat, Shadow. She
has found a safe sleeping place near a hardware store in the San Fernando
Valley. She lost her home years ago but is hoping to find a permanent place
to live.

Cathy, who works at our office, met Diana several months ago when
she stopped by the fast-food restaurant. She was impressed with the woman's upbeat attitude. When she learned Diana was homeless, Cathy and
her husband decided to help—they have since found her a room to rent.
It's one modern-day example of how Christians are not only responding to
God's plea in Isaiah 58 but are salting their communities with the preserving influence of the gospel. After all, people like Diana hold a special place
in God's heart (Matthew 25:35).

People like Cathy have a special place in God's heart too. As they
help someone like Diana, Isaiah 58:9–11 assures that "the Lord
will answer; you will cry for help, and he will say: Here am I. If
you do away with the yoke of oppression ... and if you spend
yourselves in behalf of the hungry and satisfy the needs of the
oppressed, then your light will rise in the darkness, and your night
will become like the noonday. The Lord will guide you always."

*Father God, today I will encounter all sorts of people in my community. Open
my eyes to their needs and show me how to make a difference.*

ഔ

The Truth about Suffering

For it has been granted to you on behalf of Christ not only
to believe on him, but also to suffer for him.

—PHILIPPIANS 1:29

You will hear some believers say, "Although God can turn our
trials into good, he doesn't wish hard times on us, let alone send
them. What he really wants is to bless us and to keep us from suffering.
The whole reason Jesus went through so much is so that we *wouldn't* have
to experience hurt, pain, disappointment, or affliction." The Christians
who hold this view are of sterling character—they study their Bibles, care
about non-Christians, and show love for Christ in his kingdom everywhere
they go. Nevertheless, the statement above is a hopeless mixture of truth
and error, and it misses the core of why Jesus came.

First, despite Christ's compassionate death for our sins, God's
plan—not plan B or C or D, but *his plan*—calls for all Christians to suffer, sometimes intensely. Today's verse is only one of many that point to
the fact that we are to pick up our cross daily and follow in the footsteps
of his suffering (1 Peter 2:21; 4:12). To encourage us, God will write light
moments into the script of our lives, but without fail, some scenes are
going to break your heart, some of your favorite characters will die, and
the movie may end earlier than you wish.

God's plan is specific. He doesn't say, "Into each life a little rain
must fall," then aim a hose in earth's general direction to see who
gets the wettest. He doesn't wind up nature and then sit back to
watch its sunny days and devastating hurricanes. God doesn't let
Satan prowl about totally unrestricted. Do you feel as though
God has taken a hands-off policy to certain hardships in your life?
Right now, place them under his sovereign care. Commit to trust
him with *his plan* for your life.

*Lord of wisdom, Lord of my life, I believe and trust you with every trial in
my life.*

১৬

MARCH 7
Suffering's Response

Then [Job] fell to the ground in worship and said: "Naked
I came from my mother's womb, and naked I will depart.
The Lord gave and the Lord has taken away; may the name
of the Lord be praised."

—JOB 1:20–21

God screens the trials that come to each of us—allowing only those
that accomplish his plan, because he takes no joy in human agony
(Lamentations 3:33). These trials are not evenly distributed from person to
person. This can discourage us, for we are only able to see through a glass
darkly; we are not privy to his reasons. But we can take heart that every
trial is ordained by God from eternity past, custom made for each believer's
eternal good, even when it doesn't seem like it. Nothing happens by accident . . . not even tragedy . . . not even sins committed against us.

The core of God's plan is to rescue us from our sin. Our pain, poverty, and broken hearts are not his ultimate focus. He cares about them,
but they are merely symptoms of the real problem. God cares most—not
about making us comfortable—but about teaching us to hate our sins,
grow up spiritually, and love him. To do this, he *gives us salvation's benefits
only gradually.* In other words, he lets us continue to feel much of sin's
sting while we are headed for heaven. This constantly reminds us of what
we are being delivered from, exposing sin for the poison it is. Thus evil
(suffering) is turned on its head to defeat evil (sin)—all to the praise of
God's wisdom.

What is the proper response to God's wisdom in screening our
trials and allowing particular ones—sometimes tragic ones—to
touch our lives? "May the name of the Lord be praised," says Job
in today's verse. Think of a specific heartache you are facing. Will
you follow Job in his response?

*Almighty God, may I not "waste" my sufferings today but see in my response to
them any sin of resentment, complaint, or bitterness that needs to be confessed.
I praise you for your wisdom.*

☙

MARCH 8

Jesus, Our Life and Breath

For in him we live and move and have our being.

—ACTS 17:28

Last year I struggled through a long bout against double pneumonia. While I was in the hospital, the doctors set an oxygen tank beside my bed so I could breathe easier. Never did I appreciate oxygen so! Up until my illness, I inhaled and exhaled the stuff with hardly a thought. I took breathing for granted. But in the hospital, I discovered afresh how life sustaining oxygen truly is. It's my body's life and breath.

This is often the way we relate to Jesus, our *true* life and breath. Because we live, move, and have our being in him, it is easy to take his life-sustaining grace for granted. We forget that apart from him we can't do a thing (John 15:5). Putting your Christian life on automatic pilot is the same thing as "walking in the flesh." When we forget that we live, move, and have our being in Christ, our prayers become dull, witnessing becomes dry, our jobs become routine, and relationships sag under the weight of selfishness. What's worse, our relationship to the Lord turns into a chore. The Lord seems to lose vitality, becoming a wooden icon in our hearts, and a mere measuring rod for our behavior. It all happens when we forget to inhale his life-giving Spirit on a moment-to-moment basis. It happens when we fail to see the God of grace as our very life and breath. It happens when we take our Savior for granted.

> Nothing is more mechanical than when we attempt to live a supernatural life apart from God. This is why the apostle tells us in Romans 6:11 to "count yourselves ... alive to God in Christ Jesus." To "count" means to take a daily inventory, to consciously consider yourself "alive to God in Christ Jesus." Pause often today, asking God for moment-by-moment grace.

Jesus, you are the Breath of Life. I ask your Spirit to help me lean on you moment by moment today.

ॐ

A Hard Path to Joy

> Let us fix our eyes on Jesus, the author and perfecter of
> our faith, who for the joy set before him endured the cross,
> scorning its shame, and sat down at the right hand of the
> throne of God. Consider him who endured such opposi-
> tion from sinful men, so that you will not grow weary and
> lose heart.
>
> —HEBREWS 12:2–3

The path to joy is full of pitfalls, valleys, and steep climbs. That's the way it was for Jesus. But through all the hardships he kept focused on "the joy set before him." Jesus was able to endure his cross because he kept in mind the joy of reunion with his Father, the joy of triumph over sin, the joy of all his divine rights finally restored to him, and perhaps most wonderful of all, the joy of being eternally surrounded by the very people for whom he bled and died. *This* is why Jesus Christ was able to endure the cross and scorn its shame. All for joy!

It's very much the same for you and me. Our path to joy is full of pitfalls too. But Christ has gone before us, imparting to us his enabling power to suffer with him. Jesus assures us in Matthew 5:11–12 (ESV), "Blessed [or happy and joyful] are you when others revile you and persecute you.... Rejoice and be glad, for your reward is great in heaven." And exactly what is our reward at the end of all our hardships? Our reward will be to enjoy God with the same joy that Jesus has in his Father. Oh happy day!

> Christians have no reason to be miserable or pessimistic. There
> is no room for gloom and doom when you're a believer. If your
> heart is troubled by pessimism or doubts, repeat several times
> today's verse, especially the part, "Consider him who endured ...
> so that you will not grow weary and lose heart." *This* is the secret
> to finding joy. Consider *him*.

Lord of Joy, I delight in your gladness today, and I want to honor you by taking up my cross and joyfully following you.

⟲

A Religion for Losers

Whoever tries to keep his life will lose it, and whoever loses his life will preserve it.

—LUKE 17:33

And everyone who has left houses or brothers or sisters or father or mother or children or fields for my sake will receive a hundred times as much and will inherit eternal life. But many who are first will be last, and many who are last will be first.

—MATTHEW 19:29–30

Several years ago Ted Turner, who turned a bankrupt Atlanta advertising company into a media empire, called Christianity a "religion for losers." Later on he retracted his comment and apologized for his words. But I have to wonder ... wasn't he actually right?! Christianity *is* for losers. It's a religion *of* losers. To follow Jesus Christ means to lose one's self to this world. It means losing all your winnings in this world in order to lay up treasures in the next. To be a disciple of Christ means to negate your pride, subtract your fleshly wants, and put behind you your carefully constructed plans. Jesus absolutely delights in reaching out to those who consider themselves the last, the least, the littlest, and the most lost without him. Christianity is not a religion of winners. It is a faith journey of overcomers who learn to gain by losing.

There is one respect in which Christians do not lose: we do not lose heart! Second Corinthians 4:16 and Hebrews 12:5 are just a few of the many biblical references that remind us never to lose heart. What we shake off here on earth, we accrue a hundred times more in heaven. In what ways can you "lose yourself" to this world today? Do not lose heart, but humble yourself before God and let go of that possession or relationship, title or position. Give it to the Lord, and he'll turn it into a treasure.

You are my treasure, dear Lord, and I lay my life at your feet. Keep the tentacles of the world, the flesh, and the devil from entwining around my heart. I desire to lose my life for your name's sake!

A Seventeenth-Century Prayer

Do not say, "Why were the old days better than these?"
For it is not wise to ask such questions. Wisdom, like an
inheritance, is a good thing and benefits those who see the
sun. Wisdom is a shelter.

—ECCLESIASTES 7:10–12

y mother used to say, "Getting old ain't for sissies." She
was right. I always thought it would be a cinch to grow
old gracefully; then I crested fifty and found out differently! That's why
the following prayer written by an anonymous saint from the seventeenth
century means so much to me:

*Lord, Thou knowest better than I know myself that I am growing older and
will someday be old. Keep me from the fatal habit of thinking I must say
something on every subject and on every occasion. Release me from craving to
straighten out everybody's affairs. Make me thoughtful but not moody. Helpful,
but not bossy with my vast store of wisdom—it seems a pity not to use it all,
but Thou knowest, Lord, that I want a few friends at the end....*

*Keep my mind free from the recital of endless details; give me wings to get to
the point swiftly. Seal my lips on my aches and pains. They are increasing, and
love of rehearsing them is becoming sweeter as the years go by. I dare not ask for
grace enough to enjoy the tales of others' pains, but help me to endure them with
patience. I dare not ask for improved memory, but for a growing humility and
a lessening cocksureness when my memory seems to clash with the memories of
others. Teach me the glorious lesson that occasionally I may be mistaken.*

*Keep me reasonably sweet; I do not want to be a sour old person—some of them
are so hard to live with and each one a crowning work of the devil. Give me
the ability to see good things in unexpected places, and talents in unexpected
people. And, give me, O Lord, the grace to tell them so. Amen.*

I sure do see myself in this prayer; do you? If so, "pray" it again
in your own words.

ॐ

MARCH 12

Hard Hearts

But this time also Pharaoh hardened his heart and would
not let the people go.

—EXODUS 8:32

But the Lord hardened Pharaoh's heart, and he would not
let the Israelites go.

—EXODUS 10:20

So which is it? Who did the hardening of Pharaoh's heart? As God's
ambassador to the Egyptian king, Moses went before Pharaoh's
royal throne more than once to say, "Let my people go!" Yet Pharaoh was
immovable; his heart had been hardened against the Israelites. But when
it comes to Pharaoh's stony resolve and exactly *who* did the hardening,
Scripture points to both Pharaoh and the Lord.

We know from James 1:13 that God does not inject the idea of evil
into anyone's heart. So how is it that "the Lord hardened Pharaoh's heart"?
Through the common work of grace in our world, God is constantly stav-
ing off evil, restraining the fury of Satan so that harm and calamity do
not overwhelm us. The devil can only do what God allows. Every once
in a while, however—as in the case of Pharaoh—God lifts his hand of
restraining grace to allow evil men to carry out their wicked plans, *only as it
serves God's higher purposes.* It is as though God were saying to Pharaoh, "So
you want to sin? Well, go ahead, but I'll make sure that when you do, your
evil intentions suit *my* higher purposes and plan." Even though humans
have an intellect and a will of their own, God ultimately governs all they
do—including evil intentions. And he does it *all* without impugning his
righteous and holy character.

Has someone caused you harm? Hurt or maligned you? You can
praise God today that he is in control of even *that* painful situation. No sin ever happens that God does not deliberately allow.
We may not understand his reasons, but we can rest in his goodness. Thank God today for his awesome sovereignty in your life.

*Holy and righteous Father, I bow before your infinite wisdom. Thank you for
running the universe—overseeing my life—the way you do.*

৩৶

He Works in Mysterious Ways

His father and mother replied, "Isn't there an acceptable woman among your relatives or among all our people? Must you go to the uncircumcised Philistines to get a wife?" But Samson said to his father, "Get her for me. She's the right one for me." (His parents did not know that this was from the Lord, who was seeking an occasion to confront the Philistines; for at that time they were ruling over Israel.)

—JUDGES 14:3–4

Yesterday we only began to scratch the surface of understanding the way God works out his purposes in an evil world filled with wicked people. Oh, how mysterious are his ways! Like the way he worked through Samson, the young, passionate Israelite who, although famous for his strength, was a pushover when it came to pretty girls like Delilah.

In today's verse, we learn that Samson rejected his parents' pleas that he not marry an idol-worshiping Philistine. Samson and his mom and dad assumed it was merely a matter of matrimony. But in Judges 14:3–4, we learn that God had a higher plan and purpose—a purpose that would ultimately result in a glorious victory over the Philistines. Samson and his parents never *dreamed* their little father-and-son talk about the birds and the bees played a role in foreign affairs! But God did. And God allowed Samson to have his own way, to "follow his heart" and tie the knot with a girl from a heathen nation.

God oversees people's wicked actions. No sin happens that the Lord does not deliberately permit. Don't misunderstand—he is not the source of people's evil deeds, for he despises sin. Yet he steers the sin *already in their hearts* so that sinners unwittingly fulfill his plans and not merely their own. Ponder this awesome aspect of God's sovereignty today.

Lord God, I can't pretend to understand the way you work in our world and through the hearts of both believers and pagans. But I do understand that you are good and gracious and that your plans are always perfect!

෨

Godly Questions

Will the Lord reject forever? Will he never show his favor
again? Has his unfailing love vanished forever? Has his
promise failed for all time? Has God forgotten to be merciful? Has he in anger withheld his compassion?

—PSALM 77:7–9

One night when things got as dark as dark could be, when all hope
seemed lost, I stared at the hospital ceiling from my bed and
prayed, "God, if I can't die, please show me how to live." The prayer was
short and to the point, but it left the door open for the Lord to respond.
Little did I realize he would. For "the Lord is close to the brokenhearted
and saves those who are crushed in spirit" (Psalm 34:18). Slowly, like a
hibernating animal waking up, I felt something stir in my heart. It was a
magnetic pull toward hope.

I began to sense an interest in the Bible. When I lay facedown on the
Stryker frame, I flipped the pages of a Bible with my mouth stick. I didn't
know where to turn, but the Psalms intrigued me. When I read Psalm 77,
I identified with those seven rapid-fire questions. The psalmist's despair
turned godly when it turned Godward. The irony of questioning God is
that it honors him. Honest questions turn our hearts away from despair
toward the Lord.

If you (or someone you know) are struggling against hopelessness
today, if everything seems dark, follow the psalmist's example in
today's verse. Gut-wrenching questions directed at the Lord are a
way of encountering God, opening ourselves up to the one and
only Someone who can actually do something about our plight.
If today you are frustrated, use Psalm 77 as a path toward a passionate desire to comprehend the Lord. Something awesome *has*
to happen when you choose the direct line to God.

*Father, I do not understand why you do things the way you do, but I promise
to bring my questions to you. Convict me if I start talking about you "behind
your back"!*

MARCH 15

Praying the Word

As the rain and the snow come down from heaven, and do not return to it without watering the earth and making it bud and flourish, so that it yields seed for the sower and bread for the eater, so is my word that goes out from my mouth: It will not return to me empty, but will accomplish what I desire and achieve the purpose for which I sent it.

—ISAIAH 55:10–11

Yesterday I invited you to use the Psalms—especially the questions in Psalm 77—to express your emotions toward God. Something happens when we handpick a portion of God's Word to voice our heart-wrenching questions, "for the word of God is living and active" (Hebrews 4:12). There's power in God's Word. When we search the Scriptures to find words to wrap around our wretchedness, we are speaking God's language. And God *answers*.

Jesus sets the example. When it comes to heartfelt questions and emotional pain, Jesus experienced both like no human ever has. He did not linger in the damp fog of Gethsemane. He moved in the direction of his Father and proceeded to the cross. There, he aimed his cries Godward, not choosing his own words to wrap around his wretchedness, but—you guessed it—the words of a psalm. "My God, my God, why have you forsaken me?" he groaned, quoting Psalm 22:1. Praise his name, you and I became God's answer to Jesus' plea!

This does not mean our questions get answers. It doesn't mean cancer gets cured, wars cease, and drunk drivers stay at home. But God *will* respond to his Word. Instead of answers, we will find *the* Answer. When we turn toward God in our heartache, he promises our anguished hearts will find Jesus. And he is the One who holds all the answers—and all the questions—in his hand.

I turn to you today, dear God. I voice your Word. Thank you for listening. Thank you for moving in my life.

MARCH 16

One Thing at a Time

> So whether you eat or drink or whatever you do, do it all
> for the glory of God.
>
> — 1 CORINTHIANS 10:31

One early spring day I went to visit Corrie ten Boom, the survivor of the Nazi Holocaust who shared her story in *The Hiding Place*. In her latter years, she lived in Southern California. My friends and I were able to help Pam, her companion, learn basic things about Corrie's disability and her wheelchair. After our short training session, we sat in Corrie's backyard, admiring her early spring flowers and enjoying the warm sun on our backs.

The day was filled with activity, yet relaxed and slow paced. After we enjoyed the flowers, we went into the kitchen for tea and chocolates. After tea we read the Bible and prayed. Then we retired to the parlor and talked. I was amazed how quickly the day flew by, yet how peaceful and stress free it seemed. Pam explained, "Tante Corrie and I never do lots of things at once. We don't sit outside, read, *and* enjoy tea and chocolates. We space everything out so we can truly appreciate the individual pleasures of each activity." That day I witnessed the glory of God in watching spring flowers bob in the breeze ... in savoring the taste of dark chocolate ... in smelling the fragrance of Earl Grey tea ... in listening to an elderly saint pray ... and of discovering new insights in God's Word. All because I lived the day at Corrie's pace.

Someone has pushed the fast-forward button on our days. As the microwave heats our morning Danish, we pay bills online, listen for the chime on the dryer, all the while eavesdropping on Dr. Dobson on Christian radio. Little wonder we feel stressed out. Galatians 5:25 says, "Let us keep in step with the Spirit." Often the Spirit takes very slow steps. Push the pause button, and find a way you can slow down today. Enjoy God's glory in every small thing.

Spirit of Christ, help me to keep in step with you today and not run ahead.

Good Enough?

There is no one righteous, not even one; there is no one who understands, no one who seeks God. All have turned away, they have together become worthless; there is no one who does good, not even one.

—ROMANS 3:10–12

Suppose a man works as a cook and a doctor on a pirate ship. He has never picked up a sword a day in his life. He just stays on the ship and cooks nourishing meals for the other men when they come back from a hard day's pillaging and looting. He is there to heal their cuts and put salve on their scrapes. What could be more innocent?! But if the British Crown captures the pirate ship, the doctor-cook will swing from a rope just like his shipmates. Why? Because he was doing good things in a wicked cause.

This is the way God looks at model citizens who ignore the Savior. Good people may work hard, drive their kids to soccer, keep their lawns spruced, and wave cheerily to the neighbors. But God says the first and greatest commandment is to love him with all our heart, soul, and strength. That is, to do *everything* out of a motive of pleasing him. For the nonbeliever, good acts in his life amount to nothing if he disregards God. Two factors can make an act sinful—a wrong action or a wrong motive. Often people's actions are good, but their motives are a universe away from the righteousness God underscores in Romans 3. Only Jesus is our righteousness!

Some say, "But I know some very good people. If you only knew the woman down the street. She may not claim to be a Christian, but she's the most Christian person I know." If this woman ignores Christ's claims on her, God places her in the class of Romans 3.

Lord Jesus, help me to share the gospel of your grace with people I meet today. Give me grace so that I do every good deed with a pure motive—to please you!

ॐ

MARCH 18

God Bless You

Blessed is the man who does not walk in the counsel of the wicked or stand in the way of sinners or sit in the seat of mockers.

—PSALM 1:1

When you open the Bible, you realize the first thing God does in relation to man is to bless him. When you dig a little further, you'll find the first psalm is also about blessings. Follow the lead to the New Testament, and the most famous sermon Jesus ever preached centers on blessings (Matthew 5:3–12). It is God's disposition to bless us. A blessing is an act of declaring or wishing God's favor and goodness upon others. The blessing is not only the good effect of words; inspired by the Spirit, it also has the power to bring those words to pass.

Dr. John Piper puts it this way: "When God blesses us, it is what he really loves to do. God is not acting in a generous manner in order to cloak some malicious motive. God is not saying inside, 'I will have to be generous for awhile, even though I don't want to be, because what I really want to do is bring judgment on sinners.' God is truly acting out his deepest delight when he blesses. His joy, desire, his want and wish and hope, pleasure and gladness and delight is to bless . . . to give the kingdom to his flock."[1]

It is the true inclination of God to shower his favor on our dry, shriveled souls. It is not God's duty nor his obligation to bless us. It's something he does out of the greatness of his heart. He blesses you with instruction, gentle persuasion, health, comfort, and consolation in times of hardship. He blesses you with friends, intellect, eyesight, and hearing. He blesses you with grace upon grace. Today, cultivate a personal disposition to bless others; let it be the measure of your character and heart as you shower favor and mercy on those who need his touch.

Bless the Lord, O my soul, and all that is within me, bless his holy name!

MARCH 19

Sin's Deceit

Search me, O God, and know my heart; test me and know
my anxious thoughts. See if there is any offensive way in
me, and lead me in the way everlasting.

—PSALM 139:23–24

ack in college, I recall two Christian friends of mine who had
an interesting arrangement. Knowing the warnings in Scripture
about gossip, they made a pact. They promised never to gossip—except
with each other. They didn't have loose tongues with anyone else because
they knew it would be a bad witness. But when those two closed the door
of their dorm room—oh, did they give each other earfuls!

My friends thought they had housebroken their gossip. They assumed
they had made their whispering about people respectable and under control. But now, many years later, those two friends aren't even friends anymore. I suppose they encountered the truth of Proverbs 16:28, where it
says that "gossip separates close friends." Hmmm. It's unfortunate that
Christians try to housebreak certain sins as though we can maintain control
over them. Though we might argue the point, it is usually sin that gains
control over us! It does so by deceiving us of its deadly sting. Take gossip,
for instance. It seems like a rather small and private offense, and somewhat
harmless if done discreetly. But in Romans 1:30, the Lord places gossips
and God-haters in the same sentence. I wouldn't call that harmless.

In this season of Lent, consider what Bishop J. C. Ryle wrote: "Sin
comes to us like Judas with a kiss.... Sin in its beginnings seems harmless enough—like David walking idly on his palace roof that happened
to overlook the bedroom of a woman. You and I may give wickedness
smooth-sounding names, but we cannot alter its nature and character in
the sight of God."

Ask the Holy Spirit to point out to you those attitudes and actions
that grieve his heart—and then push them away from your life
like the deadly poison they truly are.

*Forgive me, Lord, for taking a casual attitude toward the "little" sins that you
paid for with your very life.*

Unravel the Thread

Now if you are displeased, I will go back.

—NUMBERS 22:34

y friend Dave was showing me a large crocheted table runner that his wife, Patti, just completed. When I asked how long it took to make, he turned it over, pointed to a knot near the center, and said, "See this little spot? Well, I was sitting next to Patti when all of a sudden she dropped her hook and moaned, 'Oh no!' She said she had made a mistake—the ends of the threads weren't meeting like they were supposed to. It took a long time, but Patti was able to trace her crocheting way back until she located the point where she had dropped a stitch. Then she proceeded to unravel all her work until she reached the error. Before the evening was up, there was this huge mound of crinkled thread by her side. But my wife's a trooper! She just picked up the stitch and started the pattern all over again!" Most people wouldn't have noticed a dropped stitch in that table runner, but Patti noticed. As she would say, "If it's worth doing, it's worth doing right."

It's the way God calls us to live. If the Holy Spirit reveals that we have made an error, it's pointless to go on unless we go back to the place of departure.

Sometimes you get so far in life, then realize—oh no!—the threads just aren't coming together; you've made a mistake somewhere along the line. Your sins have come home to roost. We do ourselves a disservice when we merely make a quick midcourse correction. If you want the ends of the threads in your life to come together, then ask the Holy Spirit to show you where you "dropped the stitch."

Lord Jesus, you have given me a life to live, and I believe it's worth living right. May I not wink at small sins. Give me courage to go back and make things right with those I have wronged.

Who Killed Jesus?

He himself bore our sins in his body on the tree, so that we might die to sins and live for righteousness; by his wounds you have been healed.

—1 PETER 2:24

In the weeks surrounding the premiere and release of Mel Gibson's immensely successful movie, *The Passion of the Christ*, religious leaders went round and round arguing over who was responsible for the crucifixion of Jesus. Did the religious leaders kill him? The Romans? Was it our fault? Did our sins nail him to the cross? The fact is, *God did it.* Isaiah 53:10 tells us, "Yet it was the Lord's will to crush him and cause him to suffer." The Father in heaven came up with the plan that included the cross. And because of Jesus' great love for his Father—and for you and me—the Son obediently followed through on God's plan. "And the Lord has laid on him the iniquity of us all" (Isaiah 53:6).

So, yes, Herod, Pilate, the soldiers, the religious leaders, the crowd—and you and I—are morally responsible for our part in the execution of Jesus Christ. But God was behind it all! Ultimately, it was his hand that "steered" the dreadful events to serve his own ends and purposes—and that is our great salvation, so rich, full, and free! Astounding. I can't begin to explain it. I'll never understand God's wisdom, knowledge, and love. Amazing love, how can it be? That God should plunge the knife in his own chest for me. That God should overcome death by embracing it. No wonder the good news is so great!

It is true, your sins—and mine—were laid on the shoulders of Jesus as he hung on the cross, paying our debt, taking the punishment we deserve. Let the thought of his suffering keep you from falling into "the sin that so easily entangles" (Hebrews 12:1). A terrible price had to be paid for each and every sin.

Thank you, Jesus, for loving and obeying the Father. May my life forever be a thank offering as I love and obey you all the more!

MARCH 22

Passover Lamb

Tell the whole community of Israel that on the tenth day of this month each man is to take a lamb for his family, one for each household.... The animals you choose must be year-old males without defect, and you may take them from the sheep or the goats. Take care of them until the fourteenth day of the month, when all the people of the community of Israel must slaughter them at twilight.

—EXODUS 12:3, 5–6

When I was on the farm growing up, I once helped take care of a little lamb. Cute, warm, and fuzzy, he captured and melted my heart. I loved to hug him and feel his soft white fleece. This precious lamb was the picture of innocence. You can imagine my horror on the day he was taken to the slaughter house!

For Passover preparations, God wanted a family to choose a lamb, bring it into their house, and take care of it for four whole days before killing it. How awful! They were required to slaughter the little lamb they had grown to love. This heart-wrenching sacrifice demonstrated the exacting demands of God's justice, as well as how destructive and awful sin really is. It was the perfect background to "the Lamb of God who takes away the sin of the world" (John 1:29). God wants our hearts to sincerely break over the sacrifice of his perfect Lamb. *We* were the ones who put Jesus Christ to death. *Our* sin led him to the slaughter. It leads us to grief and repentance.

A Passover lamb was the picture of innocence, but the Lamb of God is the perfect picture of righteousness. Isaiah 53:7 says, "He was led like a lamb to the slaughter, and as a sheep before her shearers is silent, so he did not open his mouth." Meditate on how a lamb is a biblical "type" of the life of Christ. Remember, Jesus went to his cross as *your* sacrificial lamb.

Jesus, thank you for being the Lamb who bore my sins!

֍

MARCH 23

Nothing Hidden

> Nothing in all creation is hidden from God's sight. Everything is uncovered and laid bare before the eyes of him to whom we must give account.
>
> —HEBREWS 4:13

My friend Sherrill and I used to sit with each other in our wheelchairs and talk about heaven. We spoke fondly and wistfully about the day when we would take that first heavenly step on strong resurrected legs. But Sherrill had one reservation. It was that part where the Bible says of the Lord that "everything is uncovered and laid bare" before his eyes. She shuddered at the idea. "Joni, I'm so worried about all the mistakes I've made — the failures and the awful sins."

I understand. The fear of the Lord *is* a deterrent to sin. Our Father in heaven tells us to be holy, as he is holy. Shedding sinful habits is a key and critical sign that we're truly growing in the Lord. But that doesn't mean Sherrill needs to be afraid. On the contrary, think of the flipside of Hebrews 4:13. God's eyes don't miss the *good* you do, either. The times you hold your tongue ... the times you patiently endure suffering, leaning on Jesus ... the times you hold up under pressure with a godly response ... the times you give, secretly, with no thought of return ... the times you offer an encouraging word when you are bone tired — *all* is laid bare before his searching gaze.

Maybe Sherrill's solitary and lonely apartment seemed hidden away from the sight of others, but nothing was hidden from God's sight. He took note of her patience, her endurance, and her faithfulness.

Fear the Lord; it's the beginning of wisdom. But then *do* the wise thing: fall in love afresh with your Savior, your High Priest, who has been tested in every way like you. Live life under his gaze, knowing beyond all doubt that it's a look of love.

Lord, the servant girl Hagar once named you "the One who sees me." That was after you rescued her and provided for her in your kindness. Help me to remember today, that you never, never lose sight of me.

～

MARCH 24

No Wrestling Match

> Christ loved us and gave himself up for us as a fragrant offering and sacrifice to God.

> —EPHESIANS 5:2

*M*y father was a national champion wrestler, and even as a little girl I would love to watch him grapple an opponent on the mat. Daddy would invariably pin his challenger with time to spare. I'd giggle when they'd cry "uncle!"

This is the picture of Jesus, and God the Father, that some Christians have. Some believers imagine Jesus wrestling his angry Father to the floor of heaven until he yells "uncle!" Jesus did not force the Father to be merciful to humanity. The death of Jesus was not the begrudging consent of God to be lenient to sinners. God didn't grumble, "If it weren't for Jesus, I'd give you insolent people a good licking!" No, the cross was the Father's idea. Before the foundation of the world, God the Father conceived of the brilliant, breathtaking plan to involve his Son in rescuing sinners (2 Timothy 1:9). It's wrong to think that God the Father was dead set on obliterating sinners until Jesus intervened and offered the cross as a solution; rather, it was planned by the Blessed Trinity from before the beginning of time. And it was all inspired by the love of the Father, the obedience of the Son, and the fellowship of the Holy Spirit.

Oh, what a wonder the love of God truly is! It is not syrupy or sentimental. Rather, the love of God is rugged and awe inspiring, terrible and astounding! The death of Jesus Christ appeased the wrath of God at the same time it served as a fragrant offering and sacrifice to God. Take the rest of the day—or evening—to ponder the complex and utterly complete love of God toward you.

Father, I am humbled that you poured out your wrath on your own Son. And Jesus, I am amazed that you went to the cross out of love and obedience to the Father. And all of this is for my salvation! Oh, how happy and grateful I am!

God and the Gravy Boat

"Do you understand what you are reading?" Philip asked.
"How can I," he said, "unless someone explains it to me?"

—ACTS 8:30–31

When it comes to Bible stories, hymns, and things in the spiritual realm, children can be pretty literal. For the most part, it's benign and endearing—and can tend to excite the imagination, creating wonder and mystery. But there was nothing wonderful about the first time I sang a well-known Easter refrain. It was Easter Sunday, somewhere around the mid-1950s. I stood in the pew alongside my three older sisters, all of us in our best and frilliest garb. With hymnals in hand, Kathy, Jay, and Linda began to sing "Low in the grave he lay, Jesus my Savior...." I'd never heard the song, and it seemed kind of slow and sad. But then they hit the refrain with great gusto: "Up from the grave he arose, with a mighty triumph o'er his foes...."

What was that? "Up from the *gravy* he arose?" I couldn't imagine such a thing. *Why would Jesus be in the gravy?* I pictured the Lord buried in brown creamy sauce, the kind Aunt Lee served with her roast beef. It wasn't until later that I learned to read the refrain, and with reading, came understanding. Funny, the things we think as a child. One friend told me she thought Pontius Pilate was a "conscious pilot." Another used to imagine that "round yon virgin" meant that the virgin was young and overweight.

It's cute, yes. But just another reminder that boys and girls—and new believers too—need guidance. That's why it's always helpful to take the time to open the Word and go step by step and word by word with someone who's young in the faith. It's one sure way to keep God out of the gravy boat.

Invite a child or a young believer to come and sit. Ask, "May I explain this to you?"

Father, I bless you for those who have come alongside me at different times in my life to help me understand more about you. Help me now to be that individual for one of your younger children.

MARCH 26

What's Good in Good Friday?

His divine power has given us everything we need for life
and godliness through our knowledge of him who called us
by his own glory and goodness.

—2 PETER 1:3

addy, why do they call it Good Friday?" I whispered as I sat
next to my father in church. Up front the Communion table
was covered in black, the hymns were all somber and in the minor key, and
there was absolutely no happy chatter permitted in the narthex of our little
Reformed Episcopal church. My sisters and I even dressed in dull, colorless
jumpers—not the pretty, frilly things reserved for Easter Sunday. If Good
Friday was so good, then why be so solemn and glum?

There's a good reason. I learned early on that the cross was not a play
thing; it was not to be made light of. Jesus paid for our sins, and, yes,
that's a wonderful thing; still, the cross of Christ was an obscenity—it
was brutal torture, a mock trial, hammering hatred, blood, tears, and hard
spikes driven through hands and heels. On that breathless day, the Father
snubbed his own Son so that our sins could be wiped out. God turned his
back on Jesus so that he could say to you, "I will never turn my back on
you; I will never snub you; never leave nor forsake you." *This* is the goodness of God. This is kindness with a crown of thorns crunched down on
it. And it's all for you.

Romans 2:4 says, "God's kindness leads you toward repentance."
Stop to consider the extraordinary kindness of God on your
behalf. His love covers a multitude of your sins, whether not-so-
innocent daydreams, the fudging of facts, puffed-up pride, or the
subtle slander of a neighbor. These are the things that separated
the Son from the Father. It's why Good Friday is, indeed, good.

Lord Jesus, help me not to take your cross lightly. I humbly bow before you,
confessing my sin. Thank you for your goodness toward me.

The Greatest Spectacle

Carrying his own cross, he went out to the place of the
Skull (which in Aramaic is called Golgotha). Here they
crucified him, and with him two others—one on each side
and Jesus in the middle.

—JOHN 19:17–18

When Ken and I visited Jerusalem, we visited the garden tomb.
We entered a gate through high walls and walked into a quiet,
green oasis—a contrast to the dusty, noisy street outside. We meandered
along a flowered path and came upon an empty tomb carved into the side
of a hill. There is no solid evidence that this was the actual tomb in which
they placed Christ, but there is a curious coincidence.

The coincidence is located beyond the far wall on the other side of the
garden. It is a limestone hill with a couple of natural caves near the top;
amazingly, the side of the cliff looks just like a human skull. Golgotha,
known as "hill of the skull." At the base of the cliff is a sprawling, noisy
parking lot for public buses and beyond that, the Damascus Gate, the
eastern entrance into the old city of Jerusalem. Our guide said, "See those
people waiting for buses? This is a good picture of the way it was the day
Jesus died. There were no buses then, but Jesus was crucified in a public
place where people could see him. They made a spectacle of his death."

As I left the garden, I remembered 1 Corinthians 4:9 (KJV): "*We* are
made a spectacle unto the world, and to angels, and to men." Now it's our
turn.

The root of the Greek word for *spectacle* in the Greek means "a
place of public show." Where is your Golgotha? Can people see
that you have been crucified with Christ? You may be a fool for
Christ. Don't worry; you're in godly company.

*Lord Jesus, I want the world to see how I identify with you. I want them to see
that I am crucifying my worldly desires and wants. I consider it an honor to
be made "a spectacle."*

൪

God Suffered First

A student is not above his teacher, nor a servant above his master. It is enough for the student to be like his teacher, and the servant like his master.

—MATTHEW 10:24–25

It was a twenty-hour flight that took us from Thailand to Ethiopia. It may have been the longest, most painful flight I'd ever been on. Unable to get up and walk down the aisle, I could only shift my position once in a while in the airplane seat. It didn't help. My corset was digging into me, and it felt as though knives were stabbing my back. Ken tried to help and so did my other two traveling companions. But they could only do so much. Besides, they needed their sleep too.

Knowing there was nothing else to do, I decided not to fight the pain. I breathed slowly and deeply and tried to surrender every tense muscle in my neck and shoulders. *Others may not be able to help, but you're here, Jesus. You're not asleep. Thank you for staying up with me.* Jesus completely understood; he too once suffered. When I relaxed into that powerful and beautiful truth, an indescribable blanket of peace settled over me. I knew I had entered another level deeper into the "fellowship of sharing in his sufferings" (Philippians 3:10). I could endure. I would be able to make it. All because Jesus made his presence on that plane as near as seat 3B next to me. The next thing I knew, the sun was up and we had arrived.

Jesus did not exempt himself from affliction but lived through it and learned from it. He thus became the source of help for all those who obey him. Should we suffer? A servant is never above his master. What a privilege it is to be like our teacher ... even in affliction.

Man of Sorrows, I find complete comfort in you despite my own grief, loss, and pain. I will not resist hardship today, for I am not above you, my Master.

MARCH 29

Spit

Then some began to spit at him; they blindfolded him, struck him with their fists, and said, "Prophesy!" And the guards took him and beat him.

—MARK 14:65

As a child, my friend Glenda experienced unspeakable abuse from her father. She grew up hating him. Even as an adult, she could not shake the memory of her father spitting on her. When Glenda finally opened her heart to Christ, she realized her seething hatred was just as awful as the sins committed against her. She was no better than her father. She had spent a lifetime imagining spitting back on him. It was *this* sin—and more—that Jesus died for on his cross.

This fact softened Glenda's heart like nothing else. She understood that she could have easily been the one flinging curses and spitting on Christ as he was nailed to his cross. The memory of saliva on her seven-year-old face paled in comparison to the spit on her Savior. Glenda discovered, as few believers do, the depth of God's love "in that while we were yet sinners, Christ died for us" (Romans 5:8).

Today Glenda is one of the godliest and most remarkable Christians I know. She was able to forgive her father, all because she prayed, "God, forgive us our trespasses as we forgive those who trespass against us."

"In order to suffer without dwelling on our own affliction," Thomas Merton once contemplated, "we must think about a greater affliction, and turn to Christ on the cross. In order to suffer without hate, we must drive out bitterness from our heart by loving Jesus. In order to suffer without hope of compensation, we should find all our peace in the conviction of our union with Jesus. These things are not a matter of ascetic technique but of simple faith."[2] If there is a hint of bitterness in your heart toward anyone, think on Jesus. He bore that bitterness.

Precious Lord Jesus, give me the grace to forgive others in the same way you've forgiven me.

MARCH 30

Gray-Haired Splendor

> Gray hair [is] the splendor of the old.
>
> —PROVERBS 20:29

Ernest Barkaway, a ninety-year-old Englishman, looked bright, sprightly, and dapper in his woolen vest and British tam. He told me that when one of his kidneys was removed, he received a blood transfusion: "I watched the drops trickle through the tube, and I thought of all the people—male and female, English and foreign, black and white—who had given freely of their life blood for my need." After a pause he wistfully added, "How much more Jesus gave freely of his life blood for my *deepest* need!" I could tell he had garnered much godly wisdom in his ninety years. He proved it with a poem he gave me...

> *They say that I am growing old; I've heard them say times untold,*
> *In language plain and bold—but I am not growing old.*
> *This frail old shell in which I dwell is growing old, I know full well!*
> *But I am not the shell.*
> *What if my hair is turning gray; gray hairs are honorable they say.*
> *What if my eyesight's growing dim; I still can see to follow Him*
> *Who sacrificed His life for me—upon the Cross at Calvary!*
>
> *Why should I care if time's old plough has left its furrows on my brow?*
> *Another house, not made with hands awaits me in the Glory Land.*
> *What though I falter in my walk and though my tongue refuse to talk?*
> *I still can tread the narrow way; I still can watch and praise and pray!*
> *The robe of flesh I'll drop and rise to seize the everlasting prize.*
> *I'll meet you on the streets of gold and prove I am NOT growing old.*

As I wrote the above, I learned Ernest Barkaway went home to be with Jesus. Write a note of encouragement or call an elderly friend today. Share Mr. Barkaway's poem.

Father, reveal to me ways I can ascribe dignity and show respect to the elderly people in my life. May I never take lightly their struggles and trials.

Inadequacies

Not that we are competent in ourselves to claim anything for ourselves, but our competence comes from God. He has made us competent as ministers of a new covenant — not of the letter but of the Spirit; for the letter kills, but the Spirit gives life.

— 2 CORINTHIANS 3:5–6

Not long ago at a conference, I was introduced as "Dr. Joni Tada." When I wheeled up to speak, I told the audience, "I may have been given a couple of honorary doctorates from seminaries, but I'm only a high school graduate. I've never even been to Bible college!"

There was a time I was embarrassed by the fact that I had no *real* scholastic degrees. *I'm not competent to speak alongside Christian leaders who have actually earned their doctorates. Why am I even attempting to write a book?* Later I realized that although I am inadequate in many ways, my competence comes from God, not from four years at Bible school.

God has used my many years in a wheelchair to remind me that, yes, I am completely inadequate and anything but competent — goodness, I'm just a quadriplegic! But my weaknesses and limitations keep pointing me to the source of all authority and ability: God and God alone. Praise the Lord, *he* makes us competent as ministers of the new covenant!

You may think, *Who am I that anyone should listen to me? Why should anyone care what I have to say?* Don't fool yourself. In Christ, you are completely competent. Second Corinthians 13:4 reminds you, "For to be sure, he was crucified in weakness, yet he lives by God's power. Likewise, we are weak in him, yet by God's power we will live with him to serve you." It is by God's power I serve the Lord. And it's by his power — and his power only — you can serve too.

Father, I don't want my feelings of inferiority to limit my service to you. Remind me today that I am adequate and competent in you to serve in your kingdom.

☙

April

The Passion of the Christ

He is before all things, and in him all things hold together.

—COLOSSIANS 1:17

hen I saw the movie *The Passion of the Christ,* I was struck by the brute cruelty with which the soldiers treated Jesus. Like a bunch of poorly paid drunken legionnaires, they couldn't wait to take out all their frustrations on who they thought was a stupid, luckless Jew. They beat and abused him mercilessly.

The face that Moses had begged to see—was forbidden to see—was slapped bloody (Exodus 33:19–20). The thorns that God had sent to curse the earth's rebellion now twisted around his brow. The back of Jesus' legs felt the whip—soon the body of the Savior would look like a plowed Judean field. By the time the spitting is through, more saliva is on Jesus than in him. When the soldiers raised the mallet to sink the spikes into Jesus' hands, it occurred to me that the Son of God whom they were crucifying was the very One sustaining their lives! Someone must sustain their lives minute by minute, for no man has this power on his own. Who supplies breath to his lungs? Who gives energy to his cells? Who holds a man's molecules together? *Only by the Son* do "all things hold together" (Colossians 1:17). How amazing, how incomprehensible that the Son, the victim, is granting breath and being to his own executioners!

> Close your eyes and think deeply on the things you just read. Consider so great a Savior who would submit himself to such torture ... for your salvation. Think of the cost and sacrifice involved in Jesus' crucifixion. Then, commit afresh and anew to live on a higher, more sanctified level as you trust and obey him with new resolve. Praise your Savior for granting you breath and being, as well as life eternal.

Dear Savior, I am awestruck that you did not turn away from the cross, but traveled the road to Calvary for me. May my life today reflect my love and devotion to you.

APRIL 2

What the Son Endured

Anyone who is hung on a tree is under God's curse.

— DEUTERONOMY 21:23

The pain and humility Jesus physically suffered leading up to his death was a mere warm-up to the real dread he faced. As he hung on the cross, he began to feel a foreign sensation. Somewhere during those hours that his body was impaled, an earthly, foul odor must have wafted, not around his nose, but in his heart. He *felt* dirty. Human wickedness began to crawl upon his spotless being—the living excrement from our souls. The apple of the Father's eye began to turn brown with the rot of our sin.

From heaven, the Father roused himself like a lion disturbed, shook his mane, and must have roared against the shriveling remnant of a man hanging on a cross. *Never* has the Son seen the Father look at him so, never felt even the least of his hot breath. It was the wrath of God being poured out like hot oil on the wounded heart of the Son of Man. And the Father watched as his heart's treasure, the mirror-image of himself sank drowning into raw, liquid sin. Jehovah's stored rage against humankind exploded in a single direction. The Trinity had planned it. The Son endured it. The Spirit enabled him. The Father rejected the Son whom he loved; the God-man from Nazareth, perished.

This is who asks you to trust him when he calls you to suffer. This is the One who asks you to obey him when it's hard, when your flesh is itching to have a little worldly candy. This is the One who asks you to honor him when you face tough choices. Jesus Christ bore the wrath of hell so that you might enjoy a home in heaven with him, the Father, and the Holy Spirit. Celebrate this marvelous gift as you reflect on Easter Sunday.

Father, thank you for giving me the gift of your Son. May my life be to the praise of your glory!

೧ఎ

APRIL 3

We Always Carry ...

We always carry around in our body the death of Jesus, so that the life of Jesus may also be revealed in our body. For we who are alive are always being given over to death for Jesus' sake, so that his life may be revealed in our mortal body. So then, death is at work in us, but life is at work in you.

—2 CORINTHIANS 4:10–12

oday's verse could sound a little morbid. We *always* carry around in our body Christ's death? We are *always* being given over to death for Jesus' sake?! A hearty and happy yes! Why happy? Because then—and only then—can the vibrant, joyful life of our Savior be revealed through us. And his life is revealed in us for God's glory, our eternal advantage, and others' benefit.

We carry around Jesus' death when we daily die *to* sin in the same way he died *for* sin. It means not taking a casual greeting like "How are you doing?" as an excuse to list every minor and major casualty of your day. Not using your prayer group time as an excuse to gossip. Not painting a picture of your marriage that colors your spouse as the culprit and you the hero. Not living like a martyr and making sure everybody else knows it. These are ordinary, yet important ways of putting your flesh to death with its itchiness to rebel.

Oh, to die to sin in the same selfless, patient manner as Jesus on his cross! Oh, if we could only see that refusing sin benefits others around us (just as Jesus was thinking of us on his cross). *Then* his life would be revealed in us—his profound peace, effervescent joy, and enduring hope.

Jesus, I need the power of your resurrection to help me "die to sin" today. Help me to see how "carrying your death" will result in a livelier life for me ... and deep encouragement for others around me.

APRIL 4

A Willing Captive

Jesus commanded Peter, "Put your sword away! Shall I not drink the cup the Father has given me?"

—JOHN 18:11

I once read a heartwarming devotional in *Tabletalk* magazine about today's verse. In John 18, Jesus declared that he would no longer pray that the cup of God's wrath might pass from him. Here we see our Good Shepherd embrace the cross. First he goes to the Kidron Valley—a place well known to Judas. Jesus would not be captured like a hunted animal, but, knowing Judas would intercept him there, he gave himself up in the garden without restraint. Also, Jesus openly declared his identity to the soldiers. Some may have assumed Jesus would hide behind his disciples and have to be forcefully exposed, but not our Savior! When Jesus stepped forward to accept Judas' kiss of betrayal, he powerfully and majestically declared, "I am." With these words, the soldiers fell back in awe and intimidation.

Jesus knew he would have to stand alone in the hour of his death, and he faced it with royal resolve. Even when Peter impetuously drew his sword, Jesus admonished him, saying, "No one can stop me from the task before me." Maybe the soldiers thought they would have to drag away a reluctant captive under the cloak of darkness, but instead they faced the King of Kings who willingly took control of the situation.[1]

Jesus went to the cross with a complete devotion to obey his Father, as well as a heart full of love for his people. Do you have a difficult duty to which God has called you? Is the Lord asking you to "die" to a certain habit, wish, or circumstance? Are you following the Lord's lead reluctantly? Ask God to give you the attitude of Christ.

Lord Jesus, thank you that you laid down your life willingly for me. Thank you that you did not balk once you accepted the will of the Father. Help me to do the same today in every difficult situation.

⁋

APRIL 5

The Kiss of Peace

And he arose, and came to his father. But when he was yet a
great way off, his father saw him, and had compassion, and
ran, and fell on his neck, and kissed him.

—LUKE 15:20 KJV

*I*n the story of the prodigal son, the father runs to meet his wayward son and kisses him. What a poignant metaphor for the way
our heavenly Father receives his repentant children! That sinners such as
we should enjoy the kiss of God! What makes it especially touching is that
Jesus felt God's slap so that we would experience God's caress. Think on
this: The Son of Man endured the wrath of God so that we might have his
righteousness; he endured violence that we might share in his victory; he
faced rejection that we might be embraced in eternal fellowship with God.
Psalm 85:9–10 says, "Surely his salvation is near those who fear him.…
Love and faithfulness meet together; righteousness and peace kiss each
other." And it's all because of Jesus.

"God promised to make the arrogant drink a foaming cup of his
wrath, a reflection of God's furious hatred of sin. But the one who drank
this bitter, foaming cup of wrath was Jesus. It is beyond our comprehension—the perfect Adam, adored and loved by the Father, was also despised
by the Father … consequently, we are promised that we will never bear the
staggering weight of his fury. It has already been poured out on the perfect
human being—the glorious Son."[2]

We don't deserve the favor of God. *We* are the ones who should
have drunk the bitter, foaming cup of God's hatred of sin. But Jesus
took that cup before it ever reached our lips. We receive the kiss of
heaven. Take a few moments to let this glorious fact sink in.

*Father, Son, and Holy Spirit, I am amazed that you sacrificed so much for sin-
ners such as me. My heart is humbled by your goodness and graciousness toward
me and all those who put their trust in you.*

☙

He Speaks to Me Everywhere

You will show me the path of life; in Your presence is fullness of joy; at Your right hand are pleasures forevermore.

—PSALM 16:11 NKJV

*T*t's not often that the produce counter in Ralph's supermarket holds spiritual significance, but last week, it did. My friend Judy and I were moving toward the checkout, and just as I was passing the turnips, an odd-shaped vegetable caught my eye. It was, the sign said, an opo squash. Until that moment, I had never realized anything like an opo squash even existed on the planet. I looked up and saw an "Exotic Produce" sign. "God did that," I said as Judy examined an Asian pear. It was like no pear I had ever seen—huge, misshapen, and covered with brown speckles. "Let's try it," she said, tossing it into the basket on my lap. After we checked out and were in the parking lot, Judy pulled the exotic pear out of the bag. "Want to be the first?" She held it up to my mouth. It looked ugly and odd, but I bravely bit into it. My eyes widened in surprise. It tasted sweeter than any fruit I'd ever eaten, and it smelled like fragrant perfume.

"O taste and see that the Lord is good!" I said, while chewing. "Jesus, how in the world did you think this thing up? I am doing something brand new here.... Lord, I am experiencing something of yours I have never experienced before!" God is always introducing us to new sights, smells, sounds, and tastes, so that we might constantly enjoy original and unique reasons to praise him.

As it says in the third stanza of the old hymn, "He speaks to me everywhere." Look around you, friend. His handiwork is everywhere. Today, taste and see that the Lord is good. And when you do, you'll find you have utterly original and fresh words to tell him so.

Open my eyes, Father, to more and more reasons to praise you, to find joy and pleasure in the endless array of your divine designs.

APRIL 7

No Hypocrites!

You hypocrite, first take the plank out of your own eye,
and then you will see clearly to remove the speck from your
brother's eye.

—MATTHEW 7:5

One of my goals in life is exactly the same as yours. I don't want to
be a hypocrite. Every day I want to shorten the distance between
that which I profess and that which I actually live. I want no gaps between
my "talk" and my "walk."

It's why I'd like to repeat every day for the next month, this "Test for
Self-Evaluation," proposed by John Wesley. The questions reflect the heart
of Scripture, so every morning we should ask ourselves:

Am I consciously or unconsciously creating the impression that I'm
a better person than I really am? Do I laugh at the mistakes of others, reveling in their errors and misfortunes? Do I insist on having
my own way? Is there a tendency for me to put others down so that
I'll be thought of more highly? Do I pass on to others what is told to
me in confidence? Am I thoughtful in expressing "thanks" to people
for what they've done for me, no matter how insignificant it seems?
Am I a slave to dress, friends, work, or habits? Am I self-conscious,
self-pitying, or self-justifying? Did the Bible live in me yesterday?
Did I disobey God in anything yesterday? Did I insist on doing
something about which my conscience was uneasy? Did I handle
discouragement well or did I have to be coddled? Am I enjoying
prayer? When did I last speak to someone about Christ? Is there
anyone whom I fear, dislike, disown, criticize, or hold resentment
toward? If so, what am I doing about it?

Is Christ real to me?[3]

Copy this page, tuck it in your daily journal, and refer to John
Wesley's questions often. Purpose to shorten the gap between
what you say and what you live.

*Lord Jesus, I don't want to be a hypocrite. I pray that what I say about my walk
with you matches the way I live.*

Don't Watch the Wall

Then Peter got down out of the boat, walked on the water and came toward Jesus. But when he saw the wind, he was afraid and, beginning to sink, cried out, "Lord, save me!" Immediately Jesus reached out his hand and caught him. "You of little faith," he said, "why did you doubt?"

—MATTHEW 14:29–31

My friend Dan, a race car driver, was recently talking about a terrible accident in which a NASCAR legend was killed. The driver's car had been in first place. Slightly bumped, it appeared he overcorrected and then, in the next instant, crashed into the wall. I asked Dan if that kind of thing happens often on the racing circuit. "Oh yes," he said. "Guys in their cars get into a spin, get bumped, and they see that wall coming! I'll tell you, there's one thing they're trained to do. *They must not look at that wall.* Their training tells them to keep their eyes on the track, and steer out of the spin. If they look at the wall, they'll freeze. Your body just reacts—you can't help it. The answer is to concentrate every nerve on steering toward that open space."

That answer really spoke to me. Because lately I've been experiencing an unusual amount of aches and pains, and it's had me thinking about ... the wall. *It's not going to get easier, Joni. Old age is coming faster than you realize, and boy, you'd better brace for an impact.* As a result of my fears, I've "frozen up" at times, worrying about the future and its problems rather than the present and its opportunities.

Paul writes, "Set your heart on things above," and the Gospels say, "Lift up your head, for your salvation draws nigh." It's advice worth following ... or you just might hit the wall.

Lord Jesus, sometimes my life situation makes me afraid. I feel panic rising, my mind locks up, and my fears loom like a large wall. As best I can today, Lord, I will fix my eyes on you, and not on my problems and fears.

☙

The Night He Was Betrayed

Strike the shepherd, and the sheep will be scattered.

—ZECHARIAH 13:7

That night Jesus was betrayed, he broke the loaf and gave it to his disciples. When Judas stood to leave, the Master looked at him. Then, Judas slipped out the door. The dark presence that had awaited outside in the night now stole into Judas' very essence. For the next few hours, the most distilled evil in the universe would personally operate through the body of a disciple of the Lord.

Back in the upper room, Jesus spoke quietly to his friends; they sang a hymn, then it was time to go. Out in the darkness they slipped through a city gate, down the steep ravine, and up into the hill of olive trees—eleven lambs and a Shepherd in the night. Jesus left his friends to go pray against a solitary rock. Eleven men who would later change world history—some, accustomed to working all night on their fishing boats—could not keep awake to comfort their Shepherd and Friend. There in the dirt in the olive grove, the Son of God groaned in prayer.

It may have looked as though Jesus was alone, but the bleachers of heaven were filled to capacity that moment, and hell strained its neck to see how this prayer would end. The Father gazed down and gave his sober nod. The Son stared back and bowed his acceptance. The torches arrived. The sheep fled. And the Shepherd stood to go to his slaughter (Isaiah 53:7). Consider this: Jesus was thinking of *you* that dreadful night. He remembered *you* as the whip lashed across his back. He thought of *you* when the mallet sank spikes in his hands and heels. Make today a time of remembrance, thanksgiving, and praise for your salvation.

Precious Savior and Master, I completely yield my life to you ... after all, you completely gave your life for me, while I was full of sin and selfishness. May my walk today honor the sacrifice you gave.

෬෭

Walking through Walls

Though the doors were locked, Jesus came and stood
among them and said, "Peace be with you!"

—JOHN 20:26

ver felt like you were up against a wall? Stuck. Stalled. Stymied.
Smack-dab against a cold, hard, unyielding barrier with absolutely no way out? You can't go back, you can't go sideways, it's too high
to climb, it's impossible to tunnel underneath, and there are no detours.
What do you do? A friend once told me, "Joni, when you're up against a
wall, the only thing you can do is start walking through it." Sound impossible? Of course it is! Whoever heard of anyone walking through a wall?
Well, someone did. In the upper room, Jesus suddenly appeared in the
midst of his frightened, discouraged disciples.

The door was closed, the walls were thick, and there was no entry or
exit. But Jesus came in anyway. Jesus did the impossible. And he is constantly asking us to do the impossible. When we face the wall—whether
it be pain, an emotionally unbearable circumstance, or a difficult situation
beyond anything we've ever encountered before—God wants us to walk
through that wall. As we take that first step into impossibility, we will
find Jesus in the wall, in the most unlikely place in the most unbelievable
circumstance. And in the interior of that cold, dark, unyielding place Jesus
whispers, "Peace be with you."

No matter what my situation, I have the assurance that if Jesus walked
through walls, I can too. Besides, I *have* to follow him. I have nowhere else
to turn. And neither do you.

What is your wall today? What is the impossible situation that has
been stopping you in your tracks and turning you back? Ask the
Lord Jesus to meet you there—right in the middle of it. And then
walk hand in hand with him through that wall to the other side.

*Mighty One, nothing is impossible with you. No situation is beyond your help,
your counsel, or your strength. I choose to fix my eyes upon you this day, rather
than my obstacles.*

ᕤᕠ

Touches of Home

The heavens declare the glory of God; the skies proclaim
the work of his hands.

—PSALM 19:1

*N*ot long ago I came home exhausted from a long trip. The house
was cool and dark, the rooms were empty, and Ken carried my
suitcases into the bedroom. It was good to be home and near my husband again. But sometimes, coming off a long trip, you really want to feel
home in the deepest sense. Not just inside the four walls of your familiar
dwelling—but *home*. Home with God.

Ken flicked on the bathroom lights and I wheeled in. And there, sitting on the counter, were roses. They took my breath away—and not
simply because of their lush texture and color, but because they were so different from everything else around me. The sink is made of porcelain, the
counter, Corian, the walls, wallboard. A glance around the room revealed
brass and glass, plastic and metal, tile and paint. Everything around me was
machined and man-made. Everything but the roses.

Martin Luther once observed that "a man who could make one rose
would be accounted the greatest in the world. Yet God scatters numberless
roses around us. His gifts are so infinite that we do not see them." When I
saw those roses in the bathroom that evening, I felt instantly at home. The
flowers in that vase spoke of my Father's touch ... and my husband's love.

Nature is only a name for an effect. And the cause is God. The
touch is his ... from a lowly daisy to a queenly rose ... from a tiny
pine seedling to a towering redwood ... from the whisper of April
wind in the cherry tree to the crashing of a storm-driven surf.
Bring something into your home or office today that reminds
you of his creative touch: a vase of flowers, a colorful seashell, a
humble pinecone, or a thriving, green houseplant. Let these God-
breathed, God-caused touches remind you of your *real* home.

*Creator and Savior, you have said you are preparing a place for me in your
Father's house ... just over the horizon. One day soon, I will be home forever.*

֍

Taking Care of Mom

Clothe those who are cold, and don't hide from relatives who need your help. If you do these things, God will shed his own glorious light upon you. He will heal you.

—ISAIAH 58:7–8 TLB

*J*ust a couple of years before my mother passed away, she came out to California to visit with Ken and me for "a few days." Those "few days" stretched into many weeks, and I had to set aside commitments and actually slow down for a while!

But really, she and I did great together. I was her eyes (and sometimes her mind), and she was my hands. At the supermarket, I could carry the basket on my lap and she would reach for cans on the shelf. I laughed and told her, "Mother, together we almost make up a complete person!" On the way to the office, Mom and I enjoyed our routine. She'd look for sheep on the left side of the freeway, count the horses after the Lost Hills exit, and choose the hymn for the day that we'd sing the rest of the way to work. She helped me open the mail, fed me turkey sandwiches for lunch, and organized the colored pencils in my art studio. Back home on the Maryland farm in a lonely farmhouse, most of her days were spent puttering. Southern California and "helping Joni" was *much* more interesting.

The first night she was gone, I laid awake thinking about her, back on that isolated farm. I whispered, "God, please take care of my mom." And a deep peace settled over my heart. And he has taken care of her in the most profound way I can imagine. He has taken her into his arms and carried her home.

Do you have relatives—flesh and blood, or in the family of God—you could encourage today with a call or a card or a visit? As you bless them, I'm confident that God will also bless you in a fresh and unusual way.

Father, show me this day how to reach out to my own flesh and blood ... and to those who share the DNA of Jesus.

APRIL 13

Contemplations of the King

We make it our goal to please him, whether we are at home
in the body or away from it.

—2 CORINTHIANS 5:9

My girlfriend arrived to get me up and ready for the day.
It had been a rough night—sleeplessness, and stabbing,
razor-sharp pain in my neck and shoulders. When I told her about it, she
sighed and said, "Joni ... I'll bet you just can't wait for heaven." As she
brushed my hair, I sat and dreamed about what I've dreamed of a thousand
times: my eternal home, just over the near horizon.

I have to be careful when I speak this way. Some people look at my
wheelchair, hear my enthusiasm for heaven, and conclude that it's a death
wish. Now it's true, when I was first injured, I only viewed heaven as a
place where I could get back what I had lost. I would receive hands that
worked and feet that walked and even danced. For me, it wasn't "the Day
of Christ," it would be "the Day of Joni."

My attitude changed as I studied the Scriptures. I realized that heaven was
mainly focused on Jesus, not me. It would be his coronation day, not mine.
I also began to understand that every fringe benefit of heaven—whether
receiving my new body, a new home, new friends, whatever—really centered around the culmination of Christ's purposes and his kingdom.

Someday, not so very long from now, we will see the King of
Kings in all his radiant beauty—as surely as you will see your
pastor on Sunday, the lady at the drive-up coffee window, or your
doctor at next Tuesday's appointment. Take a few minutes to read
Revelation 1:12–18, and 19:11–16, and let your mind dwell on
the coming of the Mighty One and his great triumph over every
enemy.

*Lord Jesus, you once were the humble carpenter, the Healer, and the Friend
of sinners. Now Lord, you rule at your Father's right hand in unimaginable
splendor. I bow before you right now and acknowledge you as Lord and King.*

ଓଏ

April 14

Assurance

For this very reason, make every effort to add to your faith goodness; and to goodness, knowledge; and to knowledge, self-control; and to self-control, perseverance; and to perseverance, godliness; and to godliness, brotherly kindness; and to brotherly kindness, love.... Therefore, my brothers, be all the more eager to make your calling and election sure. For if you do these things, you will never fall.

—2 Peter 1:5–7, 10

Many Christians base their assurance of salvation on things that are not scriptural: reciting a prayer or signing a card, walking an aisle or raising their hand in a meeting. Then when hard times hit, their confidence begins to wane—the longer the trial, the more doubtful they are of the reality of their salvation.

Assurance of salvation comes from three tests. The first is looking inward: Can I look in my heart and see there is a love for Jesus Christ? Do I at least "feel" that I love Christ? The second test is looking outward: Do I see evidence in my life of this love I believe I have for Christ? Are there any good works that flow from this love to Christ? Is there any outward evidence of what I proclaim to believe inwardly? The third test is looking back: Am I able to see a growth in grace since I first professed Christ? Dr. John Gerstner would often speculate that the best Christian on his best day is only 5 percent sanctified. But he is more sanctified today than he was yesterday, if he is a true believer.

Is there a professing Christian who is engaged in a regular practice of sin? Then he has good reason to doubt his salvation (Galatians 5:21). Today, thank God that he gives *you* assurance. Ask the Holy Spirit to uncover anything that stands in the way between you and a full, lively fellowship with God.

Search me, O God, and see if there be any wicked way in me. Help me to grow in Jesus and, thereby, gain a happy assurance of my salvation.

APRIL 15

Taste and See

Taste and see that the Lord is good; blessed is the man who
takes refuge in him.

—PSALM 34:8

*M*y friend Dan Earl is a beekeeper. Recently he presented me
with a gift basket of his bee by-products—creams, candles,
and best of all, his top-selling honey. That Sunday I enjoyed a cup of Earl
Grey tea and toasted crumpets with butter and honey. I was almost in
heaven. It was so *delicious.*

The Puritan Jonathan Edwards drew a parallel between honey and
Psalm 34:8. One can conclude that honey is honey because it is golden,
has a certain viscosity, and has bits of comb in it. Therefore, it must be
honey. But Edwards said there is a superior way to know. Put a drop on
your tongue, and you'll see that knowing honey involves much more than
understanding facts about it. To truly know honey is to taste and *see* that it
is sweet, delicious, and delightful. There's nothing quite like it!

The same can be said about our knowledge of God. We can conclude
that God is God because he is omniscient, omnipresent, and omnipotent;
he is attended by thousands of angels as he sits on the throne of heaven; he
is the Supreme Ruler, the Creator of all things, and the Judge of all men.
But even the devil knows these facts about God! So truly knowing God
involves more than knowing facts about him. We must "taste and see that
the Lord is good," sweet, delightful, and all lovely. We must have a heart
that awakens to his true splendor through experiencing his beauty.

Dr. John Piper writes, "Before we met Christ we were dead, blind,
deaf and insensitive to God's glory; we couldn't taste it as beautiful.... Conversion to Christ puts within us a taste for divine
things, a taste for the glory of God. Our battle is to constantly see
him more clearly that we might delight in him more fully."[4]

*Lord Jesus, your Word is sweeter than honey, and I find you utterly delightful.
Awaken my heart further to your beauty and splendor.*

Bible Lessons

All Scripture is God-breathed and is useful for teaching, rebuking, correcting and training in righteousness, so that the man of God may be thoroughly equipped for every good work.

—2 TIMOTHY 3:16–17

Discovering God's hand in your hardships is really a discovery of God's Word. Consider these power-packed verses that serve as a lens through which we can gain a clearer perspective on our afflictions. Psalm 68:19 says, "Praise be to the Lord, to God our Savior, who daily bears our burdens." This tells us suffering is used to increase our awareness of the sustaining power of God. Second Corinthians 4:7 says, "But we have this treasure in jars of clay to show that this all-surpassing power is from God and not from us." This reminds us that suffering allows the life of Christ to show up in our mortal flesh. Second Corinthians 12:9 says, "I will boast all the more gladly about my weaknesses, so that Christ's power may rest on me." This underscores how suffering completely bankrupts us, making us totally dependent on God.

Second Corinthians 12:7 states, "To keep me from becoming conceited ... there was given me a thorn in my flesh, a messenger from Satan, to torment me." This tells us that God uses suffering to teach us humility. Actually, all of Philippians 2:1–11 shows us how God uses our hardships to impart to us the mind of Christ. The Bible is jam-packed with lessons like these.

The only way we can gain a right perspective on our headaches and hardships is to spend time meditating on such verses. All Scripture is useful for teaching us heart-pumping truths like these in order that we might be thoroughly equipped, as today's verse tells us. Meditate on these brief Bible lessons and rejoice today that God wants to conform you to his Word.

You are the great Teacher, Lord Jesus, and I thank you for instructing me from your Word today. Bring these truths to mind when I am confronted with suffering this week.

More Bible Lessons

How can a young man keep his way pure? By living according to your word. I seek you with all my heart; do not let me stray from your commands.

—PSALM 119:9–10

Oh, to live according to God's Word and to never stray from his commands! Yesterday we allowed the Bible to speak directly to us regarding a godly perspective on our afflictions. What great lessons we learned from the Word of God. Let's continue! Romans 5:3–4 states, "We rejoice in our sufferings, because we know that suffering produces perseverance; perseverance, character; and character, hope." We learn here that God is more concerned with our character than our comfort! Psalm 107:17 states, "Some became fools through their rebellious ways and suffered affliction because of their iniquities." This shows us that suffering can be a chastisement from God for sin or if we are rebellious against him. Psalm 119:67 says, "Before I was afflicted I went astray, but now I obey your word." This is a lesson on how obedience and self-control is learned from suffering.

When it comes to embracing God's will for our lives, it simply must start with lessons like these. Psalm 37:14–15 teaches us that suffering is a part of the struggle against evil. Second Thessalonians 1:6 teaches that suffering is part of the struggle for the kingdom of God. Second Timothy 2:8–9 reminds us that suffering is simply part of the struggle of the gospel. Lastly, 2 Timothy 2:12 encourages us—endurance of suffering is given as a cause for reward.

Are you tired and weary? Do you feel overwhelmed by disappointment? God will strengthen your heart today as you ponder these Bible lessons. Ask the Holy Spirit to apply each one of these truths—as well as yesterday's lessons—to your heart. Ask him to transform you by the power of his Word. And then, trust him.

I hunger and thirst after your Word, dear Lord. Thank you that the Bible has so many lessons for me to learn.

APRIL 18

Peter Alone

Simon Peter and another disciple were following Jesus. Because this disciple was known to the high priest, he went with Jesus into the high priest's courtyard, but Peter had to wait outside at the door. The other disciple, who was known to the high priest, came back, spoke to the girl on duty there and brought Peter in. "You are not one of his disciples, are you?" the girl at the door asked Peter. He replied, "I am not."

—JOHN 18:15–17

There were many burdens Jesus carried to the cross. One of them is abandonment. In the hour of his greatest need when he needed his closest friends, when he needed to know he wasn't alone, that he hadn't been forgotten, Peter forsook him. What rubbed salt into the wound was that Peter did not deny him in front of a Roman soldier, powerful official, or a priest at the temple. It happened in front of a servant girl.

We assume that the "other disciple" was John. Somehow John was able to gain entrance into the house where Jesus was being questioned. Peter entered the courtyard but did not follow John into the hearing room. Maybe he was afraid. We have to wonder whether Peter would have denied Christ had he not been alone, had another disciple been there. Would he have been bolder standing next to John? Whatever, Peter was left alone in the courtyard, surrounded by accusers and skeptics. The rest is history.

Peter allowed his fears to overcome his faith. This happens to those who are full of pride. It's not obvious rebellion that causes them to refute Christ. It is the fear and intimidation of cynics. When are you most easily tempted? Is it when you are with someone you shouldn't be with? When you are alone? Keep track of patterns of temptation and then *avoid* those people or situations.

Father, help me to always seek the company of Christian friends. Convict me if I stray into situations in which I could be tempted to forsake my Savior.

Peace Be with You

> On the evening of that first day of the week, when the disciples were together, with the doors locked for fear of the Jews, Jesus came and stood among them and said, "Peace be with you!" After he said this, he showed them his hands and side. The disciples were overjoyed when they saw the Lord.
>
> —JOHN 20:19–20

*T*he disciples were huddled together, shaking in fear for their lives—doors were locked, curtains were drawn, and lights were dimmed. Suddenly, out of nowhere, Jesus appeared in the middle of the room and announced, "Peace be with you!" This was no happy-go-lucky greeting like, "Hey everybody, I'm here!" He wasn't offering the disciples mere peace of mind by his presence. When Jesus said, "Peace be with you," he pointed to the wounds in his hands and side for a reason.

For Jesus to gesture to his wounds was another way of saying, "Friends, look at these scars. They mean that the war is over. There is no longer any conflict between God and man. I have satisfied the Father's wrath against you and the good news is, I am your peace treaty. These wounds in my hands and side are evidence of the price I paid for peace between you and my Father. Peace on earth and good will toward men has finally been secured through my cross. And the proof of it is, I'm here. I'm alive!"

What difference does the Prince of Peace make in your life? Jesus says in John 20:21, "Peace be with you! As the Father has sent me, I am sending you." The peace that Christ offers is not for our pleasure only; God is sending us to go tell the world that the war is over, the white flag is raised, the treaty has been signed and eternal peace has been secured. The proof? Simply point people to the wounds of your Savior.

May your peace rule in my heart today, Lord God. Give me courage to tell others they can have peace with God through Jesus Christ.

APRIL 20

The Real Me

See to it that no one misses the grace of God and that no bitter root grows up to cause trouble and defile many.

—HEBREWS 12:15

he other week during a long flight home, I could not get comfortable in the airline seat. My corset was digging into me and no matter what Ken did, my blood pressure continued to spike and my forehead kept sweating (signs that I am in pain). Normally, it would have been enough to drive me to pray. But not this time. I was fed up with my disability (a nice way of saying I was fed up with God's control of the situation). My thoughts were sour, and I was not about to pull my Bible out of my backpack. Instead, I tried to get my mind off my pain by watching the in-flight movie. Halfway through, I thought, *This is the stupidest film. Why am I watching it?!*

That night after the pain subsided, my first thought was, *That wasn't like me. I'm normally not like that.* But the whisper of the Holy Spirit replied, "That *is* you. You *are* like that." Suffering always tests us, examining and sifting us and asking, "Who *are* you really?" Normally, we are not faced all the time with how self-focused we are, or how sour or peevish our attitude can be. We think we're doing pretty well. But suffering strips off that veneer and shows us our true colors.

Affliction does not teach you about yourself from a textbook; it teaches you from experience. It will always show you what you love—either the God of all comfort or the comfort that can become your god. Think back on the last time you got "fed up" with your circumstances. What did this reveal about yourself? Talk to God about that today.

Lord Jesus, I may not like affliction in my life, but I am keenly aware that it constantly shows me who I really am. Thank you for covering every sin with your precious blood!

౷

Take Heed

So, if you think you are standing firm, be careful that you
don't fall!

—1 CORINTHIANS 10:12

How many times have you watched someone dive headlong
into immorality and thought, *Nope, not me; I'd never be caught
doing that.* Beware. People who view themselves as standing firm are the
most susceptible to the most gross type of sin. Upright and obedient Noah
stood alone against a carousing, lustful world that drank itself silly. Who
would have thought Noah, of all people, would end up drunk? Look at
Abraham. He was ready to push obedience to the point of sacrificing his
own son. Who would imagine he would be the one to lie straight-faced
to government officials? And do it twice! Lot closed his door against the
sexual sin in the streets of Sodom, but hardly does he get delivered from the
city's destruction than he falls into incest with his own daughters.

Bold and courageous David was brave enough to go up against Goli-
ath, but later on, he made believe he was a madman because he feared his
enemies. Then there's Elijah. We take him to be a rather brave man as he
wielded the sword of God's vengeance against tens of thousands. But the
threat of one woman sent him plummeting into suicidal despair. Finally,
there's Peter. He was part of the Lord's inner circle, following the footsteps of
Jesus closer than anyone. Yet he ended up cursing and denying his Savior.

> First Corinthians 10:6–11 cautions us further about the human
> side of Noah, Lot, David, and Elijah, "These things [are] exam-
> ples ... and were written down as warnings for us." Just when you
> think you are doing pretty well, you stumble into a sin that seems
> so out of character. But it's not. The character of our body is of
> sin and death (Romans 7:13). Remember, you won't fall as long
> as you're leaning on Jesus.

*Lord Jesus, today I stand only in your strength and grace. Keep me from falling
into sin as I keep my eye on you.*

ॐ

Devotion Distractions

Because the Sovereign Lord helps me, I will not be disgraced. Therefore have I set my face like flint, and I know I will not be put to shame.

—ISAIAH 50:7

The other morning after Carolyn and Dana got me dressed and up in my wheelchair, we had our usual Bible reading together. We had just finished a hymn, our devotions, and were in the middle of praying by my bedroom bay window. I occasionally pray with my eyes open and on this particular morning, my gaze fell upon a huge spider crawling toward Carolyn. Without thinking, I gasped. My friends opened their eyes, and when they saw how big the spider was, we three screamed out loud together.

Dana took off her shoe to smack it, Carolyn raced for tissue paper, and I kept my eye on the intruder so it wouldn't vanish under the bay window cushion. Seconds later, the spider was history. After the kafuffle, we had the hardest time remembering where we were in our prayers, what hymn we sang, and which part of the Bible we read. Our minds were blank slates. We had forgotten all about our time with God! It was a useful lesson on how devilishly disrupting distractions can be. Everyday interruptions may be Satan's most useful tool in diverting our attention from godly pursuits.

Start praying and you can be sure the microwave will beep, the doorbell will chime, the phone will ring, the dryer will buzz, or a spider will appear. For me, a good defense is to now pray with my eyes closed. My husband goes into our guest room, takes the phone off the hook, and closes the door. Don't let interruptions be your shame when communing with your Savior. Put the blinders on, stick with the program, and set your face like flint.

I ask you, dear Lord, to be a watchdog over my mind and heart when I pray or read your Word. Keep me from any disturbance that the Enemy might place before me.

෴

APRIL 23

Where Jesus Is

We give thee thanks, O Lord God Almighty, which art, and wast, and art to come.

—REVELATION 11:17 KJV

To walk where Jesus walked is a thrill. I've experienced it as I've wheeled over the cobblestone streets of old Jerusalem, wandered the narrow roads of Bethany, and sat outside the home of Mary, Martha, and Lazarus. Oh, to be where Jesus was.

It was late in the day when my husband, Ken, stood on the spot where Jesus preached his Sermon on the Mount, overlooking the Sea of Galilee. As Ken stood facing the west, he began to recite Jesus' Sermon on the Mount: "Blessed are the poor in spirit, for theirs is the kingdom of heaven ... blessed are those who hunger and thirst for righteousness, for they will be filled...." I was gripped by the moment. Not so much to be where Jesus *was,* but to be where he *is* right now, showing up through the eyes and smile of my husband. Jesus was alive then, but he's alive now as Ken gives voice to the words of the Savior. Oh, to be where Jesus *is*!

Yet the double joy is that Jesus also *will be.* He's coming back. Heaven's about to break on the horizon, and soon God's feet will touch this earth once more. To be where Jesus *was* is heartwarming; to know that he is to come soon is heart-pumping. But the most poignant and powerful reality is this: *Jesus is!*

Notice the order of Revelation 11:17 (KJV), "O Lord God Almighty, which art, and wast, and art to come." Living in the present reality of Christ breathing life and vitality into our souls is matchless; by his spirit *alive* within you right now, Jesus *is.* Your past and the future can't compare with the power of his immediate presence. I know. I saw it that day on the hill above the Sea of Galilee.

Matchless Savior, awaken my heart to the possibilities and opportunities to fragrance my world with the truth that Jesus is ... within me.

༄

APRIL 24

God Sees ... God Knows

> Do not curse the deaf or put a stumbling block in front of
> the blind, but fear your God. I am the Lord.
>
> —LEVITICUS 19:14

What a strange thing for God to say: "Do not curse the deaf."
Even if you did bad-mouth a deaf person, he wouldn't be able
to hear you. And if you placed a stumbling block in front of a blind person,
he wouldn't be able to see you do it, right? What's God saying here?

First, he is saying that he takes the side of the poor, the lame, and those
who are deaf or blind. He is the guardian and protector of those who are
weak and infirm. God takes the position of their *advocate*, which literally
means to "give voice to those who have no voice." But is there a broader
application of Leviticus 19:14?

Yes, there is: God wants you to grasp the fact that he hears your hurtful
comments, even though others are out of earshot. God sees your mischievous behavior, even though others can't observe what you're doing. God
says in Numbers 32:23 that "you will be sinning against the Lord; and you
may be sure that your sin will find you out." Though the people you are
plotting against or gossiping about may not be aware of your malice, God
is aware. It's why he says in today's verse, "*Fear* God. I am the *Lord*."

Find a way you can take the side of the poor, the elderly, or the
disabled today. Several couples at my church take turns on Sunday mornings to drive to a local assisted-living center to pick up
Mr. and Mrs. Hill, an elderly couple who is separated from their
family. These friends from my church are true advocates ... they
are true friends of God.

*Lord Jesus, keep me from harmful conduct this day ... and help me to reach out
to those who are poor or disabled. I want to join you in serving as a guardian
and protector of those in need.*

He Is Your Shield

> The eternal God is your refuge, and underneath are the everlasting arms. He will drive out your enemy before you.... Blessed are you, O Israel! Who is like you, a people saved by the Lord? He is your shield and helper and your glorious sword.
>
> —DEUTERONOMY 33:27, 29

*J*eff was miffed. He wrote, "Joni, to even say that God allows bad things to happen goes against his loving nature. God is good, and he has absolutely nothing to do with the tragedies and awful things that happen in this world!" I thought back to the early days of my paralysis when I believed the same way. But it made me feel *less* trustful of God, not *more*. God seemed to be held hostage by bad things—things that were happening in my life! *Surely the Bible has more to say about this.* That's when I stumbled upon Deuteronomy 33:27–29. There I found a sturdy, wonderfully awesome view of God. He *definitely* has something to do with the awful things that happen in the world!

God is *constantly* protecting us from the full force of the Fall and the evil and suffering that goes with it. He is relentlessly shielding us. Time and again, he drives the devil away and rescues us from his wicked schemes. This sin-stained planet would have ripped apart at the seams long ago were it not for the restraining hand of God.

Second Thessalonians 2:6–7 says, "And now you know what is holding [the evil one] back.... For the secret power of lawlessness is already at work; but the one who now holds it back will continue to do so till he is taken out of the way." The Spirit of the Living God is the One who is "holding back" Satan and the suffering he instigates. Moment by moment God is engaged with suffering, restraining it, and only allowing those harmful things to reach us that ultimately fit into his plan for your life!

Lord God, bless you for shielding, protecting, and preserving me this day. I rest in your everlasting arms for you are my refuge in this world of sin and woe.

Cowboys in Wheelchairs

> Carry each other's burdens, and in this way you will fulfill
> the law of Christ.
>
> —GALATIANS 6:2

*L*ittle Matthew and Stephen came to one of our Family Retreats to volunteer alongside their mom and dad. They pushed wheelchairs, carried lunch trays, held Bibles, and played games with kids in wheelchairs. The boys had a blast, plus it provided great insight as to how disabled kids deal with daily struggles.

After the retreat was over, Matthew received a Lego City for his birthday. Their father observed his boys snap together a cowboy and Indian fort. They built walls, watchtowers, and a group of teepees. "What's that?" Dad pointed to an odd conglomeration of blocks.

"It's a ramp," they replied. "It's there so people in wheelchairs can get in the fort." The boys started snapping together little wheelchairs with square wheels. (Square? It's the thought that counts.) The cowboys rode wheelchairs instead of horses. So did the Indians. The boys constructed ramps into the general store, livery stable, and the jail. (I suppose that shows disabled people are sinners too.)

"They came up with the idea themselves," their father told me. "It came naturally." Hobnobbing for a week with kids in wheelchairs changed Matthew and Stephen. They will grow up to be adults who think, *What can I do to make life easier for my disabled friend?* It won't be a fearful world of "us" and "them," but a world where it comes naturally to put in a ramp, widen a door, reach out a hand, or open a heart. It will be a great world when it happens, and Matthew and Stephen are paving the way.

> Think of a family member, neighbor, or coworker who has a disability. Is there anything you can do to make his or her life a little easier for them? If so, you will fulfill the law of Christ.

Lord, open my eyes to the needs of others. Help me to carry their burdens and so fulfill your law ... the law of love.

Seasoned Conversation

Be wise in the way you act toward outsiders; make the most of every opportunity. Let your conversation be always full of grace, seasoned with salt, so that you may know how to answer everyone.

—COLOSSIANS 4:5–6

D o you have a driver's license for that thing? Ha! Ha!" My wheelchair elicits lots of comments. I'm surprised how many people initiate communication with me. I really don't mind. In fact, I love it. Usually the ambassador of Christ is the one who must jump-start conversations, hoping to engage the interest of the other. That's hardly the case with me. The wheelchair does the "initiating." I merely sit back and respond.

People don't *expect* me to look happy sitting in a wheelchair. Saying "I have a reason for living," in response to their remarks about my singing or my smile, always evokes a curious look. That's when I add, "Jesus has blessed me! By the way, what's *your* reason for living?" Sure it catches people off guard, sometimes delighting them, sometimes making them curious, and sometimes sending them running for the nearest exit. But one thing's for certain ... it got them thinking!

The truth is I've never heard of one certain style of giving the gospel that was a surefire success. I've learned that it has a lot more to do with the Holy Spirit's work in a person's heart than it does with a certain tool or technique. And so we do the best we can, grabbing a bit of opportunity here, nurturing a conversation there, sprinkling it with prayer, seasoning it with our testimony ... and leaving the results to God.

My friend, quit looking for a "guaranteed" method of sharing the gospel. Just ask the Holy Spirit to fill you, and tell him you're ready and available to touch the life of another. Then start sprinkling the conversational salt! Believe me, thirsty souls will be drawn to the Living Water.

Father, please bring a prepared, hungry heart across my path today. Put a smile on my face, a song in my heart, and fill my mouth with words that will open a padlocked heart.

Can You Stand the Test?

> We also rejoice in our sufferings, because we know that suffering produces perseverance; perseverance, character; and character, hope.
>
> —ROMANS 5:3

Six months ago, Ken and I began our home-remodeling project with big plans, high hopes, and glorious visions. Believe me, the glory has departed. It stopped being fun two weeks ago. Gone are the days when optimism oozed.

For the past four months, Ken has been sleeping in the middle of our living room surrounded by boxes covered with plastic sheeting, covered in turn by a quarter inch of drywall dust. I've remained in our bedroom, despite the floor-to-ceiling plyboard that's smack up against the mattress. Somewhere between wrangling over the color of stain for the ceiling molding and that night when we almost lost it at Carpets-R-Us, we knew we needed help. No, not with a second mortgage or an interior decorator or a marriage counselor. What we needed was a new perspective. Our gratitude had grown tired, and we needed grace.

We found it when we stumbled across today's verse, Romans 5:3. There is something wonderfully man-sized about the apostle's response to his hardships. *Stand the test, friends, for the end is in sight. Hope is on the horizon.* A right approach to problems—whether great or small—is a wonderful thing to have hammered into your character.

Sometimes we think of the suffering in Romans 5 as the huge life catastrophes. We forget that God's grace-giving power is mostly for everyday sorts of tests and trials—like adding square footage to your home.

What are your tests today? Where do you need perseverance, staying power, and hope? Ask God to help you step back and see a bigger picture than the trial right in front of your nose. He uses everything in our lives to mold our character and make us more like his Son.

Just for today, Lord, keep me and guide me, just for today. For the next twenty-four hours, fill me with the grace to face each setback with patience and joy beyond my own.

APRIL 29

Rich in Faith

Listen, my dear brothers: Has not God chosen those who
are poor in the eyes of theworld to be rich in faith and to
inherit the kingdom he promised those who love him?

—JAMES 2:5

When Ken and I traveled to Cuba with our Wheels for the World
team to deliver wheelchairs and Bibles, I met a fourteen-year-
old girl named Isis who had a brittle bone disease. Earlier that morning,
her mother had pushed her down the long dirt road in a rickety old adult-
sized wheelchair with flat tires. Isis sat quietly as she watched others receive
wheelchairs. She didn't smile all day. I'm sure this little girl wasn't so certain
we would be able to give her a different or better wheelchair.

As it turned out, Isis was delighted with the sleek and streamlined little
turquoise-colored wheelchair we gave her. But she was more delighted in
something else. When I gave her a copy of the Bible in Spanish, she gasped
with delight. Ken flipped open to the book of James, and I asked her to
read one verse. Isis began reading aloud the entire first chapter. Physical
therapists and mechanics put down their work. Tears welled as we all listened. It was clear Isis was far happier with the gift of the Word than with
her new wheels.

Perhaps God has made the poor of this world to be rich in faith,
because the poor have so little. What they do have, they treasure—like Isis with her first Bible. Psalm 119:47 says, "For I
delight in your commands because I love them." Is the Word of
God a place where your spirit dwells? Are your prayers peppered
with verses from the Bible? Do you prefer the Scriptures over
other things? Faith comes by hearing, and hearing by the Word of
God; therefore, rich faith comes from much study in his Word.

*Dear Word of Life, may I treasure your decrees and consider them precious.
Increase my faith as I increase my time in the Scriptures.*

℘

An Answer for Loneliness

> Turn to me and be gracious to me, for I am lonely and
> afflicted.
>
> —PSALM 25:16

sat on the porch trying to console Jennifer, a twenty-three-year-old
woman with cerebral palsy. Earlier in the day a few volunteers at
our Family Retreat tried to send her to the "children's group." With her
girlish grin and short blonde hair, Jennifer looked ten years old. Feeling
sullen and discouraged, she cried, "Joni, I don't have any friends. I'm so
lonely."

I couldn't imagine the gut-wrenching emptiness Jennifer was feeling.
When it comes to loneliness, though, "God has said, 'Never will I leave
you; never will I forsake you'" (Hebrews 13:5). That's a promise from
the lips of Jesus himself. He is especially near to Jennifer, for Psalm 10:17
assures her, "You hear, O Lord, the desire of the afflicted; you encourage
them, and you listen to their cry." After our talk Jennifer and I bowed our
heads in prayer and asked God to fill her void.

Three weeks later, Jennifer was enlisted in a volunteer position at a
local center for children with cerebral palsy. It was her job, as she told me
later with a proud smile, to go from crib to crib, pick up the little ones
in diapers, and "just love on them all!" Jennifer found the answer to her
prayer *and* her loneliness. It was others with cerebral palsy.

First Kings 22:5 says, "First seek the counsel of the Lord." We
feel we must have the love of others to fill the void in our hearts.
God says that as we cultivate an intimacy with him, we will not
only realize we're never alone, but we will see we can reach out
to others more in need. Nothing fills the void quite like getting
the focus off you, onto God, then on someone else in greater
distress.

*May my soul find rest in God alone, for my hope comes from him. You alone
are my rock and my salvation. Help me to point others to you today.*

May

The Beauty of Holiness

Your eyes will see the king in his beauty.

—ISAIAH 33:17

*M*y pastor recently asked me to share a few words during the worship service about the beauty of Christ. But how can one *talk* about the beauty and majesty of our great King? To grasp the beauty of something or someone, you have to experience it. Psalm 29:2 tells us: "Worship the Lord in the splendor of his holiness."

God's holiness? *Beautiful?* That would be like staring at the sun with your naked eye, hoping to find its beauty. You can't! It would blind you. But as the writer to the Hebrews reminds us, "We see Jesus, who was made a little lower than the angels, now crowned with glory and honor because he suffered death, so that by the grace of God he might taste death for everyone" (Hebrews 2:9). Scripture invites us to turn our gaze on Jesus, remembering his holiness and allowing his indwelling life to burn away the doubts and fears, anxieties and worries about the future, or bitterness and resentment. We take up our cross and follow him. He died *for* sin, and we die *to* sin. When that happens, in due time the dark, thick clouds will part and we will see the Savior in all of his full-orbed splendor.

> You and I grasp his beauty when we die to the very sins he died for. At that point, the comeliness of Christ strikes a tuning fork in our sanctified souls, and we resonate with his freshness and purity. Jesus said, "Take up your cross *daily*." So today is the day to cast your sins aside, embrace the deep-down cleansing of his blood, and seek him with a life scrubbed clean. It feels beautiful. So beautiful you can't talk about it—you have to experience it for yourself.

King Jesus, I praise you for removing my sins far from me. I pause to worship you with a purified heart, a clean conscience, and a fresh desire. Help me to stay on my knees until, once again, I catch a glimpse of your radiant beauty.

☙

MAY 2

Putting Pleasure on Hold

I wait for you, O Lord; you will answer, O Lord my God.
—PSALM 38:15

ave you ever had a cup of the coffee they serve in hotel hallways or lobbies? Early in the morning the people at the front desk put a pot of coffee out on a little table with powdered creamers next to some Styrofoam cups. It's not the best-tasting stuff—and may have been sitting there for hours. Sometimes when I'm traveling, I'll spot the coffee, sniff the aroma, and often I'm tempted to scarf down a cup. If I'm in a hurry, I'm thinking less about quality and more about caffeine!

Ah, but if I know there's a gourmet coffee kiosk at the airport, serving up a fresh ground heavenly brew, then I say, "Hmmm, I think I can wait a half hour." I know it will pay off. I think of that which is higher quality. It takes a little self-control, and it means putting pleasure on hold, but I do it in anticipation of an even greater pleasure on the horizon.

This is at least some of what it means to "wait on the Lord." Waiting on God does *not* mean passive indifference—hanging around and doing nothing. It has more to do with saying no to impulsive, spur-of-the-moment actions or decisions, and by so doing, saying yes to something you know will satisfy much better on down the line. Those who have not yet learned how to wait on the Lord may tend to indulge in something immediate that only half satisfies. But Christians who have fostered a degree of self-control—Christians who know God better—don't mind putting pleasure on hold. They know something better is brewing down the line.

God is always worth waiting for. Take time to be still before him, seeking his mind and his desire for your today ... and all your tomorrows.

Lord, I praise you for what Peter called your "precious and magnificent promises." I wait on you today, believing what you have planned for me is so much better than what I could ever grab for myself.

ᡠᡃ

First Response

Paul and Timothy, servants of Christ Jesus, to all the saints in Christ Jesus at Philippi, together with the overseers and deacons: Grace and peace to you from God our Father and the Lord Jesus Christ. I thank my God every time I remember you. In all my prayers for all of you, I always pray with joy because of your partnership in the gospel from the first day until now.... Now I want you to know, brothers, that what has happened to me has really served to advance the gospel. As a result, it has become clear throughout the whole palace guard and to everyone else that I am in chains for Christ.

—PHILIPPIANS 1:1–5, 12–13

This was Paul's first letter from prison to the church at Philippi. Obviously the Philippians were anxious to hear how Paul was doing. The apostle could have started off his letter, "I'm glad you're praying because I need it. The prison guards are mean, my chains are chafing, the grub is lousy, the nights are freezing, my bed is hard, I can't sleep, and the other inmates are bullies. This place ain't no picnic!" That's how some people might have responded, but not Paul. He was not about to drag the Philippians down with a long list of complaints. Rather, he strove to encourage the church with his prayers and to assure them the gospel was going forth.

Paul writes in Acts 20:24, "I consider my life worth nothing to me, if only I may finish the race and complete the task the Lord Jesus has given me—the task of testifying to the gospel of God's grace." His focus in good times and bad was the going-forth of the gospel. What an example! Throughout your day, think of how your circumstances and encounters with others serve to advance the good news of Jesus.

Lord God, the good news is the goal of my day. Help me not to complain about my problems, but to see them as opportunities to share the gospel.

☙

The Owls

Give me a sign of your goodness ... for you, O Lord, have
helped me and comforted me.

—PSALM 86:17

*D*riving home one late afternoon, I felt empty, dry, and bone
weary. From that perspective, everything I had done during the
day seemed pointless ... just so much wasted time. Pulling into my drive-
way, I whispered, "Lord, I need to see you at work. I need you to touch me
in some special, unusual way tonight."

In my bedroom an hour later, still fighting the blues, I paused by the
bay window overlooking our backyard. Suddenly I spotted something in
the twilight—two somethings!—with large wingspans, fluttering on a
branch of my neighbor's pine tree. Then I saw yet a third great bird, even
larger, perched on one of our pines. They were huge great-horned owls.
Before long, the owl from my yard joined the other two. My visiting friend
came into the room, grabbing binoculars. Peering into the neighbor's tree,
she said, "Joni, those are baby owls!" They had been bobbing, flapping,
and hopping back and forth on the branch waiting for their mother—
obviously the larger owl who had been in my tree. We even saw the mother
fly away and, within minutes, come back with a mouse to feed her babies.
(At which point we put the binoculars away.)

What a thrill to watch these unusual representatives of God's creation
up close and personal! I forgot all about my dreary mood of a few moments
before. When the whole escapade was over, I remembered my prayer. I
would have thought God would have given me his "fresh touch" through
special words from my visiting friend ... or maybe a verse of Scripture ...
or perhaps a vase of flowers surprising me at the kitchen sink. Who would
have thought owls would have been his emissaries of encouragement?

Ask the Lord to show himself to you in new and unexpected ways
today. And prepare to be surprised!

*Lord, I don't want to miss those little "calling cards" of your presence, your inter-
est, and your care. Please keep me alert to all the ways you speak your love.*

What God Wants

Set your minds on things above, not on earthly things.

—COLOSSIANS 3:2

This is what God wants—hearts burning with a passion for future things, on fire for kingdom realities that are out of this world. God wants his people aflame with his hope, a "consider it pure joy" outlook that affects the way we live on earth. God wants us to be "cities on a hill" and "lights on a lamp stand" so that everyone around us will be encouraged to look heavenward (Matthew 5:14–15).

A perspective like this doesn't happen without suffering. It is affliction that fuels the furnace of heaven-hearted hope. People whose lives are unscathed by affliction have a less energetic hope. Oh, they are glad to know they are going to heaven; for them, accepting Jesus was a buy-and-sell agreement—place your sins on the counter and get an asbestos-lined soul. Once that's taken care of, they feel they can get back to life as usual—dating and marrying, working and vacationing, spending and saving.

But suffering obliterates such preoccupation with earthly things. Suffering wakes us up from our spiritual slumber and turns our hearts toward the future, like a mother turning the face of her child, insisting, "Look this way!" Once heaven has our attention, earth's pleasures begin to pale in comparison.

What has suffering taken away from you? What has it diminished or robbed? Don't allow your heart to dwell on earthly disappointments. God permits suffering to draw our attention on heaven where that which was lost—and more—shall be restored. Suffering forces us to look forward to the day when God will close the curtain on *all* disease, death, sorrow, and pain. Until then, we have work to do! John 9:4 says, "As long as it is day, we must do the work of him who sent me. Night is coming, when no one can work."

Lord of heaven, turn my heart toward you this day. I set my mind right now on things above.

MAY 6
Mother's Day

"Sing, O barren woman, you who never bore a child; burst into song, shout for joy, you who were never in labor; because more are the children of the desolate woman than of her who has a husband," says the Lord.

—ISAIAH 54:1

For years Ken and I tried to conceive a child. I knew of other spinal-cord-injured women who gave birth to children, and I was convinced I could do the same. I planned to turn my art studio into a nursery and my wheelchair into a "stroller." I could even envision holding my baby in a "kangaroo carrier" on my wheelchair. But it wasn't to be. After many tests at an infertility clinic, Ken and I realized we would not be able to have a child.

At first, I was devastated. But then we realized we already had a family. A *worldwide* family. We began to rejoice anew over the thousands of spiritual children—especially children with disabilities—who had been touched by my story over the years. Ken and I began to pray in a deeper, more specific way for these young people. Almost overnight God took away the pain and emptiness of my barren womb. I almost plastered an Isaiah 54:1 bumper sticker on the back of my wheelchair!

There's a reason for every woman to celebrate Mother's Day—even those who, like me, do not have children. Any woman can enjoy rich relationships with boys and girls in their neighborhoods, churches, and extended family. If you have never given birth to a child, ask God to show you a young person whose life you can spiritually nurture. It'll be a reason to "burst into song and shout for joy." Look up Child Evangelism Fellowship at www.childevangelismfellowship.org to find ways you can share Christ with young people.

Lord God, I'm glad you take delight when we provide spiritual parenting to children in our sphere of influence. Use me to bring more boys and girls into your kingdom!

Perplexities

> He was wounded and crushed for our sins. He was beaten that we might have peace.... The Lord laid on him the guilt and sins of us all.
>
> —ISAIAH 55:5–6 NLT

Ravaged by a degenerative nerve disease, my friend John is no longer able to sit up. Not long ago, on his bed in the middle of the night, he got some unexpected visitors. An ant found him. Then others. Then thousands, fanning out over his body ... and he was too weak to call out. The next morning the nurse threw back his blanket and gasped. His entire body was red and badly bitten. Those who know John were shocked and aghast. *How could God allow this to happen to one of his children?*

To be honest, I have wondered the same on many occasions. We ask, "Why God?" But clear-cut answers aren't always easy to discern. When we honestly ask God the "why" question, he doesn't give us answers as much as he gives us himself. If you are the One at the center of the universe, holding it together so it doesn't split apart at the seams, if everything that lives and breathes has its being in you, you can do no more than give yourself. And God has done that! In order to defuse our anger over the suffering of loved ones, we must focus on a greater suffering—Jesus on the cross.

Some people look at John's life with all he suffers and think, *How does God get off the hook on this one?* But John knows the answer. He keeps pointing people to Jesus. As someone once said, Jesus is God *on* the hook.

Have you been asking the "why" question lately? Instead of allowing the question to push you away from God, let it push you deeper into his arms. The God who gave the greatest Gift delights to give more and more of himself.

Father, you know and understand the perplexities of my heart. When my mind can't trace your ways, may my heart simply trust in your love.

᠙

Rejoice Always!

Rejoice in the Lord always. I will say it again: Rejoice!

— PHILIPPIANS 4:4

*L*iving the Christian life is so opposite, so against the grain of our human nature. When today's verse tells me to rejoice always, my inclination is to be glum-faced, thank you. A little bit of whining, huffing and puffing, scowling and sighing is more to my liking. But common sense warns me it will only make things worse.

Philippians 4:4 is a triple whammy: we are to rejoice in the Lord *always,* and then *again,* rejoice with an *exclamation mark.* Perhaps Paul felt he should underscore the command because circumstances in Philippi were so bad as to make the exhortation utterly unreasonable. But Christians can be commanded to rejoice because their ground for doing so is not in circumstances but "in the Lord." The command may be contrary to our old nature, but remember it's not Paul's command. It is the command of Jesus Christ. When Paul insisted we rejoice always, he was no doubt thinking of the words of Jesus who said, "Take heart! I have overcome the world," and "Blessed are you when men hate you. Rejoice in that day and leap for joy for great is your reward in heaven" (John 16:33; Luke 6:22–23). We rejoice not only because Jesus told us to, but because he himself rejoiced. And that's with an exclamation mark!

How can we rejoice in every circumstance? In chronic pain or cancer? In rejection and bankruptcy? The next verse provides motive, perspective, encouragement, and reason enough: *The Lord is near* (Philippians 4:5). You can keep a bright outlook in the midst of any hardship; you can have peace of mind and heart when you know that the Lord Jesus is close at hand. Think of a situation you've been grumbling about; choose today to rejoice in the Lord in the midst of it all.

Lord, I bring before you the circumstance of _____. I purpose by your grace to rejoice always, and again I will say, "I rejoice!"

ᦉ

May 9

Shine Like Stars

Do everything without complaining or arguing, so that you
may become blameless and pure, children of God without
fault in a crooked and depraved generation, in which you
shine like stars in the universe.

— PHILIPPIANS 2:14 – 15

e saw yesterday that the book of Philippians is filled with commands to be joyful in suffering. And to be joyful *always.* Today's
verse echoes that theme as the Spirit of Christ, through Paul, commands us
to do everything without complaining or arguing. That means *everything.*
Paul was writing to the congregation at Philippi who were facing enormous
hardship, and the temptation to murmur or grumble must have been great.
The apostle was not so much scolding Christians for their sour attitudes;
rather, he had a bigger picture and purpose in mind ...

Evangelism. Paul's heart — and the heart of Christ — was focused on
wooing others into the kingdom. His passion was for the salvation of the
crooked and depraved generation in Philippi. Paul wanted the power of
God to be showcased to those lost in darkness. By not grumbling, we
become "blameless and pure" before others. No one can point a finger.
This shakes a skeptic to the core. Nothing makes a scornful, cynical world
sit up and take notice of God more than when it observes believers actually
rejoicing in their hardships, without a hint of complaint.

"Do everything without complaining or arguing *so that you may
... shine like stars in the universe."* Paul's unswerving focus in Philippians is evangelism. Every admonishment, warning, counsel,
and instruction is always for the purpose of somehow reaching
others for Christ. Think of how complaints or grumblings may
have diminished your witness to those around you. You will shine
like a star in a dark world today as you put behind you any grumblings or murmurings.

*Lord Jesus, for the sake of your gospel, for the sake of the advancement of your
kingdom, for the sake of this crooked generation in which I live, please convict
me if I complain today.*

MAY 10

An Ever-Present Help

God is our refuge and strength, an ever-present help in trouble.

—PSALM 46:1

Nothing is more suffocating, more soul stifling than the feeling of hopelessness. When you've tried every option, it's despairing to think that you've come to the end of your rope with no aid in sight. Hopelessness breeds when we fail to sense God's hand in the hardship, or the presence of his help. It's demoralizing to feel as though God is off somewhere, distracted by the needs of more obedient saints.

Hope is built on fact. And the fact is God *never* becomes distracted from your life. He *never* takes time off from tending to your needs. When troubles come, he doesn't back away to allow Satan a free hand. Today's verse assures that not only is the help of God available and accessible at all times, but *God himself is* the always-present help in every trial.

"God understands the darkness that we face. He is right there in it with us, 'an ever-present help in trouble.' The Lord of light is your friend in darkness. The Lord of life stands beside you in death. The Lord of hope is your companion in your despair. The Prince of Peace supports you when no peace can be found. The God of all comfort waits faithfully near you. The Source of all joy is close by when death has robbed you of joy."[1]

When we've hit rock bottom or are up against a wall, we are easy prey for the lies of the adversary. When we are emotionally distraught, we believe the lie that God has become a casual observer, standing at arm's length from our pain. Write out today's verse and underline the adjective. God is always present with help and hope.

You are my refuge and my strength, dear Lord. When troubles assault, may I never be deceived into thinking that I am beyond your tender compassion. Thank you for being always and ever present in my trials. I praise you for being in control!

Jesus Came for This Reason

Very early in the morning, while it was still dark, Jesus got up, left the house and went off to a solitary place, where he prayed. Simon and his companions went to look for him, and when they found him, they exclaimed: "Everyone is looking for you!" Jesus replied, "Let us go somewhere else—to the nearby villages—so I can preach there also. That is why I have come."

—MARK 1:35–38

In the early years of my paralysis, I traveled to many faith-healing services. My fingers and feet never seemed to get the message, though. After one healing service, I went home and read the first chapter of the gospel of Mark.

Although it was still early in the morning, crowds of disabled and sick people came to Capernaum to find Jesus. He wasn't there. He was up in the hills praying. When the disciples found him, Jesus refused to meet with the crowd; he simply said, "Let's go somewhere else. Let's go to other villages so I can preach in those places *for this is why I have come.*" It's not that Jesus didn't care about the cancer-ridden people or the blind or the disabled; it's just that their illnesses weren't his focus. The gospel was. His message was: God is holy and you are not. He is just, your soul is in risk of hell, but the Father sent me to show his love. Now believe in me and you will be saved. Whenever people missed this—whenever they started coming to him to have their pains and problems removed—the Savior backed away.

On a scale of one to ten, how often do you ask God to remove a painful situation? On the same scale, how quick are you to tell people about the gospel, the real focus of Jesus' coming? Remember, God saved you to tell others his good news. Your painful situation just may be his best platform to showcase the gospel.

Jesus, may I have the same sense of urgency about the kingdom message today as you do!

෨

Heaven's Incentives

The man who plants and the man who waters have one purpose, and each will be rewarded according to his own labor.

—1 CORINTHIANS 3:8

The Gospels are packed with parables of kings honoring servants for their diligence, landlords showering bonuses on faithful workers, monarchs placing loyal subjects in charge of many cities, and owners of vineyards paying top wages to the lowliest of laborers. These parables teach us that God *wants* to reward us. God is the king and the landlord who has every intention of giving us more than we deserve. He takes great delight in showering bonuses and blessings upon us.

Heaven has its incentives, and as we remain faithful in the midst of pain or problems, we are not only accruing eternal reward, we are giving greater glory to God. God is worth it! The more faithful we are to him, the more our reward and joy in heaven. Our reward will be our capacity for joy, service, and worship. Whatever suffering you are going through this minute, your reaction to it affects the happiness of your eternal state. Heaven will be more heavenly to the degree that you have followed Christ on earth.

Gospel parables are reminders for us to remain faithful ... to not give up ... to hang in there ... and to do so willingly and happily. God is more generous than we can possibly imagine, and he intends to recompense and more than repay every hurt and tear. If today you are lacking resolve to obey through tough times, remember—God is worth it.

Father God, I'm amazed that you want to reward us in heaven. Thank you that when you bestow heavenly benefits and blessings, I will have the honor and privilege of turning right around to shower the blessings on my precious Savior. I want to follow you here on earth ... so that I can cast more crowns at Jesus' feet.

ॐ

Open My Eyes

The cross ... is the power of God.

—1 CORINTHIANS 1:18

Startling things happened shortly after that first resurrection Sunday. For example, Luke 24, where Jesus is having supper with the two he met on the road to Emmaus. It says, "When he was at the table with them, he took bread, gave thanks, broke it and began to give it to them. Then their eyes were opened and they recognized him." They recognized Jesus when he broke the bread. Imagine it. What brought that "Aha!" moment? Their eyes saw his hands reach for the loaf, then tear it apart. Something seemed familiar. Suddenly, I think that's when they knew. How could they miss the nail prints in his hands as he passed the chunks of bread?

There's a powerful lesson in this for us. If we want people to recognize Jesus, to see the characteristics that reveal him as Savior, our conversation about God with others must always point to Christ. And when we talk about Christ, we must always point to the cross, where Jesus reveals himself as Savior, Deliverer, Triumphant King. The Father will open the eyes of seekers when they contemplate the cross. It is what makes the Christian faith utterly unique. When we point people to Calvary, they cannot miss the glory of the cross. For what other man died upon such a tree, yet still lives?

If you want an "Aha!" moment, remember that the cross is the power of God. It is in the nail prints where Jesus reveals who he is. It's not difficult to recognize him. Then, like the women at his empty tomb, let us run with joy to tell others of his victory — *our* victory. "Because I live, you also live," he said. We know the promise, and we've felt the touch of his nail-scarred hand. Now gaze at the empty cross. Recognize him?

Lord Jesus, use me to point hearts toward the cross ... where one glimpse will change everything, for all eternity.

MAY 14
Jerry's Place

As for man, his days are as grass: as a flower of the field, so
he flourisheth. For the wind passeth over it, and it is gone;
and the place thereof shall know it no more.

—PSALM 103:15–16 KJV

Francie, my secretary, lost her husband, Jerry, this year, and like
most widows she shivers to think that his place will be forgotten.
Even Ecclesiastes 9:5 underscores, "For the living know that they will die,
but the dead know nothing; they have no further reward, and even the
memory of them is forgotten." The world deals a cruel blow to people who
die. It does its best to make sure their place will be forgotten.

Perhaps Jesus was thinking of this when he assured, "I am going there
to prepare a place for you. And if I go and prepare a place for you, I will
come back and take you to be with me that you also may be where I am.
You know the way to the place where I am going" (John 14:2–4). In the
span of three sentences, our Savior speaks of a man's "place" three times.
The Carpenter of Nazareth has built Jerry a place in heaven. Not one made
with hands but by God's eternal decree. The world might erase Jerry from
its memory, but not heaven. He will *never* be forgotten. That's because he
has a *place* by Jesus' side.

Perhaps you know a widow who is still grieving the loss of a loved
one who has gone on to heaven. Those who are grieving want
you to mention their spouse. Today, jot that person a note, sharing a special memory and letting her know you haven't forgotten.
Assure your friend that heaven has a far grander place for their
mate, hand made by Jesus Christ himself!

Lord Jesus, thank you that you have designed a specific, hand-tailored, custom-
constructed place in heaven for me. Thank you for building my home—my
special place—in heaven.

෨

MAY 15
Washing Wheels

After that, [Jesus] poured water into a basin and began to wash his disciples' feet, drying them with the towel that was wrapped around him.

—JOHN 13:5

Ken and I invited two couples from out of town over for a backyard dinner last night. It was candlelight, music, and dining under the stars. It was going to be *great*. To situate my legs under the table, I had to wheel back and forth over wet grass. After getting in place, I looked down and groaned. Chunks of mud, stones, and dirt were thickly wedged between the tread in my tires. I imagined what that would do to my new cream-colored carpet when later I would wheel inside my house.

But after dinner and without any prompting from me, Peter and John, the two husbands, left our table and ran inside to get a pail of hot water. Pouring it over my dirty tires, they began scrubbing with a dish brush and picking away mud with a knife. I felt embarrassed that our special dinner guests were on their hands and knees, getting dirty and wet. One of the fellows laughed and said, "Hey, what we're doing is very biblical. When Jesus told us to wash each other's feet, I'm sure he meant your wheels too!" Immediately I sensed an outpouring of God's humility and grace. Humility in seeing our honored visitors on their hands and knees ... and grace in that these men had a chance to jump in and follow the Savior's example from John 13:5.

I learned two things last night. Nothing works better than hot water for getting mud off anything; plus, I learned that to wash my feet is to wash my wheels. Today, find a unique and unusual way to "wash the feet" of another. When you serve, you'll experience both humility and grace.

Lord Jesus, when I see a need today—no matter how unusual or unique—give me humility and grace to serve and make a difference.

MAY 16

It Hurts So Good!

> God disciplines us for our good, that we may share in his holiness. No discipline seems pleasant at the time, but painful. Later on, however, it produces a harvest of righteousness and peace for those who have been trained by it.
>
> —HEBREWS 12:10–11

As time marches on in my paralysis, I'm struggling with more pain (knifing pain in my neck and shoulders) than I used to have. Paulette, my physical therapist, helps me with pain management. She twists, turns, and stretches my arms and shoulders, pushing and kneading my muscles. She works on my shoulder area with a small rubber-tipped instrument I call "the torture tool," pressing it between my muscles. And it *hurts*. When she first started using the torture tool, I hated it. It felt as though my muscles were being ripped away from their tendons. After many sessions, however, I have learned that it was that very tool that made the biggest difference in my pain. It hurts a lot—but it hurts real good.

God has a tool, and holding it in his own hand, he digs and presses into our lives. The tool is called suffering, and we hate it! It *hurts*. And yet the apostle Peter tells us, "Those who suffer according to God's will should commit themselves to their faithful Creator and continue to do good" (1 Peter 4:19). We really can commit ourselves to him and have utter trust and confidence in his expertise with that tool in his hands. He knows what he is doing, he knows what we need, and he knows the "harvest of righteousness and peace" it will produce in our lives. It hurts—but it hurts good.

Are you enduring emotional or physical suffering in these days? Don't yield and bend to the situation, but rather submit to your Father who loves you, and who will use these circumstances for a future harvest in your life you can't begin to foresee.

Thank you, Jesus, that you went before me in my suffering and understand so well what I'm going through. Be my comfort, my courage, and my strength this day.

∾

Speech Writing

And the words of the Lord are flawless, like silver refined in
a furnace of clay, purified seven times.

—PSALM 12:6

I read an article recently about the president's speechwriter. It
described the intensity and scrutiny that goes into writing a speech
for the president. When crafting an important address, the writer goes to
great pains selecting the exact verbs, adverbs, nouns, and adjectives. Every
word is carefully scrutinized to fit the overall strategy of the administration.
No word appears in a speech by accident. No pronoun is used carelessly.
Each subject and predicate fits perfectly.

Now if a president goes to such lengths to handcraft every solitary
word so that his message comes across clear and concise, when can we say
about the Word of God, the Bible? Would there be any throwaway words?
Any thoughtless expressions? Of course not. Everything fits perfectly. If a
presidential speechwriter sweats over every word, then you know the Holy
Spirit has taken far greater pains with the living, eternal Word of God.

Friend, this is helpful to remember as we come to the Lord in prayer.
First Peter 4:11 tells us that "if anyone speaks, he should do it as one
speaking the very words of God." We don't need a speechwriter to remind
us of the importance of preparing our hearts and minds before praying,
or of seeking God's heart before speaking, or of searching for his overall
strategy before petitioning ... or of weighing our words before offering
them before the throne of the Almighty. Your words have power before the
Lord—more power than you realize.

Surrender your soul, center your thoughts, ask the Spirit for help,
weigh your words. Then pray with joy and certainty that God will
take those words to accomplish his grand and glorious purpose!

*Forgive me, Lord, for rote, thoughtless, or distracted prayers. Thank you for the
grace that though you are the awesome Sovereign of the universe, you are also
Abba Father, and you treasure the words of your child.*

MAY 18

Making God Glad

All Your garments are scented with myrrh and aloes and cassia, out of the ivory palaces, by which they have made You glad.

—PSALM 45:8 NKJV

We tend to think God exists to make us glad; but in truth, we exist to make him glad. Unbelievable! Oh, that we can actually make God happy. We can give him delight and pleasure by our simple acts of obedience, songs of praise, words of gratitude, and pure and godly thoughts.

Charles Spurgeon writes, "When you lean your head on His bosom, you not only receive, but you give Him joy; when you gaze with love upon His all-glorious face, you not only obtain comfort, but impart delight. Our *praise* too gives Him joy—not the song of the lips alone, but the melody of the heart's deep gratitude. Our *gifts* too are very pleasant to Him; He loves to see us lay our time, our talents, our substance upon the altar, not for the value of what we give, but for the sake of the motive from which the gift springs. To Him the lowly offerings of His saints are more acceptable than the thousands of gold and silver. *Holiness* is like frankincense and myrrh to Him. Forgive your enemy, and you make Christ glad; distribute of your substance to the poor, and He rejoices; be the means of saving souls, and you give Him to see of the travail of His soul; proclaim His gospel, and you are a sweet savour unto Him; go among the ignorant and lift up the cross, and you have given Him honour."[2]

Read in Mark 14:3–6 the story of the woman who made Jesus glad. It is in your power today to break the alabaster box and pour the precious oil of joy on your Savior's head. Find ways to make God glad today through your obedience and praise.

Lord Jesus, I commit this day to finding opportunities to bring you delight and joy. Thank you for giving me the privilege of serving you in this special way.

☙

MAY 19

Anger's Focus

He replied, "I saw Satan fall like lightning from heaven."
—LUKE 10:18

The first time I visited Birkenau, the Nazi death camp in Poland, I was asked to pray at a large memorial erected near the crumpled ruins of the gas chambers. People around me bowed their heads, but I had to first ask the Lord to show me what he wanted me to say. After all, millions of people were put to death just a few feet from where we stood. What could—what *should*—I say to God?

I stared at a piece of rusted barbwire at our feet and considered the evil that fueled those gas chambers. All I could think of was my disgust for Satan and his hordes. So I wrapped my prayer around Psalm 139:21–22, "Do I not hate those who hate you, oh Lord, and abhor those who rise up against you? I have nothing but hatred for them; I count them my enemies."

There is an accurate focus for our anger over the injustice and violence in this world: Satan. He was the one who started the whole mess. He was the one who, because of pride, brought on himself—us included—every horror of the curse of Eden.

"Our struggle is never that we are too angry; but that we are never angry enough. Our anger is always pitifully small when it is focused against a person or object; it is meant to be turned against all evil and all sin—beginning first with our own failure of love."[3] Turn your anger into action. It's how organizations like Mothers Against Drunk Driving, Child Help, and Battered Wives Anonymous began, to name a few. Today, find a way to push back Satan's darkness with deeds of mercy and love.

Father God, I resist the devil and his lies. I purpose to spread the good works of your kingdom, bringing justice and hope, help and relief to all those in need I meet today.

ഇൗ

Reckless Words

Reckless words pierce like a sword, but the tongue of the
wise brings healing.

—PROVERBS 12:18

hen God created the world, he spoke it into being. When Jesus
walked the earth, he spoke and the lame were healed. When
Peter preached his first sermon, he spoke and thousands were gathered
into the kingdom. Powerful things happen when we *speak*. Our words can
either accomplish great good or inflict terrible damage. God has arranged
that words are granted incredible clout. Proverbs 18:21 says, "The tongue
has the power of life and death, and those who love it will eat its fruit." Dr.
Dan Allender gives us a profound purpose for our speech: "I am to sow
words like seeds to bring a harvest of fruit that blesses God."[4]

Repeatedly in Scripture, we are admonished to choose and use words
carefully in healing and holiness. However, our words are not only instruments of health but hurt. Words create division; they can wound or create
distance through subtle inflection. James 3:6 warns, "The tongue also is a
fire, a world of evil among the parts of the body." It's interesting that the
book of James does not give us any advice about stopping our tongues.
Instead, God's Word asks us to develop a sense of horror over the damage
our tongue can inflict. The sobering reality of how such a small part of
the body can do so much good or harm should wake us up to the power
of our words.

> Look for ways today you can exalt Christ through your speech.
> Find opportunities to sincerely encourage and commend your
> coworkers, family members, neighbors, or pastor and members
> of your congregation. Have you spoken damaging words? Do you
> need to make repairs? Remember, the tongue of the wise brings
> healing.

*Lord, today I commit to seriously considering the power of my speech. Show
me ways I can speak words of healing and holiness. Most of all, help me to
think—and pray for wisdom—before I say anything.*

ॐ

Sequoias

Stay here and keep watch with me.

—MATTHEW 26:38

Sequoia National Park is just a four-hour drive north from where Ken and I live. I feel so small when I sit at the base of one of those towering, ancient trees. Some are over three hundred feet tall—the size of a thirty-story building. I am told that sequoias have relatively shallow root systems considering their height. This is why you don't see many standing alone; they stand in groves. The roots of sequoia trees entwine and together the added support prevents winds from uprooting any one tree. Separate and standing apart from the rest, a sequoia wouldn't last long; with its shallow roots, it would fall prey to the harsh winds that blow against the Sierra Mountains.

We can learn a lot from those trees. We might look strong; we may seem independent, but any thinking Christian knows he simply can't survive apart from the body of Christ. When bitter winds of adversity blow, we need the support of each other. God engineered us so that we require the intertwining of genuine give-and-take fellowship. Even Jesus needed this. On the last night of his life when the storms of devilish opposition began howling around him, he asked for help: "Stay here and keep watch with me." If Jesus sought support in the midst of trials, how much more do we need our brothers and sisters in hard times!

First Thessalonians 5:11, 14 says, "Therefore encourage one another and build each other up, just as in fact you are doing. . . . And we urge you, brothers, warn those who are idle, encourage the timid, help the weak, be patient with everyone." Who is timid? Who is the friend who is weak? Create a "sequoia grove" around that individual today. Think of creative ways you can minister to your neighbor or coworker who needs support.

Father, keep me from living my life so independently, so separately from others. Show me how I can support those in need around me.

Give Careful Thought

Now this is what the Lord Almighty says: "Give careful thought to your ways. You have planted much, but have harvested little. You eat, but never have enough. You drink, but never have your fill. You put on clothes, but are not warm. You earn wages, only to put them in a purse with holes in it." This is what the Lord Almighty says: "Give careful thought to your ways."

—HAGGAI 1:5–7

We have our ranch-style homes and unemployment insurance, three meals a day on the table, and supermarket double coupons, if not food stamps, but isn't it odd how we still want more? If we're single, we want marriage. If we're married, we want the perfect spouse. If we have the perfect mate, we want the time to enjoy life.

Other times we have too much. Sky-high medical bills. Fourteen visits to the Mayo Clinic and eight surgeries. A stroke renders our husband speechless or chromosomes retard our grandchild. The funeral was yesterday and we wonder how we'll face the future alone. We are baffled at why the abundant life elludes us and lands in the laps of others. We want what we do not have. We have what we do not want. And we are unhappy. Why is it our human nature never seems satisfied?

When God tells us *twice* in Haggai 1:5–7 to give careful thought to our ways, he is telling us to thoroughly examine our perspective on life, as well as our lifestyle. First Peter 4:3 warns, "For you have spent enough time in the past doing what pagans choose to do." As Christians we need to learn that Christ is our sufficiency. "The fear of the Lord leads to life: Then one rests content." (Proverbs 19:23). Ask God to show you how to rest content in him — then *believe* what he says and obey him.

Forgive me, Lord, when I concentrate too much on "things" in my life, rather than on you. You are my source of happiness and may I rest content in that fact today.

∾

Hints of Heaven

You have made known to me the path of life; you will fill
me with joy in your presence, with eternal pleasures at your
right hand.

—PSALM 16:11

Will heaven's ecstasy go on forever? Is it true we will never become
bored? Will it really be as glorious as the Bible insists? God
sprinkles hints of heaven on earth to give us an inkling—just a small
glimpse—of how *pleasurable* heaven will be. I catch hints of heaven in
magnificent sunsets that leave me breathless. I hear it in the haunting
strains of Dvořák's *New World Symphony*. I recognize it in the soft gaze of
someone I love. I smell it in the ocean air when dark, gray clouds brew in
the distance. If these are mere glimpses and hints of heaven, what will the
real thing be like?

C. S. Lewis wrote, "The faint, far-off results of those energies which
God's creative rapture implanted in matter when he made the worlds, are
what we now call physical pleasures; and even thus filtered, they are too
much for our present management. What would it be to taste at the foun-
tainhead that stream of which even these lower reaches prove so intoxicat-
ing? Yet that, I believe, is what lies before us [in heaven]. The whole man is
to drink joy from the fountain of joy. In the light of our depraved appetites
we cannot imagine this."[5]

Every beautiful sunset, breathtaking symphony, or exhilarating
taste of salt air at the ocean is not merely for your present inspiration. It is a God-sent gift to whet your appetite for your true home
in heaven. Earthly pleasures never quite satisfy; God wants you to
sing "This world is not my home; I'm just a-passin' through." In
heaven we will keep getting smarter, wiser, younger, and happier.
The unfolding of the story of redemption will have us taking one
gasp after another, with our joy and amazement ever increasing.

*Oh God, open my eyes and heart that I might recognize "heaven" here on
earth!*

MAY 24
Chris's Poem

How long must I wrestle with my thoughts and every day
have sorrow in my heart? How long will my enemy triumph
over me? Look on me and answer, O Lord my God.
— PSALM 13:2–3

*T*he last time I saw Chris Kelly, he was a little freckle-faced kid. He
has a ready smile *and* cerebral palsy. Chris is now grown and in college. Like many young adults with disabilities, he has struggled to reconcile
his faith in Christ with the enormous barriers he faces, plus pressure from
his peers. He sent me a poem last week, written straight from his heart ...

Do you know what I am ... do you understand
the severity sealed in clarity of my failure as your child
no longer meek and mild, but tainted and perverted
by the sins now burdened upon my heart ... as evidence of the prevalence
that Darkness has in me ... my arrogance has not been Free
I wander now at the cost of walking forever lost
but even now, I'm led to bow my head and pray
though I have no right to say
I'm sorry, Lord.

And it's a wonder that your grace gets under
all my rotting skin and takes the sin off my heart
because I'm to be a part of your Family above
because I am one that Jesus gave his all that I might not fall
head first into the abyss of condemned ... insignificance.

Take a moment to imagine what any young person in a wheelchair
must face as he grows up. Think of the challenges he must deal
with in college — if he has the wherewithal to go to college. Think
of the hurdles he'll face out in the world. May Chris's example
of perseverance inspire us never to complain *ever*. Philippians
2:14–15 puts it this way: "Do everything without complaining ...
so that you may become blameless and pure children of God."

Lord of all, I pray for the many young people like Chris who need your grace
today. May their examples inspire and encourage me always to persevere.

❧

One More Stepping-Stone

About midnight Paul and Silas were praying and singing hymns to God, and the other prisoners were listening to them.

—ACTS 16:25

Anika was our German shuttle-bus driver who carted us and our luggage from the Munich airport to our hotel. As we pulled away from the curbside, I said, "Anika, we're going to pray here in the back seat. But you're driving, so don't close your eyes!" The look she gave us in the rearview mirror said it all: *You people are odd.* We were wonderful examples of 1 Peter 2:9 (KJV), "A peculiar people; that ye should shew forth the praises of him who hath called you out of darkness into his marvellous light."

But it's the odd things that stick in your mind. And sometimes your heart. The next morning when Anika loaded us up to take us back to the airport, she thanked us after we prayed out loud for her (we also interceded for her live-in boyfriend, as well as her parents, whom she hadn't seen for years). When we said goodbye, she commented with wet eyes, "I like you people. There's something about you that makes me happy. I wish I could go with you."

"You can," I said. "One of these days we're going to lift off, and we'll go higher than any airplane could ever take us. It's all about following Christ." Anika smiled. We were one more stepping-stone in her long journey that, I'm convinced, will land her in heaven.

Sometimes evangelism doesn't mean delivering the whole gospel message at a curbside and asking for a response before the light turns green. Everything we say or do that moves an individual one step closer to Jesus and salvation is evangelism. And allowing our joy in Christ to just spill over and splash on others is as powerful a witness as a three-point sermon.

Holy Spirit, fill me with your joy today as I walk in your presence and lean on your strength. I pray for the opportunity to move at least one person at least one step closer to heaven.

༄

MAY 26
Higher Ground

Therefore, strengthen your feeble arms and weak knees. "Make level paths for your feet," so that the lame may not be disabled, but rather healed.

—HEBREWS 12:12–13

was on my way to the airport when a car suddenly veered in front of us on the freeway. Ken slammed on the brakes, my chest restraint snapped, and my body tumbled forward. I landed on the floor! We quickly pulled over, and Ken carefully lifted me back in my wheelchair. Breathless and nervous, we waited to see if I would develop "sweats," a pain signal that indicates whether or not I've sprained or broken something. All seemed fine, so we cautiously proceeded on to the airport. Midway through our flight, my leg began to swell. When we arrived at our destination, an ambulance took me to the hospital where X-rays confirmed I had broken my leg. It was 3:30 a.m. by the time they put on a cast and released me to go back to our hotel.

To calm my nerves, I asked God if he would give me a hymn to sing. Immediately, I began humming, "Lord, lift me up and let me stand, / by faith on heaven's tableland; / a higher plane than I have found / —Lord, plant my feet on higher ground." The next day I traveled on to Lancaster Bible College to give the commencement address. As I sat on the platform, the graduation program began with a hymn. The audience stood and sang—I couldn't believe it!—"Still praying as I'm onward bound, / 'Lord, plant my feet on higher ground.'"

During the most difficult challenges of the day, God will give us an assurance of his presence through a phone call from a friend, a flower by our path, a butterfly flitting across the yard, or an inspirational song on the radio. Today, if you are facing hardship or heartache, ask God to open your eyes to recognize the many evidences of his nearness (2 Kings 6:17).

Oh God, you are constantly near me, always with me. Give me eyes to see your presence today.

ଉⱱ

A Spirit of Humility

> When you bow down before the Lord and admit your dependence on him, he will lift you up and give you honor.
>
> —JAMES 4:10 NLT

*P*ride always blows our cover. In case you doubt that, hit the concordance key on your computer Bible software, type in the word "pride" or "proud," and watch a zillion verses pop up. All of them detail how the Lord detests haughty eyes, boastful tongues, and hearts bloated by ego. Never was there a character trait more opposite of God.

In our best moments, we want very much to be like God, to be godly … yet what an invitation to pride! That's why it always requires humility. When our pride has caused us to wound our friend or spouse, we walk over to them and say, "I am so sorry for hurting you. What you have observed about me is true: I am stubborn and very much 'in the wrong.' Please forgive me." Oh, it is never easy! But it is richly rewarded.

An old Puritan wrote: "Let me never forget that the heinousness of sin lies not so much in the nature of sin committed, as in the greatness of the person sinned against." If we're looking for humility, we don't gaze inward to see how greatly we've missed the mark. We gaze at the Lord Jesus. We drag ourselves to the cross … where our pride is suffocated! "Self" becomes "hid with Christ in God," and humility is the result.

Asking the Holy Spirit to roll up his sleeves and deal with pride in your heart may involve several things (I speak from experience!). It may include opening yourself to the valid criticism of others, openly confessing your faults, or inviting your spouse or close friend to point out your blind spots. Easy? Never! Rewarding? Always.

Lord, as the old hymn says, "When I survey the wondrous cross, / on which the Prince of Glory died, / my richest gain I count but loss, / and pour contempt on all my pride." Keep me on my knees today, until I get a fresh vision of your cross.

The Big Story

> But you are a chosen people, a royal priesthood, a holy
> nation, a people belonging to God, that you may declare
> the praises of him who called you out of darkness into his
> wonderful light.
>
> —1 PETER 2:9

In their book *The Sacred Romance* Brent Curtis and John Eldridge explain how the cathedral was the center of everyday life in the High Middle Ages. Church bells marked the passing of the hours. People celebrated Pentecost, not the opening of baseball season. Christian expressions like, "the year of our Lord," "pray tell," "God be with you," and "by Christ's blood" peppered normal conversation, reminding young and old alike that their lives were entwined in a drama greater than the daily events of their lives, in the big story of God's redemptive purposes in the world.

But we don't live in the Middle Ages, we live in the postmodern era, and the transcendence of the big story has been splintered and subdivided into many smaller stories, seemingly without direction or purpose. Tragedy still moves us to tears and heroism still lifts our spirits, but as the authors explain, "We have no larger context in which to fit these events." Our culture is unable to fit all the fragments and pieces of individual life stories into any kind of a meaningful, larger framework. It's what happens when we forget the Author and the big story of his greatness, holiness, and sacrificial love.

Does your life ever seem fragmented, random, and without real direction or meaning? That's a lie of the enemy! You truly are a part of God's great story, and every day of your life—whether you realize it or feel like it or not—is weighted with kingdom purpose, eternal significance, and high destiny. You have a role to play today as you walk in his will and speak of his love and salvation to those who cross your path.

Lord Jesus, I praise you for being "the Author and Finisher" of my faith. Open my eyes to my part, my contribution to your desires and plans for this broken, unhappy world.

Wise Singing

I will pray with my spirit, but I will also pray with my mind; I will sing with my spirit, but I will also sing with my mind.

— 1 CORINTHIANS 14:15 – 16

The other week during Sunday worship service, I was singing, "Take my voice and let me sing, always, only for my King. / Take my silver and my gold, not a mite would I withhold. / Take my will and make it Thine, it shall be no longer mine...." Suddenly I was jolted, *What in the world am I singing?! These are powerful words!*

I have glossed over the text to that hymn — and others — many times. Sometimes if I know the song, I'll sing by rote. I'll put myself on automatic and just let the music carry me. Other times, the tune becomes the focus and I work hard to get the harmony notes just right. But I often fail to "sing with my mind," as today's verse says.

If only people in the pews could stand on the platform and observe the congregation singing during an average church service. It would reveal many who have come to church without the express purpose of encountering God or truly worshiping him. What does it mean to sing with our spirits and our minds? It means happy, intelligent praise. In short, to sing with your mind is to sing what you mean ... and mean what you sing.

This Sunday when you sing praise choruses or hymns, ask the Lord to prepare your heart and mind before each song. Ask the Spirit of Christ to quicken the words on the page, illumine your understanding of the text, and make your worship of him pure and purposeful as you sing. Pray that others around you will sing the same way!

Help me to worship you in spirit and in truth, dear Lord. And when I worship you in song — no matter what day of the week — I want to sing with my spirit, as well as sing with my mind.

The Name of the Lord

The name of the Lord is a strong tower; the righteous run
to it and are safe.

—PROVERBS 18:10

heological convocations are not usually scintillating. According
to Dr. R. C. Sproul, they tend to be academic and sometimes
tedious. But he will never forget one incredible speaker at a convocation
at a prestigious seminary. The topic centered on Jesus Christ. The well-
respected, elderly professor climbed the steps to the podium, cleared his
throat, smiled, and then spent the entire forty-five minutes slowly repeat-
ing by heart every name and title of Jesus Christ.

Rock of Ages ... Redeemer ... King of Kings ... Bread of Heaven ...
Living Water ... Son of God ... our Sure Foundation ... Good Shepherd
... Fairest of Ten Thousand ... Savior ... Mediator ... our Advocate ...
Alpha and Omega ... the Stone the Builders Rejected ... Beginning and
End ... Wonderful Counselor ... Friend of Sinners ... Great Physician ...
Anointed One ... Healer of Broken Hearts ... Lamb of God ... Prince of
Peace ... Blessed Hope ... our Atonement ... Mighty Fortress ... Shelter
... the Narrow Gate ... Lord of Grace ... God of All Comfort ... Word of
Life ... Rose of Sharon ... Lily of the Valley ... Bright and Morning Star
... Glorious Lord ... Immanuel ... Living Word ... Chief Cornerstone ...
Creator ... Ancient of Days ... the Eternal One ... Author and Finisher
of our Faith ... First and the Last ... Son of Man ... Almighty God ... the
Resurrection and the Life ... the Way, the Truth, and the Life ... Everlast-
ing Father ... Captain of the Lord's Army ...

And that's just scratching the surface.

At the end of the forty-five-minute litany of the names and titles
of Jesus, the entire audience was reduced to quiet tears. This is
what happens when we focus on Jesus and all that he has accomplished. This Sunday, meditate on each of these names—and
more, if you have a concordance—and express your appreciation
to God for all that the Lord Christ achieved on your behalf.

*Jesus, you are my all in all. You are everything to me. Thank you that I can hold
fast to any of your precious names or titles and in them find safety. For, indeed,
the name of the Lord is a strong tower!*

Flight Rules

> To keep me from becoming conceited because of these sur-
> passingly great revelations, there was given me a thorn in
> my flesh.
>
> —2 CORINTHIANS 12:7

*T*once talked to a pilot who described how he lands his plane in a
deep fog. He has to be extremely alert as he guides his plane on
what are called Instrument Flight Rules (IFR). He's flying blind, so the
pilot must be totally dependent on his instruments and the signals from
the control tower. He is extra careful to listen and respond to directions:
check altimeter; check air speed; check flaps, yaw and pitch, navigation
indicators, radar; check speed again. Suddenly the fog lifts, the pilot sees
the runway beneath his plane, and the landing is smooth and safe.

The next day when the sky is clear, the pilot comes in for a landing on
what is called Visual Flight Rules. Because he can easily spot the landing
strip ahead, the pilot isn't glued to all the gauges. As a result, he comes in a
bit too fast, which makes for a bumpy landing. The apparent ease of using
Visual Flight Rules caused the pilot to be a little laxer, when he should have
been just as alert.

God often sends a fog our way and we find ourselves "flying blind,"
unable to discern what's ahead. God does this so we will pay closer attention to the way we are flying through life. When I'm in a fog, when my
thoughts are clouded and confused, I *have* to live my life on Instrument
Flight Rules. I think: check mission, check attitude, check source of
strength, check perspective on the day, check, check. If I don't live life
using Scripture and prayer—God's Instrument Flight Rules—it'll be a
hard landing at the end of a bumpy day.

Feeling under the fog? Make doubly sure you are *dependent* on
prayer and God's Word to guide you through the day.

*Father God, please keep me from becoming conceited. Keep me from being too
sure of myself. Keep me utterly dependent on you.*

June

Let Me Not Shrink

His intent was that now, through [Christians], the manifold
wisdom of God should be made known to the rulers and
authorities in the heavenly realms, according to his eternal
purpose which he accomplished in Christ Jesus our Lord.

—EPHESIANS 3:10–11

oneliness mixed with affliction can be a dangerous potion.
You lie awake, persistently needled by pain. Physical pain, yes,
but also mental. The mountains you face are unknown to others. Quite
frankly, you are tired of always talking about your problems to others.
You'd really rather bear the burden alone. Yet that thought too can add a
more dangerous element to the potion: if we get the feeling that no one
notices our hardships or sorrows, it can drive us to emotional numbness,
if not downright despair.

If I am describing you, I want you to be encouraged. Something
dynamic and electrifying is abuzz all around you. It is filling the air and
agitating the atmosphere above you. Angels, along with powers and prin-
cipalities in the heavenly realms, are watching, listening, and best of all,
learning. Angels — even demons — are intensely fascinated in the thoughts
and affections of every human being. Especially Christians like you who
bear up quietly under pain and loneliness.

I can hear you thinking, *Angels eavesdropping on me? Demons wringing
their hands in glee, hoping I'll yell at my kids when they cross me? Principali-
ties and powers watching to see whether I turn to God or turn away?* This
isn't science fiction. The Bible tells us that angels get emotionally charged
whenever one sinner repents — they get excited when God's people choose
to trust him (Luke 15:10; Ephesians 3:10). You are *not* alone.

Make this poem by Amy Carmichael your prayer today:

*O Prince of Glory, who dost bring Thy sons to glory through Thy Cross,
Let me not shrink from suffering, reproach, or loss.*

*And by the borders of my day the river of Thy pleasure flows;
The flowers that blossom by the way, who loves Thee knows.*[1]

Riches in Secret Places

I will give you the treasures of darkness, riches stored in secret places, so that you may know that I am the Lord.

—ISAIAH 45:3

My friend Vicky is one rich person. She's got it all, yet she sits paralyzed in a wheelchair, having been shot in an attempted rape many years ago. At first, this tragedy plunged her into dark despair. Yet during her darkest hour, she discovered rich, spiritual treasure. She was able to mine precious insights hidden in secret places. Through her affliction, Vicky found the seven-fold riches of God.

In Ephesians 3:8 she discovered she was blessed with "the unsearchable riches of Christ." In Romans 2:4, she found "the riches of his kindness." In Romans 9:23 she took hold of "the riches of his glory." There's the "riches of wisdom and knowledge" mentioned in Romans 11:33 and "the riches of God's grace" given in Ephesians 1:7. The "riches of his glorious inheritance" is mentioned in Ephesians 1:18. And, finally, "the riches of his glory" is listed four times in Scripture.

Priceless, spiritual treasures are often discovered during our darkest times. Our afflictions are the pick and ax that help us unearth the unsearchable riches of Christ. Vicky is a rich woman—she has mined priceless insights that far outweigh all the pain and inconvenience of her paralysis.

Matthew 13:44 explains that, "The kingdom of heaven is like treasure hidden in a field. When a man found it, he hid it again, and then in his joy went and sold all he had and bought that field." Affliction often forces us to search for wisdom and mercy, goodness and kindness. Oh, how rich we are when we discover Jesus, the Pearl of Great Price!

Do you consider yourself "wealthy" in the Lord? If you feel impoverished today, remember this encouragement from Philippians 4:19, "And my God will meet all your needs according to his glorious riches in Christ Jesus."

You are the precious Pearl of Great Price, Lord Jesus. I promise to keep searching for wisdom and knowledge. I want to be rich in your mercy and grace!

JUNE 3

Always Grateful

As he was going into a village, ten men who had leprosy met him. They stood at a distance and called out in a loud voice, "Jesus, Master, have pity on us!" When he saw them, he said, "Go, show yourselves to the priests." And as they went, they were cleansed. One of them, when he saw he was healed, came back, praising God in a loud voice. He threw himself at Jesus' feet and thanked him — and he was a Samaritan. Jesus asked, "Were not all ten cleansed? Where are the other nine? Was no one found to return and give praise to God except this foreigner?"

—LUKE 17:12–18

The ten lepers were anxious and impatient to be healed. Jesus showed mercy and healed them, telling them to go show themselves to the priests. One of the lepers ran back to Jesus, overwhelmed with praise to God and heartfelt gratitude to his benefactor. The other nine were more interested in following the religious prescription — to show oneself to the priest meant receiving a "certificate of cleansing," being reinstated into the synagogue, reentering society, and regaining acceptance from family and neighbors. It meant a social, religious, and medical "clean bill of health."

Rather than seek approval and acceptance from the priests and society, one leper chose to rush back to Jesus with happy abandon. He was less interested in "getting on with his life" and more concerned with acknowledging God's mercy and pouring out gratitude to his Savior.

God is not impressed with religious duty; he is more interested in our spiritual gratitude. The Lord is always looking for the heart that is effusive in expressing thanks for his great mercies. Even Romans 1:21 warns that God gave sinful man over to his own wickedness because "he neither glorified him as God nor gave thanks to him." Purpose today to pour out your gratitude to God for every small and great mercy.

Thank you, Lord Jesus, for the countless blessings and innumerable mercies you pour out upon me every day.

JUNE 4
The Hedge

Therefore I will block her path with thornbushes; I will wall her in so that she cannot find her way. She will chase after her lovers but not catch them; she will look for them but not find them. Then she will say, "I will go back to my husband as at first, for then I was better off than now."

—HOSEA 2:6–7

When I was a little girl, my mother would take me to Grandmother's every Wednesday morning. While she cleaned house, Mother gave me free range in the spacious backyard, which was lined with a tall, thick hedge. I had plenty of room in which to play. I didn't know what was on the other side of the hedge, but I wasn't about to trespass beyond the watchful eye of Mom. Who knew what dangers lurked beyond the safe, secure wall of thorny leaves that defined my family's property?

I often think of Grandmother's hedge when I look at my wheelchair. It may be a thorn in my side, but it is God's barrier; otherwise, I would be reaching for and running toward a lot of wrong things! I thank my wise God for placing this hedge in my life. It may hurt and sometimes humiliate me, but it keeps me within the safe, secure boundaries of God's protection and provision. It keeps me out of the worse kind of danger: *moral* trouble.

Today's verse describes a rebellious, headstrong person who is ruled by desire, a person who looks for ways to trespass God's boundaries of safety and borders of protection. Don't invite the Lord to block your path with a taller, thornier hedge. Be content within the confines of his commands. The Bible's precepts give you room enough in which to grow. What hedges has God placed in your life? How has "hedging in" helped you?

Lord Jesus, I desire to trust and obey you with a willing and contented spirit. I am thankful for the hedges you place in my life.

෨

JUNE 5

Stay on Course

Whether you turn to the right or to the left, your ears will hear a voice behind you, saying, "This is the way; walk in it."

—ISAIAH 30:21

Ken and I were standing with a group of friends on a high bluff, overlooking Chesapeake Bay, when we got into a friendly argument about directions. One person stabbed his finger in the air and said, "*That* is south." Another countered, "No, it isn't. I would swear that's due east." Others threw in their two cents worth, and people began to take sides, becoming entrenched in their opinions.

Finally Ken reached into his duffle bag and said, "I'll solve this one fast." Within seconds the compass confirmed that we had been facing west the whole time. And you know what? Not one of us was about to argue with the compass. We knew it had the final say. In the same way, if we only look at circumstances around us, we can easily become disoriented. Just a couple of wrong cues and our bearings can get turned upside down, making north look like south, making evil look like good. We risk dangerous wrong conclusions when we try to ascertain God's purpose and plans in our life using only our circumstances for cues.

I have never forgotten that lesson. The longer I am in this wheel-chair, the more I need help in keeping my bearings. More and more pain encroaching into my life can turn my feelings "this way and that." I need the Holy Spirit to remind me that there is "a way I should go." Despite the backaches and headaches, I need to hold fast to the blessed Word of God.

As you walk through this day, determine that you will make no decision without first consulting the Lord. Ask him to bring Scriptures to your mind that will help you find—and keep—your bearings.

Father, how can I be so foolish as to think I can plan my own life itinerary apart from your strong counsel? Guide me, O thou great Jehovah.

Days Like Grass ...

The Lord knows the days of the upright, and their inheritance shall be forever.

—PSALM 37:18 NKJV

*I*t was one of those moments that stands out in memory with high-definition clarity. Former President Ronald Reagan had died on June 6, and now his body lay in a flag-draped casket in the Capitol rotunda.

Margaret Thatcher entered the rotunda, leaning on the arm of a senator. She walked slowly with a mature dignity, but she looked so frail. I held my breath as she neared the coffin, bowed her head, and placed her hand on the flag. One old warrior saying goodbye to another. Images of both of them flashed through my mind ... so much younger ... filled with courage, optimism, and seemingly boundless strength. And now, one was hardly a shadow of her former stalwart self, and the other had breathed his last. As I watched Mrs. Thatcher back away from the coffin, James 4:14 came to mind: "What is your life? You are a mist that appears for a little while then vanishes." And then another floated to the surface, Isaiah 40:7–8: "Surely the people are grass. The grass withers and the flowers fall, but the word of our God stands forever."

Presidents and prime ministers—for all their charisma, power, and authority—come and go. But we who are in Christ are related to a Redeemer who will never age, never change, and who walks with us through all our days.

Where were you and what were you doing this time last year? Does it seem possible that an entire *year* has flown by since that time? Where do the years fly to? Our days may be like grass and our glory may fade like a flower, but, oh, that we might hold fast to the Word of Life, our precious Savior. May you and I press on to the high calling of him better—much better—Christ Jesus, the Captain of our salvation and our mighty Warrior.

Lord Jesus, by your Spirit who dwells within me, remind me to make the very most I can out of this twenty-four hours that lies before me.

JUNE 7

The Visitor

Praise be to the Lord, for he showed his wonderful love to
me when I was in a besieged city.

—PSALM 31:21

Last year at about this time, I was flat out with the flu. And I do
mean *flat*. Being paralyzed in a wheelchair is one thing, but in
a bed ...? A stuffy head only adds to the claustrophobic feelings. Still, I
held on to the truth that God is truly in control and that he permits trials
for my good.

So where's the good? I wondered, looking out at my window bird feeder.
The answer was sprightly and pale gray, with a jaunty little crest on his
head. It was unlike any bird I had ever seen. He looked like a charged-
up rocket with that "space cadet" hat on his head. Out came my friend's
binoculars and bird book. "I came prepared," she said gleefully. Plopping
onto the bed next to me, she opened the book and the search for my little
crested visitor was on. We crossed off finches and wrens, juncos and nut-
hatches, and half a dozen sparrows. Thankfully, the little bird lingered long
enough for us to track him down.

"Here he is!" My friend jabbed her finger on the page. "A titmouse!"
we chimed together. It was the cutest, most innocuous name for one of
the most darling birds I'd ever been introduced to. Mr. Titmouse was the
first of many others whose names I came to know that week. *So where is
the good?* First Peter 4:10 describes "God's grace in its various forms." That
week in bed, I saw not only birds in various forms but the delightful, inex-
haustible, infinitely winsome grace of God.

Sometimes you and I become so deeply committed to our
own self-pity that we refuse to see the "good" when God sends
it—whether a card from a friend, a kind remark from a stranger,
a rainbow ... or even a humble titmouse paying a call to your
windowsill.

*Lift my heart, Father, from the shadows of self-absorption and self-pity. Open
my eyes to the multitude of good gifts you send into my life every day.*

ᕙ

JUNE 8

Magnify the Lord with Me

Oh, magnify the Lord with me, And let us exalt His name together.

—PSALM 34:3 NKJV

t's time for the NBA basketball finals. When Ken and I went to a playoff game in the Los Angeles Staples Center, we sat in the cheap seats—up so high in the stadium we had a difficult time seeing the basketball players on the court. They looked so *small*. But then I glanced at the towering jumbo screen above the court. What a difference! We could see every player up close. Even facial expressions!

The screen magnified what was already there. The magnification didn't actually make the players bigger, they just *seemed* bigger to our eyes. Every aspect of each player could be enjoyed. Here's my point: when we "magnify" the Lord, we make the God who looks small in the world's eyes seem ... huge! No, we could never *change* anything about him. He's the same size he has always been. We can't make him any grander or greater or more powerful than he already is. We just enlarge him before the world's eyes so they can see him up close.

As Christians, our lives are a little like that jumbo screen. Through our actions and attitudes, we enable others to see God better. When we let the Lord showcase his grace and power in our lives, when we display his peace and patience and joy in our daily attitudes and circumstances, then we truly are magnifying him.

The world has such a diminished impression of God. He appears so insignificant to so many. Most people don't even take notice of him. This is why the world needs to see the true details about who God actually is. They need to see Jesus, in his love, his strength, his majesty, and his tender care. Ask the Lord this day to be magnified through your life—in your joy, in your diligence, even in your setbacks and disappointments.

Lord, reveal yourself to a watching world through me! As your life radiates through me, may people catch a glimpse of how large and wondrous you truly are.

ॐ

The Rose of Sharon

I am a rose of Sharon, a lily of the valleys.

—SONG OF SONGS 2:1

*I*t's June, the month of roses. Nothing is more beautiful than the gradual unfolding of a rosebud into its full glory. Each petal unfurls, layer by layer, revealing ever-increasing loveliness. At each stage you say to yourself, *How could it be more beautiful? Right now it's at its best. I've got to get my camera!*

When I consider the way God reveals his glory to us, I picture a rose. In Genesis, the bud of God's plan opened just enough to show the promise of salvation. Through successive chapters of history, the bloom opened more and more before the wondering eyes of God's people. One glory followed another. God's glory as a warrior striking Egypt with plagues; God's glory at Mount Sinai with trumpet, quaking earth, and laws for living; his glory blazing between the cheribum in the wilderness tabernacle; his glory filling the temple of Solomon. At each stage, as the rose unfurled petal by petal, there were probably those who reasoned, "This is the ultimate. It can't get any better!"

But finally the glory of God was fully revealed, and his name was Jesus. John 1:14 says, "The Word became flesh and lived for awhile among us. We have seen his glory, the glory of the One and Only." It was certainly no mistake that Jesus was called "the Rose of Sharon." (Sharon is the celebrated plain from Joppa to Caesarea, between the hill country and the sea, and travelers have remarked on the abundance of flowers with which this plain is still carpeted in spring.)

God wants to reveal his glory to you. Jesus lives in you, and as you take time to draw closer to him today, he will unfold himself to you. At times you will think, *It doesn't get any better*. But it will.

Lord Jesus, I take time today to inhale the fragrance of your nearness. My eyes linger on your beauty. You are altogether lovely.

ॐ

From Bud to Blossom

And we, who with unveiled faces all reflect the Lord's glory,
are being transformed into his likeness with ever-increasing
glory, which comes from the Lord, who is the Spirit.

—2 CORINTHIANS 3:18

esterday we enjoyed picturing Jesus as the Rose of Sharon in
whom the fullness of God's glory was revealed, just like a beautiful flower in full bloom. People marveled at each new turn, each new facet, each unfolding and unfurling of his nature and character. Beholding the glory of God in the life of Jesus must have been breathtaking beyond description—no wonder people wanted to be near him.

In the same way, the Father desires that you reveal the glory of the Son in ever-increasing measures. Second Corinthians 4:6 says that God has given *you* "the light of the knowledge of the glory of God in the face of Christ." With every small obedience and with every drastic trust in him, you grow from bud to blossom, just like a rose. As you reflect the Lord's glory, you are being transformed into his likeness *with ever-increasing glory,* just like a flower unfurling. I want people to marvel at Christ's character in your life; I want people to be drawn to you by the fragrance of Christ's life; I want you to grow in him, change, and be transformed, from bud to blossom.

If the season is right, clip a rosebud from a backyard bush. Or splurge and purchase an American Beauty bud from your florist. Place it in a vase near your desk or near your kitchen sink. Watch it blossom from day to day. As you see it change, take that moment to glory in one of Christ's amazing and lovely attributes … take that moment to welcome change and transformation in your own life … take that moment to commit to trust and obedience in the Rose of Sharon.

Lord Jesus, you are full of grace and truth. I covenant with you today to reflect those wonderful qualities. Transform me. Change me. From bud to blossom.

JUNE 11

Much Fruit

I am the vine; you are the branches. If a man remains in me and I in him, he will bear much fruit.... This is to my Father's glory, that you bear much fruit, showing yourselves to be my disciples.

—JOHN 15:5, 8

A careful owner of a vineyard watches for all the signs of budding fruit. He has spent months tilling, furrowing, fertilizing, pruning, watering, and testing everything from the acidity of the soil to the humidity of the air. And now he is expecting his vines to bear big, luscious prize-winning grapes.

Don't think the Almighty is any less meticulous. He wrote the book on growing fruit! And he wants *you* to bear *much* fruit. He notices every time you sow seeds in the lives of others. He keeps tabs every time you water that seed with your prayers. If something good stirs in a soul, even in the souls of onlookers, God chalks it up to your account. He records it on your balance sheet when he observes faith flowering and fruit ripening in the life of someone in whom you have invested your Christian witness.

If they profit, you gain. If they are rewarded, you reap. If they are lifted up, you are raised up with them. You share in the blue ribbon for the fruit born in their lives. This is why the apostle Paul spoke of those in whom he invested his life as his "joy and crown" (Philippians 4:1). Other people are *our* crown.

Be vigilant about people in your sphere of influence. You are sowing seeds; your prayers are having an impact. So "let us not become weary in doing good, for at the proper time we will reap a harvest if we do not give up. Therefore, as we have opportunity, *let us do good to all people*" (Galatians 6:9–10, italics mine).

Lord of the vineyard, I want to bear much fruit to the Father's glory. Help me to invest my life in others whom I encounter today. They are my crown!

ൟ

A Way to Wholeness

I have come that they may have life, and have it to the full.

—JOHN 10:10

*L*ast weekend Ken and I welcomed twenty-six of his high school students for a graduation day barbeque. A sunny day ... the aroma of burgers sizzling on the grill ... the sounds of kids laughing and throwing Frisbees. It was a great time to connect with these young people.

I asked one girl, "So ... what does the summer hold for you?" She responded, "I want to work on becoming more whole, more fulfilled, more *myself*." She thinks it will all come together when she finds a boyfriend. She said, "I just know there's somebody out there who matches the other side of me, someone who is my perfect complement." I stifled a giggle, and then replied, "A lot of us are seeking that. We're looking for that person or that situation in life which will make us feel complete." I then proceeded to gently explain what really does make us complete: God.

Life isn't going to get completely fixed. We're never going to experience wholeness this side of eternity. Someone once said, "In worshiping God we realize we were never created to be whole. What we were created to enjoy is fellowship with God, who alone is whole and complete. Nowhere in the Bible are we told that God wants to give us wholeness. What God wants to give us is himself."

This is good news for each of those students who left our barbeque last weekend, many of them thinking seriously about the insights Ken and I shared. This is also good news for you, if today you are struggling with feeling incomplete in your marriage or restless with where you live. And it is great news if you are looking for something beyond romance or riches, aching to be whole and complete. There is an answer and there is a complement that makes us whole. His name is Jesus.

Father, help me to fill those aching, empty places in my soul with more and more of you.

ᐯ

JUNE 13

To This You Were Called

To this you were called, because Christ suffered for you, leaving you an example, that you should follow in his steps.

—1 PETER 2:21

ften during a single day I will have to make twenty-six different adjustments in my wheelchair. When pain begins to burn between my shoulders, it's, "Judy, would you please push my hips this way ... lift up on that side ... move my knee to the right ... would you please stretch my arm up? Thank you for shoving that pad down further behind me." Usually I have to lie down and make an adjustment that way. Sometimes I think I'll drive me and my friends crazy!

That's when I need to remember today's verse. To *this* I have been called. The Man of Sorrows acquainted with grief is my example. Life is supposed to be difficult. Jesus said in this world we would have trouble. Philippians 1:29 reinforces that it has been granted—that is, it has been gifted—on behalf of Christ not only to believe on him, but to suffer for him. Sometimes I don't want that gift, but I remember that discomfort is God's way of keeping me close to him. If Jesus learned obedience through the things he suffered, then I can learn from twenty-six different adjustments in my sitting position (Hebrews 5:8).

God desires our intimacy, but he shares that intimacy on his terms. And those terms require for us to in some way suffer as his Son suffered. The next time you get hit broadside with a bruising disappointment, remember the example of Jesus Christ. God is asking you to follow in his steps.

Lord Jesus, it goes against my human nature to look at hardship as a gift. Today, help me to unwrap that painful gift and learn obedience through the things I suffer. Help me to seek intimacy with you through disappointment. Help me to understand that life is supposed to be difficult. Most of all, may I realize you are worth it.

ॐ

"For My Daddy Showed Me So ..."

This is how we know what love is: Jesus Christ laid down
his life for us.

— 1 JOHN 3:16

everal years ago Nancy wrote to tell me the deep struggles she and
her husband wrestled with over placing their severely handicapped
son, Brad, in a residential facility. Should they bring him home? Did the
family have enough support?

I tried to give the family some tools to make those critical decisions,
and she recently wrote back to express her appreciation. They'd made their
decision; Brad was home again. "Joni," she wrote, "incredible fruit has
resulted in our lives from that decision. God used Brad to change my husband and me, helping us see the Lord in a way we never could have had
Brad not lived in our midst."

Nancy also enclosed a beautiful three-page tribute to her husband,
written from Brad's point of view. Every paragraph was a powerful testimony to a father's flexibility, integrity, love, and devotion to his disabled
child. Little Brad "wrote," "Dad, I can't give anything back to you except
my smiles when I hear your voice, or my giggles when you whistle. I can't
even say, 'I love you.'" But I think the best part of the tribute is the close:
"Maybe I can't read the Bible, but I can 'say' Jesus loves me, this I know,
for my daddy *showed* me so."

Greeting card makers employ countless poets and writers to come
up with clever, funny, poignant, or romantic ways to say, "I love you; I'm
thinking about you." But God didn't send a greeting card to show his
love—he came himself. He didn't just tell us he loved us—he gave up
his own life on our behalf. You can talk and sing about love until the cows
come home. But at the end of the day, real love means sacrifice.

How can you show the love of Jesus today by what you sacrifice
for another?

*Thank you, God, for those who have showed me the true love of Christ by what
they gave up to teach, encourage, help, and support me.*

JUNE 15

A Covenant with Man

So the Lord said to him, "Bring me a heifer, a goat and a ram, each three years old, along with a dove and a young pigeon." Abram brought all these to him, cut them in two and arranged the halves opposite each other; the birds, however, he did not cut in half.... When the sun had set and darkness had fallen, a smoking firepot with a blazing torch appeared and passed between the pieces.

—GENESIS 15:9–10, 17

In Genesis 15 God appears to Abraham and promises him more great-grandchildren than the old man can count stars. How can Abraham know for sure that God will keep his word? The Lord tells Abraham to cut some animals and birds in two and lay the pieces end to end. It was a bloody mess! When the sun sets, God appears as a burning torch and small firepot passing between the pieces—the Lord is "cutting a covenant" with Abraham, saying inasmuch, "If I fail to keep my word to you, I will make myself like these animals!" God was swearing by himself that he would fulfill his promise, or else cease being God.

Can God cut himself in two? Can he divide himself in half? Is it possible that God could bleed? God was showing Abraham through this "cutting of a covenant" that he was as good as his promises. God was saying he would *never* forget his people—he swore it.

What promises of God's do you lean on for peace of mind? The promise of forgiveness of sins? A home in heaven? That God will take care of your needs? Remember that God put his divinity on the line when he cut a covenant with man. The Lord loves you and has engraved your name on the palm of his hand. He is the original promise keeper—he stakes his reputation on that and he signed it in blood.

Father God, I hold fast to each and every one of your promises this day. I am humbled that you would cut such a covenant with your people!

JUNE 16

The Blood of the New Covenant

"The time is coming," declares the Lord, "when I will make a new covenant with the house of Israel and with the house of Judah. It will not be like the covenant I made with their forefathers when I took them by the hand to lead them out of Egypt, because they broke my covenant, though I was a husband to them," declares the Lord. "This is the covenant I will make with the house of Israel after that time," declares the Lord. "I will put my law in their minds and write it on their hearts. I will be their God, and they will be my people."

—JEREMIAH 31:31–33

In the old covenant God made with Abraham, he swore he would *never* forget his people. But just a casual reading of the Old Testament shows *they* forgot *him*. One sin led to another, and soon there wasn't a commandment Israel hadn't broken. Who *now* deserved to be cut in two?!

But God had created his people to mirror him, not to be miniatures of Lucifer. It would take great wisdom and compassion on the part of God to save his people without trivializing their guilt, to cure them without letting the horror of sin ever be forgotten, to mingle mercy with justice. Hebrews 9:15 explains how he did it: "For this reason Christ is the mediator of a new covenant. . . . He has died as a ransom to set them free from the sins committed under the first covenant."

Amazing love! Remember the old covenant? God "cut himself" and bled so that man might not be cut off from him. Jesus Christ, the Son of Man, fulfilled the old covenant and made a new one, a better one, hallelujah, and "you have come to God, the judge of all men . . . to Jesus the mediator of a new covenant, and to the sprinkled blood that speaks a better word" (Hebrews 12:23–24).

I am humbled, precious Lord, that you bled and died so that I might be rescued. Thank you!

Hedges and Walls

Why is life given to a man whose way is hidden, whom
God has hedged in?

—JOB 3:23

The four walls of a sick room can feel terribly confining, even if you
are only in bed a short time. When I was stuck in a hospital room
for over a year, those four walls felt like a jail. I resonated with the prophet
who wrote, "He has walled me in so I cannot escape; he has weighed me
down with chains" (Lamentations 3:7). There's a lot of lament in that
verse, and in today's.

There is also comfort. For it is *God's* hedge. Those are *God's* walls. It
is God who has confined you in. He is the one who has surrounded you
with that high hedge. It is only when we view our restricting circumstances
as being placed there by God's hand that we find courage to face the wall
and the hedge. Walls are cold and hard. Hedges are unyielding and thorny.
But the love of your God is supreme and matchless, and he only confines
you 'round for a wise and timely purpose. For those who believe in the
love and wisdom of a sovereign God, even a terrible confinement can be a
place of building trust.

A high hedge cannot shut out our view of the skies nor can it prevent the soul from looking up into the face of God. That's what
happened to me in the hospital. During the year within those
four walls, I earnestly wrestled with God, pleading and praying
to him. Looking back, it was dreadfully difficult—but it was a
rich and deep spiritual time, which I wouldn't trade for anything.
Because there is so little else to see, the hedged-in Christian may
possibly apprehend God more fully than the disciple who moves
about freely and unconfined.

*Today I need to remember that the "four walls" of a difficult situation force me
to look up. Lord Jesus, please help me to see you in the confining situation.*

JUNE 18

A Marriage Mission

God blessed them and said to them, "Be fruitful and increase in number; fill the earth and subdue it. Rule over the fish of the sea and the birds of the air and over every living creature that moves on the ground."

—GENESIS 1:28

What a mission God gives in this verse! We are to increase, fill the earth, subdue, and rule. In other words, we are to give shape to the world around us and take on the glorious responsibility of making and owning it. We are to create, produce, and shape the creation into a higher order of beauty and usefulness. We are to rule; that is, to serve and give, sacrifice and look to the interests of others. What a breathtaking mission for a marriage of two people.

Pastor Steve Muzio states, "Marriage is designed as an alliance of two souls knit and working together to obey these commands. However, because of sin's entrance into the world, marriage is now more likely a battlefield of two individuals seeking to gain an advantage on the other. Too few are willing to lay down their arms ... as they approach the other with offers of love and peace. Life is a battle and, unfortunately, in selfishness we make marriage yet another battleground instead of a holy alliance with a glorious purpose."[2]

You have a purpose in your marriage—in any relationship—no matter its stage or state. The purpose is to create and nurture good, produce righteousness, and cultivate spiritual beauty in the other.

You can either contribute to the good in your relationships or to the decay. Find a way today to shape the world around you by giving, serving, and sacrificing. Confess to your friend or spouse any selfishness that may have eroded your relationship. Nurture the good. Create, produce, and shape into a higher order of loveliness, your world around you and the people in it.

Oh God, help me to regain your magnificent mission in my marriage ... in my relationships with those for whom I care.

☙

June 19

Courageous Grace

He put a new song in my mouth, a hymn of praise to our
God. Many will see and fear and put their trust in the
Lord.

—Psalm 40:3

*I*t was talent night at one of our Family Retreats, and Cindy, a
young woman with severe cerebral palsy, was the last one sched-
uled to perform. Cindy's mother pushed her daughter in her wheelchair
out onto the platform. Cindy, she told us, had been working hard all week
on her song, "Amazing Grace." But how was this going to work? Because of
her disability, Cindy couldn't speak. Then her mother walked off stage and
left Cindy alone. The young woman laboriously stretched out her twisted
fingers and pushed a button on her communication device attached to her
chair. And out came the monotone computerized voice, "Amazing grace,
how sweet the sound, that saved a wretch like me."

As the computer continued the hymn, Cindy turned her head to face
us, the audience, and with enormous effort, began to mouth all the words,
as best she could. What's more, her smile lit up the entire place. It was a
performance that any opera star or top Christian recording artist would
envy. "Amazing Grace" is not a new song, but that night, it was sung in an
entirely new way. Although Cindy was unable to sing the words, it rose up
as a ringing hymn of praise to God. I can imagine the angels leaning over
the edge of heaven, filled with wonder, to catch every word.

In some parts of the world today, people risk their very lives to
praise Jesus in public. And there are men and women like Cindy
who unashamedly lift up his name with physical and emotional
difficulty we can't begin to understand. The question is, if we are
so easily able to praise the name of Jesus without physical struggle
or fear of reprisal ... why don't we?

*Thank you, Lord, for the courageous example of this young woman who
declared your praise even when it was very difficult. Teach me, Lord, from her
example.*

JUNE 20

The Cross-Centered Life

> Put to death, therefore, whatever belongs to your earthly nature: sexual immorality, impurity, lust, evil desires and greed, which is idolatry. Because of these, the wrath of God is coming.
>
> —COLOSSIANS 3:5–6

I enjoy my morning routine—two kiwis and a hot bran cereal followed by a cup of coffee at work. I haven't altered that routine in years. That's because we build habits around the things that matter to us. This is an important principle to remember as we seek to daily build our lives around the gospel. C. J. Mahaney writes, "Do you want to live a cross centered life? A cross centered life is made up of *cross centered days.*"[3]

My friend C. J. tells us how to keep the flame of the gospel burning brightly in the drizzle of our everyday lives. As I begin my day, you and I must *preach the gospel to ourselves*—our audience is our heart, reminding us of those things that matter most to God. Next, *memorize the gospel*—God wants us to tuck his promises into our hearts so that wherever we are, we can be strengthened by their eternal truth. Every day we should *pray the gospel*—never forget to thank God for the forgiveness of sins, the cross of Christ; always acknowledge transgressions and speak to your Lord about eternal things. Finally, *sing the gospel*—lift to the Lord songs that center on the cross. Choose a worship CD that includes a variety of songs about what Jesus accomplished on the cross. And don't forget to *study the gospel*—it's the only way to grow in your passion for Jesus and all that he has done; never be content with your current grasp of the gospel.

It's hard to put to death old ways, but these five practical recommendations from C. J. Mahaney will give you a clearer understanding of how to make every day cross centered. You can't do it on your own, though. Ask the Holy Spirit to help you. It will mean your life will totally focus on Jesus' cross!

Jesus keep me near the cross, hoping, trusting ever . . .

෬෬

Judging Scripture

For the word of God is living and active. Sharper than any double-edged sword, it penetrates even to dividing soul and spirit, joints and marrow; it judges the thoughts and attitudes of the heart. Nothing in all creation is hidden from God's sight. Everything is uncovered and laid bare before the eyes of him to whom we must give account.

—HEBREWS 4:12–13

The other day my friend and I were discussing parts of Scripture we liked best. She preferred reading the Psalms for her quiet times. She liked the poetry. The epistles were nice to read, but not the book of Romans so much: "That one's too hard. And forget the book of Revelation!" I shared that I like the parts of the Bible that tell stories — like in Genesis, Exodus, or the book of Ruth. And Luke or Mark were nice to read in one sitting.

Afterward, something about our discussion kept needling me. We had been judging the parts of God's Word we liked, what spoke to us, what parts we were drawn to, and what parts we avoided. We were picking it apart, missing the whole point of the Word of God. Hebrews 4:12 reminds me that God's Word judges us; we don't judge it.

God's Word in all its entirety forces us to understand things about ourselves that we would never grasp did we not spend time in *all* parts of the Bible. The Word of God scolds, comforts, assures, and reveals life-changing truth. Are there parts of the Bible you pass over? Perhaps it's those sections God wants to use to reveal things about you that are hidden or secret. There is not one place in Scripture that lacks a voice. Whether it's the book of Amos or 2 Chronicles, God has something to say to you.

Spirit of Christ, open my heart and mind today to parts of the Bible I'm not acquainted with. Tell me what I should hear. May all your Word speak to all of me today.

෨

JUNE 22
Mustard Seeds

[The kingdom of God] is like a mustard seed, which is the smallest seed you plant in the ground. Yet when planted, it grows and becomes the largest of all garden plants, with such big branches that the birds of the air can perch in its shade.

—MARK 4:31–32

When we were in Israel, one day we took a drive beyond the city of Jerusalem. Three miles later, down the back side of the Mount of Olives, we entered Bethany—a little whitewashed village that hadn't changed since the days of Lazarus, Mary, and Martha. While I waited in the van, my friend Bunny spied an old, bearded Arab sitting at a table. "I'm going to go see what he's selling," she exclaimed. Moments later she returned holding out her hand to show me pea-sized brown dried seeds. "Would you look at these?! They're mustard seeds! If we have faith the size of one of these," she said, picking one up, "we can move mountains."

"But they look kind of big," I frowned. "I thought the mustard seed was the smallest of all seeds." Bunny told me she said the same thing to the Arab vendor. "Let me show you what he did," she said. She then cracked one of the seeds open and gently spread its contents across her palm. Bunny cupped her hands so the breeze would not disturb the infinitesimally tiny black specks ... mustard seeds. The pea-sized pod contained thousands of breathlessly small seeds. Bunny dusted off her hand and sealed the package of pods. "And we're going to scatter these wherever we pray on this trip!"

Short, faint prayers, small acts of obedience, little expressions of kindness and encouragement ... all of these are like mustard seeds. When inspired and empowered by the Spirit, they have great impact in the kingdom of God. Today, plan to "scatter mustard seeds" of encouragement, prayer, kindness, and obedience, knowing that God will plant each seed ... resulting in great glory to his name.

Though my faith be as small as a mustard seed, I praise you, dear Lord, for "growing" your kingdom through my life, witness, prayers, and ministry today.

JUNE 23

Being One in Christ

> Now you are the body of Christ, and each one of you is a part of it.
>
> — 1 CORINTHIANS 12:27

*L*ast Sunday during Communion, I watched the plate of little crackers being passed down my row. I took note of how the well-dressed people in the pew ever so carefully lift their "pinkie" and aim for a cracker piece so as to not touch the others. My friend sitting next to me reached in to get crackers for us both. At the appropriate time, she lifted my piece to my mouth, and afterward, the other piece to hers. The fact is I just can't take Communion by myself. I'm forced to depend on another Christian friend to handle my bread for me. The wine too.

I used to feel embarrassed that I couldn't so much as pick up a cracker, but that's changed. I've learned to look at my situation differently. Asking for help makes me feel connected. Interdependent. One with others. It's a happy symbol of how closely I must live my life with fellow believers. I can't live my life alone and isolated. In fact, I couldn't even survive. Here's the point: Communion celebrates this sort of unity in the body. It's something we have to learn and relearn every day of our lives as we humbly lean hard on others for help. You and I desperately need Jesus Christ. And you and I desperately need his people.

You may not have any physical disabilities. But it would be a sad mistake to imagine you can live isolated and independent from fellow believers. Since we are one body in Christ, the hand needs the eye, the ear needs the feet, and the brain needs the heart. You have deep needs, and you are deeply needed. Remember that next time you lift the Communion bread to your lips.

Lord, help me celebrate my need of others in the body of Christ rather than being ashamed. And give me grace to make my brothers and sisters feel welcome and at ease enough in my presence to ask for help from me.

ॐ

JUNE 24

It Is Written

As soon as Jesus was baptized, he went up out of the water.... And a voice from heaven said, "This is my Son, whom I love; with him I am well pleased." Then Jesus was led by the Spirit into the desert to be tempted by the devil. After fasting forty days and forty nights, he was hungry. The tempter came to him and said, "If you are the Son of God, tell these stones to become bread."

—MATTHEW 3:16–4:3

You can't be a Christian. You're a nobody. God would never make time for the likes of you! It's an accusation the devil persistently throws at believers. Our adversary is constantly trying to get us to doubt our sonship in Christ and citizenship in heaven. The same thing happened to Jesus. No sooner had God the Father said, "This is my Son," than Satan countered with, *"If* you are the Son of God ..." Satan is still doing the same with us today.

Jesus' response in Matthew 4:4 was simply to say, "It is written ..." The Word of God is called the sword of the Spirit because it is our primary offensive weapon (Ephesians 6:17). When Jesus returns, asserting his right to reign on earth, he will defeat the Enemy with a sword that comes from his mouth (Revelation 19:15). From beginning to end, our Savior has given us the highest example: be ready to speak forth the Word of God. When Scripture is in our mouth, on the tip of our tongue, it will defeat the devil and doubts every time.

The devil's first strategy is to get you to doubt, ignore, second-guess, belittle, rationalize away, or forget about God's Word. Today be aware that as soon as a snippet of the Word of God sinks into your heart, the devil will try his utmost to undermine it. But here's your offensive weapon: "Resist the devil and he will flee from you" (James 4:7).

Lord Jesus, thank you for giving me your example in always using the Word of God to defeat the Enemy's tactics.

☙

Eternal Life

"Where, O death, is your victory? Where, O death, is your sting?" The sting of death is sin, and the power of sin is the law. But thanks be to God! He gives us the victory through our Lord Jesus Christ.

—1 CORINTHIANS 15:55–57

Not long ago I visited a funeral home and was stunned to see the way they "advertised" their services. Funerals are now portrayed as "celebrations of life." Funeral services now have themes: if the deceased enjoyed fishing, then funeral directors offer a display of rods, reels, nets, and other fishing doodads to decorate the casket. If the dead person liked gardening, then it's watering cans, hoes, and rakes, and sunflowers with a floppy straw hat cocked sideways on the coffin.

We are kidding ourselves when we romanticize death as the beautiful climax of a life well lived. It is an enemy. It is an even greater enemy to the unbeliever, for death then becomes his threshold to hell (that's nothing to celebrate)! Jesus spoke of hell more than anybody, and he made plain that rejecting his offer of eternal life would result not in nonlife, but the misery of God's wrath (John 3:36). As hell is the worst outcome of this life, so eternal life is the best. It is the supreme and ever-increasing happiness where all sin and all sadness will be erased, all that is evil in this fallen world will be removed, and all that is good will be preserved and intensified. We will be changed so that we are capable of more happiness than we could possibly conceive in this life. *That's* something to celebrate!

Oh, if only unbelievers could see the unspeakable horror of treating God with indifference or contempt in this life. Unbelievers have only this earthly life in which to hear the gospel and respond to Christ's invitation. Today, will you be encountering someone who doesn't believe in Christ? Share with them your testimony and pray for their salvation.

Blessed Redeemer, today make me mindful of every opportunity to share your love with those who don't know you.

The Power of Example

Join with others in following my example, brothers, and take note of those who live according to the pattern we gave you.

—PHILIPPIANS 3:17

One of the reasons God may have chosen Paul to write most of the New Testament is that he wanted us to know him *well*. The Holy Spirit may have wanted us to grasp Paul's thinking, motives, attitudes, and choices all the way from the book of Acts through his epistles. Paul's life ambition was evangelism, his focus was the cross, and his motive was Christ and Christ alone. No wonder the Spirit of God inspired Paul to say to us, "Join with others in following my example." And Paul could say that without a hint of smug self-righteousness.

Faced with accusers? Paul holds his tongue and points to the facts. Assaulted by hardships? He says they will all fit together for good. Confronted with injustice? He patiently states his case and moves forward. Slapped with false imprisonment? He sings praises to God in his cell. Harassed by death threats? He says it would merely send him home sooner to glory. Hounded by loneliness? Paul fixes his eyes on heavenly glories above.

This week read the book of Philippians with an eye on Paul's example. See how in Philippians 3:4–8 he lists all his religious credentials and then calls them "rubbish." Not only did he consider his religious achievements and awards worthless, he thought they were damning (there is nothing God hates more than a religious spirit). Follow Paul's example. Let's not take pleasure in our regular church attendance or pride in how many committees we serve on. Let's take pleasure in pleasing Christ and Christ alone. Remember, you *are* an example to others—whether for good or bad.

Lord God, thank you for the example of godly men like the apostle Paul. Help me to learn from his life and make the cross my focus, evangelism my motive, and the glory of Christ my goal.

ௐ

JUNE 27
He Is Able

Therefore he is able to save completely those who come to
God through him, because he always lives to intercede for
them.

—HEBREWS 7:25

*A*ble ... able-bodied ... disabled ... disability. As a quadriplegic, I am very familiar with the word *able*. There is so much
I am not able to do, whether it's playing the piano, embroidering, vac-
uuming, holding a pen or pencil, or peeling an orange. My muscles simply
aren't capable (another one of those words with *able* in it).

This is why I love the many verses in Scripture that describe our God
as *able*. Today's verse reminds us God is able to save *completely*. Because
Jesus lives and is no longer subject to death, he is able to utterly save and
to extend his salvation to anyone who comes to God through him. Second
Timothy 1:12 assures us God is able to keep saving us all the way until the
day we go to glory. First Chronicles 17:10 tells us God is able to subdue all
of our enemies, including the powers of darkness who try to erode our joy
and peace of mind. Philippians 3:21 reminds us God is the authoritative
ruler, able to subdue all things to himself. Finally in Matthew 9:28, Jesus
asks a troubled blind man, "Do you believe that I am able to do this?"

I want to be like that blind man. I may have a disability, but my confidence rests in the Savior. I say with the blind man, "Yes, Lord, have your
way in my life."

If you have a disability, God can be your "ability." Plan a study
around the verses listed today and celebrate Ephesians 3:20–21,
"Now to him who is *able* to do immeasurably more than all we
ask or imagine ... to him be glory in the church and in Christ
Jesus throughout all generations, for ever and ever! Amen."

*Lord Jesus, there is nothing missing in your character or your ability to save,
sustain, succor, and subdue. I praise you because you are ABLE!*

JUNE 28

Dancin' Shoes

We have heard of your faith in Christ Jesus and of the love
you have for all the saints—the faith and love that spring
from the hope that is stored up for you in heaven.

—COLOSSIANS 1:4–5

One of the highlights of our five-day Joni and Friends' Family Retreats is Family Celebration Night, on our last evening together. It always ends with a kicky, upbeat song of praise that gets us folks in our wheelchairs out on the floor, wheelin' and swingin' to the music. It's the next best thing to doing a jig!

Where does the joy come from? The inspiration always effervesces on that last night because that is when we underscore the happy-hearted hope of Isaiah 35:3–6: "Strengthen the feeble hands, steady the knees that give way. Be strong and do not fear; your God will come. Then will the eyes of the blind be opened and the ears of the deaf unstopped. Then will the lame leap like deer, and the mute tongue shout for joy." If you were in a wheelchair, wouldn't hope like that make you want to kick up your heels? But this year, I was doubly blessed. Right after our celebration night was over, the mother of a disabled child presented me with a special gift: a pair of red, high-topped tennis shoes! The mom explained, "Joni, all the parents chipped in for this gift for you. We've all signed our names to the shoes—they are your dancing shoes for when you get to heaven!"

In that moment, I burst out laughing. But that night, as I laid in bed, I was blinking back tears of gratitude. *One day soon, Lord, I will dance ... and leap like a deer ...*

The promise is for you too, with all the challenges and trials you may be facing today. Friend, strengthen your feeble hands and steady those shaky knees. Soon our God will come. And together we will leap for joy.

Praise you, Lord, for the promise of health and strength and overflowing joy that you have given us as an inheritance.

❧

Oh, for Leaders!

And what more shall I say? I do not have time to tell about Gideon, Barak, Samson, Jephthah, David, Samuel and the prophets, who through faith conquered kingdoms, administered justice, and gained what was promised; who shut the mouths of lions, quenched the fury of the flames, and escaped the edge of the sword; whose weakness was turned to strength; and who became powerful in battle and routed foreign armies.... The world was not worthy of them.

—HEBREWS 11:32–34, 38

Once I was waiting with a group of people for the pedestrian signal to turn green on a street corner. While it was still red, one man decided to stride across the street. Within seconds, two people followed him, then three, and then the whole group. My friend and I remained on the corner, feeling almost silly standing there by ourselves. It was the classic example of "But everybody's doing it!" But we stood alone, happy to wait until the light turned green.

People love to play Follow the Leader, even if it means doing the wrong thing. The world is waiting for leaders to break the law, trash the standard, and throw caution to the wind—that way, the world's conscience is eased and people can feel their wrong actions are justified. In Hebrews chapter 11, the Lord has given us a roll call of great, godly leaders from whom we can draw courage and resolve. The world was not worthy of David or Gideon, the apostle Paul or Peter, but God tells us to look to them as life examples of valor and nerve. Today's verse shows us how righteous people can make a *huge* difference in this world.

Give the world around you a godly example to follow. Everyone else may be "doing it," others may follow fallen leaders, but not you. Look for ways you can swim against the tide, go against the grain, and give people something, or I should say, *Someone* to follow!

Give me courage, Lord God, to be a leader today for the people around me.

This One Thing

No, dear brothers, I am still not all I should be but I am
bringing all my energies to bear on this one thing: For-
getting the past and looking forward to what lies ahead,
I strain to reach the end of the race and receive the prize
for which God is calling us up to heaven because of what
Christ Jesus did for us.

—PHILIPPIANS 3:13–14 TLB

In the movie *City Slickers* a man in midlife crisis and several of his
friends find renewal and "purpose" for their lives on a cattle-driv-
ing vacation. In one key scene, a gritty, crusty old cowboy named Curly
sits straight on his horse, spits a stream of tobacco juice, and tells them,
"Boys, ya gotta find that one thing." The rest of the movie is about these
city slickers in pursuit of their "one thing," their reason for living.

The movie got me thinking: *What's God's idea of that one thing?* I went
on a search ... and it didn't take long to find "echoes of Curly" in Psalm
27:4: "One thing I ask of the Lord, this is what I seek: that I may dwell in
the house of the Lord all the days of my life, to gaze on the beauty of the
Lord and to seek him in his temple." In short, the really *important* "one
thing" is being near Jesus and seeking him no matter where we are or what
we're doing.

Whether you're graduating from school, commencing a new job,
entering marriage, or counting the days to the birth of a new
child, remember, it's all about focusing on Jesus — pressing with
all our strength toward him. Real life, life that satisfies no matter
what, means staying hot on the heels of our Savior.

*Lord, I have to admit that sometimes I feel so frazzled and distracted that I
don't know which way to turn. Help me to remember that the road to purpose
in life is a one-way street. Holy Spirit, help me to focus all of my energies and
desires on pleasing Jesus first.*

July

Dad Huffman

But my eyes are fixed on you, O Sovereign Lord; in you I take refuge—do not give me over to death.

—PSALM 141:8

Remember when you were a child your mother would hold your face and say, "I want you to look at me when I'm speaking." It was impossible not to give her your attention. I thought of this when Dad Huffman—my secretary's father—was in a hospital intensive care unit. Because he was "fixed" in one position with a bulky ventilator down his throat, he was very anxious. My secretary had a great idea. She printed out in large letters several Bible verses of encouragement and taped them in his line of sight. Everywhere his eyesight was fixed, she put a Scripture—on the bar overhead, on the corkboard, and hanging from the wall-mounted TV.

Like a horse with blinders, like a child whose parent is holding his face, Dad Huffman couldn't miss the message: "I am your Lord, your comforter and encourager. Listen to my words. I want you to look at me when I'm speaking." With his head stuck in one position with the ventilator, only one glorious thing filled his view: the Word of God.

These Scriptures served as a powerful witness to the nurses and doctors who came to check on Dad Huffman, including the respiratory therapist and the little Mexican lady who mopped the floor every day. They were able to see firsthand how anxiety and fear dissipated from Dad Huffman's countenance. Isaiah 50:7 underscores how one directional we should be: "I set my face like flint, and I know I will not be put to shame." Write your favorite Scriptures on three-by-five cards and place them at work, in the kitchen, or inside your closet. Keep the Word of God in your line of sight today.

Lord, I don't want to turn to the right or the left; I want to keep Scripture front and center in my thinking. Bring your Word often to mind as I go throughout my day.

JULY 2

Growing the Glory

For this reason a man will leave his father and mother and
be united to his wife, and the two will become one flesh.
This is a profound mystery—but I am talking about Christ
and the church. However, each one of you also must love
his wife as he loves himself, and the wife must respect her
husband.

—EPHESIANS 5:31–33

Ken and I will celebrate our wedding anniversary tomorrow.
Over dinner and candlelight, I will be reminded of my goal in
marriage: to grow the glory of my husband. Ken may be human and full of
faults and shortcomings like us all, but I am committed to be a tool in the
Father's hands to restore my husband to greater heights of reflecting God's
glory. Yes, Ken is fallen—as am I—but he has residual glory because he is
made in the image of God. It's my goal as Ken's wife to enhance his glory.

Dr. Dan Allender has said, "Marriage is the soil for growing glory.
We must see our spouse in light of what they are meant to become, without turning bitter or complacent about who they are."[1] Marriage has a
task—to grow the glory of the other. Marriage also has a challenge—it is
tempting to become bitter or complacent about the distance your spouse
is from the glory they ought to exude. Every day we have a choice of
either encouraging our partner's journey toward Christ, or degrading and
stripping him or her of splendor as well as obscuring what little glory
remains.

The challenge is to delight in, respect, and learn from each other.
Men and women reflect different features of God, and we should
be on the edge of wonder as we consider the glorious image of our
great Creator God reflected—even if ever so dimly—in the life
of our spouse. Watch for that today.

*Jesus, help me to see my goal in any relationship. I want to join you in helping
to grow the glory of the other.*

JULY 3

A Word from Ken

Glorify the Lord with me; let us exalt his name together.

— PSALM 34:3

I've never written one of my wife's devotionals before, but I wanted to do it today. July 3 is our anniversary. I also want to write because Joni recently arrived home from the hospital where she survived a struggle against double pneumonia.

Those nine days in the hospital were extremely difficult for Joni. They were difficult for me too. I felt helpless, unable to do much for her except to press on her abdomen to help her cough. I stayed at the hospital every night, making sure she had someone to be her "muscles" when she needed help breathing. Quadriplegics like Joni have limited lung capacity, and many don't live through such an ordeal. It's amazing she recovered. Obviously God has much more work for her to do.

And me too. For all these years, we've shared a marvelous mission together. And underline that word *together*. Joni and I were never more "together" than when she and I were battling against her pneumonia in the hospital. One would think a feeling of togetherness would occur over a candlelight dinner or a romantic vacation. But isn't it just like God to strengthen our unity, deepen our commitment, and breathe fresh romance into our marriage through, well . . . dealing with pneumonia in a hospital?!

> The sense of being together is never stronger than when you are in the trenches with a loved one battling a common enemy side by side. Stressful situations can bring us closer *together*. Ephesians 2:22 says, "And in him you too are being built *together* to become a dwelling in which God lives by his Spirit."

Father, help me find someone today with whom I can exalt your name. If an affliction, disappointment, or illness is separating me from a loved one, give me the grace and wisdom to embrace them in the midst of hardship. I want to be built up "together" with them . . . all for the praise of your glory.

ॐ

July 4

Is It Coincidence ... or God?

In him we were also chosen, having been predestined
according to the plan of him who works out everything
in conformity with the purpose of his will, in order that
we, who were the first to hope in Christ, might be for the
praise of his glory.

—Ephesians 1:11–12

God delights in arranging coincidences. Consider your big Fourth of July picnic. The sun is warm and the grill is working and everyone's bringing salad and watermelon, but unknown to you, God wants it to rain. He wants your friends to leave early before the storm hits. He wants your brother-in-law, Ed, to help you hurry the grill into the garage where you two will stand leaning against the car, listening to the downpour. There you will get into a long conversation leading into spiritual things that will eventually lead to your brother-in-law's conversion to Christ.

How does God pull this off? Earlier in the day, it may have been warm, but five miles above your house a polar jet stream was bringing colder air from the northwest. Yesterday, the jet stream was two hundred miles north, but a disturbance over the Canadian Rockies three days ago pushed it your way. What caused the disturbance? Merely a complicated sequence of atmospheric twists and the proper Pacific Ocean water temperature three weeks ago. Yet that temperature was being affected back in April. Whew! God has been thinking about your brother-in-law for a long, long time.

God is doing the exact same thing with people all over the country who need a little sunshine—or rain—to further the Lord's work in their lives. How does God manage it all? He does it totally naturally. But it's mind-bogglingly complicated. These sorts of divine coincidences happen every day. Today, meditate on how he works out everything in conformity with the purpose of his will in your life.

God of wonder, I cannot begin to fathom the way you work in this world to advance your purposes, but thank you for running things. I submit my will to you, happy to know that your plan for me is perfect.

JULY 5

A Reminder over the Rockies

Be very careful, then, how you live—not as unwise but as
wise, making the most of every opportunity.... Therefore
do not be foolish, but understand what the Lord's will is.

—EPHESIANS 5:15–17

Somewhere over Colorado, the plane went completely dark. At the
same moment, the audio channels died and the movie screen went
blank. I gave a serious—almost frightened—look to my friend Judy, sitting next to me. It didn't help that we were encountering turbulence over
the Rocky Mountains.

The captain came on with the usual bland assurances. But I don't
think many of us felt assured. After a few more minutes I heard a passen-
ger say, "Do you smell something burning?" You could sense the tension
in the cabin. And just then we began to descend. Judy and I huddled our
heads and began softly saying the Lord's Prayer. The captain came on and
explained that due to the power failure, we would be making an emergency
landing in St. Louis. As our plane slowly lost altitude, Judy and I began
praying for the other passengers. If we were going to die, we wanted to
cover as many people as possible with our intercessions.

When we finally touched down in St. Louis, applause erupted from
the passengers. Relieved as I was, I found a Scripture from the book of Job
slipping into my thoughts. "Man's days are determined; you have decreed
the number of his months and have set limits he cannot exceed" (Job 14:5).
In short, God can take us home any old way and any time he wants. That
"limit" for me might have been that very afternoon over the Rockies. It was
yet another reminder that *today* is the most important day of my life.

Don't look at today as "just another day." Think of it as one more
priceless opportunity to love people to Jesus. We really don't know
if there will be another.

*Father, I don't want to waste this precious day of life. I want to walk with you
step-by-step and enter into all your will and desire for me.*

Ꮗ

JULY 6

Two Lenses

Though he brings grief, he will show compassion, so great
is his unfailing love. For he does not willingly bring affliction or grief to the children of men.

— LAMENTATIONS 3:32–33

The Lord took no pleasure in my broken neck. Like any father who
has compassion on his children, it pained his heart to see me hurt.
Yet at the same time, it pleased the Lord to permit my accident. My spinal
cord injury was something he sovereignly designed in and for his good
pleasure.

God's ways are so much higher than ours, he has the capacity to look
at the world through two lenses — through a narrow lens *and* a wide-angle
one. When God looks at a painful event through a narrow lens, he sees
the tragedy for what it is. He is deeply grieved. In Ezekiel 18:32 he says, "I
take no pleasure in the death of anyone." God feels the sting in his chest
when a child dies of cancer or a husband is killed in an accident. When
God looks at that same event through his wide-angle lens, however, he sees
the tragedy in relation to everything leading up to it, as well as flowing out
from it. He sees a mosaic stretching into eternity. It is this mosaic with all
its parts, both good and evil, that brings him delight.

In the span of a single verse, the Bible asserts "the Lord brings
grief," yet "he does not willingly bring ... grief." God tried this
out on himself. He willed the death of his own Son, but he took
no delight in it. God saw how Jesus' death would demonstrate his
incomprehensible mercy, as well as bring his people to glory. God
often wills what he despises because — and only because — he has
a wide-angle view on the world.

*Lord, too often I have only a narrow-lens view of my world. Give me your per-
spective, and may I rejoice in the beautiful mosaic I will one day understand.*

☙

God Weeping

Jesus wept.

—JOHN 11:35

hen God looks at our suffering through his narrow lens, his heart is moved. Jesus wept at the graveside of Lazarus. He often wept when he prayed, pouring out tears in the garden of Gethsemane. Reading through the Gospels, it is clear that emotion choked his throat and empathy filled his eyes as he looked out on suffering people, like a shepherd gathering bewildered, sick, and lost sheep. Our sufferings matter to the Almighty, and he has wept in empathy time and again.

But heaven will reveal something different. The mosaic, which I spoke about yesterday, will reveal an eternal plan that was never for a moment threatened, never in jeopardy of collapsing, and never on the edge of defeat. People whose suffering seemed confounding on earth will see this marvelous mosaic. God will personally flip right side up the tangled embroidery of that scarred life to reveal the delicate and beautiful pattern never observed on earth. Those who have been martyred or tortured—the Christians in the genocide of south Sudan, Armenia, and China—will stand and adore God for his plan in their suffering.

We will experience love like we never imagined. This is good news for people who have never been "the most important person" in anyone's life. But in heaven, "all shall have as much love as they desire ... as much as they can bear. Such will be the sweet and perfect harmony among the heavenly saints, perfect love reigning in every heart toward every other, without limit or restriction or interruption."[2]

> Best of all, Jesus Christ and his bride will no longer taste tears (unless they are tears of joy?!). The grand and glorious mosaic—the wide-angle way of looking at life—will be revealed and we shall finally *understand*. In the meantime, Psalm 56:8 promises, "Record my lament; list my tears on your scroll—are they not in your record?"

Lord Jesus, your tears are very precious to me. Thank you that you wept on my behalf when you interceded for me and all those you love.

JULY 8

The Sufferings of Jesus

> In a loud voice they sang: "Worthy is the Lamb, who was
> slain, to receive power and wealth and wisdom and strength
> and honor and glory and praise!"
>
> — REVELATION 5:12

In heaven, not only will our sufferings win us merit, the sufferings
of Jesus will have an eternal perspective too. Our Lord will be honored as the slain Lamb. His sufferings will *never* be forgotten. Unlike us, he
will always visibly bare his wounds to the universe, and for that, God the
Father, Son, and Holy Spirit will enjoy praise as never before!

If any dark demon in the corner of the universe ever doubted the righteousness of God in stooping to rescue debased sinners, he'll be set straight.
No evil spirit will dare accuse God of having defiled his purity in order to
redeem wicked men. No one will question God's righteous reputation for
having condescended to save sinners. God's righteousness will be beyond
question! In fact, the sacrifice and suffering of Jesus was of such massive
worth and supreme value that God's righteousness will shine even brighter.
For it will be shown that God in his wisdom was able to rescue sinners,
redeem suffering, crush the rebellion, restore all things, vindicate his holy
name, and provide restitution . . . and come out all the more glorious for it!
Heaven will show this. And we will praise him for it for all of eternity.

You have something eternally precious in common with
Christ—suffering! No angel or archangel will ever fully grasp the
sweet union that affliction has refined between you and your Savior. In heaven you won't praise the suffering, but you *will* praise
the wisdom and the power of God in using it to drive you to the
cross, as well as showcase his righteousness and mercy for all of
eternity.

How unsearchable is your wisdom, O God! I praise you for your awesome plan
of salvation and the way you use affliction to showcase your mercy and grace. I
look forward to heaven where it will all be made plain!

Windows of the Soul

> Your eye is the lamp of your body. When your eyes are good, your whole body also is full of light. But when they are bad, your body also is full of darkness.
>
> —LUKE 11:34

It was a warm July afternoon, and Ken and I were floating down a lazy river on a pontoon boat with our friends. A new couple, Ed and Gale, had joined us. The sun sparkled off the river, so all of us kept our sunglasses on as we talked. We anchored under a big shade tree, ate sandwiches, and shared what we had been learning from the Bible. I was fascinated by Ed and Gale's testimony—their adult children had recently led them to Christ! It was an amazing story of one neighbor influencing a brother, then a son's witness and a daughter's marriage, all woven together to bring not only Ed and Gale to the Lord, but a wide circle of neighbors and relatives. My heart was drawn to theirs, and I was struck by their tender spirits.

We pulled anchor when we noticed a storm starting to brew in the distance. We got back to the dock just when the first drops started. Although we were rushed to say goodbye before the downpour, I called to Ed and Gale as they climbed into their van. "Wait! Take off your sunglasses ... I need to see you!" I had learned so much about them, but I couldn't say I knew them or had really *met* them until we looked each other in the eyes. For the eyes are the lamp of the body and the window of the soul.

Your eyes are a private place where the "who" of who you are is revealed. Be transparent; cultivate a see-through soul. Get in the habit of looking into the eyes of others when you talk about Christ. Your eyes will shine his brightness!

Give me confidence, Lord, to look at people straight in the eyes today when I speak about Jesus. May others see his light in my eyes.

A Real Friendship

I have called you friends, for everything that I learned from
my Father I have made known to you.

—JOHN 15:15

*I*n the film *Sleeper,* Woody Allen plays a character who wakes up
in another century, having been frozen in a scientific experiment.
He is given a stack of photographs from our century to identify, which
prompts a series of hilarious one-liners. Billy Graham's picture comes
up. Allen pauses, then says, "Billy Graham ... claimed to have a personal
relationship with God." The audience, of course, cracks up. That is how
absurd the idea sounds to many people.[3]

What is more astonishing is that God doesn't think it's absurd. He is
very interested in relating to us. He's a host issuing party invitations left
and right. He's a shepherd leaving the ninety-nine in the field to seek the
one lost lamb. He's a wealthy king lavishing a party on lowlifes. He seeks
friendship.

We should be that passionate. But often we seek a church, or a style of
worship, or a way of studying the Bible, or a method of prayer. We make
these things the focus rather than him. Study methods and worship tech-
niques are helpful, but even Jesus was astounded that people could devote
their entire lives to studying Scripture yet fail to know the One to whom
Scripture was pointing (John 5:39–40).

Even in the best relationships, we are still left aching for someone
to enter our struggle—to embrace us with a passion that seizes
and melts us into a union that will never be broken. We want
friendship, real and deep. Intimacy with God blossoms when we
enter "the fellowship of sharing in his sufferings." When suffering
is shared, hearts can't help but be pressed together. Relationship is
then no longer a routine ... it's *real.*

*Lord God, I want to seek you in the way you seek a relationship with me. And
not just a "relationship" but a true and glad friendship. That's what I want
with you.*

For the Sake of Christ

> That is why, for Christ's sake, I delight in weaknesses, in insults, in hardships, in persecutions, in difficulties. For when I am weak, then I am strong.
>
> —2 CORINTHIANS 12:10

It's one thing to muster a submissive attitude toward God when we bring troubles on ourselves, but it's a different matter when unexpected trials hit us broadside—trials not of our own making. Like when a drunk driver veers across the yellow line. Or a grim-faced doctor diagnoses cancer. Or reassessment slaps your property into a higher tax bracket. Or a clumsy linebacker breaks your high-school kid's leg in football practice. Or an old friend drags your name through the mud. You didn't bring any of these troubles on yourself; these are circumstances over which you have no control—and for that reason, they're the hardest with which to deal.

But look at the apostle Paul. He didn't bring that shipwreck on himself. He didn't instigate a death threat in Damascus. He didn't orchestrate mob scenes that left him smashed by stones. Paul may not have been responsible for his circumstances, but he *was* responsible for the way he reacted. He never groaned, "Oh, for Pete's sake, here we go again!" Instead, he said, "For Christ's sake, I delight in hardships." Another response? He said in 2 Timothy 2:10, "Therefore I endure everything for the sake of the elect." These were the first words out of Paul's mouth when he was pelted by stones, blindsided by brutal floggings, and thrown into dark dungeons. He endured hardships for Christ's sake, as well as the sake of the church.

When trials assault you, bite your tongue from saying, "Oh, for Pete's sake!" Instead, whisper a word or two of praise. No matter what the circumstances at home or at the office, praise is possible when we win the battle with words that bless our Lord.

Lord God, for the sake of your Son, Jesus, and for the sake of my friends and family watching me, I give you praise today in the midst of my hardships.

The Graft

> I am the vine; you are the branches. If a man remains in me and I in him, he will bear much fruit; apart from me you can do nothing.
>
> —JOHN 15:5

As a child, I remember early spring and grafting time in my Uncle Don's apple orchard. My uncle would run his hand over the bark of the apple tree, finding just the right place to peel it away and make a slanting cut into the heart of the wood. He would then take a small branch and push the graft down into the damp wood of the tree. Later that spring, new life would emerge: blossoms to buds to fruit. I've heard that one tree can bear over one hundred different kinds of apples. But it does not come without a wounding in both tree and branch.

Years later I would understand John Bunyan's words: "Conversion is not the smooth, easy-going process some men seem to think.... It is wounding work, this breaking of the hearts, but without wounding there is no saving. Where there is grafting there is a cutting, the graft must be let in with a wound.... Heart must be set to heart ... or there will be no sap from root to branch."[4]

Never would I have dreamed as I wandered through that orchard as a little girl, sensing the Spirit's promptings to draw nearer, that my journey to know God would be filled with such cutting and wounding. The diving accident in which I became paralyzed was yet in the future, but it would force my wound to his wound, my heart to his heart. Years later I would understand the lesson of the graft: the wounding is where divine sap flows and spiritual fruit blossoms.

In affliction and suffering, our hearts are pressed into his. And the life of God flows into us, wound to wound. In those times of brokenness, remember that in Christ, the result is life, life, and more life.

Help me, Lord, to remain, to abide in you this day, no matter what my circumstances.

The Lord Your Helper

Jesus left the synagogue and went to the home of Simon.
Now Simon's mother-in-law was suffering from a high
fever, and they asked Jesus to help her.

—LUKE 4:38

*P*icture the scene. When Jesus entered the home of Simon Peter
and learned his mother-in-law was sick, the people made a
beautiful and simple request. They asked Jesus to help her. No fanfare, no
digging deep into the matter, no extended discussions and wondering if it
was the will of God or not. Jesus was under their roof, and they knew he
had the power to help a sick woman. And he did.

Sometimes it's hard to know what or how to pray. Ken and I have felt
that way lately. For several months, we have been praying nightly for a list
of friends who have cancer. Some of the cases are pretty extensive, others
look hopeful. Through it all, our friends are struggling through pain and
disappointment. Often we don't know how to pray, but we can't go wrong
following the lead of Luke 4:38, "Lord, help her." It's simple, to the point,
direct, and sincere. Jesus is under the roof in the homes of our friends, and
we don't have to dig deep into the matter or question God's will.

There's something else I like about that simple prayer, "Lord, help
her." It sums up our bewilderment. It describes how we've come
to the end of our understanding and that we have nowhere or no
one else to whom we can turn. To pray "Lord, help her" is to have
your focus on Jesus. Whether it's healing in the here and now or
hope for the hereafter, there's one thing utterly true of the Lord:
"He is your shield and helper and your glorious sword" (Deuteronomy 33:29).

*Jesus, I pray that you will be a help today to my friends or family members who
are dealing with illnesses. I may not be certain how each sickness will turn out,
but I know for sure you will shower your help and hope today. So be it.*

God Is Worth It

> Whatever you do, work at it with all your heart, as working for the Lord, not for men, since you know that you will receive an inheritance from the Lord as a reward. It is the Lord Christ you are serving.
>
> —COLOSSIANS 3:23–24

My friend Judy Butler has served as my administrative assistant for decades. She not only invests long hours at Joni and Friends but helps me get up for church on Sunday mornings and often cooks dinner for Ken and me. Sometimes people say to her, "It's wonderful the way you help Joni," to which she replies, "God is worth it!"

And he is. Judy is keenly aware that when she helps me, she is working for the Lord, not for the praise of others. She also knows that when she books my travel tickets, answers the phone, makes my appointments, and travels with me near and far, she is making an eternal investment, advancing the kingdom of Christ, fulfilling God's purpose for her life, and setting the stage for others to hear the gospel. Also, when Judy picks up things for me at the market, helps me with my personal routines, and whips up her famous lamb curry for me and my husband, she is serving the least of the brethren (that's how I think of myself).

Is Judy simply helping a disabled lady? No, she is serving God. And he's *worth* it!

Judy really is an amazing woman. What is most amazing is the grace of God in her life. First Corinthians 15:10 says, "But by the grace of God I am what I am, and his grace to me was not without effect. No, I worked harder than all of them—yet not I, but the grace of God that was with me." Work hard in the kingdom today—God's worth it.

Lord God, you are my focus as I serve today. Energize me with your grace and enable me to be diligent in my work—for you are worth it!

ॐ

The Wall Won't Hurt You

For by You I can run against a troop, by my God I can leap
over a wall.

—PSALM 18:29 NKJV

Corie is nineteen years old, a little under five feet tall, has one of the most winsome smiles I've ever encountered, *and* she has Down syndrome. Corie's speech is a little slurred, and her nouns and verbs don't always match. But that just adds to her charm. One summer at a Family Retreat she asked me excitedly, "Are you going rock wall and come down and watching me climb it all the way to the top and back down okay?" I replied, "You bet!"

I watched the conference staff workers strap my new friend into her helmet and climbing harness. Corie was ready! She gave me a happy "thumbs up," turned to the wall, grabbed a rock, and away she went. She was so fast! This girl had no fear! After she had conquered her goal and scooted back down the wall, everyone cheered.

But Heather, who was next, was too nervous to cheer. It was her very first climb . . . and she has Down syndrome too. "Are you ready?" the staff worker asked her. She could only stare at him with a blank expression. But then Corie stepped in. "Headder, you are going too, up?" she said. Slipping an arm around her friend, Corie said softly, "Okay it is, Headder. The wall won't hurt you." That was all Heather needed to hear. In the next instant she was scrambling up the wall. Halfway up, she meekly called down, "It doesn't hurt!"

Are you facing an intimidating wall right now . . . a medical problem, an unexpected bill, a strained relationship, or a wrestling match with temptation? God has a purpose and knows all about what you're facing. Look up, take heart, and say, "I can do everything through him who gives me strength" (Philippians 4:13).

Thank you, Lord Jesus, that you are the Master of every wall in life. Help me to take courage from little Corie's courage and counsel. With your help, I'll grip that first rock and begin to climb.

No Tear Wasted

> There is a time for everything, and a season for every activity under heaven: ... a time to weep and a time to laugh, a time to mourn and a time to dance.
>
> —ECCLESIASTES 3:1, 4

An old devotional book movingly says, "How can God dry your tears in the next world if you have not wept in this one?" The image of God tenderly wiping away your tears describes a loving and utterly compassionate moment in heaven between you and your Savior. Your earthly sorrows have a profound purpose in eternity: they are setting the stage for God to engage himself wholly and completely in your eternal comfort. No wonder David prayed in Psalm 56:8 (KJV) for God to "put thou my tears into thy bottle: are they not in thy book?"

God will atone for every single one of your tears. First, the reason behind your suffering will be made plain as God reveals something so glorious in his purpose that it will completely suffice for all your hurt. Next, as God dries your tears, it will showcase the intimate, sweet affection of God toward you personally—much more so than if you never cried!

I'm not glorifying weeping, but I'm glorifying the God whose purpose will be exalted and whose tenderhearted compassion will be *glorified* through your weeping. Søren Kierkegaard said, "In the language of eternity, the suffering that helped you to the highest, is certainly not useless. It is useless and unused only if you do not allow yourself to be helped by it to the highest."[5]

When time comes for weeping, comfort yourself with these assurances from God's Word. No tear will be wasted. Share today's thoughts with a friend who is grieving or hurting. And don't forget ... bring Kleenex.

Lord, I am amazed that you have recorded in detail every time I've cried. Help me not to hide my tears. Help me also not to waste my sorrows, remembering they are aiding me for all of eternity.

ᕮᕲ

Harbor Lights ... Lower Lights

"Should you not fear me?" declares the Lord. "Should you not tremble in my presence? I made the sand a boundary for the sea, an everlasting barrier it cannot cross. The waves may roll, but they cannot prevail; they may roar, but they cannot cross it."

—JEREMIAH 5:22

When I was a little girl, I loved beach camping with my family along the dunes of the Delaware shore. We would huddle around the campfire on the sand and sing:

Brightly beams our Father's mercies from his lighthouse evermore;
But to us he gives the keeping of the lights along the shore.
Let the lower lights keep burning, send a beam across the waves.
Some poor fainting, struggling seaman, you may rescue, you may save.

When the mist began to overtake our campfire, we trekked back to our tent on the other side of the barrier dunes. At the crest of the dune, we could see the Fenwick Island lighthouse and, straight ahead, the red and green channel markers on Indian River Bay. When I asked about the lights in the channel, Daddy explained, "They mark where the water is deep enough for a boat to safely sail. If those lights go out, sailors won't be able to tell where the sandbar is." When I asked why they were called lower lights in the hymn, he told me that, "God is the lighthouse and we are his lower lights. We point the way. We show where it's safe to go. That's what you do, Joni," he smiled as we slid down the other side of the big dune.

What way can you "mark a safe channel" for others who are younger in the faith? Don't be afraid to point the way. Show others where to find the safe harbor. You are the Father's "lower light"; after all, Jesus said, "You are the light of the world.... Let your light shine before men, that they may ... praise your Father in heaven" (Matthew 5:14, 16).

Keep your mercies brightly beaming, Father. Thank you for being our safe harbor.

The Legacy of Mary Rose

> Well done, good and faithful servant! You have been faithful in a few things.... Come and share your Master's happiness!
>
> —MATTHEW 25:23

Just minutes before I was called up to the platform to address the overflowing convention, I met Mary Rose. She shuffled toward me, leaning on the arm of her escort, her gait stiff and her arm curled against her chest. I guessed she had cerebral palsy. She wore a tan cardigan over a yellow cotton dress. Nothing fancy. Her glasses sat askew on her nose. "Joni," her escort said, "this is my friend Mary Rose, and she's been waiting so long to meet you." Mary Rose stretched out her rigid arm to greet me. Her body may have been stiff, but her smile was warm. She was excited to meet me, the person who had written the book that had meant so much to her decades earlier. "And Joni," her escort said, "Mary Rose has something to tell you."

"I-have-been-pray-ing-for-you-ev-ery-day," she said with great effort, "ev-er-since-I-read-your-book." Praying for me? *Every day?* I did some quick math in my head. Seven thousand times this woman had lifted me up to the Savior! I watched her shuffle away, back into the shadows, as I wheeled out into the light and the applause. But I didn't feel important at that moment. God isn't impressed by my books, paintings, speeches, and world travel. When it comes to "entering the Master's happiness," the highest accolades will go to godly people who have labored loyally yet received no recognition. Someday on the Other Side, when Mary Rose receives her magnificent reward, I'll stand happily on the sidelines, cheering and applauding.

Do you ever feel that your service for Christ has been inconspicuous—hardly noticed by anyone? Be encouraged. Your reward has nothing to do with being bigger or better, well known or well watched. But it has everything to do with faithfulness.

Lord, empower me to serve you steadily and faithfully this day, this week, this year. Thank you for the promise of 1 Corinthians 15:58, that my "labor in the Lord is not in vain."

A Word from Joni's Sister ...

In him we were also chosen, having been predestined according to the plan of him who works out everything in conformity with the purpose of his will.

—EPHESIANS 1:11

My name is Kathy Eareckson, and Joni is my little sister. I'm the one who was at the beach that day when Joni dove off the raft and broke her neck. I will never forget that Saturday afternoon in July 1967. I was a teenager, like Joni, and had planned a swimming date with my boyfriend. I knew Joni had hoped to play tennis with her friend that afternoon, but when the match fell through, I asked if she wanted to join us.

We drove to the beach on Chesapeake Bay and wasted no time in heading for the cool water. I stayed near shore, but Joni made a beeline for a raft anchored further out in the water. Suddenly, I felt a sharp pinch. A crab pinched my toe! Startled, I shouted to Joni, "Watch out for crabs!" She didn't respond. In fact, she was nowhere in sight. Not on the raft. Not in the water. Something told me to go find her—*quickly*. I reached her just when she was beginning to drown! What are the chances of a crab pinching someone's toe and getting her attention just in time to respond to an emergency? A million to one. Every time I've been tempted to doubt God's hand in those terrible circumstances that day, God brings that humble little crab to mind. From the big events in life down to the tiniest of details, he is great, he is sovereign, and he is in control.

I've learned from Joni (actually, the Bible) that though our circumstances are puzzling, perplexing, and even heartbreaking, we can trust him. Bow low before the throne of your Father who loves you and cares about every detail of your life.

Praise you, Father. It's so amazing that a God who spins great galaxies across the void of space would care about the seemingly small events of my day.

Sharing the Manna

Freely you have received, freely give.

—MATTHEW 10:8

What does it mean to glorify the Lord? It means showing off Jesus! Talking about him, thinking about him, singing about his goodness, pointing people to him, letting all his attributes and character qualities shine through our lives. *That's* what it means to glorify him.

The other night while lying in bed, I had the chance to glorify him by just thinking about his goodness. I was pondering 1 Timothy 6:17 (NKJV), which says that he "gives us richly all things to enjoy." Lying there, I magnified the Lord in my thoughts. I recalled how God's hand of blessing often stopped and started in the Old Testament depending on the Israelites' obedience.

But then I thought of God's New Testament way of doing things. Always blessing. Always giving. And *always* richly giving us all things to enjoy. Jesus is the manna always falling on the camp. He is the rock in the desert, ever sending out streams of life. He is the bronze serpent, lifted high, and always healing. He is the sun always shining. He is the well of grace constantly overflowing. Who ever returned from his door unblessed? Who ever rose from his table unsatisfied? Scripture says, "Praise the Lord, O my soul, and forget not all his benefits" (Psalm 103:2). The Lord Jesus is so *good*. Taste and see how good he really is. Drink deeply from the Living Water today . . . and glorify his name.

I think we glorify the Lord best when we pass on his goodness to others. By God's grace, *you* are his manna to others. *You* are his light shining in the darkness. *You* are the vessel through which his grace overflows. And out of *you* flow streams, rivers of life touching the thirsty world around you. The charge to us today is to richly *give* all things for others to enjoy.

Father, help me to glorify your Son this day as I watch for opportunities to touch, encourage, help, and strengthen other lives by your empowering and in your great joy.

He Hideth My Soul

One thing I ask of the Lord, this is what I seek: that I may
dwell in the house of the Lord ... and to seek him in his
temple. For in the day of trouble he will keep me safe in
his dwelling; he will hide me in the shelter of his tabernacle
and set me high upon a rock.

— PSALM 27:4–5

Fanny Crosby suffered much as a blind person living in the nine-
teenth century. She wrote that she often found solace in the book
of Psalms. Miss Crosby especially liked those psalms that pointed her to
the future, encouraging her to hold on tightly for heaven was just around
the corner. She needed that reminder — she realized her physical limitations exposed her to powerful emotions that, if left unattended, could
sway her faith. When she leaned on the Psalms, she found them to be a
wellspring of inspiration, and they provided the basis for many of her six
thousand hymns. Psalm 27 was, in fact, the inspiration for:

He hideth my soul in the cleft of the rock
  That shadows a dry, thirsty land;
He hideth my life in the depths of His love,
  And covers me there with His hand
  And covers me there with His hand.

When clothed in His brightness transported I rise,
  To meet Him in clouds of the sky,
His perfect salvation, His wonderful love,
  I'll shout with the millions on high.[6]

Turn Fanny Crosby's beautiful old hymn into a prayer today, saying, "Lord Jesus, *you* hide my soul in the cleft of the rock; and *you*,
Savior, are that Rock! *You* hide my life in the depths of your love.
You cover me with your hand." Today, open a hymnal and enjoy
using the words of several timeless hymns as prayers of praise and
thanksgiving.

*Thank you, Lord God, for the Psalms. You have provided these wonderful
Scriptures to help stabilize my feelings when I feel overwhelmed. Thank you,
especially, for Psalm 27.*

☙

Horsey Obedience

Do you give the horse his strength or clothe his neck with a flowing mane? Do you make him leap like a locust, striking terror with his proud snorting? He paws fiercely, rejoicing in his strength, and charges into the fray. He laughs at fear, afraid of nothing; he does not shy away from the sword.

—JOB 39:19–22

very morning on the way to work, I pass a horse-show ring. Today I pulled over to watch a woman exercise a big chestnut thoroughbred. They were all alone, the horse slowly cantering with his head down. The rider moved one foot forward, barely touching his shoulder, and he immediately switched his lead, stretching out his right foreleg. She moved her other foot, and he switched to the other lead. She didn't use a crop or wear spurs. She didn't even pull on the reins. Her commands were imperceptible—a tightening of the knees against the saddle, a nudging with the toe of her boot, or perhaps a soft click with her tongue. The big thoroughbred was alert to her commands; he got the message every time.

Because of the two-way communication between horse and rider, the woman and her steed seemed to blend as one. They appeared to share one mind, one purpose. They looked indivisible. Wouldn't it be wonderful if we could always be sensitive and alert to God's commands, responding to his promptings without delay?!

You can tell from today's Bible passage that God takes delight in one of his most elegant creations, the horse. God also takes delight when he puts a little pressure here or there—almost imperceptibly—and *we* respond, switching our lead. God wants us to be so at one with him that we appear indivisible with our Savior, having one mind and purpose. Today, make it the joy of your heart to do God's will. Instantly obey. *Get* his message.

Lord, train me in godliness that I might respond happily and instantly to every one of your commands.

JULY 23

I'm Full

> Whom have I in heaven but you? And earth has nothing I
> desire besides you. My flesh and my heart may fail, but God
> is the strength of my heart and my portion forever.
>
> —PSALM 73:25–26

Wouldn't it be wonderful to be able to say with the psalmist, "God, I am *full*! I'm stuffed full of blessings, and I can't think of anything else I desire on earth besides you." Oh, to be that satisfied. When you become satiated in Christ, it is evidence that contentment has the definite upper hand in your heart. When Jesus says to you, "I am the bread of life. He who comes to me will never go hungry," he is talking about gratification of the soul (John 6:35). To be satisfied in Christ means being full. Never wanting more. We need not ever be hungry for "man does not live on bread alone but on every word that comes from the mouth of the Lord" (Deuteronomy 8:3). The role of the Word of God is to feed faith's appetite for Christ.

Contentment consists not in great wealth but in having very few wants in this life. A divine arithmetic for contentment is to subtract your earthly wants so that something of greater value can be attained: satisfaction in the Lord.

> Francis Quarles has stated, "As there is no worldly gain without some loss, so there is no worldly loss without some gain. If thou hast lost thy wealth, thou hast lost some trouble with it. If thou art degraded from thy honor, thou art likewise freed from the stroke of envy. If sickness hath blurred thy beauty, it hath delivered thee from pride. Set the allowance against the loss and thou shalt find no loss great."[7]

Father, not everything I desire is necessarily good for my soul. I pray that you will only give me what is good for my eternal well-being and my happiness in this life. Help me to subtract my wants, so that eternal rewards might be added. Then I shall be content.

Women of Influence

Neither do people light a lamp and put it under a bowl. Instead they put it on its stand, and it gives light to everyone in the house.

—MATTHEW 5:15

*M*ore than two hundred years ago, two average, rather frail women became concerned by the spiritual state of their small church in a little Minnesota town. They decided to meet together regularly and pray for God to work. A short time later their pastor noticed that his heart seemed more open to the Word of God—and that his preaching had fresh power. Several families in the congregation fell under conviction and confessed their sin. Other families began witnessing to their neighbors. Before long, people were traveling from far away to become involved in the many Bible studies springing up in the church community. Soon wholesale spiritual revival broke out, and God's Spirit moved powerfully across the state of Minnesota, changing the landscape for decades to come.

These two women never wrote a book or traveled to other cities to tell their story. They didn't even want their names known! But they were powerful women of influence, substantial saints who let God exercise spiritual clout through them. And you are no different. God is not looking for famous individuals who can speak eloquently before thousands. God is looking for someone like you. Daniel 11:32 (NASB) says: "The people who know their God will display strength and take action."

The passage doesn't say you have to join the talk-show circuit or do noteworthy things. If you know God, display his strength and take action! It may be as simple as taking a meal to family with a sick mom, leading a Bible study, or just meeting with a few friends to pray. First make sure you know him, know his heart. And then just do what he says!

Father God, I do know you and love you. Empower me by your Holy Spirit and show me how to take action—wherever and however you lead—to advance your kingdom.

☙

JULY 25

That Other Place

[Hell] has long been prepared; it has been made ready for
the king. Its fire pit has been made deep and wide, with an
abundance of fire and wood; the breath of the Lord, like a
stream of burning sulfur, sets it ablaze.

—ISAIAH 30:33

ell's stock has fallen lately from lack of public confidence. Of
course, atheists have never bought into it anyway, but millions reject hell yet still believe in heaven and cherish fond hopes of going
there. Some draw comfort from biblical descriptions of a compassionate
God and the joys awaiting his children in the world to come. Surely if *we*
hate suffering, God must hate it worse and could never have founded a
place as horrible as described in Dante's *Inferno*.

But the same Jesus who gave heaven a five-star rating also described
an otherworldly chamber of horrors. And he made clear that Satan doesn't
top the list of people to be feared. For the determined evildoer, God is the
one to shudder at. Today's verse states that it's the *breath of the Lord* that
sets hell ablaze. Those who prefer their dark deeds, better beware! Matthew
10:28 warns, "Do not be afraid of those who kill the body but cannot kill
the soul. Rather, be afraid of the One who can destroy both soul and body
in hell." But remember, God did not originally make hell for people. Jesus
said it was "prepared for the devil and his angels" (Matthew 25:41). It's
unnatural for humans to be there—as unnatural as turning our backs on
a Creator who loves us.

God takes no joy in sending anyone to eternal misery; his Son was
a lifeguard, urgently warning swimmers of treacherous waters. But
in dozens of passages, God warns he will hurl everyone into that
unthinkable pit who persists in challenging or ignoring him.

*Oh God, give me boldness to talk about the gift of salvation. I don't want my
friends and neighbors to die without having the chance to respond to your Son!*

July 26

Beach Towels and Hymns

> But let all who take refuge in you be glad; let them ever sing for joy. Spread your protection over them, that those who love your name may rejoice in you.
>
> —Psalm 5:11

The fire crackles and pops, and a burst of sparks swirl in the smoke. The surf pounds the beach, and the hissing of retreating foam sounds soothing. Is there any sweeter satisfaction than to lie on the blanket with hands under head and gaze at the starry dome above while singing a hymn? These are my favorite childhood memories of summer. And on that Delaware beach around the campfire, my father, with all his warmth and tenderness, would lead us in singing.

"On a hill far away stood an old rugged cross, the emblem of suffering and shame...." When the rest of the family finished the verse and went on to the chorus, I stopped singing. I was listening to a larger song coming from the star-splattered heavens. With knees bent, the front of my legs caught the heat and light, casting over me a deep cool shadow as I laid face up listening to the universe drift by.

Safe, secure, and significant. I could not imagine a kid anywhere on the planet that night, anywhere among the sand dunes along the Delaware coast, who felt as safe as I. Part of it was my daddy's stories. Most of it, the hymns. When someone started singing, "I come to the garden alone while the dew is still on the roses ...," I felt as though God himself were among us, breathing a sigh with each wave, illuminating his presence with the flames.

> Do you know any of the old hymns of the faith? How about one of the newer worship songs? Find a quiet corner—by a fire, on the back patio in a lawn chair, or out on the grass under the stars—and sing to the God who loves you.

Lord, how good it is to realize that no matter what happens in my life, I am safe, eternally safe, with you.

Ryan Leads the Way

Therefore, my brothers, you whom I love and long for, my joy and crown, that is how you should stand firm in the Lord, dear friends!

— PHILIPPIANS 4:1

Ryan Mazza is a profoundly disabled man who lives in a care center. He was born with Crouzon's syndrome and has endured countless setbacks that have left him blind, mentally handicapped, paralyzed, and unable to feed himself. But he can hear. He *loves* the sound of his father's voice — especially when his dad reads to him from the Bible. In fact, his father used to work as senior American executive for the Suzuki Motor Company located near Ryan's care center. Many times the nurse would call Doug Mazza out of a meeting: "We are having trouble getting Ryan to eat his lunch. Would you please come over? He'll respond to you!" No matter if it was a top-management meeting or a marketing presentation, Doug was out the door to go help his son. To this day, Doug reflects, "No one has impacted me more for Christ than Ryan." This young man inspires not only Doug, but thousands who hear his story.

Does this make Ryan nothing more than an audiovisual aid in the hands of a utilitarian God who only uses him for inspiring others? Are Ryan's severe hardships merely "object lessons" from which we can learn? What does Ryan stand to gain? Plenty! What others gain from observing Ryan's sweet attitude gets credited to his eternal account (Galatians 6:9–10).

Almighty God notices when Ryan's life encourages others — if they profit, Ryan gains. If his dad is rewarded, Ryan reaps. Ryan's "joy and crown" are people who are blessed by his example. Think of the crowns being reserved for Ryan Mazza! By the way, his father left Suzuki years ago ... N. Douglas Mazza serves as our president at the Joni and Friends International Disability Center. And yes, Ryan keeps leading the way.

Lord Jesus, I need this perspective in my life. I pray for all the "Ryans" who are persevering through pain. Thank you for the rewards they'll receive in heaven for inspiring people like me.

ↄ

JULY 28

Praise Him with Every Part

Praise the Lord, O my soul; all my inmost being, praise his
holy name. Praise the Lord, O my soul, and forget not all
his benefits—who forgives all your sins and heals all your
diseases, who redeems your life from the pit and crowns
you with love and compassion, who satisfies your desires
with good things so that your youth is renewed like the
eagle's.

—PSALM 103:1–5

After years of quadriplegia, my bones are feeling tired. But
whenever I struggle with pain, I pray, "Bless the Lord, O my
soul, and *all* that is within me, bless his holy name." I force *all* parts of
me to bless the Lord, even my lower back when it's aching. It's one way of
making certain God receives glory during physically agonizing times.

Physical pain can cloud our convictions about God's benefits, which is
why I must continually stir my soul to remember them. God has pardoned
all my sin, rescued, restored, crowned me with his love, and healed all my
diseases. Does this mean the pain goes away? Not immediately, but I have
the sure promise that just as Jesus rose from the grave with a new body, so
I will one day rise with no more pain or heartache. For now, as Paul says in
Romans 8, we groan, waiting for the redemption God has promised.

Nevertheless, our groans can glorify God! Next time your muscles
ache, your head throbs, or your feet cramp, force these body parts
to join your soul in praising God: "Praise the Lord, O my soul;
and even my sore back blesses you. *Every* part of me blesses your
holy name!" You will be stirring your soul to recall God's benefits.
You will be offering a "sacrifice of praise" (Hebrews 13:15).

*Lord Jesus, I want to praise you in body, soul, and spirit. I bless you from that
part of me that "hurts" today. May it be a sacrifice of praise for every part of
me delights in every part of you!*

JULY 29

Escape

Our God is a God who saves; from the Sovereign Lord comes escape from death.

—PSALM 68:20

Tomorrow marks the anniversary of my diving accident. Decades have passed since that fateful day I crunched my neck, then floated helplessly paralyzed, face down in shallow water. Someone once asked, "Didn't you panic when you were in the water? You were running out of breath . . . weren't you frightened?"

Strange as it may seem, I wasn't frightened. Although I knew that in the next few seconds water would flood my lungs, a deep and powerful peace held fear at bay. Today's verse explains why. Our sovereign Lord is an "escape artist" when it comes to death. "All that pertains to deliverance from death, all that prepares for it, all that makes it easy to be borne, all that constitutes a rescue from its pains and horrors, all that follows death in a higher and more blessed world, all that makes death 'final,' and places us in a condition where death is no more to be dreaded—all this belongs to God. All this is under his control. He only can enable us to bear death; he only can conduct us from a bed of death to a world where we shall never die."[8]

As it turned out, my sister Kathy rescued me seconds before I began to drown. Psalm 18:4–6 says, "The cords of death entangled me; the torrents of destruction overwhelmed me. The cords of the grave coiled around me; the snares of death confronted me. In my distress I called to the Lord; I cried to my God for help."

Only heaven will reveal the countless times we escape death every day. Thank him for his sovereign protection over your life—whether broken necks, broken arms, or broken fingernails, God blankets you with his protection. When your time comes to leave this earth for the next, he will provide the same "escape"!

Sovereign God, thank you for keeping death at bay until it's your time to call me home. Until then, give me grace to serve you wholeheartedly.

A Long Time

Some time later, Jesus went up to Jerusalem for a feast of the Jews. Now there is in Jerusalem near the Sheep Gate a pool, which in Aramaic is called Bethesda and which is surrounded by five covered colonnades. Here a great number of disabled people used to lie—the blind, the lame, the paralyzed. One who was there had been an invalid for thirty-eight years. When Jesus saw him lying there and learned that he had been in this condition for a long time, he asked him, "Do you want to get well?"

—JOHN 5:1–6

Today marks the anniversary of the diving accident. A few years ago when I reached my thirty-eighth year of living in a wheelchair, my sister Jay called on the phone to read today's Scripture to me: "Joni, you've been paralyzed for as many years as the man by the Pool of Bethesda! Isn't that amazing?" It gave me goosebumps! Later in the day, I showed the passage to a friend. As I read John 5:1–6 aloud, I got a lump in my throat when I read the words, "When Jesus ... learned he had been in this condition *for a long time* ..." I paused while tears of amazement and wonder filled my eyes. I looked up from the Bible and said, "Thirty-eight years in this wheelchair is a long time. And it touches me that Jesus thinks thirty-eight years of paralysis *is* a long time too. He understands!"

The Lord Jesus understands the weight of every burden you quietly bear. Nothing escapes his notice, for he empathizes with our weaknesses and, in fact, understands them better than we ever will! Hebrews 4:15 assures us that "we do not have a high priest who is unable to sympathize with our weaknesses, but we have one who has been tempted in every way, just as we are—yet was without sin."

God of all comfort, keep me from complaining if my burden seems heavy. Help me to follow in your footsteps and endure every weakness without the sin of resentment or complaint.

Bold Words

Now, Lord ... enable your servants to speak your word with
great boldness.

—ACTS 4:29

*S*teve Estes was a sixteen-year-old "nobody"; a paper boy, sitting
across from me, his paralyzed neighbor who just got out of the
hospital. He had heard from kids in high school that I had big questions
about God since I had broken my neck; he came to visit and offer help. I
noticed he was *very* nervous.

Many years later Steve would tell me, "Joni, when I sat across from
you that first day, I was scared. You were out of my league. The crowd you
ran with I saw only from across the gymnasium. Plus, I had never met
another teenager in a wheelchair. I knew what the Bible said about your
questions and a dozen passages came to mind from years of church. But
sitting across from you in your wheelchair, I realized I had never test-driven
those truths on such a difficult course. Nothing worse than a D in Algebra
had ever happened to me. But I kept thinking, *If the Bible can't work in
this paralyzed girl's life—it never was for real.* So I cleared my throat and
jumped off the cliff. I remember telling you, 'God put you in that chair,
Joni. I don't know why, but if you will trust him instead of fighting him,
you'll find out why—if not in this life, then in the next. He let you break
your neck, and he has good reasons. I want to help you find out what those
reasons are!'"

It was a bold thing for Steve to say to me, but his courage peaked
my interest. From that day on, I had my nose in the Bible, searching for God's wisdom. In what ways do you lack boldness for
Christ? Ask God to give you fresh courage to share his Word with
those in need.

*You are the Word of Life, Lord Jesus. Help me to speak your words with boldness
yet kindness; courage mixed with compassion. Speak through me this day!*

෨

August

Peculiar People

> Looking for that blessed hope, and the glorious appearing
> of the great God and our Saviour Jesus Christ; who gave
> himself for us, that he might redeem us ... and purify unto
> himself a peculiar people, zealous of good works.
>
> —TITUS 2:13–14 KJV

His name is David, and he may be the best-looking seventeen-year-old I've ever seen—tall and blonde, with clear blue eyes and the biggest smile ever. Yet this is not what distinguishes him. It's the way he volunteered at not just *one* of our Joni and Friends' Family Retreats for disabled people, but two right in a row.

He had a fantastic attitude about helping Michael, a tall, muscular kid with severe cerebral palsy. Everywhere Michael went, David was hot on his heels. During Talent Night, the two of them dressed up as clowns and sang at the top of their lungs: "I'm not cool but that's okay, Jesus loves me anyway!" They were having a blast. David was simply doing what a volunteer *should* do. And doing it with zeal and passion.

Titus 2:14 describes that passion: "Jesus ... redeem[ed] us ... to purify unto himself a peculiar people, zealous of good works." Jesus did not save us to merely "do" good works, but to be *passionate* about doing them. He wants us to "have a blast" helping others.

God has saved some to open medical clinics, run shelters for homeless people, work in Africa, write books, and speak from platforms. These constitute "good works." But for most, God has saved us to wipe the nose, prepare the dinner, run an errand for a sick neighbor, clean the toilet, drive a relative to a hospital, hold the Bible for, or even play chess with, a lonely friend. Look around your church or neighborhood today—Jesus saved you to be *excited* about helping others. Just ask David.

Lord Jesus, I don't want to perform good works as a duty; I want to be eager about serving others in your name. Help me to do that today.

AUGUST 2

One of a Kind

Who is like You among the gods, O Lord? Who is like
You, majestic in holiness, awesome in praises, working
wonders?

—EXODUS 15:11 NASB

One of the definitions of *rare* might be "valuable." Like two-carat
diamonds. Or black pearls. Or a blue moon. Or Bengal tigers,
dinosaur fossils, double rainbows, snow leopards, or rain on the Sahara.
Rare speaks of that which is utterly unusual. Never to be replaced. One
of a kind.

This is good to remember when we speak of the holiness of God.
When we say he is *holy*, we mean that he is one of a kind. There is none like
him. He is in a class by himself. Our God is holy in his absolute unique-
ness. Dr. John Piper puts it this way: "Everything else besides God belongs
to a class. We are human. Rover is a dog. The oak is a tree. The earth is
a planet. The Milky Way is one of a million galaxies. Gabriel is an angel,
Satan is a demon. But only God is God." The holiness of God is synony-
mous with his infinite value. God is infinitely valuable because he is the
rarest of all beings and cannot be made, duplicated, or even imagined in
our wildest dreams. And—wonder of all wonders—he has moved heaven
and earth to find a way to pay for our sins, forgive us, redeem us, and adopt
us into his very family circle!

Many of us try to put our God in a box or convince ourselves
we've got him figured out, imagining in our arrogance that he
should see things and do things "our way." Take a moment today,
to remember that God is *infinitely beyond* our every conception of
him. Let that thought lead you into awe and worship.

*Holy, holy, holy ... I worship you, triune God. Truly there is no one like you.
And I am in awe that because of Jesus, I now have the privilege to declare your
praises along with the saints of all ages and the holy angels of heaven.*

෨

AUGUST 3

We Were Made for This

I will say to the north, "Give them up!" and to the south, "Do not hold them back." Bring my sons from afar and my daughters from the ends of the earth — everyone who is called by my name, whom I created for my glory, whom I formed and made.

— ISAIAH 43:6 – 7

*E*ver wonder exactly why God created you? Or why he placed children in *your* specific family? God couldn't have spelled it out any plainer than in Isaiah 43:6 – 7. He created you and me for one purpose: to showcase his glory, to enjoy it, display it, and demonstrate it every day to all those we encounter.

What does it mean to put his glory on display? It means highlighting his attributes and characteristics. It means making hard choices to do the right — that is, the righteous — thing. It means biting your tongue from gossiping, going out of your way for a neighbor in need, telling the truth even when it's hard, not snapping back when someone hurts you, or speaking freely and openly about your Father in heaven. In short, it's living like Jesus lived when he walked on earth.

God is invisible. In the Old Testament, whenever he wanted to display his character, his innermost being, he did so through something visible like a burning bush, a pillar of cloud or of fire, or a "theophany" (an appearance of the pre-incarnate Christ). In the New Testament, God displayed his glory through his Son, Jesus. But Jesus doesn't physically walk on earth anymore, and bushes that burn are only in prairie fires or piles of raked leaves. So how does an invisible God display his glory in this age? Through *you*. What a privilege.

Father God, what an honor I've been given! You no longer choose burning bushes through which to speak, you choose people like me. Point out ways I can showcase your character and glorious qualities to others today. In so doing, I'll be glorifying you ... I'll be living the life I was created to live.

AUGUST 4

Blessed Blows

Blows and wounds cleanse away evil, and beatings purge
the inmost being.

— PROVERBS 20:30

The first time I read this verse, I cringed. It brought up contorted images of the Spanish Inquisition and the Salem Witch Trials — or at best, stern, tight-lipped schoolmarms walking the classroom aisles with a rod in hand. Proverbs may be a book filled with wisdom and godly instruction, but this verse seemed better suited for the sixteenth century.

But my heart has warmed to Proverbs 20:30. That's because I'm writing this vignette from my bed where I have been spending long days dealing with severe back pain. The encroachment of my disability has humbled me of late: My pride has taken a severe beating as I've missed deadlines; I feel humiliated doing "business" from my bed; and I've had to bite my tongue from grumbling. God is forcing me to learn the deeper meaning of Psalm 119:67, 71, "Before I was afflicted I went astray, but now I obey your word.... It was good for me to be afflicted so that I might learn your decrees."

God may land a knockout blow to your puffed-up pride. He may wound your heart through a deep disappointment. He will go to great lengths to beat hateful habits out of your character and purge selfishness from your soul. Your ego may feel trampled. But that's not bad. I, for one, know I will come out the other end all the richer and happier for the wounding. It's what Proverbs 20:30 is all about.

Your God is not a stern, tight-lipped celestial ogre. He's not on a witch hunt. He is the kind Father who has *compassion* on his children (Psalm 103:13). He's also the wise and wonderful God described in Hebrews 12:10 who "disciplines us for our good, that we may share in his holiness." Join me today in saying, "Though he slay me, yet will I hope in him" (Job 13:15).

Lord God, remind me when I feel beaten or wounded that you are disciplining me for my good. I hope and trust in you!

It Came to Pass

But it came to pass within a while after . . .

—JUDGES 15:1 KJV

W hen I was talking with an African sister in Christ in a small Ghanaian village, I was impressed with her quiet, humble spirit. She wore brightly colored tribal clothes with a turbanlike headdress. Although I guessed she was young, her hands were weathered and lined. After she shared her testimony, I asked what her favorite Bible verse was. A knowing smile spread across her face and her eyes lit up. Without hesitation, she replied, "And it came to pass." I gave her a puzzled look. She added, "Everywhere you look in the Bible, there it is, my favorite verse." It was a familiar phrase from God's Word, but I had never heard anyone claim it as their favorite. I asked her to explain.

"Joni, it is a hard life we live in our country. The weather is harsh and our crops sometimes fail. It's at those times we don't know where the next meal is coming from. We have no money, nothing to offer our children. But we have God!" she said in a hearty voice. "And we know he will take care of us. We can look at the misery around us and know that God will see us through. Then we can smile and say, 'It came to pass.'"

"And it came to pass" reminds me of 1 Peter 5:10, "And the God of all grace, who called you to his eternal glory in Christ, after you have suffered a little while, will himself restore you." I don't face drought and failing crops, but I am in a wheelchair; it's why I appreciate the words, "After you have suffered for *a little while*." Our troubles are but momentary according to 2 Corinthians 4:17, and very soon hardships will be behind us. What hardship are you facing? Thank the Lord that you'll soon say, "It came to pass."

Lord, keep me from a complaining spirit. Give me the courage to trust you no matter what I lack in life.

ᘒ

AUGUST 6

The Dam

> But because of your stubbornness and your unrepentant heart, you are storing up wrath against yourself for the day of God's wrath, when his righteous judgment will be revealed.
>
> —ROMANS 2:5

I used to ride my horse near Liberty Dam, which held back a huge lake. Whenever I would cross the stream at its base, I'd get the jitters. *That dam is storing up a lot of water ... what if it bursts?* I thought about this when I read today's verse. It's hard to imagine God storing up holy anger against us, but it's true. Without Christ and his awesome salvation, we would be frightfully exposed on the day of God's wrath when his judgment comes against those who deny his Son. Dr. John MacArthur describes it this way: "God's wrath is a holy raging torrent and only his grace, like a dam, prevents it from spilling on us sinful human beings. The good news is that when we embrace Christ as Lord and Savior, the dam of God's righteous anger breaks upon Jesus, not us. When he bore our sins on the cross, the Lord was our substitute. Jesus Christ endured the white-hot fury that the Father had been storing up for us."

This is the love of God. Sadly, we forget this. So God may occasionally sprinkle "a little wrath" in the form of suffering. Yet even this is an expression of his goodness for it cultivates a fear of God, reminding us of his holiness, as well as what we are being saved from.

Romans 5:10 provides heartwarming encouragement: "For if, when we were God's enemies, we were reconciled to him through the death of his Son, how much more, having been reconciled, shall we be saved through his life!" Such love floods my heart with deep respect for God the Father and overwhelming gratitude for God the Son!

Lord God, I tremble to think that you've rescued me from your wrath! How I thank you for sending Jesus Christ to bear your judgment against me!

The Patience of God

He is patient with you, not wanting anyone to perish, but everyone to come to repentance. But the day of the Lord will come like a thief. The heavens will disappear with a roar; the elements will be destroyed by fire, and the earth and everything in it will be laid bare. Since everything will be destroyed in this way, what kind of people ought you to be? You ought to live holy and godly lives.... Bear in mind that our Lord's patience means salvation.

—2 PETER 3:9–11, 15

Yesterday we saw how suffering—"a little bit of wrath"—can serve as evidence of the goodness of God. When viewed from a heavenly perspective, suffering cultivates a proper fear of God in our hearts. It helps us to understand the hell from which we have been delivered. Most of all, it fills our hearts with adoration and gratitude to Jesus who bore our sins, as well as his Father's righteous anger.

Personal suffering can also remind us of God's patience and loving-kindness toward the unbelieving world. It is only by the restraining hand of God that the world has not disappeared with a fiery roar. Soon the Lord's patience will be spent. The heavens will disintegrate and the earth will be destroyed by fire—everything and *everybody* in it will be laid bare. Such a fact fills me with holy dread. So join me in reading today's verse again and let the Spirit of God ask, "Since everything will be destroyed in this way, what kind of person ought you to be?"

Do not coddle secret sin or private iniquities. Confess these things and be filled with the Spirit of God to go and say that God so loved the world that he gave his only Son so that whoever would believe on him would never perish.

I confess my sins, dear Lord. Thank you for your patience toward me and toward the people of this world. Energize me to share your good news with them!

☙

August 8

He Leadeth Me

Lead me, O Lord, in your righteousness because of my enemies—make straight your way before me.

—Psalm 5:8

Please, Daddy, I don't need the lead line! I can steer Thunder by myself!" My father refused to listen to his five-year-old daughter on top of her sixteen-hands-high horse, even if it was an old gray mare. And so Daddy would snap the lead line on Thunder's bit. Down the trail we ambled, my father ahead on his horse and me tethered to him by a long leather strap. I fumed and folded my arms as Thunder clip-clopped along. One day Daddy gave in and unclipped the lead line. I could now kick and steer to my heart's content. I was grown up. Ready for adventure. That is, until we reached a swift running river. When we got to the middle, Thunder put her head down to drink. "Daddy, help!" I screamed. My father came cantering toward me in a spray of water and grabbed Thunder's reins just before she wandered into the deep part.

I was greatly relieved when he reached into his saddle bag and snapped a lead line on Thunder's bit. I was back to being tethered, but it was okay. I was safe. Daddy was in front of me and we were bound together. Many years later, I sometimes wish I were still on that lead line. Then again, I am. Faith is the invisible connection between me and my heavenly Father: "Faith is being ... certain of what we do not see" (Hebrews 11:1). Take advice from the little kid on the big horse: stay tethered to our Father. *Nothing* can snatch you out of his hand (John 10:28).

> Lord, I would clasp Thy hand in mine, nor ever murmur nor repine,
> Content, whatever lot I see, since 'tis Thine hand that leadeth me!
> He leadeth me, He leadeth me, by His own hand He leadeth me:
> His faithful foll'wer I would be, for by His hand He leadeth me.

Lead me, Lord, in your paths of righteousness. Thank you for never letting go of me!

ᏇᎳ

August 9

Let the Truth Be Told

> Truth is nowhere to be found, and whoever shuns evil becomes a prey. The Lord looked and was displeased that there was no justice. He saw that there was no one, he was appalled that there was no one to intervene.
>
> —Isaiah 59:15–16

*T*was at a loss for words when a young disabled girl in Bangalore, India, told me, "My aunt said I would have to go through eight reincarnations before I could become a whole person." A doctor from New Dehli said, "Most people do not consider autistic children to be human." On that same trip while I was in Africa, I met mothers who were beaten because they gave birth to a child who was blind or disabled. A man told me his cerebral-palsied sister was left out in the jungle for the animals to take. "My parents thought it would appease the animist spirits," he said. In southeast Asia I met people who thought disabilities were "curses from the shamans in the village." My heart broke when several disabled women told me they were "easy targets for abuse."

Isaiah lamented, "Truth is nowhere to be found.... There was no one to intervene." This is the commission God has given us. Jesus is "the way, the truth and the life" (John 14:6). When we follow his way and carry the truth into the dark corners of the world, we bring light, hope, and deliverance. Jesus tells the truth about everything from the atonement to autism, from the resurrection to rickets, from sanctification to spina bifida.

The overwhelming needs of people in less-developed nations can either make you shake your head and walk away or fill your heart with Christ's compassion. Support the work of your church's missionaries who labor among the world's neediest. Ask God to raise up those who will intervene and bring justice, mercy, and the hope of Christ's love.

Empower and resource your missionaries around the world, dear Lord. For the sake of truth, mercy, and justice. For the sake of the world's neediest.

AUGUST 10

Not in Vain

Though the fig tree does not bud and there are no grapes on the vines, though the olive crop fails and the fields produce no food, though there are no sheep in the pen and no cattle in the stalls, yet I will rejoice in the Lord, I will be joyful in God my Savior.

—HABAKKUK 3:17–18

Joan Liggins married John without a hint of love in her heart. She was pregnant and assumed it was the right thing to do. After she delivered her child, frustrations mounted. Joan found release at work hanging out with a male coworker from another department. Occasional work lunches led to a secret rendezvous in a hotel. She was back to her old ways. "I want a divorce," she told John, and her husband yielded.

Joan hit rock bottom in 1968. When her cousin invited her to church, she decided to go. Sitting on the red-cushioned pew, she opened her heart to Jesus. Under the conviction of the Holy Spirit, she knew what she must do. Joan must remarry her ex-husband, a man she did not love. *And I must marry John because of my love for God.* That was forty years ago. Forty long years of praying for the salvation of her husband whom she now loves very much. All of us pray alongside Joan who has now worked for Joni and Friends almost twenty years. Her prayers remind me of the following poem by Amy Carmichael:

> *Not in vain, the tedious toil, on an unresponsive soil,*
> *Travail, tears in secret shed, over hopes that lay as dead.*
> *All in vain, thy faint heart cries. Not in vain, thy Lord replies:*
> *Nothing is to good to be; then believe, believe to see.*[3]

Do not give up on praying for your loved ones ... no prayer is ever offered in vain!

Lord Jesus, I lift up before you today _____ who does not know you as personal Savior and Lord. Rescue this dear one out of the kingdom of darkness. Give this person a spirit of repentance and a home in heaven.

❧

God's Spy Within

The goal of this command is love, which comes from a pure heart and a good conscience and a sincere faith. Some have wandered away from these and turned to meaningless talk.

—1 TIMOTHY 1:5–6

The apostle Paul took his clear conscience seriously. He would not allow his conscience to criticize or reprimand him, censure or blame him. Paul purposed to live "rightly" so that his conscience would not scold him. Oh, that we would take *our* conscience that seriously.

The Puritans did the same thing as Paul. They sat "close to self-scrutiny," as they called it. It meant "communing with your conscience" every day, examining your actions and attitudes. The Puritans called the conscience "God's spy within our bosoms" or "God's deputy and vice-regent within us." They believed that the conscience was like a mirror, catching the light of God's Word and reflecting its concentrated focus on one's deeds, desires, goals, and choices.

Our conscience speaks independently of our will. And when it speaks, it is in a strange way distinct from us—it stands over us, addressing us with an authority that we did not give it. We can suppress or stifle the conscience, but its voice will continue to speak to us if its volume has been turned up through daily times in God's Word.

When was the last time you listened—and responded—to your conscience? Try the Puritan habit. When you read God's Word today, ask the Lord to make your conscience tender toward anything evil or unlovely in your life. If it whispers, "Turn off the TV and spend some time with Jesus," be sure to not only listen, but act. It's one way to make sure your conscience will continue to speak ... and speak in clear and convicting tones!

Spirit of the Living God, please continue to inform my conscience—I want your "vice regent" within my heart to keep me on the right track. And when my conscience convicts me today, help me to respond and obey your Word.

৹৶

Majoring in the Minors

Well done, my good and faithful servant! Because you have
been trustworthy in a very small matter, take charge of ten
cities.

—LUKE 19:17

*I*t's midseason for professional baseball, and it's always interesting
to watch which pitchers the major league teams will call up from
the minor leagues. It's great that these hardworking young rookies finally
get a chance to pitch in the majors!

Have you ever thought of life on this earth as the "minor leagues"—with
Christians working hard to gain a berth high up in the major leagues of
heaven? I'm *not* talking about earning salvation. That's already been paid
for with the blood of our Savior, and we can add nothing to it. But we *do*
have the opportunity to earn eternal rewards in this life. Scripture tells us
that "we must all appear before the judgment seat of Christ, that each one
may receive what is due him for things done while in the body" (2 Corinthians 5:10). The way I live life on earth *will* affect my responsibilities,
opportunities, and even my joy—in ways beyond my ability to imagine.

This is what makes our present life so exciting. It's a training gymnasium! Your nine-to-five job isn't merely an occupation, it's a proving
ground for your faith. Every earthly problem, affliction, task, household
chore—and all the relationships that go with them—*everything* is a minor
league exercise to prepare you for the major leagues. My longing for heaven
is not a pie-in-the-sky desire to leave this tiresome old wheelchair behind.
No, I see my earthly afflictions as opportunities to demonstrate my faithfulness.

Stand firm, my friend. The dawn is coming. Life everlasting.
Oceans of light. Joy unspeakable. Be trustworthy and remain
faithful. Because there will be no sweeter music in time or eternity than the words "Well done" from the smiling face of our
Savior and King.

*Remind me, Lord, how quickly my life passes. Help me to see the events of my
day—even the disappointments—as the very things that will make heaven all
the sweeter as I trust in you.*

August 13

Forgiving God?

> While he was still speaking, yet another messenger came and said, "Your sons and daughters were feasting and drinking wine at the oldest brother's house, when suddenly a mighty wind swept in from the desert and struck the four corners of the house. It collapsed on them and they are dead, and I am the only one who has escaped to tell you!" At this, Job got up and tore his robe and shaved his head. Then he fell to the ground in worship.... In all this, Job did not sin by charging God with wrongdoing.
>
> —Job 1:18–20, 22

My elderly friend Roy is struggling against the last stages of macular degeneration. That's not all. The city of Toronto is buying up the property his house is built on; he may lose his home. He's also losing his son-in-law to cancer. Although a Christian, Roy is confused. Some people have counseled him, "You need to forgive God for all this!"

Forgive God? Don't those counselors have it backward?! The Bible never directs us to do such a thing. To "forgive" God implies that he has done something wrong. But has he? The Bible says that nothing—not cancer, blindness, or eviction from our homes—can separate us from the *love* of God. So are we to forgive him for loving us too hard? Our darkest emotions may want to charge God with wrongdoing, but God's dealings with us are always motivated by love and concern for our souls.

Hebrews 12:3 provides correct counsel: "Consider him who endured such opposition from sinful men, so that you will not grow weary and lose heart." Amy Carmichael once said, "If I forget that the way of the Cross leads to the Cross and not to a bank of flowers; if I regulate my life on these lines ... so that I am surprised when the way is rough and think it strange, 'Think it not strange, Count it all joy,' then I know nothing of Calvary love."

Forgive me, God, if ever my emotions deceive me into charging you with wrongdoing. May it never be!

The Question of Good

All of us have become like one who is unclean, and all our
righteous acts are like filthy rags; we all shrivel up like a leaf,
and like the wind our sins sweep us away.

—ISAIAH 64:6

This world is full of pain. People look at the anguish of those
who hurt and insist, "Good people deserve better." But do we?
It's a tough question, and the Bible has a hard answer. It paints a sobering picture: people are *not* innately good. It also says that people—all of
us—cannot begin to comprehend how our sin has offended God. In fact,
the Bible states that God is just to send rebellious creatures to hell. Thus, as
incomprehensible as it may sound, he is fair to start that hell in this life.

But wait; there is a hidden mercy here! By tasting suffering in this
life—hell's splash over—people are driven to ponder what may face them
in the next life. In this way, suffering may be our greatest mercy; for many,
suffering becomes God's roadblock on their headlong rush to hell. If we
experienced nothing but ease and comfort, we would soon forget that
we are eternal creatures—but suffering won't allow that. It persistently
reminds us that something immense and cosmic is at stake—a heaven to
be reached for Christ's sake, and a hell to be avoided.

Every day of our short life has eternal consequences for good or
ill. Thus, it is only fitting that a merciful and wise God should
give us some sense of the stakes involved, some sense of the magnitude of the spiritual battle. He does this by giving us foretastes
of heaven in the joys we experience, and foretastes of hell in our
suffering.

*Open my eyes, Father, so that I might grasp how holy you are. Help me to see
how cosmic and grand the eternal stakes really are in this life. And then, help
me to live circumspectly and wisely!*

ॐ

Ripe for Glory

You [God] have set mankind so brief a span of life—months
is all you give him! Not one bit longer may he live.

—JOB 14:5 TLB

I am a banana expert. I know exactly when a banana is too green,
and I also know "just the right time" when it's ready to be peeled.
Who can tolerate a banana that's gone mushy, covered with brown spots?
When I go to the market, I normally buy my bananas hard and green.
Then I place the fruit on the kitchen counter and wait for that just-right
time when the color turns a yellow-green. It's a signal! It's a sign! And I'm
ready to eat the whole bunch.

When the Puritan pastor Richard Cameron was ill and in bed, it was
said that he was "ripe for glory." Reading that statement made me pause
and consider. I often say, "Boy, I wish the Lord Jesus would come back
soon—I'm ready to leave this wheelchair behind and dance on those
streets of gold!" But I'm *not* in heaven yet, I'm still here on earth. Doesn't
that prove I'm still a green banana, not yet ripe for glory?

And if you are moving and breathing, you're not ripe, either. You've
got a ways to go. God has determined the exact number of our days on
earth. That means all our days and hours—and even our moments—have
meaning and purpose. God has a design, a plan. He waters us with his
Word, tills the soil of our heart through trials, sweetens our disposition
over time, and ripens our faith. He knows the exact moment when we are
no longer green, but ready!

God has something to finish in you, and until he does, every
day is packed with purpose. Ask the Lord to reveal his desire and
intentions for the way you live your life over the next twenty-four
hours. It's your chance to ripen.

*Fill me, Lord Jesus, with your Holy Spirit, that I might make the choices that
please you this day and seize every opportunity you lay at my feet.*

August 16

The Good Answer

For God so loved the world that he gave his one and only Son, that whoever believes in him shall not perish but have eternal life. For God did not send his Son into the world to condemn the world, but to save the world through him. Whoever believes in him is not condemned, but whoever does not believe stands condemned already because he has not believed in the name of God's one and only Son.

—John 3:16–18

*I*f God is so good, why doesn't he get rid of the awful suffering in the world?!* If God were to get rid of suffering, he would get rid of sinners—suffering is one of the consequences of our rebellion against God back in the garden. God does not want to obliterate sinners; he wants to save them (2 Peter 3:9).

The kingdom of heaven came to earth with the arrival of King Jesus. When Christ died, God opened the way for sinners to be rescued. God was wise, however, in not finishing the kingdom when Christ was on earth. If he had closed the curtain on suffering, doing away with all pain and heartache, what would have become of us? God is rich in mercy toward us! He is delaying closing the curtain on sin and suffering so that more people—millions more over the last two thousand years—might come to know Christ.

And I promise you—the Bible promises you—five minutes of heaven will be worth the pain. Until then, our sufferings drive us to reach out toward unbelieving friends and neighbors with the good news that God so loved the world, that he gave his only begotten Son that whoever should believe on him should not perish, but have eternal life. The cost of suffering may be great, but people's souls are worth it.

Lord, I believe the eternal state of my neighbors and coworkers is worth the suffering I face in this world. Give boldness as I share John 3:16 today.

AUGUST 17

Rescue the Perishing

Be merciful to those who doubt; snatch others from the fire and save them; to others show mercy, mixed with fear — hating even the clothing stained by corrupted flesh.

— JUDE vv. 22–23

The movie *Titanic* launched me into one of the liveliest — and longest — prayer times I've ever had. With images of that great sinking ship in my mind ... and the frantic families trapped by locked hatches down in second class ... and men resigned to the inevitable, drinking brandy and toasting their fate ... I left the movie crying to God to show mercy to those who didn't know him. "Oh Lord," I prayed, "rescue the perishing! Please remember my neighbor, the lady at the salad counter in Gelson's, the checkout guys at the drugstore, and ..." On and on I went, listing men, women, and children, some who I knew by name, but most, only by face.

The movie was a powerful metaphor of a frightening reality. This tiny planet has absorbed a mortal blow, a gash in its side. Rebellion against God has set it on a crash course with hell, and whether we like it or not, it's going down — dragging a vast multitude of people with it. Stop and listen. Do you feel the tremor? The down-deep rumbling of something gone terribly wrong?

God didn't make hell for people. Jesus said it was "prepared for the devil and his angels" (Matthew 25:41). It's unnatural for humans to be there — as unnatural as our turning our backs on a Creator who loves us. God takes no joy in anyone heading for eternal misery. His Son, Jesus, is the lifeboat, the ark, big enough and wide enough to rescue the perishing.

If you had the opportunity to warn people who were about to board the *Titanic* in England, what would you do? Shrug your shoulders and go back to your novel? Ask the Lord to open your eyes to the urgency of telling men, women, and children about the Lifeboat that will bear them safely into eternity.

Lord, forgive me for my nonchalant attitude toward the eternal destiny of my friends, neighbors, coworkers, and family.

☙

The Thief

Serve wholeheartedly, as if you were serving the Lord not men, because you know that the Lord will reward everyone for whatever good he does, whether he is slave or free.

—EPHESIANS 6:7–8

The iron gate clanged behind me. A flood of prison memories washed over me in my wheelchair. I smiled weakly at the guard who looked a little like the uniformed guard at my old state institution where I lived for two years. No, it wasn't a prison. It was a rehab center. Oh, the irony. Here I was confined by my own set of bars, yet freewheeling. And these men were free to walk, yet confined behind bars.

I had come to cut the ribbon at our Wheels for the World restoration center, where prisoners were refurbishing wheelchairs for our teams to deliver overseas to disabled children and adults. The inmates had seen the videos of children shut away in dark huts. Each child was given a new wheelchair worked on by these prisoners. I entered the restoration area and gasped. Everything was immaculate and organized. I flashed a smile at four inmates who stood proudly by their workbenches. "Why are you doing this?" I asked Jose. He fiddled with his wrench. "Because somebody needs help," he replied, as if the answer were obvious. "It's good to do something that will help somebody. Like those kids in that video." It was Ephesians 4:28 in action: "He who has been stealing must steal no longer, but must work, doing something useful with his own hands, that he may have something to share with those in need."

Perhaps you need fresh resolve to "do something that will help somebody." In a lonely prison, there are inmates who turn down minimum wage jobs in the prison's work program to restore wheelchairs for disabled children. They are finding new meaning to their lives, "doing something useful" so that they "have something to share with those in need." What do you have to share?

Lord, you have placed your tools in my hands. I want to do something useful ... to share with someone in need today.

☙

Friendship Has a Purpose

And let us consider how we may spur one another on toward love and good deeds.

—HEBREWS 10:24

oday's verse underscores why there's such a thing as friendship. It's what we do in the body of Christ. We are to consider—think creatively about—spurring one another on in our Christian walk. Christian friendships are never idle. Our relationships with our brothers and sisters in the Lord are either moving onward and upward, or we are diminishing each other.

We are to see our friends in the light of what God intends for them to become. We must not become complacent or disillusioned when friends disappoint us—like anyone, our friends are fallen image-bearers, marred and defaced by the world, the flesh, and the devil. But God is in the business of re-creating them. His goal is to restore his image—the image of Christ—in our loved ones. It is our role to join with God in his glorious work to redeem the people we love, as we encourage them with vision for their growth in Christ (Ephesians 4:15). We can help enhance the "new creation" in them (2 Corinthians 5:17). We can push and prod our friends through our prayers (James 5:16). We must never let our passion for our friendships wane because we lose this marvelous sense of purpose. We must constantly consider ways we can spur one another on.

Who are your best friends and how have you been able to spur them on lately in their walk with Christ? Do not lose your sense of calling when it comes to those you love and spend time with. God has designed all friendships to have a magnificent purpose. Think of a way you can "grow God's glory" in the lives of your friends today.

Lord Jesus, help me not to become complacent or lazy about my friendships. Show me fresh new ways I can spur my friends on in their growth in you. What a joy it is to partner with you in your redemptive work.

AUGUST 20

Jars and Boxes

But we have this treasure in jars of clay to show that this
all-surpassing power is from God and not from us.

— 2 CORINTHIANS 4:7

uthor Robert Jewitt imagines a dialogue between the apostle
Paul and our popular culture. He talks about 2 Corinthians
4, where Paul compares our earthly bodies to common earthenware jars.
Back in the first century, these pots were just ordinary containers. Nothing
special, nothing spectacular. After all, you had to carry your belongings in
something, and back then, it was a clay pot.

What is it in our culture, the author asks, that would carry the same
common insignificance? How about a cardboard box? Our bodies, to paraphrase 2 Corinthians, are like the box your new shoes came in. Like the
box they use at the department store to wrap your new sweater. But *within*
that box, as with Paul's jars of clay, we hold a priceless treasure.

Several years ago, my own dear mother, Lindy Eareckson, left this
earth for heaven. In that moment, she had no more need of the box that
had wrapped her life for eighty-seven years. It was empty, with worn-out
corners, bends, and wrinkles. And yet ... it had been the vessel in which
the treasure of the Spirit of Christ had dwelt. And he had shone all the
more brightly through the edges and thin places of that box as it began to
collapse with age. He was radiant in her, shining mightily, as she served our
family, as she stuck by my side all the years I was in the hospital, and as she
gave, gave, and gave. But now, praise God, the treasure is safely home.

Just think, the circumstances that crush you, wear you down,
or stretch you at the seams are the very forces that release God's
beautiful light, pouring out from within you.

*Who would place treasure in a cardboard box? How amazing, Lord, to think
that you would entrust the very wealth of heaven into a common container like
me. Shine brightly, I pray, through every gap, joint, seam, and crevice!*

☙

AUGUST 21

Familiarity

Love the Lord your God with all your heart and with all
your soul and with all your strength.

—DEUTERONOMY 6:5

When Tim, an elder at our church, moved into his home in the
Santa Monica Mountains five years ago, he was awestruck by an
enormous rock formation that was set back from the main highway. The
rock citadel towered majestically over the waters of a sparkling lake. "That
first year I nearly ran myself off the road and into that lake half a dozen
times, rubbernecking to get every view possible of its grandeur, at every
time of day, in every different kind of light," Tim said. "The sun illumi-
nated its dramatic cracks and crevices in so many diverse and magnificent
ways. If that rock were in the middle of Kansas, it would draw a million
visitors every year!" A few months ago he was driving a visitor from the
airport to his home. They came around a corner and his guest exclaimed,
"Look at that rock!" to which Tim replied "What rock? Oh, *that* rock!"

The next week in church, Tim blushed as he told us about the inci-
dent. "It reminded me of the 'sin of familiarity'—a sin that only those who
have seen and loved the grandeur of *our* Rock of Salvation, Jesus Christ,
can commit."

> My elder-friend went on to say that familiarity with Christ keeps
> us from enjoying true intimacy with the Lord. We listen to Chris-
> tian talk radio, thinking it suffices for our daily devotions. Or we
> reach for an article on the latest theological controversy and fail
> to reach for the Word of God itself. Ask the Lord to give you a
> new sense of his presence and a fresh touch of his Spirit. Renew
> your commitment to love him with your whole heart, soul, and
> strength.

Lord Jesus, you are my Rock and Fortress. You tower over everything in my life.
Forgive me when I take for granted your grace and strength in my life, and may
I never, ever allow your death and resurrection to become "familiar."

Reasons!

> In this you greatly rejoice, though now for a little while you may have had to suffer grief in all kinds of trials. These have come so that your faith—of greater worth than gold, which perishes even though refined by fire—may be proved genuine and may result in praise, glory and honor when Jesus Christ is revealed.
>
> —1 Peter 1:6–7

*S*omewhere after my first decade in my wheelchair, I was gratified by the changes in my life. All things were working together for my good and God's glory—it didn't mean being an author or speaker; it meant being like Christ. Hardships were forcing me to make decisions about God—my faith was becoming more muscular. Suffering was doing a job on my character—I was able to stick to promises, not be sloppy in relationships, quit whining, and be more patient. My thoughts were being jerked right side up—I couldn't reach for the common temptations like before (having no hands helped with that). Also . . .

Suffering was making me more sensitive to others. I couldn't have cared less about people like me before my accident, but now it was a different story. Being paralyzed was making heaven come alive—not in a cop-out way, but in a way that made me want to live better here on earth because greater things were coming in the next life.

A checklist like this sounds dry and technical, but years ago it helped answer—at least in part—that sticky question, "Why does God pile on hardships so high?" Well—hey!—God is more concerned with conforming us to the likeness of his Son than leaving us in our comfort zones. God is more interested in inward qualities than outward circumstances. Today, look for the "reasons" God has for *your* hardship. When you find them, you will "leave the elementary teachings about Christ and go on to maturity" (Hebrews 6:1).

Lord, you are the One who holds all the reasons in your hands. I can trust you with every reason!

AUGUST 23

And Reasons Lead to . . .

Yet for us there is but one God, the Father, from whom
all things came and for whom we live; and there is but
one Lord, Jesus Christ, through whom all things came and
through whom we live.

— 1 CORINTHIANS 8:6

Yesterday we saw how appreciating God's reasons behind suffering can lead to Christian maturity. God uses hardships to
improve our character, remove sinful habits, make us heaven-hearted, and
instill compassion toward others, to name a few.

But answers and reasons, no matter how good and true they are, cannot be the coup de grace. Purified faith should never be an end in itself—it
should culminate in God. Stronger character is made muscular not for its
own sake, but God's. A livelier hope is more spirited because its focus is
not on "things getting better," but on God. To forget this is to tarnish faith,
weaken character, and deflate hope. As the Phillips' paraphrase puts 2 Peter
1:8, "If you have these qualities existing and growing in you then it means
that *knowing our Lord Jesus Christ* has not made your lives either complacent or unproductive." It really is all about Jesus. Simply Jesus. As today's
verse says, "There is but one Lord, Jesus Christ, through whom we live."

We must never distance the Bible's reasons from God. The problem of suffering is not about some *thing,* but *Someone.* It follows that the answers and reasons must not be some thing, but
Someone. The Bible never bids us to keep our eyes on suffering,
or even suffering's benefits. Only on God, the One who wrote
the book on suffering. Consider the good and valued benefits for
the hardship in your life. Can you say with the apostle Paul, "I
consider them rubbish, that I may gain Christ and be found in
him" (Philippians 3:8–9)?

*Lord Jesus, keep my focus off not only my hardships, but even whatever ben-
efits might come of those hardships. May my focus always and only be on you.
Especially today.*

AUGUST 24

Closer to the Other Side

> I press on to take hold of that for which Christ Jesus has
> taken hold of me.
>
> —PHILIPPIANS 3:12

For me in this wheelchair, shampooing my hair requires parking in front of my bathroom sink, leaning forward, and letting my friend Dana "go at it" as she stands to one side and lathers my hair.

"Joni, would you like me to wash your face while you're under the faucet?" she asked. "Sure," I gurgled. She took her soapy hands and began lathering my cheeks, using the flat of her fingers to gently wash around my eyes. I gasped. "Am I hurting you?" Dana asked. "Oh, no, not at all!" I said. "Please ... please keep going!" How could I explain? For that brief moment, it felt as though her hands were *mine*! She was rubbing my face exactly the way I used to do with my own hands, decades ago. Those few brief moments were about as close as I've ever felt to being healed! When we finished, Dana patted my face and hair dry with a towel. She also had to wipe away my tears. But they weren't tears of sadness or regret. They were tears of joy about the future. I told her, "This was a reminder that soon I will be able to wash my own face with new, glorified hands!"

There is less distance between me and the future than me and the past, before I was injured. I have come to the place where a memory can push me joyfully into the future rather than pull me somberly back into a sad past.

Because we are believers, the future has a happy, magnetic pull on our hearts. Take just a few minutes today (maybe while you're on a walk in the sunlight) to think about the new, marvelous, perfect, immortal body that awaits you—really, just a few years away on the Other Side.

Lord how good you are! The promises you have given us for that radiant tomorrow help us walk through the darkest of days on this side of heaven.

❧

A Lesson from Atlas

God made him who had no sin to be sin for us, so that in
him we might become the righteousness of God.

—2 CORINTHIANS 5:21

In New York City, in front of Rockefeller Plaza, there's a famous statue depicting a Greek god named Atlas, bearing the earth and the heavens on his shoulders. The huge globe Atlas carries looks terribly heavy, and his knees buckle under the weight. Atlas was condemned to carry the awful burden as a punishment from Zeus, the head honcho in Greek mythology.

That mythological depiction reminds me of something real and important. Peter says of the Lord Jesus, "He himself bore our sins in his body on the tree, so that we might die to sins and live for righteousness" (1 Peter 2:24). Sometimes when we hear people talk about Jesus bearing the sins of the world, we imagine him carrying those sins like Atlas bearing the weight of the world on his shoulders. But is that a true picture of what Jesus was doing?

Actually, that passage explains that Jesus carried our sins "in his own body" on the tree. It was something that happened to him on the inside. He *became* sin. Soaked through and through with our transgressions, he had to endure the righteous and unrestrained wrath of his Father against sin. No wonder Jesus was heartbroken when he went to the cross. The awful load he bore wasn't something he could shrug off his shoulders. Jesus knew our sin would affect him personally—that when his Father would look upon him on the cross, God would see every one of our awful sins. How unbearable that must have been.

But what an astonishing gift, as well! Jesus takes *our* sin, and we receive *his* righteousness. He takes on the debt we could never pay, and credits our account beyond what we could ever earn. Today ask God to change you on the *inside*!

Lord, when I ponder a gift of this magnitude, it stirs my desire to live in a way that pleases and honors you.

ॐ

Behind the Scenes Miracles

Because you have seen me, you have believed; blessed are
those who have not seen and yet have believed.

—John 20:29

Many Christians don't see God in their trials. If no miracles are happening—if the floods aren't receding or the cancer is not in remission—God must not be at work. We think of miracles as the kind we witnessed in the movie *The Ten Commandments*. "Those ten plagues on Egypt, now *that* was God up to something." Agreed, frogs and lice in Pharaoh's bed made for a great film years ago. Ah, but if we could only watch the real movie of how God runs the world from behind the scenes ...

Oh, the infinite complexity of it all! The wrenching of good out of evil like blood from a turnip; the clandestine exploiting of Satan's worst escapades; the balancing act of weather systems across the globe that assure the arrival of summer; the infiltration of grace and salvation behind even the barbwire of Russian death camps; the exact number of white blood cells called into action to defeat your illness—*that* will win an Oscar. The delicately balanced, invisible workings of our great God—*this* is real drama. Meanwhile, he wants us to trust him. As Jesus told skeptical Thomas after the resurrection, "Blessed are those who have not seen and yet have believed."

So why do we still doubt? Perhaps we cannot find wrapping paper wide enough to package these truths neatly. No one can grasp the Almighty and his miracles. "Even angels long to look into these things" (1 Peter 1:12). However, our inability to comprehend something doesn't make it untrue or any less miraculous. As Paul put it, "How unsearchable his judgments, and his paths beyond tracing out!" (Romans 11:33). Count his miracles today ... and thank him.

Lord, thank you for every miracle today, whether it is to heal or spread encouragement, or to defeat the works of darkness. I believe!

෨

A Gift for a Gypsy Girl

He was despised and forsaken of men, a man of sorrows
and acquainted with grief.

—ISAIAH 53:3 NASB

Our Wheels for the World team was in Romania recently. As we
were setting up our distribution site, disabled people and their
families were already streaming in from near and far, hoping to receive a
new wheelchair. One was a Gypsy father and his disabled daughter, slowly
making their way up the street.

Their pace was hampered by the dilapidated old wheelchair with flat
tires and bent spokes. Before they reached the doors, however, a government official turned them away. Gypsies are social outcasts and considered
a blight on society in some parts of Romania. A few minutes later, however,
two of our team members ran down the street after the Gypsies, pushing
a nice, brand-new wheelchair. Minutes later, they lifted the paralyzed girl
out of her tattered chair and placed her in the new one. It fit perfectly!
Then, as the father shook his head, amazed, they presented the girl with a
brand-new Romanian-language Bible.

The gospel is meant for the hopeless and helpless. Time and again
God brings stories such as this one to light so that we might be convinced
of his compassion and tender mercy.

Perhaps the Lord would like to stretch you out of your comfort
zone today. Maybe there is a social outcast in your town—someone you know who has been shunned. Remember the paralyzed
Gypsy girl from the mountains of Romania. Remember her
wheeling down the street in a new wheelchair, pressing a blue
leather Bible to her chest. Remember how God loves to reach
beyond every human barrier to love and deliver people. And then,
take a deep breath and offer to help that scorned, rejected person.
As you do, the life you change may be your own.

Dear Lord, you also were scorned and rejected. No wonder your heart is moved
by those who are outcast and shunned! Help me to touch the lives of such as
these, and do it as unto you.

❧

AUGUST 28

Living under the Curse

> But he was pierced for our transgressions, he was crushed
> for our iniquities; the punishment that brought us peace
> was upon him, and by his wounds we are healed.
>
> —ISAIAH 53:5

*I*t is true that disease flows from the curse God pronounced on us after Adam's rebellion. It is also true that Jesus came to reverse this curse. But does this mean Christians shouldn't have to put up with cancer, Down syndrome, Lyme disease, or Alzheimer's? We'd like to think that since Jesus came to take up our diseases, there should be healing for everything from migraines to menopausal sweats. But that's akin to saying, "There's an oak in every acorn—so take this acorn and start sawing planks for picnic tables." Or it's like saying, "Congress just passed a Clean Water Act, so tomorrow morning Manhattan residents can start drinking from the East River." Forty years will pass before that oak is ready for lumbering. Purging industrial ooze out of a river will take decades.

And so it is with Jesus' reversal of sin's curse (and the suffering that goes with it). What Jesus began doing to sin and its results won't be complete until the second coming. The purchase of salvation was complete, and the outcome was settled with certainty. But the application of salvation to God's people was anything but finished. God "*has* saved" us, yet we are still "being saved" (1 Corinthians 1:18). We are still on earth; this means we're still going to feel the influence of that old curse. At least until heaven!

First Corinthians 15:45 calls Jesus "the last Adam" who came to undo the curse triggered in the garden of Eden—but this summer you'll still be wrestling with weeds in your backyard, as well as a backache from all that hoeing. Only in paradise will it be said, "No longer will there be any curse" (Revelation 22:3).

Jesus, thank you that you saved me ... and that I am still being saved. I look to that day in heaven when there will be no more sorrow, sickness, disease, or death!

ᘕ

He Carried Our Sorrows

Surely he took up our infirmities and carried our sorrows ...

—ISAIAH 53:4

Nobody likes to be sad. No Christian welcomes grief. So aren't you glad that Jesus carried our sorrows when he went to the cross?! But sorrow did not cease with the death and resurrection of Christ. Think of the apostle Paul who confessed to "great sorrow and unceasing anguish in my heart" over the spiritual lostness of his race. He also described Christ's apostles as "*sorrowful,* yet always rejoicing." Jesus' death did not hinder him from saying, "Blessed are you who weep now." It did not hinder James from advising us to "grieve, mourn and wail" when we sin. Sorrow and tears, disappointment and grief are written into God's plan for you and me. To be sure, he lightens and brightens our days with glimpses of paradise; he ladles out foretastes of bliss through a thousand blessings large and small. But they are all just that—glimpses and foretastes. We are not in heaven yet. We are destined to experience earth's sorrow.

But when tears and sorrow come, we look to Jesus—he bore to the cross the very tears you cry. He blamed no one when he felt the weight of grief and disappointment. He did not shrink from sorrow, nor sink under the burden of sadness. The load was heavy and the way was long, but he persevered. *And he gives you power to do the same.*

When we grieve and feel deep sorrow, we must look to Jesus who endured a greater grief and sorrow. There's a reason Jesus says "Blessed are those who mourn": sorrow forces you and me to identify more deeply with the Savior when he carried his cross. If you are experiencing sorrow, if your tears seem to flow endlessly over a deep disappointment, remember the Savior. He persevered. That means you can too.

When I grieve, thank you, Lord God, for supporting me with your presence and consolation. My tears help me to know you better. They drive me into your comforting arms. Thank you for that.

Out-of-the-Box Thinking

> Yes, I try to find common ground with everyone so that I
> might bring them to Christ.
>
> — 1 CORINTHIANS 9:22 NLT

When Ken and I landed in Havana on one of our Wheels for the World trips, officials escorted me to an airport doctor's office. They thought I was "sick" and needed supervision before boarding our connecting flight to Santiago de Cuba. After I met two female doctors and a disabled woman who was also waiting (no one spoke English), I realized, *This is a unique opportunity, Lord . . . a chance to think outside the box. I have a feeling you want me to do an "outreach" right here in this office.*

I began to sing out loud—the only Christian song I knew in Spanish. *That* got people's attention. I then asked in halting Spanish, "Do you know songs about Christ?" The two doctors stared at one another. One asked in Spanish, "We see you are an American. Why are you in our country?" I explained in my high school Spanish that we were bringing wheelchairs and Bibles as gifts to the disabled people of Cuba. I went on to describe the mandate of our Savior to go into all the world and share the good news. "What is this good news?" she asked in a softer voice.

At that, her fellow doctor brightened, ran back to her cubicle, and returned holding a battered, bent-paged Bible. Before I knew it, this doctor began explaining the gospel in sixty-mile-an-hour Spanish to her coworker. It was clear the Christian doctor had suddenly found the courage to share her faith!

Who knows what you might get started once you take that first step of faith and share a word about your Savior! The challenge is to think outside the box, go beyond the program, and reach the people God places in your path each day.

Lord, it's that first step that's so hard for me sometimes. Give me the strength and the boldness to break the inertia to at least begin the conversations, and then look for an opening to speak about my faith in you.

August 31

Wake Up!

> He who gathers crops in summer is a wise son, but he who
> sleeps during harvest is a disgraceful son.
>
> —Proverbs 10:5

*S*ome years ago I was in Australia serving as a chaplain to the disabled athletes in the 2000 Paralympic Games in Sydney. Fred, our host, was in charge of organizing our schedule. For two weeks, we were going nonstop! From morning to night, we visited hospitals and churches. I was speaking to groups, large and small, passing out gospel tracts, and witnessing one-on-one to everyone from taxi drivers to wheelchair athletes in the Olympic village.

On our way to the hotel after a late-night meeting, we were bumping along in the van with Fred, feeling exhausted but happy. I could see his face in the light of oncoming cars. His eyes were at half-mast. "I bet you are going to be glad to see the back of us when we leave," I said, "then you'll be able to get some rest." To which Fred replied with a grin, "I may be weary, but I'm a Proverbs 10:5 kind of guy . . . look it up when you get back to your room." Later, we collapsed in bed without giving Fred's verse a thought. The next morning we were up and out the door. Proverbs 10:5 got scribbled on a card and forgotten. When I returned to California and was unpacking, I found the card with the verse! I smiled when I read it, and pictured Fred with his passion for lost souls. Even now, I know he is praying, singing, fasting, working on his computer and cell phone, traveling, witnessing, calling sinners to come home, and shaking the world for Christ.

Jesus says in John 4:35, "I tell you, open your eyes and look at the fields! They are ripe for harvest." Now is not the time to sleep; it's the time to gather a crop for the kingdom. John 9:4 says, "As long as it is day, we must do the work of him who sent me. Night is coming, when no one can work."

Lord of the Harvest, strengthen me as today I head into the fields white for harvest.

❧

September

September 1

A Good Kind of Anger

You have put me in the lowest pit, in the darkest depths.
Your wrath lies heavily upon me; you have overwhelmed
me with all your waves.... But I cry to you for help, O
Lord; in the morning my prayer comes before you. Why, O
Lord, do you reject me and hide your face from me?

—Psalm 88:6–7, 13–14

The author of Psalm 88 doesn't complain *about* God, but he sure does complain *to* God. He abruptly stops his psalm on a note of resentment. No setup for a hopeful ending. No hand-is-quicker-than-the-eye move from moaning to praise. Not even a sniff of joy in the entire eighteen verses. God seems snide and cruel, smashing underfoot helpless humans as though they were cigarette butts. The words are ugly. Then again, so is life.

God is big enough to take on anger. He knows stuff happens. He said, "In this world you will have trouble." He does not tiptoe around ugly things, embarrassed at wit's end to explain our woes. He doesn't cover up the guts of a person's rage—he invited people like the one who wrote Psalm 88 to be his coauthors. In so doing, he invited frustrated, angry people to air their complaints.

Too often we choose the polite routine and repress our deep emotions toward God. But anger pushes the problem to the front burner. Strong emotions open the door to asking the really hard questions: Does life make sense? Is God good? Anger often reveals whether we are moving toward the Almighty or away from him.

Take your complaints to God. Like the psalmist, move toward him, not away from him. Don't sow seeds of discord or incite rebellion among your friends against God, but allow your hurt to engage him head-on. This makes anger a *good* kind of anger. It's the point behind Ephesians 4:26, "In your anger do not sin."

Lord, may my anger drive me into your arms. Help me to point my anger, frustration, and bewilderment Godward.

❧

SEPTEMBER 2

Glimpses of Glory

Blessed be His glorious name forever! And let the whole
earth be filled with His glory. Amen and Amen.

—PSALM 72:19 NKJV

As our plane began its approach to the runway, I marveled at
the way the lowering sun reflected off everything wet and
metallic. Streams became ribbons of molten silver, car windows flashed
like golden shields, and puddles shone like shiny pennies. As a cemetery
rushed toward me on the left side, I briefly noted that there were no head-
stones—only plates of brass, marking each grave. But I wasn't prepared
for what happened next.

As we flew over, suddenly the sun exploded off the tops of hundreds
of the brass markers in quick-fire succession. Bam! Bam! Bam! As the plane
tilted, each marker ignited with a flash bright as a diamond. And then
it was over, and our plane touched down. It happened so fast, as if in a
twinkling of an eye. I had been looking out the window, dreaming about
heaven, and the Lord opened the eyes of my heart to glimpse heaven's
glory. I got a bird's-eye view of 1 Corinthians 15:51–52 when "we will not
all sleep, but we will all be changed—in a flash—in the twinkling of an
eye, at the last trumpet. For the trumpet will sound, the dead will be raised
imperishable, and we will be changed."

Some would insist that all I saw was the sun reflecting at a 45-degree
angle into my eyes. But it was more than that. Our God is an intentional
God, brimming over with purpose, infusing meaning into everything
around us. He has sprinkled earth with calling cards of his presence and
purpose ... whether in parking lots, airport terminals, or cemeteries.

Moses once prayed, "Show me your glory." You, also, can pray
that prayer. But be prepared to catch those glimpses at most
unusual times in most unusual places.

*Lord, as the hymn writer said, you "shine in all that's fair." Thank you for the
little flashes, the brief glances out of the corner of our eyes of that which will
one day fill the earth.*

Believe *It!*

For God so loved the world that he gave his one and only
Son, that whoever believes in him shall not perish but have
eternal life.

—JOHN 3:16

Chuck, a forty-two-year-old man with Down syndrome, stood
proudly in front of church and recited John 3:16. He and his
friends had come from a nearby group home that Sunday to help the congregation learn more about disabled people. Chuck boomed out the verse
loud and clear, bowing when he finished. More than a few people laughed
heartily. That's when he stepped forward, stuck out his chest and insisted,
"Don't laugh, I mean it! I *really* believe it!" It took the people aback. But
Chuck made his point. This wasn't a fun game meant to entertain, and he
wasn't a trained seal doing tricks. He was a grown man with a mind and
a will to choose. He believed the gift of eternal life was serious, offered to
him through the solemn sacrifice of Jesus Christ. His defense of the gospel
gave pause to the congregation.

First Corinthians 1:27 says, "God chose the foolish things of the world
to shame the wise; God chose the weak things of the world to shame the
strong." Perhaps Chuck "shamed" those who might have become complacent about the soul-riveting reality of their salvation. John 3:16 underscores
that sin kills, hell is real, people are perishing, and Jesus Christ delivers.
Chuck's mental retardation may have been his greatest spiritual asset. No
intellectual smugness for him! Rather, with spiritual zeal, he insisted the
church take both him *and* God's Word seriously.

How about us? All our brain cells are firing and most of us don't
wrestle with retardation. Do we believe—and act upon—the
Word of God with all our heart, soul, and mind? Do people
around us know we mean it? Do they take us seriously? Step
forward. Be insistent. Let your assurance in God's Word show
through your words and actions.

*Lord Jesus, convict me when my intellect gets in the way of a pure, simple trust
in you.*

SEPTEMBER 4

John 3:16

For God so loved the world that he gave his one and only Son, that whoever believes in him shall not perish but have eternal life.

—JOHN 3:16

Yesterday we saw that John 3:16 is my friend Chuck's favorite verse from the Bible. It's a beloved verse for many Christians. Perhaps that's because this short sentence sums up the gospel so well.

I once heard a speaker give an excellent word-by-word treatise on John 3:16. God (the greatest Giver) so loved (the greatest motive) the world (which has the greatest spiritual poverty) that he gave (the greatest act of all) his only Son (the greatest gift), that whoever (the all-time greatest invitation) believes in him (the greatest opportunity) should not perish (the greatest deliverance) but have eternal life (the greatest joy).

In one short verse, we meet the greatest Giver who has the highest motive to meet the most exacting demands of justice by the most powerful act of giving. His is the most breathtaking invitation for the greatest deliverance from the worst of hells to the highest of joys—eternal fellowship with God.

Most striking is how *sinful* and *wicked* "whoever" is in this verse! It makes John 3:16 all the more astounding. And so, "God demonstrates his own love for us in this: While we were still sinners, Christ died for us" (Romans 5:8). Later on, Romans 8:32 expounds on his love, for "he who did not spare his own Son, but gave him up for us all—how will he not also, along with him, graciously give us all things?"

Meditate on the words of this time-honored hymn:

> *Could we with the ink the ocean fill and were the skies of parchment made,*
> *Were every stalk on earth a quill and every man a scribe by trade*
> *To write the love of God above would drain the ocean dry,*
> *Nor could the scroll contain the whole tho stretched from sky to sky.*[1]

I humbly bow my knee before you today. What great love you have for sinful man!

SEPTEMBER 5

Rubbish

If anyone else thinks he has reasons to put confidence in the flesh, I have more: circumcised on the eighth day, of the people of Israel, of the tribe of Benjamin, a Hebrew of Hebrews; in regard to the law, a Pharisee; as for zeal, persecuting the church; as for legalistic righteousness, faultless. But whatever was to my profit I now consider loss for the sake of Christ. What is more, I consider everything a loss compared to the surpassing greatness of knowing Christ Jesus my Lord, for whose sake I have lost all things. I consider them rubbish, that I may gain Christ.

— PHILIPPIANS 3:4–8

Climbing the social and religious ladder was no longer Paul's focus—he was glad to "lose" his earthly awards, accolades, and achievements. He considered them rubbish. However, there's a deeper, more serious reason he calls these things trash. Earthly accolades are *dangerous*. Social and religious props are downright deterrents to a fervent faith in his Savior. Paul will no longer allow himself to be defined by his earthly credentials; it's why he considers *everything*—the whole package—a loss compared to knowing Jesus. For him, it's Christ and Christ alone.

This speaks to me as a quadriplegic. I consider a strong, sleek, athletic, and beautiful body rubbish, that I may gain Christ and be found in him. It's not only that I have lost these things; I simply recognize they were—and can be—disincentives to an intimate, lively and needy dependence on the Lord Jesus.

When an easy and trouble-free life entices us to place confidence in the flesh, when comfort zones breed self-assurance, it's high time we label these things rubbish. How highly do you value your appearance, background, abilities, and achievements? Do you lean on, cleave to, treasure, or secretly delight in them? Then you may be putting "confidence in the flesh." Happily toss those earthly props today on the trash heap.

Jesus, you are my confidence! I invite your Spirit to kick the props out from under me if I lean on my appearance, abilities, or achievements.

SEPTEMBER 6

My Own Baggage

> But when they measure themselves by one another, and
> compare themselves with one another, they are without
> understanding.
>
> —2 CORINTHIANS 10:12 RSV

have been at countless airport luggage carousels, watching as
bags innumerable drop from the chute. Some of those pieces are
very nice. Smart leather trim. Clean. New. In my daydreams I wonder
what would happen if I swapped my old, scuffed-up luggage for one of
those fancy new pieces? I wouldn't, of course. But *if* I did, what might I
find inside? Elegant clothes that don't fit. Shoes I don't like. Makeup that
doesn't match my skin tone. Jewelry that's clunky and overdone. And what
might I *lose* in this hypothetical deal? I'd lose my speaking notes, my favorite dress jeans, and treasured personal jewelry. I would lose the devotional
book I love to read in the morning. In fact, while the bag I took might look
better on the *outside*, it's a no-brainer that the stuff on the *inside* wouldn't
be a good fit at all.

Sometimes we like to imagine ourselves swapping lives with
others—lives that look so much more attractive and desirable than our
own. But the truth is, we really don't know what's *inside* their lives. We
forget that God has equipped and enabled us with special abilities to cope,
grow, and thrive through life's challenges. We forget the loyal friends and
wonderful people he has placed around us, and we forget the incompa-
rable, eternal purposes he is working through our lives. I may have difficulties in my life because of my disability, but I wouldn't trade my "baggage"
for anyone else's!

Sometimes when we long to escape the life we have, it's because
we have failed to take stock of our blessings and resources. Think
through the friendships, life experiences, encouragement from
other believers, and gracious provisions from the Lord that are
part of your "baggage" today.

*Father God, I thank you for the unique way you have provided for me, showing
me your tender love through the years. Help me to keep my eyes focused on Jesus,
rather than comparing myself to others.*

SEPTEMBER 7

The Defeat of Disease and Death

When evening came, many who were demon-possessed were brought to him, and he drove out the spirits with a word and healed all the sick. This was to fulfill what was spoken through the prophet Isaiah: "He took up our infirmities and carried our diseases."

— MATTHEW 8:16 – 17

My friend Skip and I are the same age, plus he broke his neck the same day I did. What's more, his diving accident also occurred in the Chesapeake Bay! I dove into the Maryland side of the bay; he, the Virginia side. You can see why I've always felt a special kinship with Skip. And my heart broke when I learned he recently died from complications connected with his quadriplegia. It made me angry at death and disease!

At the same time, I felt a sense of joy. Christ defeated death and disease by taking them with him to the grave. God's judgment on the sin that ushered disease into the world was endured by Jesus when he died. The prophet Isaiah explained, "He was wounded for our transgressions; he was crushed for our iniquities; upon him was the chastisement that brought us peace, and with his stripes we are healed" (Isaiah 53:5 ESV). The horrible blows on Jesus' back purchased a world without disease — that world is still in the future, but it's coming soon (Romans 8:23 – 24). And Skip and I can't wait!

When Christ came into the world, he was on a mission to accomplish global redemption. He signaled his purposes by healing the sick and raising the dead. These were previews of what was coming at the end of history when "he will wipe away every tear from their eyes, and death shall be no more ... nor pain anymore" (Revelation 21:4 ESV). Do you know someone who is gravely ill? A friend or family member who recently died? Take a moment to praise God that one day all disease and death will be banished!

Praise to the Conqueror of death! Praise be to the Healer of the sick! Lord, I look forward to the new heavens and new earth. No more disease or death!

Battle Plan

> The weapons we fight with are not the weapons of the
> world.
>
> —2 CORINTHIANS 10:4

The other night I had a little daydream going ... about a story I made up between the Duke of Endor and Prince Elohim. In my imagination, tension had been building between them for weeks—and finally came to a head in the castle banqueting hall.

There was a shout, a shoving of chairs. Ladies screamed and huddled against the walls as Prince Elohim drew his jewel-encrusted sword, the weapon given him by his father, the king. Saber in hand, the duke circled him, waiting to catch the prince off his guard. Suddenly, the duke lunged, and steel met steel. A stab ... a wound ... blood! Prince Elohim had been struck in the fray, his magnificent sword knocked from his hand. But wait! With deerlike speed, the prince leaped beyond the sweep of his enemy's blade, grabbing a heavy brass candlestick holder on the table. Armed with a frightfully inferior weapon, he sprang again into battle, diverting the lunges and stabs. Swinging his crude weapon, he connected with his opponent, crushing the adversary's skull.

Okay, maybe the way I tell it is a tad melodramatic. But the real thing is much more dramatic than this! The Bible tells the story of how the good Ruler sent his only Son to invade Satan's territory in order to free the captives and retake the kingdom under the family banner. But what is most poignant is that the Son defeated the enemy using "inferior" tactics—servanthood and death on a Roman cross. It is this that proves him mightier still.

In the battle against Satan, are you and I a jeweled sword in the Prince's hand? Hardly. We're more like a clunky candlestick—a most unlikely weapon. It's the One who wields us that makes all the difference. And when we overcome despite the odds, the King gains twice the glory!

Lord, at times I feel so inadequate for the task, so weak in the battle. But in your strong and skillful grip, I will overcome against all odds.

Facts of Life ... and of Death

For the wages of sin is death, but the gift of God is eternal
life in Christ Jesus our Lord.

—ROMANS 6:23

When my mother reached her late eighties, she suffered a series
of strokes that left her very confused mentally. She didn't know
who my sisters and I were. Mother became a shadow of her former self. I
would sit by her and recall happier days of standing with her in the backyard to watch the sun go down or harmonizing with her on her favorite
hymn.

Strange how we expect the parade of life to go on forever; when it
finally runs out of steam, we feel cheated, as though someone should have
told us it was this short, this hard, this ... final. But death is supposed to
be hard. Perhaps it's supposed to be a taste of hell. The wages of our sin
is death; could God have in mind for us to feel—really *feel*—a little of
what the Savior bore? God may want to remind us of what sin would have
earned us, had it not been for Christ. I guess the throes of death are our
birth pangs before we enter heaven's bliss. These are sobering thoughts. But
the facts of death often can be as harsh as facts of life.

When a loved one dies, it should be an alarm clock, a waving red
flag, warning us, "Wake up! Examine yourself! Have you made
your peace with God?" When a natural disaster strikes, killing
many, the alarm should sound louder. I can't say what God has in
mind with untimely deaths, but I *can* say we are *all* heading for
the grave, some of us sooner than others. And that should make
us sit up and take notice: What have we done with Jesus? Will we
be ready? Think about this today. Are you ready? How can you
help prepare a loved one or friend who is facing death?

*Almighty God, help me to grasp how brief our days really are, and give me
a sense of urgency to share the gospel with friends and loved ones who do not
know Jesus!*

☙

Casey Reds

Do not be like the horse or the mule, which have no understanding but must be controlled by bit and bridle.

—PSALM 32:9

My sister Kathy owned a quarter horse named Casey Reds—only she could ride him. Reds was a beautiful sorrel gelding, but he had been abused as a colt. He was shy and skittish. When Kathy rode Reds, she sometimes put racing blinders on him. Although just a horse, you could detect sadness in his eyes. He had lost his spirit.

"Do not be like the horse ... which has no understanding," today's verse says. A lot of people are like Casey Reds. They've suffered great sadness in their lives. The heart of God breaks when he sees us put blinders on, like horses with spirits broken. He never intended that we should live lives of solemn resignation. Maybe horses can resign themselves to a life of sadness, but not humans. We are not animals. Our souls are too significant. Humans bear the image of God. Unlike animals, "God did not give us a spirit of timidity" (2 Timothy 1:7). He wants his followers to *understand* something important about life eternal, grace overflowing, healing assured, contentment given, peace promised, hope everlasting, and joy that can surely brighten *any* countenance.

Are you feeling timid and fearful? Shy and skittish? Take off the blinders. Proverbs 2:2–5 says, "[Turn] your ear to wisdom and [apply] your heart to understanding, and if you call out for insight and cry aloud for understanding, and if you look for it as for silver and search for it as for hidden treasure, then you will understand the fear of the Lord and find the knowledge of God." The word *understand* is repeated three times here. "Cry aloud for understanding" and ask God to show you his wisdom regarding your situation. Jesus the Redeemer assures, "He has sent me to bind up the brokenhearted."

Lord God, I want to be able to follow you without "bit and bridle." Help me to do that.

September 11

Terror Tactics

In addition to all this, take up the shield of faith, with which you can extinguish all the flaming arrows of the evil one.

— Ephesians 6:16

*T*oday is Patriot Day, and I am reminded of the spiritual lessons I am learning from this war on terror. Terrorism is a devilish kind of warfare. A group like Al-Qaeda knows it could never stand toe-to-toe against a power like the United States because they would be outgunned, outmanned, and outmaneuvered. So what does Al-Qaeda do? They throw hand grenades here, take sniper shots there, and they hijack and hold hostages. It's not conventional warfare. They know they would lose if they ever went one-on-one against coalition forces.

Terrorism spreads fear and chips away at our resolve until we become demoralized. When that happens, good people cave in. We make appeasements, all in the name of being left alone. Just leave us alone. Go away!

The devil fights like that. He knows he would lose if ever he went directly up against God. He'd be outmaneuvered by the Almighty and he knows it. So what does our adversary do? He gets at God by needling us. He takes potshots at our peace of heart and fires off shots of discouragement or frustration. He throws hand grenades into our joy and robs us of our confidence in the Lord. The devil doesn't come out with guns blazing. He pricks at us with fiery darts and spreads fear and terror, little by little, until we make appeasements. We compromise our testimony — just sinning a little — hoping that the devil will quit bugging us and leave us alone.

Christians must remain focused against the devil. His goal is to demoralize and defeat us by guerrilla warfare. Ephesians 6:16, however, gives great advice. Christian, take faith! The war has been won! So please don't let the daily battle wear you down. Terrorism must not win ... and it won't!

Captain of the Lord's Army, I take my shield of faith and sword of the Spirit today. Fit me for battle against the forces of darkness. Be my victory, O Lord!

SEPTEMBER 12

Speak Up

I looked for a man among them who would build up the
wall and stand before me in the gap on behalf of the land so
I would not have to destroy it, but I found none.

—EZEKIEL 22:30

The horrors that occurred on September 11, 2001, shook not only
our country but the world. Several thousand people lost their lives,
and the fireball images that flashed around the world became unforget-
table. As deeply moving and heart wrenching as 9/11 was, its evil pales
beside other entries in the dark catalog of recent history. In the Rwandan
bloodbath in 1994, for example, Hutus ferociously slaughtered more than
800,000 Tutsis in less than three months. It was the clearest case of genocide since the Holocaust and three times the speed of Hitler's extermina-
tion of the Jews and Gypsies. In Rwandan terms, it was the equivalent
of more than two World Trade Center slaughters every single day for a
hundred straight days.[2]

That's sobering. Especially when you consider how the world
responded to America's plight after 9/11, yet turned a blind eye to—and
often weren't aware of—what happened in Rwanda. "Never again," the
civilized world intoned after the Nazi Holocaust. "You never know," might
be more realistic. God is looking for individuals who will stand in the gap
on behalf of the people of the world who are struggling against injustice
and genocide.

Edmund Burke said, "The only thing necessary for the triumph
of evil is for good men to do nothing."[3] When evil threatens, we
can take measures to prevent it, take action against it, inform
others about it, help those being oppressed by it, encourage those
who work against it, and much more. What examples of costly
stands against evil have you experienced in your own life? How is
God asking you to stand in the gap today?

*Lord God, I know that evil abounds in this world. Empower me to make a
stand where I am able and to encourage those who are struggling against injustice around the world.*

ର

Least in the Kingdom

> Anyone who breaks one of the least of these command-
> ments and teaches others to do the same will be called
> least in the kingdom of heaven, but whoever practices and
> teaches these commands will be called great in the kingdom
> of heaven.
>
> —MATTHEW 5:19

*H*erb had served as a leader in Christian ministry for years; so I was stunned when he confided to my husband that he was planning to leave his wife. "Martha and I have lived separate lives for years; the kids are grown ... why not? It won't really hurt anybody." He thought a minute, then added, "Sure, I feel bad about it and I wish it would have worked, but I know in the long run that, well ... God will forgive me."

If so, he won't be the same Herb. Charging ahead into sin while betting on God's forgiveness is a prescription for disaster. Herb will diminish his capacity for service in God's kingdom. He will break his marriage vows—the commandment to love and honor his wife—and through his example he will be teaching others to do the same. Young couples struggling to stay together will lose their resolve when they hear about Herb. This is why he will be called least in the kingdom of heaven. Herb, why risk your eternal state? Is escape from your dead-end marriage worth being demoted to least in the kingdom of heaven? May it never be!

> Anyone who breaks God's commandments and teaches others to
> do the same will be called least in the kingdom of heaven. It
> should send shivers down our spine! Don't forget, we teach by not
> only our words, but by our example. Think of the people who will
> observe your actions today. Will you unwittingly be encouraging
> them to join you in sinning? What will you be teaching them
> about God?

Lord Jesus, I realize I don't take your commandments seriously enough. Help me to respect your commands, live soberly, and look forward to a greater capacity of joy, worship, and service in heaven.

SEPTEMBER 14

Jake's Story

> Many are the plans in a man's heart, but it is the Lord's purpose that prevails.
>
> —PROVERBS 19:21

Our Wheels for the World team arrived in a small town in Poland to distribute 225 wheelchairs and Bibles. Before the day had hardly begun, however, their plans were in shreds. The assigned room was tiny and cramped. But before anyone could come up with a plan B, streams of families with disabled children began pouring through the doors. The place quickly became packed and noisy. Everything was thrown into confusion. "Lord Jesus," the team prayed together, "may your purpose prevail here." Then they went to work greeting families, assessing needs, locating pre-assigned wheelchairs, and sharing the gospel of Jesus at every opportunity.

The afternoon wore on. A tired father, carrying his little five-year-old disabled boy on his back, finally reached the head of the line. But when he lifted his son into the pre-assigned chair, his shoulders slumped. It didn't fit! "I am so sorry!" our seating specialist exclaimed, "this is the wrong chair." But there were only a few chairs left. Pushing aside several adult chairs, she reached for a child-sized one. But it was highly customized, with side supports — including blue leather backing with "Jake" stitched across the middle. In the end, there was no other choice. It was that chair or nothing. When the father lifted his boy into the new chair, it fit perfectly! An interpreter exclaimed, "It's like it was *made* for him!"

"By the way, what is your son's name?" someone asked the boy's mother. "Jakob," she replied — and everyone gasped! When an interpreter explained to the boy's mystified parents that "Jake" is the shortened version of Jakob, they too cried for joy. The whole family, along with almost sixty others, opened their hearts to receive Jesus that day. The Lord's purpose had prevailed!

If you are struggling today with a plan gone haywire in your life, take comfort in Proverbs 19:21. The Lord's purpose *will* prevail.

Father, help me to see through the strands of my shredded plans that if my purposes are truly your purposes, your heart's desire will prevail.

☙

A Little Girl's Gift

A gift opens the way for the giver and ushers him into the
presence of the great.

—PROVERBS 18:16

When I wheeled up to the cashier's counter in the airport gift shop,
I asked the clerk to reach into my handbag behind my chair,
open up my wallet, and take out the correct currency and change. "Sure,"
the clerk replied. And so, while standing next to me and holding my wallet,
she began to count out the bills and coins, laying them on the counter one
by one. Suddenly a little girl darted up and—clink!—dropped a penny
into my change purse. Then she ran back to her daddy. "What was all that
about?" the clerk said with surprise.

Then I put two and two together. The child, who must have been
watching me the whole time from behind her daddy's legs, saw the clerk
rummaging through my wallet. She must have thought I was poor and
didn't have enough money. Should I go over and tell that little girl the truth?
Should I say, "No honey, I don't need your pennies. I am a self-sufficient
person"?

I wheeled over to the child, smiled, and said, "I want to thank you
very much for helping me. You have the wonderful quality of Christlike
compassion, and if you don't know what that means, ask your daddy." Her
father gave me a wink. As I left the store, I realized it wasn't only the right
response, it was the *only* response. God must have been looking down and
smiling. A child's generous spirit was reinforced, her compassion encouraged, a father was made proud, a proud person was made humble, and
God received the glory. A little penny opened the way for a young girl to
be ushered into the presence of God, the giver of all gifts.

Today, reinforce the gift of compassion and generosity in the life
of someone who has been kind to you—no matter how small
that gesture of kindness.

*Father, I humble myself in your presence. Show me how to humbly receive, and
to encourage hearts with my gratitude.*

೨

SEPTEMBER 16

No Accident!

The Lord has decreed disaster for you.

—1 KINGS 22:23

These words from God's prophet made wicked King Ahab very nervous. After all, he was going into battle the next day. So for precaution, King Ahab forced an allied king to take the battlefield decked out in royal attire, while he himself dressed like a common soldier. King Ahab thought he had everybody fooled. But the switch-the-armor plot failed. Second Chronicles 18:33–34 describes how Ahab bit the dust: "But someone drew his bow at random and hit the king of Israel between the sections of his armor.... Then at sunset he died."

Amazing. An enemy archer shot "at random," yet if ever an arrow had someone's name on it, his did. How did God do that? How does God decree that something should happen—plan for it to happen—but accomplish his ends through a willy-nilly arbitrary act?! There were dozens of troops within the range of that archer on the battlefield. He took his pick and—twang!—what luck! He just killed his nation's foremost enemy, the wicked King Ahab, achieved his army's top priority, and he didn't even know it.

What we do know is that it was no accident. God somehow planted a thought in the archer's mind to aim "thataway," and the arrow did the rest. And it all fell securely within God's amazing and mysterious decree.

Let it sink in: there are no accidents in the Christian's life. God doesn't take his hand off the wheel of your life for a nanosecond. What appear to be "random crazy acts," God says fall within his purview. Have cruel or careless people broken your heart or stolen your dreams? By the time their sin splashed onto your life, it was the will of God for you—the God who loves you intensely.

Sovereign God, thank you for all that your sovereignty means. Thank you that every haphazard or hit-and-miss circumstance in my life falls under your over-arching decrees. For that, I am truly thankful.

ᕗᐁ

Somebody's Watching

His intent was that now, through the church, the manifold
wisdom of God should be made known to the rulers and
authorities in the heavenly realms.

—EPHESIANS 3:10

Last week I received a letter from Beth, a middle-aged woman
with multiple sclerosis who lives in a nursing home. She wrote,
"God has taken me out of the battle; I may be a Christian, but I don't have
a real ministry anymore." I think of Beth whenever I visit people who
languish in nursing homes. Many are women who, because of a debilitating injury, find themselves without a husband, and their children gone.
They think, *My life in God doesn't mean a thing. Nobody notices me. Nobody
cares.*

That's not true. A great many "somebodies" are observing and gaining
from the examples of persevering Christians. I'm not talking about nurses
or volunteers who stop by with a juice cart or medication. I'm talking
about God and the entire spiritual world of angels and demons. Spiritual
beings are intensely interested in our response to suffering. Luke 15:10
says, "There is rejoicing in the presence of the angels of God over one sinner who repents." If angels rejoice over that, you know they jump up and
down with excitement when a suffering Christian hangs on to God despite
loneliness or pain. Ephesians 3:10 reminds us God actually uses the life
examples of his children to teach angels and demons about how wise and
powerful he is.

When a young mother in her wheelchair perseveres through
loneliness, when an elderly widow keeps leaning on Christ, when
Christians in dark corners of the world hold on to God's grace,
the entire spiritual world stands on tiptoe, wondering, *How great
their God must be to inspire such loyalty!* If you're alone, thinking
no one cares, don't give up the battle. Remember, somebody is
watching, somebody cares. And you might even hear the rustling
of their wings.

*Father, thank you for using my life to show the unseen world how your grace
sustains a simple believer like me.*

∽

There's Always a Way

For Christ's love compels us.

—2 CORINTHIANS 5:14

Glenda Heisley and her family are Mennonites who tend a small farm in the pasturelands of Lancaster County, Pennsylvania. The Heisleys have a herd of goats and cows, besides their modest fields of corn. Glenda loves to sing, and she's a member of her church's choir. Shortly after the terrorist attacks of 2001, she and her choir friends wondered, *How can we help the people of New York City? Our denomination has already sent medical supplies, but what can our church do?*

They asked God to show them how a few farmers from the cornfields might encourage the city folk of New York. God gave them a wonderful idea. Early one Friday morning, Glenda and her church friends boarded a bus for New York. They took with them a stack of CDs, recordings they had done of all their favorite old hymns.

When they arrived, their bus stopped at a subway station, and they disembarked. They looked quite a sight in their simple farming clothes—including traditional white caps for the women and straw hats for the men. Standing near the station, they took a deep breath ... and began to sing. In rich, deep, four-part harmony, they sang "Rock of Ages" and "Dwelling in Beulah Land." Suddenly the stockbrokers rushing by slowed their pace. Students, exiting the subway to run to class at Columbia University, paused. Shoppers hesitated. All turned their heads as they walked by, catching lovely strains of hymns from what must have seemed to them like another planet. As they sang, they held out the free CDs. Gifts of love, straight from the heart, in the name of Jesus.

There is *always* a way—a creative, sincere way—to share the love of Christ. For these Mennonites, it started with prayer, asking God for direction and fresh ideas. And that's a good place for you to start today too.

Use me, Holy Spirit—who I am and where I am—to show people an alternative to a shallow, empty life without God.

෨

SEPTEMBER 19

Rescued through the Flames

> For it became him, for whom are all things, and by whom
> are all things, in bringing many sons unto glory, to make
> the captain of their salvation perfect through sufferings.
>
> — HEBREWS 2:10 KJV

The fireman's angry gaze held mine. "So God 'understands,' does he?
Well, *big deal*! What good does that do me?" He raised his arms
out from under the table, revealing the smooth ends of two stumps where
hands should be. "Burned off in a blaze," he said. "Lost my job."

Fresh out of the hospital myself, I was taken aback. Still young in the
faith, I was no expert on the Bible. But I looked into those smoldering
eyes and answered as honestly as I knew how. "Listen ... I'm not saying I
know all the answers. But I do know the One who has the answers. And
knowing him has made all the difference." This grieving man didn't need a
bunch of words. He needed *the* Word. The Word made flesh, gouged, nails
piercing wrists nearly ripping hands off. Spat upon, beaten bloody, buzzing
flies, and hammering hatred. As a saint of old described it, "Love poured
out like wine as strong as fire." The fireman stopped thinking about God
as some distant being in a galaxy far, far away. He realized God got messy
when he smeared his blood on a cross to save people from hellfire. In a
sense, Jesus ran into a burning building to save everyone he could. This
fact had a strange appeal for this fireman who had injured himself rescuing
others from the flames.

> If you want to be held steady in the midst of your anxiety or suf-
> fering, you want to be held — but not by a "doctrine" or a cause.
> You want to be held in the embrace of the most powerful Person
> in the universe, the very One who says, "Come to me."

*Savior, I come to you, you who know my weariness, my burden, and my pain.
You rescued me from the fires of hell, and now your wounded hands are outstretched. Jesus, I come. Jesus, I come.*

☙

The Correct Path

> Direct me in the path of your commands, for there I find delight.
>
> —PSALM 119:35

hree-year-old Thaddeus is a little boy with many disabling conditions. He had barely gotten out of diapers and had already endured eight surgeries. A few months ago his parents got quite a scare. While Thad was napping in his crib, his ventilator came undone. When his mother checked on him, Thad was unconscious. Quickly they administered CPR and called 9-1-1. Because their town is so small, the rescue squad was there almost immediately.

The paramedics swept Thad up in their arms, continued CPR, and told the parents to follow the ambulance in their car. Where were they heading? "To the cemetery," the paramedics shouted back. What a strange, eerie destination! As Thad's parents sped behind the ambulance, they kept thinking, *Why the cemetery? How awful! What's going on?* You can understand. A cemetery is the last place you would think to go if your child's life is hanging in the balance. When the paramedics pulled up to the gates of the cemetery, it became clear. The paramedics had called ahead, and just yards away was the life-flight helicopter from a nearby city. The only place for it to land with no trees around was the town cemetery!

Thad is okay now. His parents have a new appreciation for the town cemetery and the strange way God often asks us to trust him. Sometimes it definitely feels as though God is leading us down the wrong path to the wrong place at the wrong time. Today's verse should be our prayer every day. What path is God leading you on? Does it feel "right"? Don't allow your emotions to alter your confidence in God. When he is leading the way, we not only find life, but *delight*.

O God, forgive me for doubting you when the path you take me on seems dark and indiscernible. Forgive me for questioning you when the destination you are leading me to seems "wrong." Increase my trust this day!

SEPTEMBER 21

A Different Kind of Leprosy

A man with leprosy came and knelt before him and said,
"Lord, if you are willing, you can make me clean." Jesus
reached out his hand and touched the man. "I am willing,"
he said. "Be clean!"

—MATTHEW 8:2–3

Though we rarely hear about it in the Western world, diseases like leprosy still blight and mar many lives in developing nations. The disfigurement of leprosy, as you have no doubt heard, happens when people lose their sensation of pain. And so, with no pain to warn them, people badly damage their fingers or feet, ultimately destroying them.

In the book of Hebrews, the author writes: "See to it, brothers, that none of you has a sinful, unbelieving heart that turns away from the living God. But encourage one another daily, as long as it is called Today, so that none of you may be hardened by sin's deceitfulness" (Hebrews 3:12–13). Right there you have a diagnosis of spiritual leprosy. It's when your soul becomes hardened by sin's deceitfulness. It is when you spiritually lose all sensation of pain, especially things that pain God. It's when you become actually dull and deadened to sin — when your sensitivity to wrongdoing becomes so numb that you end up ripping your soul apart and don't even realize it. You sin — even blatantly sin — and you don't feel it. White becomes black, black becomes white (or at least gray), and you end up thinking that what others call rebellion in your life isn't really all that bad.

My friend, leprosy is something you don't want to fool around with — spiritual or otherwise. If it's a lie, go back and make it right before you become hardened. If it's a fantasy, shelve it! Don't let it fossilize your conscience. Don't turn away from the Lord, as it says in Hebrews 3:12. Let me encourage you today: do a double-check to see if you've got any leprous spots on your soul.

Touch me, Lord Jesus, and clean my heart, just as you willingly touched the leper and made him whole.

SEPTEMBER 22

Prone to Wander

But the more I called Israel, the further they went from me. They sacrificed to the Baals and they burned incense to images. It was I who taught Ephraim to walk, taking them by the arms; but they did not realize it was I who healed them. I led them with cords of human kindness, with ties of love; I lifted the yoke from their neck and bent down to feed them.

—HOSEA 11:2–4

Whenever I visit my sister Jay on her Maryland farm, we always find time to sing our favorite hymns. We love to harmonize on the old hymn, "Come Thou Fount." My heart aches so as we sing the third verse: "Oh, to grace how great a debtor, / daily I'm constrained to be! / Let Thy goodness, like a fetter, / bind my wandering heart to Thee. / Prone to wander, Lord, I feel it, / prone to leave the God I love; / here's my heart, oh, take and seal it, / seal it for Thy courts above!"

Tears come easily when I sing that familiar verse. I cry because it's true. I am *so* prone to wander. I'm inclined to roam away from God. I know myself all too well! The poignant thing is, God knows me too. Hosea 11:2–4 reflects God's thoughts on our wandering hearts.

Read today's verse again. God is the One who taught you to take your first steps in your Christian life. During times of confusion and tumult, God took you by the arms and led you. In all your illnesses, it is God who healed you. He led you with cords of human kindness and ties of love. When your burden seemed overwhelming, when you felt trapped by your circumstances, it was he who lifted the yoke from your neck. God is the One who has condescended time and again to bend down to feed you, provide for you, and take care of you. Oh, what a fountain of love he is!

Jehovah-Jireh, you are my provider. With tenderhearted care, you teach me and lead me. Oh, may I never wander! Here's my heart! Take and seal it for thy courts above!

SEPTEMBER 23

Mrs. Sherman's Treasures

Do not store up for yourselves treasures on earth, where
moth and rust destroy, and where thieves break in and steal.
But store up for yourselves treasures in heaven, where moth
and rust do not destroy, and where thieves do not break in
and steal. For where your treasure is, there your heart will
be also.

—MATTHEW 6:19–21

My friend Charlotte Sherman will turn ninety-one today. I
first met Randy and Charlotte through Young Life when
they served on the local committee. They prayed for hundreds of young
people in the Baltimore area who came to Christ.

Many years ago Mr. and Mrs. Sherman sold their beautiful Maryland
farm and moved into a retirement community. They took as many photos,
furniture, and mementoes as they could squeeze in their apartment. After
about eleven years Randy began a long struggle with chronic pneumonia;
unfortunately, it meant a second move into a much smaller assisted living
unit.

It was nowhere near as spacious as their other apartment and Charlotte
found herself "getting rid of lots of stuff," as she put it. My heart broke to
think of her selling their furniture and giving away family treasures. When
I asked her over the phone how she was able to manage it, she said with a
smile, "All these earthly treasures will disappear one day anyway; I know
my real treasure is in heaven." I couldn't see her, but I could picture the
twinkle in her blue eyes. What an inspiration!

Americans are experts at accumulating "stuff." Earthly things
can sink anchors deep in our hearts; we feel we could never live
without that new exercise equipment, that second car, or the
Chico's charge card. What are the possessions you treasure in
life? Let Charlotte Sherman inspire you today. Find ways you
can downsize; it's the sure way to upgrade devotion to Christ in
your heart.

*Lord Jesus, may the way I deal with stuff in my life reflect how you and you
alone are my treasure.*

SEPTEMBER 24

Steering Sin

The Lord works out everything for his own ends—even the wicked for a day of disaster.

—PROVERBS 16:4

God is a lot bigger than we think. A whole lot bigger. Most Christians willingly acknowledge God's hand in people's good deeds, even the good deeds of serious atheists. But God also oversees people's wicked actions. No sin happens that God doesn't deliberately allow. (A statement like that will take your breath away!) Don't misunderstand—he is not the source of people's bad deeds, for he despises sin. He hates it. James 1:13 says that God never tempts anyone to do wrong. Nevertheless, his overarching decrees allow for God to turn wicked hearts and evil motives this way and that, all to suit his higher purpose. It's what today's verse is all about.

So how does our big God pull it off? He steers the sin *already in people's hearts* so that sinners unwittingly fulfill God's plans and not merely their own. Look at wicked King Ahab of Israel. As he was mustering his troops for war, a courageous prophet tells him what he does not want to hear: "The Lord has decreed disaster for you." Decreed, mind you—Ahab's death in battle is not a suggestion-box item that God is merely considering. Jehovah plotted Ahab's demise. And even when the wicked king tried to cleverly subvert God's decree, he still ended up dying in battle (2 Chronicles 18:33–34). How did God *do* that?! He accomplished it, and countless similar circumstances by infinite wisdom far beyond our grasp.

Little wonder God's Word tells us to cultivate a fear of the Lord (Psalm 111:10; Proverbs 1:7). A proper fear begins with understanding how big God really is. Reread today's devotional with that in mind.

Lord God, there is no way I can understand the way you do things. I don't pretend to comprehend how you work through people's evil deeds to serve your own ends. But I know this: I believe you are far more kind and gracious than I could possibly imagine.

☙

Fruit Comes through Struggle

This is to my Father's glory, that you bear much fruit, showing yourselves to be my disciples.

—JOHN 15:8

Last week Ken and I visited Tim, a friend from church, who grows several rare varieties of grapes on the hillside behind his house. I was surprised that Tim had planted his vines along a steep and rocky portion of the hill. "Why didn't you plant the vines at the base of the hill?" I asked him. "The soil certainly looks a lot better—and there's more sun."

Tim smiled. "There's a rule you need to remember when it comes to growing these special varieties of grapes," he said. "When you feed them luxuriously with lots of nutrients and fertilizer, the vine produces a pro-fuse bush of leaves and cane. But the fruit it grows is sparse and very poor. Oh, make no mistake," he laughed, "the plant *loves* lots of fertilizer. But it invests all those nutrients into growing lush, dark, beautiful leaves. And when the vine has finished doing that, it has very little energy left to produce fruit. It certainly looks like a beautiful vine. But that's it. It just looks good."

How, then, do you get good grapes? As Tim explained it, you have to make sure the grapevine struggles! You plant it in rocky, flinty soil, or you girdle the vine by wrapping wires around the cordons, forcing the plant to struggle as it tries to draw nutrients from its roots. This causes the dis-tressed vine to divert most all of its prized and hard-won nutrients into the fruit, instead of the leaves. The result of these trials and tribulations is the sweetest fruit possible!

So ... maybe the rocky soil and steep inclines in your life aren't so bad after all. The trials and struggles, disappointments and set-backs you face, this "girdling" that presses you in from all sides ... is a bruising of blessing. And you won't bear a crop without it.

Lord, when this life is all over and I stand before you, I want you to find sweet fruit in my life ... and not just leaves.

Prayer Dogs

Jesus asked them, "Which is lawful on the Sabbath: to do good or to do evil, to save life or to kill?" But they remained silent. He looked around at them in anger and, deeply distressed at their stubborn hearts, said to the man, "Stretch out your hand."

—MARK 3:4–5

*M*y friend Marlys, who heads up a Christian disabilities group, recently visited an internationally renowned prayer center. As she was sitting in the prayer room, interceding and enjoying the peaceful atmosphere, a staff member from the prayer center motioned to her and asked her to step outside. "Ma'am," he said, "we're a little concerned about two blind members in your group. The two blind people went into the prayer room *with their guide dogs*. I don't think that's proper. I'm concerned that having a dog in the room would grieve the Holy Spirit. How do you think the Lord feels about this?"

Marlys could hardly believe her ears. It was all she could do to stifle her anger. What she said was, "I think God is saying, 'Hallelujah! I'm glad they're here!' " Still, the man persisted. He thought someone should remove the dogs and let the blind individuals remain in the room to pray. After ten minutes of haggling, the staff member finally relented.

The whole affair reminded me of Jesus' words in Matthew 23:23–24, "You give a tenth of your spices—mint, dill and cummin. But you have neglected the more important matters of the law—justice, mercy and faithfulness. You should have practiced the latter, without neglecting the former. You blind guides! You strain out a gnat but swallow a camel." Thank heavens, there is a higher law that incorporates prudence, compassion, and a more exalted perspective!

How often we believers lose our focus and put more emphasis on externals, rules, and practices rather than on God's passion for lost and hopeless people. Which means more to the Lord ... religious decorum or eternal souls?

Dear Father, keep me from becoming distracted by minor issues and trivial infractions, so that I fail to walk in your great yearning for men and women to turn back to you. As David prayed so long ago, "Renew a right spirit within me."

Job's Trials

> Then the Lord said to Satan, "Have you considered my
> servant Job?"
>
> —JOB 1:8

The Bible infers that God always eventually gets his way. But what does that say about him? God's favorite planet has experienced a lot of evil over the years. Why hasn't he stopped it ... or at least curbed it? If God's the boss, is Satan his employee? Let's look at Job.

Job had it all—money, land, status, family. One day in God's throne room, Satan broached his disgust over Job's pious reputation. "The man loves you because you bribe him," the devil argued. "But stretch out your hand and strike everything he has, and he will surely curse you to your face." God answered, "Job is yours, only don't lay a finger on his person." The words were scarcely out of God's mouth when lightning killed Job's sheep and shepherds, a Chaldean raiding party plundered the cattle and herdsmen, then a mighty wind collapsed a roof on Job's children. So we ask, who caused Job's trials?

At the most basic level, *natural forces* did—desert winds blew and lightning struck. On the same level, *evil people* caused Job's trials—greedy men killed and plundered. On another level, *Satan* caused Job's problems—he leaves God's presence, we scarcely blink, and carnage is everywhere; Satan engineered it all: the fire, the wind, and the sword. But on the deepest level, *nothing happened that God did not decree.* God permitted what he hated, to accomplish something he loved: the worship of a wiser Job.

Satan's motive was to wreck Job's life and mock God. God's reaction to the devil was merely to lengthen his leash. God's decree made room for evil to occur, but God didn't *do* it. He simply exploited the deliberate evil of wicked people, as well as the impersonal evil of some bad storms *without forcing anyone's hands.* How does God pull it off? Welcome to the world of finite human beings trying to comprehend an infinite God!

Almighty God, how unsearchable are your judgments and your ways past finding out! I simply praise you that your decrees are perfect.

ॐ

SEPTEMBER 28

Prepare to Meet Your God

> I know that everything God does will endure forever; nothing can be added to it and nothing taken from it. God does it so that men will revere him. Whatever is has already been, and what will be has been before; and God will call the past to account.
>
> —ECCLESIASTES 3:14–15

Don't be afraid of this verse. It's good news! God will one day call your past into account, and he will no doubt see smudges and stains, sins and faults. He will also see the blood of his Son, which will cover all (Hebrews 9:14). What else about your past? God will see countless times of obedience and perseverance, trust and confidence in him; he will recognize your doggedness through hardship and your resolve against temptation. Again, it will be his Son who made the provision of grace upon grace. When God calls everything about you into account, you will praise God for the blood and the blessings of Jesus as never before!

You will drop to your knees before Jesus to express thanks and gratitude. The Man of Sorrows will walk from his throne and approach you. He will have absolutely no doubt of your appreciation, for he knows what you have suffered, what you have endured, the temptations to which you said no. He will reach toward you with his nail-scarred hands, and when you feel your hands in his, you will not be embarrassed. That's because your own scars, and all those times you felt rejection and pain, have given you at least a tiny taste of what the Savior endured to purchase your redemption.

Your hardships, like nothing else, are preparing you to meet your God. Your suffering is getting you ready—for what proof could you bring of your love for Jesus if this life left you totally unscarred?

Gracious God, I am full of praise for Jesus Christ. His blood covers my sins, and his blessings of grace help me live righteously. He deserves all the praise!

The Exaltation of Christ

> Therefore God exalted him to the highest place and gave
> him the name that is above every name, that at the name
> of Jesus every knee should bow, in heaven and on earth and
> under the earth, and every tongue confess that Jesus Christ
> is Lord, to the glory of God the Father.
>
> —PHILIPPIANS 2:9–11

I can't wait for the day described in our verse. It will be a glorious, grand day for Jesus! Christ's status as the God-man means that the Father will give his Son privileges he did not have prior to the incarnation. He will be crowned King of Kings and Lord of Lords. He will receive back his glory because he crushed the adversary. He will be honored for having rescued sinful man by his own sacrifice. "Jesus" was the name bestowed at his birth, but "Lord" is what *everyone* will call him after his exaltation.

When every knee finally bows and every tongue confesses that Jesus Christ is Lord, we will confess him as the undisputed Sovereign Ruler of the universe. These confessions will not only come from the saints and angels but from the demons and lost humanity in hell—*everyone* will eventually agree that Jesus is Lord. They will do so willfully and happily, or unwillfully and painfully. But they'll do it. Not everyone will be saved, but everyone will acknowledge Jesus as the rightful Ruler of the universe, never to be contested again. What a glorious day that will be!

You can begin practicing for the wonderful "day of Christ," a day described three times in the book of Philippians—a day of rewards for believers, final salvation, and glorification. But remember, it's Jesus' day. You will be among those who willfully and happily bow the knee to confess that Jesus is Lord!

Father, thank you for all the privileges and honors you will bestow upon your Son on that awesome day. May I bow my knee in submission to him even now while I'm on earth.

The God of Hope

> May the God of hope fill you with all joy and peace as you trust in him, so that you may overflow with hope by the power of the Holy Spirit.
>
> —ROMANS 15:13

I was on the phone an hour with Ron. His wife had contacted me, distraught that he was depressed and had been lying in bed since he broke his neck. Ron was a former pastor and probably knew more Scripture than I did. When he didn't respond after an hour, I took a different tack. "Did you see the movie *The Shawshank Redemption*?" He seemed surprised at my question. "Remember when Andy DuPhrane said to his fellow prisoner, 'Hope is a good thing, maybe the best of things, and no good thing ever dies ... so get busy living, or get busy dying.'" Ron was quiet for a long moment then said softly, "Hope *is* a good thing." From then on, he got busy living.

It's amazing how far we can go on a little bit of hope. Hope means "I know I can make it!" The source of all hope is none other than Jesus Christ. Titus 2:13 (KJV) says, "Looking for that blessed hope, and the glorious appearing of the great God and our Savior Jesus Christ." No wonder today's verse tells us to trust in "the God of hope." From the Lord alone flows all joy and peace. I saw hope overflow in Ron's life when he and his wife finally came to one of our Family Retreats. There they were, passing on hope to others!

Hope happens when we gently point people to Jesus, whether through a few encouraging words, a Scripture in a note card, or just spending an hour on the phone together. Today, nudge people toward "the Blessed Hope," the Lord Jesus.

Father, because you are the God of Hope, I have assurance that I can make it through the toughest of times. Help me to pass on your hope to a hurting friend today.

October

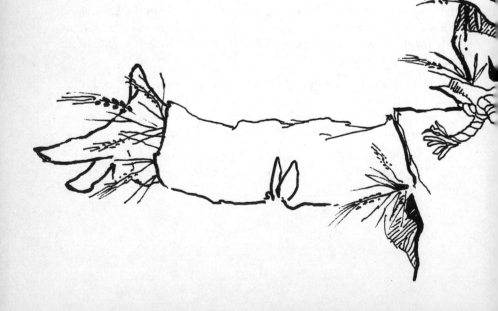

October 1

Waiting in Prayer

In the morning, O Lord, you hear my voice; in the morning I lay my requests before you and wait in expectation.

—Psalm 5:3

When our Wheels for the World team was in Peru, we met Angelica Ramirez, a twenty-five-year-old woman who had cerebral palsy and epilepsy since birth. For most of her life, she had laid in bed all day—her only entertainment was watching the shaft of the sun move across her room. On the morning of our wheelchair distribution, Angelica's mother wrapped her daughter in a white mattress pad so that her brother could carry her down the mountain. They were hoping to receive a wheelchair.

Our team happened to have a recliner wheelchair with an extended headrest (we don't usually take these sorts of highly customized chairs on trips). As Angelica was placed in this particular chair, everyone gasped. It fit perfectly. When our team gave Angelica's mother a Bible in the Spanish language, she broke down and began sobbing. "God has answered my prayer," she said through an interpreter. We smiled, thinking she meant the Bible. But the woman shook her head and explained, "I want you to understand that I have been praying for twenty years for a wheelchair for my daughter and today—*Gloria al Dios*—God has answered my plea. Now I can take my daughter to church. I won't have to worry about carrying her!"

If God answers your prayer immediately, be thankful; if it's denied, be patient; if you are to wait, remain eager and expectant. Angelica's story taught me something fresh about laying our requests before God: he invites us to have an expectant attitude when we pray. He wants us to be hopeful and eager—even if the answer is delayed for twenty years! Why such a delay? Only God knows, but I know this: he provided a perfect wheelchair hand tailored for Angelica, and that Peruvian mother experienced twenty times the joy.

Thank you for hearing my voice in prayer, O Lord. I trust you with the answer and I wait eagerly—not impatiently—for your reply.

෨

OCTOBER 2

A Lesson in Humiliation

> All of you, clothe yourselves with humility toward one
> another, because, "God opposes the proud but gives grace
> to the humble."
>
> —1 PETER 5:5

*S*everal disabled people in our workshop complained about the insensitive, ignorant comments able-bodied people seemed to repeat to them. Rana, my coleader, suggested, "If you keep getting the same comments, why don't you memorize a short, to-the-point response you can give without giving it a second thought."

That's when my mother, sitting in the third row, raised her hand. "I want you all to know," she said, "that Joni has a pat reply she always uses." Panic clutched my throat. *What was she going to say?* "Sometimes people stop Joni to ask for her autograph—at the most inconvenient times! So rather than say an outright 'No,' she says, 'I'm sorry, I must sign holding my special pen between my teeth. And I don't think I have my pen with me. Bother!' And there are times when she really *does* have her pen with her!"

The class belly laughed as I died a thousand deaths. They read the situation well. A mother had just embarrassed her daughter in front of a lot of people. It's just like Mother to do that. And it's just like God. He steps into our tightly managed public persona and says, "Pardon me, everyone, I have something to reveal about this person." He brushes aside our smooth talk and cultivated image. He boldly intrudes into our sin, naming it for what it is. It's called humiliation, and we *need* it. If we remain unaware of our sin and hypocrisy, it will become a barrier in our relationship with God ... and with one another.

If we humble ourselves before God, he will have no need of humbling us before others. Follow Peter's advice today, and "humble yourselves ... under God's mighty hand, that he may lift you up in due time" (1 Peter 5:6).

Lord, I bow low before you, confessing my sinful, prideful attitudes. I freely admit that all that I have and all that I am—my very life—is in your hand this day.

OCTOBER 3

Confined Contentment

> I am not saying this because I am in need, for I have learned to be content whatever the circumstances.
>
> —PHILIPPIANS 4:11

Will I ever be happy again? It's all I could think of after I got out of the hospital and wheeled through the front door of my home. Doorways were too narrow and sinks were too high. I sat at the dining room table, my knees hitting the edge. A plate of food was placed in front of me, but my hands remained limp in my lap. Someone else—at least for the first few months—fed me. I felt confined and trapped.

My confinement forced me to look at another captive. The apostle Paul had seen the inside of more than one small room from which there was no escape. For over two years, he was shifted from "pillar to post" until finally he arrived in Rome where he remained under house arrest. When Paul wrote to thank the church in Philippi for their concern, he reassured them with the words of today's verse. Paul became my example in my own "prison." I learned—and am still learning—the secret of being content. The apostle writes about this secret in Philippians 4:13, "I can do everything through him who gives me strength." Contentment in confinement has an internal quietness of heart that gladly submits to God in all circumstances.

When I say "quietness of heart," I'm not ruling out the prison bars and wheelchairs. What I *am* ruling out is peevish thoughts, plotting ways of escape, and fretting that only leads to anxiety. Contentment is a sedate spirit that finds its strength in Jesus. Contentment comes from many great and small *acceptances* in life. As the saying goes, when life isn't the way you like it, like it the way it is ... one day at a time with Christ.

Father, I don't want to plot ways to escape my circumstances. Help me to be content, knowing that your Son is with me. He—and he alone—will give me strength.

෨

It Could Be Worse

The eternal God is your refuge, underneath are the everlasting arms.

— DEUTERONOMY 33:27

*Y*ou've heard that old cliché, "It could be worse!" It's not a phrase we like to hear. The words can sound rather trite and empty at times. But it's *true*. Things truly could be much worse for all of us. Picture God holding up his hands like the flood-control locks on a canal, holding back a dark tidal wave of suffering and harm. His everlasting arms shield us. He is our refuge and protector. Were it not for the influence of the Spirit of Christ in this world, we would see much more calamity, violence, natural catastrophes, war, and crime. Most of all, thank God we don't get the sentence of death we deserve for our sins, but rather the rescue and salvation he so freely offered to us in his Son!

Are you experiencing hardship today? God promises that absolutely nothing will penetrate his sheltering hands to touch us except that which has been weighed and measured, so as to not ultimately harm us. And when troubles do encroach on our lives, God promises to flood us with his sustaining grace.

And though our world can be a dark and sorrowful place at times, we can still experience our Father's goodness in the simple pleasures of a rainbow burning against a dark sky, a honeybee exploring a daffodil, the soft morning sunlight, a cup of cocoa by a cherrywood fire on a stormy night, the whisper of a summer wind in the pines, the companionship of a loved one, and the hope of a wondrous new dawn in our heavenly home, just around the corner.

Take a moment to think through the good in your life—the things and the people you love and value. Then spend some time thanking the one who sends us "every good and perfect gift" (James 1:17).

Bless you, my Father, for your guarding and shielding me from so much evil, so much harm and grief. Grant me a grateful, thankful heart through the hours of this day.

OCTOBER 5

God Meant It for Good

> But God sent me ahead of you to preserve for you a rem-
> nant on earth and to save your lives by a great deliverance.
> So then, it was not you who sent me here, but God.
> —GENESIS 45:7–8

Whenever I become troubled by crazy things that happen to me, I turn to the story of Joseph in the Bible. *There* was somebody who *really* went through bizarre circumstances! But think about it . . .

If Joseph had not been sold to those caravan traders by his wicked brothers, he would not have been sold as a slave to Pharaoh. And if Joseph had not become Pharaoh's right-hand man, no one would have thought to build giant grain silos to ward off the seven-year famine. And if the famine hadn't happened, Jacob and his family would never have come to Egypt for food and safety. And if Jacob's family weren't in Egypt, there would have been no slave laborers. And if no slaves, no exodus. And no Mount Sinai and the giving of the law to Moses. And no Promised Land. And, finally, no line of Judah from which the Messiah, Jesus Christ, would come.

It is enthralling to see how the troubles of one young man named Joseph could kick-start a whole chain of earthshaking events that would ultimately lead to our salvation. Oh, the wisdom and knowledge of God!

Joseph's story could be yours. Only heaven will reveal the incredibly complex intertwining of events in which you have played a pivotal role. Like Joseph, you may not be able to discern it at the time, but God has it all in hand . . . he has it all in control . . . and you, dear friend, are needed in his marvelous plan to spread his kingdom in your corner of the world.

God of Abraham, Isaac, and Jacob, thank you for the awe-inspiring lessons about your sovereignty that you teach us through the story of Joseph. Thank you for your dominion and rule, not only in his life, but mine.

Jesus' Social Life

For the Son of Man came to seek and to save what was lost.

—LUKE 19:10

Jesus had a clear and concise mission — to seek out and save those who were lost. To carry out his mission, he connected with virtually every person the Father put in his path, every kind of individual in every strata of society. He did not allow himself to bypass *anyone.*

If we are to follow in Christ's steps and carry out his mission, we must do the same. It won't be easy, and we will be tempted to relate only to those with whom we identify, with whom we are comfortable. But if we want to follow Christ's lifestyle, then it will mean making inroads — that is, seeking out people we don't normally connect with.

Look at the ones Jesus sought out. In Mark 5:1–5, he befriends a guy with a serious mental illness — something no Jewish fellow would be caught dead doing. In Luke 5:27–30, he starts up a relationship with a tax collector, a conniver and a known cheater. In Luke 7:36–39, Jesus befriends a loose woman whose reputation was the talk of the town. In John 4:5–9, he connects with a Samaritan: a real outsider, a loner, an oddball. In Luke 15:1–2, we see Jesus going to parties with bums and lowlifes. He goes out of his way to get to know people riddled with disease and wracked with mental illness.

Every day we bypass people who are considered outsiders and oddballs, loners and second-class citizens. Yet God has put these individuals around us in our neighborhoods, on our street corners, and in the mall parking lot. My coworker Cathy has befriended a homeless woman who works part-time at the local Taco Bell — she's taking her to dinner this week! Cathy is making inroads in our community "mission field" and is seeking out the lost. Can you do the same?

Jesus, help me not to overlook anyone today. May I seek out people the way you would!

৶

OCTOBER 7
Hand-Tailored Grace

Before I formed you in the womb I knew you, before you
were born I set you apart.

—JEREMIAH 1:5

*I*n China, generations of Communism has taken its toll on the way
people think. Uniformity is a basic value—everyone looking, acting, and thinking like everyone else. No one standing out. The individual
person isn't important ... it's the country as a whole that counts.

In a crowded residential facility for the elderly outside Shanghai, our
Wheels for the World director, John Wern, had just lined up a weird and
wonderful assortment of wheelchairs—large and small—in front of the
room. One had a tall back with a headrest. Another, movable footrests.
Another was wide with angled wheels. It was a wild array, and John, speaking to the people and staff, said, "Each of these chairs is totally unique,
because people and their needs are unique. Each person here is an *individual*, and we're committed to finding the right chair for each specific need."

A murmuring began among the staff. One staff worker replied, "What
you're saying is a new concept." He was right. Because just days later when
I was in Beijing and visiting a rehabilitation center, I went into the patients'
rooms and introduced myself to them one-on-one. The doctors seemed
mystified. Why would I take the time? "You're an important person. You're
a visitor from America." True. But I wasn't there just to give wheelchairs. I
wanted to connect with the people who needed them.

First Peter 4:10 describes the manifold—literally, "multicolored"—grace
of God. Just like those varied wheelchairs, the grace God brings to your life
today is hand tailored and custom designed for your individual needs.

God's grace is not one-size-fits-all. He relates to you as an individual—a unique person created in his image. Don't fall into
the trap of comparing your situation to that of others. Tell your
Father your specific needs and desires, and he will fulfill you as
no one else ever could.

*Bless you, Father, that though you have many children, you know my name,
my circumstances, and the hidden needs of my heart.*

☙

OCTOBER 8
Real Dignity

Choose life and not death!

— 2 KINGS 18:32

His name was Nathan. He was severely brain-injured, and I couldn't help but notice the way his elderly parents doted over him. While Dad pushed him around the Joni and Friends' Family Retreat, Mom constantly had her hand on Nathan's arm. They were at his side, wiping his mouth, smoothing his hair, and taking him to every Bible study and snack-shop fellowship. Nathan couldn't speak, but that didn't stop his folks from introducing him to every attendee of the retreat.

As I watched this incredible threesome, I thought, *Many people would think Nathan would be better off dead than so severely disabled. They'd pity him ... his elderly parents too.* That's why the physician-assisted suicide laws that are cropping up in various states are so dangerous. It's bad enough that doctors can help people with terminal illnesses commit suicide. But now, the lines between a terminal illness and a disability like Nathan's are beginning to blur. That's bad news for people like him.

No one should feel they have to die to have dignity ... or to be relieved of pain or depression ... or to stop being a burden to their family or society. This is why it's so important for Christians to work to promote the gospel; it's a way of promoting a culture of life. Nathan's parents left our Family Retreat refreshed, believing God had a plan and purpose for their son's disability. *This* is what gives a person dignity!

Consider volunteering at a Joni and Friends' Family Retreat next year. You'll spread the love of Christ among people like Nathan, as well as lob a hand grenade into society's pity-the-poor-unfortunate mentality. You'll be obliterating fundamental fears about disability. You'll be reinforcing the God-honoring truth that people are *not* better off dead than disabled. *Thank you* for promoting a culture of life today. If he were able, Nathan would say the same.

Lord Jesus, thank you for being the Prince of Life, the Resurrection and the Life, and the Way, the Truth, and the Life.

༖

OCTOBER 9

One with Him

Holy Father, protect them … so that they may be one as
we are one.

—JOHN 17:11

Jesus wants his followers to be one in the same intimate, sweet
way that he and the Father experience oneness. Think of the
immense satisfaction and gladness the Father and Son experience in each
other. Think of their agreement and delight, how each rejoices in pleasing
the other. Jesus always deferred to the Father, always pointed to him, and
lifted him up. They have the same mind and share the same heart about
absolutely everything. Now ponder this: *we are destined to enjoy this same
intimacy with one another.*

The best of friendships are only embryonic on earth, snatching only
a few short years to mature. There's never enough time. Words can never
convey the overflow of our hearts. I experience this bittersweet sadness
with intimate friends. I love them so much that I want to pass through
them, to know them fully, and be one with them. Not to possess, but to
meld with them. I can't on earth. I am on the outside of their heart's door,
always wanting to get closer, even while relishing their company. My longings are eased knowing that in heaven I will "get in." In heaven we shall
experience the oneness that God intended all along.

> God wants you to get a head start on heaven by cultivating right
> now a deep and abiding oneness with your Christian friends.
> Romans 12:5 says, "Each member belongs to all the others."
> Ephesians 4:3–4 adds, "Make every effort to keep the unity of
> the Spirit through the bond of peace. There is one body and one
> Spirit." We already are one, and earth merely provides the green-
> house where our oneness begins to flower. Ask the Lord to show
> you how you can glorify him through the refinement of your
> relationships with your brothers and sisters in Christ.

*Father God, Lord Jesus Christ, show me how I can serve and glorify you more
completely through deepening my friendships with other Christians!*

ॐ

"Doorkeeping" Tasks

For a day in thy courts is better than a thousand. I had rather be a doorkeeper in the house of my God, than to dwell in the tents of wickedness.

—PSALM 84:10 KJV

Elsie runs a Christian home for young girls who have left behind lives of prostitution and drug dealing on the streets of Hollywood. Elsie walks the streets, shares the gospel, and leads these girls to Christ. If these new converts truly desire to change their lives and commit to new responsibilities, they have a place in Elsie's home. Pam is one such convert. Although a Christian with a sweet spirit, Pam bears scars from knife fights and heroin needles. Her arms are marred with tattoos. I sensed her joy and deep appreciation when she explained her role at the home. "I scrub the toilets and bathrooms," Pam beamed. "That's my job and I love it!" This young woman was so grateful to have structure in her life, safety in her surroundings, and an honest-to-goodness job of service in Christ's kingdom. For Pam, a day of ministry in Elsie's home was far better than a thousand days lived in the sordid pursuit of self-destructive pleasures.

I was struck by Pam's humble spirit toward her job. Her delight in cleaning toilets sprang from a keen awareness of her role in the body of Christ. Few believers reading this devotional book have a background like Pam's, but every day, each of us rolls our sleeves up to accomplish menial, basic tasks—changing oil at Jiffy Lube, changing ink cartridges in printers, or changing a diaper (perhaps on an elderly parent). Like Pam, when we consider these jobs as service to Christ, we discover the joy of being a "doorkeeper in the house of God." We experience 1 Corinthians 10:31, "Whether you eat or drink or whatever you do, do it all for the glory of God."

Lord God, I want to be a doorkeeper in your kingdom. I want to tackle the menial tasks of my day with an eye to your glory.

෴

The Price of Identifying

Since the children have flesh and blood, he too shared in
their humanity.

—HEBREWS 2:14

When we are hurting, if there is one thing that eases our pain or grief, it is this: we want someone to *understand*. We want somebody to really identify with us, to have some idea of what we're enduring.

It is certainly like that for me. I hate feeling alone and alienated in those dark times when my paralysis seems overwhelming. On my really rough days it helps to remember what the Bible tells us about Jesus identifying with us in our sufferings. It says that he was tested and tried in every way like us. That helps! When it comes to suffering, the Lord Jesus has gone ahead of us and has intimate, experiential, firsthand knowledge of the pain, the weight, the frustration, and the struggle. He appreciates. He understands. He connects.

But it works both ways! Not only does Christ identify with us in our suffering, we identify with him in *his* suffering. He identifies with us, and we identify with him. He appreciates all that it means to be human, and we appreciate all that his divine grace supplies. Through suffering, he participates in our humanity; through suffering, we participate in his divinity.

So why do we struggle so to escape our suffering? Why do we look so desperately for release? I suppose this is why I'm not earnestly seeking to be healed and raised up out of this wheelchair. I see this trial of mine as a window into the heart of Jesus. Suffering is a connecting point between my Savior and me. And when I see his great love on the cross, it gives me courage to take up my cross and follow him.

Do you want someone to understand what you are going through today? Turn to Jesus. When you do, you will better understand what he has gone through for you.

Lord Jesus, sometimes in my grief or suffering I just want to run away and hide. Help me, Savior, to run away to you and to hide in you.

☙

OCTOBER 12

A Triumphal Procession

But thanks be to God, who always leads us in triumphal procession in Christ and through us spreads everywhere the fragrance of the knowledge of him. For we are to God the aroma of Christ among those who are being saved and those who are perishing.

—2 CORINTHIANS 2:14–15

*S*ometimes large Christian conferences can get a little stuffy. It happens when Christians rehearse theology *at* one another rather than live it *with* one another. Like the time I was at a large conference at a fancy resort with thirty-six other disabled people. Our workshop group—the paralyzed, blind, deaf, and the lame—were enjoying fantastic times of worship and prayer. In contrast, the other groups seemed studious and quiet.

During the last session of the conference, our team of thirty-six happy, ragtag people had so much fun praising the Lord, our joy spilled out of the workshop room, flooded down the hallway, and splashed over the hotel mezzanine level. All thirty-six of us with white canes, walkers, crutches, and wheelchairs began conga-lining through the elegant hotel lobby, singing, "We are marching in the light of God, we are marching in the light of God." Before we knew it, onlookers dropped their briefcases and joined us in our procession of praise. We were an audiovisual of 2 Corinthians 2:14–15: "Thanks be to God, who always leads us in triumphal procession in Christ and through us spreads everywhere the fragrance of the knowledge of him."

Every time we exhibit joy in the face of suffering, we remind the Father of Jesus. The world can't see Jesus endure suffering with gladness because he's not here on earth. But you and I are. We can fill up in our flesh what is lacking in his afflictions (Colossians 1:24), and in so doing become that sweet fragrance, that perfume, that aroma of Christ to God. What a way to *live* theology . . . and encourage others to do the same.

Father, I want my life to remind you of your precious Son. Help me to live with that in mind today.

OCTOBER 13

When Pain Moves In

My back is filled with searing pain; there is no health in my body. I am feeble and utterly crushed; I groan in anguish of heart.... I wait for you, O Lord; you will answer, O Lord my God.

—PSALM 38:7–8, 15

The realization may have been years in the making, or it may have come in one swift, devastating stroke. But at last you know that pain—your pain, whatever it may be—is here to stay. Perhaps it is an illness, a rebellious child, a chronic muscle problem, the death of a loved one, or a severe disability in the family. Whatever form it takes, it's the common experience of all people. Human pain wears a thousand guises.

After four decades of permanent paralysis, I can attest that only a daily, hourly, even momentary placing of our throbbing into God's strong hands can protect us from the crippling ravages of fear. There are countless "fear nots" in Scripture, each one of them covering the whole spectrum of human experience. Every "fear not" can be embraced and impressed on our hearts and repeated in the presence of our adversary. Then we will press to our hearts this poem by Miss Margaret Clarkson, a woman who was bedridden for years with chronic pain:

> *Lord Jesus, King of pain,*
> *Thy subject I; Thy right it is to reign:*
> *Oh, hear my cry, and bid in me all longings cease;*
> *save for Thy holy will's increase.*
> *Thy right it is to reign o'er all Thine own;*
> *then, if Thy love send pain, find there Thy throne,*
> *and help me bear it unto Thee,*
> *who didst bear death and hell for me.*
> *Lord Jesus, King of pain, my heart's adored,*
> *teach me eternal gain is love's reward:*
> *in Thee I hide me; hold me still*
> *till pain work all Thy perfect will.*[1]

When I struggle with pain, dear Lord, teach me to wait on thee and remember the example of Jesus, the King of Pain.

☙

OCTOBER 14
The Lord's Right Hand

> In his right hand he held seven stars, and out of his mouth
> came a sharp double-edged sword. His face was like the sun
> shining in all its brilliance. When I saw him, I fell at his feet
> as though dead. Then he placed his right hand on me and
> said: "Do not be afraid."
>
> — REVELATION 1:16–17

Every year I plunge into the book of Revelation (daunting as it may be), asking God to show me something fresh about himself. Well, this year, he answered my prayer in the very first chapter.

Beginning in verse 12, the apostle John describes a stunning vision of the resurrected Christ. I stopped my reading here and tried hard to visualize the actual moment. I saw Jesus, the Ancient of Days, the First and the Last, standing there holding seven stars in his right hand. And not just any stars — these represent the seven angels of the seven churches. Now, here's what amazes me. When John is overcome by the vision (and who wouldn't be?) he falls at Jesus' feet, nearly frightened to death. The text says that the Lord takes his right hand — the hand still holding up the stars and the churches (he doesn't let them go or set them down) — and gently bends down to touch and comfort John.

This is astonishing! Our Savior stoops to give us his right hand, not the left, but his righteous right hand. This is the same hand that keeps stars and suns and planets spinning in motion, and the hand that upholds his church and its messengers all over the world.

Do you see it? Even though the Son of God is awesome in his glory and power, he does not think your needs — your hurts, your fears, your emotions — are beneath him. High and exalted as he now is, he still takes delight in bending low. His right hand may perform great and wondrous things beyond description, but he also reserves that same hand to gently touch you at your deepest point of need.

Lord, thank you for this picture of your majesty and your tenderness.

☙

OCTOBER 15

The Shiny, Sharp Tool

> But Zerubbabel, Jeshua and the rest of the heads of the
> families of Israel answered, "You have no part with us in
> building a temple to our God. We alone will build it for the
> Lord, the God of Israel...." Then the peoples around them
> set out to discourage the people of Judah and make them
> afraid to go on building. They hired counselors to work
> against them and frustrate their plans.
>
> —EZRA 4:3–5

Dorothy Williams was a British missionary who served in West
Africa during the 1930s. She was a nurse from Wales and spent
her time on the mission field training African nurses. This amazed her mission
board back home—Dorothy was very frail; they didn't expect her to
last but a year or two working in Africa! But with God's help, she refused to
be discouraged by her limitations. This inspired the young African nurses
under her charge who were often disheartened by their own poverty and
lack of resources.

One day a young nurse was carrying a tray of surgical instruments,
and Dorothy noticed a sad look in her student's eyes. "Oh, Mum, I am
feeling much afraid today," to which Dorothy replied, "Dearie, look at
these shiny instruments on your tray." The British missionary picked up
the pointiest one, then added, "The devil has a tray of instruments too, and
the shiniest and sharpest is his tool of discouragement—it's sharp because
he uses it so often." The student nurse smiled, blushed, and then went on
her way with fresh resolve.

Ezra 4:4 describes the devil's strategy against God's people. It is
"to discourage the people ... and make them afraid ... to work
against them and frustrate their plans." Do not be fearful, for the
Bible repeats 112 times, "Do not be afraid." And Dorothy would
add, "Don't be discouraged." You have your own shiny, sharp
tool: the Word of God (Hebrews 4:12). Keep it sharp and use it
often against your adversary!

God of all encouragement, thank you that I never have a reason to be afraid!

OCTOBER 16
What Do I Have?

I have learned to be content whatever the circumstances....
I have learned the secret of being content in any and every
situation.

—PHILIPPIANS 4:11–12

All I need, I already have." Do you believe that statement? It is one I have wrestled with in recent days.

What do I have? Well, I *don't* have use of my hands, legs, or the sense of touch to feel Ken's embrace. But I do have a voice, a wheelchair, and a husband who loves me. And that, according to the Lord, is all I need. For if there was anything more I needed, he would have given it to me. *Am I using what I have?* God never gives us a task without supplying the need. His command never comes without empowerment. *Am I prepared to lose what I have?* This is the litmus test of contentment. Despite Job's agony, he declared, "Though he slay me, yet will I hope in him" (Job 13:15). He was prepared to believe, even to the point of death. To be honest, when I think of the future, I sometimes get scared. I know my good health won't last forever. But my calling is not only to abandon my future wants, but to trust in God and hand over what I already possess. *Am I ready to receive what I do not have?* Well, my friend, it's not as though I'm looking to "enlarge my borders" like Jabez and expand my spiritual territory. I'd just be happy if God would simply make my *heart* larger, to receive more of his peace and joy.

All you need, you already have. What do you have? How long has it been since you did a thoughtful inventory of your possessions? The secret of contentment is wrapped up in simple gratitude for what God has already provided you.

Father, I'm so often like the ungrateful Israelites, who even complained about the sweet, nourishing "bread of angels" that appeared at their feet each morning. Forgive me for looking down on your "manna" in my life, and hankering after more exotic fare.

OCTOBER 17

A Prompting from the Spirit

I tell you, now is the time of God's favor, now is the day
of salvation.

—2 CORINTHIANS 6:2

Rush from work. Scarf dinner at Hamburger Hamlet with Judy.
Dash into van. Oh! Stop and pray before heading to church
to speak.

Pulling out, I noticed a woman leaving the restaurant with a baseball
cap over her scraggly hair. I sensed a powerful urge to invite her to church.
She needs to hear what I have to say. "Ridiculous," I thought. "What am I
supposed to do, God? Yell out, 'Hey, follow me to church!'?"

Heading out, I berated myself for not following through. "Lord,
next time I promise I'll obey your promptings!" Ten minutes later, Judy
screeched up behind me in the church parking lot—the woman in the
baseball cap right behind her! Apparently, after I'd left the restaurant, she
had asked Judy who I was. "Joni is speaking nearby," Judy replied. "Would
you like to go?"

In the parking lot I heard her story. "I have breast cancer. Two hours
ago I learned that it has spread to my brain. It's inoperable. I don't know
where to turn." My mouth dropped open. I now understood why the
Spirit had urged me to stop and invite her, a complete stranger, to hear
me speak.

That night as I talked about heaven and the gospel, Joyce and her
husband opened their hearts to Jesus. I shudder to think it all was nearly
lost because I let embarrassment override God's voice. That night, I learned
that *every prompting to share the gospel is a prompting from God.* Oh, that
we would be quick to obey ... for that one whom God loves may never
pass our way again.

This week, God's voice may whisper, "Make that call ... forgive
him of ... apologize for ... check on her." Don't brush it off.
Today is the day of salvation.

Lord, give me an undivided heart to obey. Open my eyes to see those around me
through your eyes. And may I be quick to say, "Here I am Lord ... send me!"

Take It by Force

From the days of John the Baptist until now, the kingdom of heaven has been forcefully advancing, and forceful men lay hold of it.

—MATTHEW 11:12

Although tall, blonde, and beautiful, my friend Shawna fell into depression during her days in college. She flirted with alcohol to ease the pain. One night in a stupor, she climbed into her car and drove up the exit ramp on the northbound 101 Freeway. After a horrible head-on collision and the death of a southbound driver, Shawna landed in prison. In a cell with prostitutes and drug pushers, this young woman who once professed faith in Christ, suddenly woke up. God pierced her heart. She gave her broken life to Christ. After that, Shawna became a light for the gospel to all her fellow inmates.

She wrote, "Joni, prison is hard. My crime was awful, and the situation here is overwhelming, but that doesn't mean God will deliver peace on a silver platter—I have to believe, fight, and 'take by force' that which is promised us in Scripture despite all the obstacles, including the sin in my own heart. I know the truth now. I know what's mine as a child of God, and I am taking back by force what I lost—I'm taking my rightful place in the body of Christ as more than a conqueror through Jesus who strengthens me."

The apostle Paul "fought the good fight" in prison (2 Timothy 4:7). Like him, Shawna is in the battle fray in jail. Her adversary is not about to relinquish his claim on her life. Yours, neither. The devil will not go down quietly without stirring up a struggle in your life. Scriptural promises are yours, but often you must push through spiritual opposition. Today, purpose to persevere, strive, press on, fight, believe, and lay hold of your place in the kingdom. Remember, the reign of Christ advances by force. And *you* are on the front lines.

Lord, I press on, determined today to advance your kingdom by grace and by force.

The Fear of the Lord

Do not let your heart envy sinners, but always be zealous
for the fear of the Lord.

—PROVERBS 23:17

*S*ometimes Christians fall into the habit of envying evildoers. But
stop for a moment and think of what awaits people who ignore or
challenge God. Such a person is no one to envy! Consider the sinner's state:
What could be more terrifying than having as your prosecutor, judge, jury,
then jailer a Father whose Son you murdered? Someone you've ignored and
offended all your days? Someone whose mercies you have inhaled over a
lifetime without a word of gratitude—like the spoiled kid on Christmas
morning tearing through his gifts with no thought about who gave them?
Someone whose reputation you only cared about when it served your purpose? Someone who can never be outwitted, sweet-talked, or negotiated
into accepting a plea bargain? Someone who cannot be talked into showing
mercy, because the time for mercy has passed?

Little wonder today's verse tells us to always be zealous for the fear of
the Lord. The eternal state of the believer is blessed beyond belief! That
we who at one time scorned God should now be showered with his favor
and pleasure! May we never take lightly our salvation or shrug the Father's
kind arm from our shoulders while caressing Eden's serpent coiled around
our hearts! May we *never* envy sinners, but always respect the fear of the
Lord.

Psalm 111:10 says, "The fear of the Lord is the beginning of
wisdom; all who follow his precepts have good understanding."
The truly wise Christian is the one who invests time in cultivat-
ing an awesome respect and a reverent fear of the Lord. Our sins
nailed the Father's Son to the tree; it is only by God's grace that
we are rescued.

*Holy Father, I bow in humble respect for the unspeakable mercy you have
shown me in that you have given me heaven rather than hell. Give me courage
to tell others about the good news of your grace!*

ॐ

OCTOBER 20

Clothed in Righteousness

> For all of you who were baptized into Christ have clothed
> yourselves with Christ.
>
> —GALATIANS 3:27

I often wish I could dress myself. I can't pull on a sweater, button
a jacket, or hike up a pair of slacks. This frustrating predicament
has driven me at times to God for help. And isn't it like the Lord to give
not only grace but insight? I was reading today's verse and decided to hunt
down other references to clothes. Isaiah 61:10 says, "I delight greatly in the
Lord ... for he has clothed me with garments of salvation and arrayed me
in a robe of righteousness." There's a similar reference in Revelation 19:8.
Even back at the garden of Eden, it was God who provided skins to clothe
Adam and Eve after the Fall.

Why does the Bible say that God clothes us when it speaks of our righteousness? Then it hit me. Garments of salvation and robes of righteousness are things we cannot provide for ourselves. God provides the salvation
and the righteousness. Yes, we can clothe ourselves with Christ as it says
in today's reading, but it's *his* righteousness, not ours. Righteousness is
something that God does to us and for us. In fact, when we try to impress
God by our own acts of righteousness, the Bible doesn't call them clothes,
but "filthy rags" (Isaiah 64:6). Can you imagine putting on a garment that
you sewed out of smelly, soiled rags? I now have a whole new perspective
on my "robe of righteousness" whenever someone dresses me!

The Lord Jesus Christ is our garment of praise, our robe of righteousness, our garment of salvation. Put him on today and delight
in all that he sacrificed to clothe you in something so precious, so
priceless ... *his* righteousness.

*Lord God, I want to head into this day clothed in your righteousness, not righ-
teous acts performed through my fleshly effort. I put you on today. Help me to
put off sin and self-centeredness and anything that detracts from your glory. You
are my robe of salvation, and I couldn't be dressed in a finer garment!*

ଙ୍ଚ

OCTOBER 21

A Weaned Child

My heart is not proud, O Lord, my eyes are not haughty;
I do not concern myself with great matters or things too
wonderful for me. But I have stilled and quieted my soul;
like a weaned child with its mother, like a weaned child is
my soul within me. O Israel, put your hope in the Lord
both now and forevermore.

—PSALM 131:1–3

My nephew Cody is his mommy's little boy. He's a toddler and still enjoys sitting in his mother's lap and sucking his thumb. He loves to snuggle. My sister-in-law, Carol, says that occasionally, her five-year-old son, Kyle, will want to snuggle too. It steals Carol's heart; she nearly cries. It's one thing for a toddler to want to be close to his mother; you'd expect that. But it's another thing for a child who has been weaned—who is independent—to want to cuddle. It's something you don't expect and that makes it all the more precious.

This is what Psalm 131 is all about. It's one thing to go to God because we want something, much like a baby might want his mother's breast. But it's another thing to go to God because you enjoy being close to him ... you want to be near. When that happens, Psalm 131 describes us as weaned children with still, calm souls. Not only does it please us to be close to God during those times ... it pleases God. It delights him when we desire to draw close to him, feel his embrace, and hear his heartbeat. What more could a child of God want!

When you approach God, would you consider yourself a weaned child as Psalm 131 describes? In what ways today can you show God that you desire to be close to him? Carve out time to recite a favorite hymn or Scripture song to the Lord. Thank him for little things, like the beauty outside your window, the crisp fall air and colorful leaves.

Lord Jesus, draw me close to you this day and quiet my soul. I love you, Lord Jesus, and want to be near.

Future Memories

"For I know the plans I have for you," declares the Lord, "plans to prosper you and not to harm you, plans to give you hope and a future."

—JEREMIAH 29:11

I love a good memory. The older I get, the more I enjoy them. Talking about favorite vacation spots, childhood jaunts, and my dear mother who has long since gone to heaven. My sweetest memories are those that inspire hope. I recall what it was like to peel an orange, pluck a guitar, hold a cold glass of Coke, and feel my fingers tap the cool ivory keys of a piano. Why do memories like these inspire hope? They remind me that one day I will have new hands. Fingers that work, feel, touch, pluck and pick, scrub and dig. I can't wait to reach for the glorified hand of Ken in heaven. It'll happen! Today's verse promises it.

My best memories give shape to that hopeful future. Your memories—especially if you've lost a loved one, or your health, or your ability to think clearly—should inspire hope in you too. For as wonderful as the world was when all those special remembrances occurred, as wonderful as it was when my hands worked, these things are only foreshadowings of more delightful, pleasurable experiences to come. Jesus is the one who makes our future bright. Jesus assures us that our best memories will one day blossom into a more joyous reality than we ever imagined. *He* is our hope. First Timothy 1:1 (KJV) speaks of "our Saviour, and Lord Jesus Christ, which is our hope." In Titus 2:13, he is called our "blessed hope."

What are the memories of things you've lost? How might those memories inspire hope in you today? How might these remembrances draw you closer to Jesus, the God of all hope? Grab hold of today's verse and so many other Scriptures that promise the world. Oh, not this world, but the world to come!

Lord of hope, thank you for the promise of hope and a future.

Therefore . . .

Your attitude should be the same as that of Christ Jesus: Who, being in very nature God, did not consider equality with God something to be grasped, but made himself nothing, taking the very nature of a servant, being made in human likeness. And being found in appearance as a man, he humbled himself and became obedient to death—even death on a cross! Therefore God exalted him to the highest place and gave him the name that is above every name.

—PHILIPPIANS 2:5–9

Notice the "therefore" in today's reading. Jesus was on a journey of humility—he was God, but he made himself nothing. He was a servant, and he was utterly obedient, even unto death. And not only an average death, but death on the cross. At each level, Jesus humbles himself more. And the point? "Your attitude should be the same as that of Christ Jesus." You may be a "somebody," but God would have you make yourself a "nobody" in the world's eyes. But does it end there?

No! *Therefore* God exalted Jesus . . . and God will exalt you to be a co-heir with Christ. "We are co-heirs of God and co-heirs with Christ, if indeed we share in his sufferings in order that we may also share in his glory" (Romans 8:17). It's like a math formula or an inverse proportion. The more we humble ourselves, the more God will raise us up not to just any old high place but as a co-heir seated alongside our Savior. Astounding! We suffer with Christ—that we may share in Christ's *highest glory.* Believers who face the greatest conflict, yet hold on to God with all their hearts—these are the ones who have the greatest confidence in sharing Christ's glory.

In what way can you humble yourself today? Is an apology owed to a friend or a family member? Is there an elderly person in your apartment unit you can help with a chore? Can you volunteer as a teacher's aid in the special needs class at church?

I humble myself today in the sight of you, oh Lord.

☙

OCTOBER 24

Hearts Fully Committed

For the eyes of the Lord range throughout the earth to strengthen those whose hearts are fully committed to him.

—2 CHRONICLES 16:9

It all began when I received a letter from a quadriplegic in China. He had recently come to Christ and now saw his disabled friends as his mission field. He couldn't use his hands, and so he needed a power wheelchair to get around. He wrote, asking for help. *Where am I going to get such a chair, and how will we get it to China?* At the same time, I received a late-night call from John, a friend in Ohio. His disabled wife had recently passed away. "We just purchased a new $20,000 power chair. My wife hardly used it. Think you can find someone who needs it?" Remembering the quadriplegic in China, I blurted, "Of course!" Then I wondered, *How are we going to get a hold of this wheelchair? There's crating and shipping and ...*

Before I could say another thing, John added, "We received some financial gifts at the funeral.... I'd love to cover the costs of sending this chair to whoever needs it, no matter how far away." I was breathless. I told John about the man in China. We rejoiced together, utterly amazed at how the eyes of the Lord were on a quadriplegic on the other side of the earth, and his eyes were on a widower in Ohio with a slightly used wheelchair too. And the Lord wanted to strengthen the hearts of both!

It happens in China. It happens in Ohio. And it can happen to you. Of all the places in the earth, God has his eyes on *you*. He desires to strengthen the hearts of those who are fully committed to him. How can you demonstrate to the Lord today that he has your undivided heart? Is there anything hindering you from being fully committed to Christ?

Dear Lord Jesus, I want my heart to be completely focused on you. Please look upon me today, and in your great mercy, strengthen my faith and give me an undivided heart!

ᕲᕳ

God's Wedding Ring

So Abraham called that place The Lord Will Provide.
—GENESIS 22:14

My wedding ring has seen a lot of abuse over the more than seventeen years I've been wearing it. Because I can't feel my fingers, it gets knocked around and battered. Recently, Ken looked at that scarred up ring and said, "Let me take this to the jewelers and get it fixed." So for seven days I was without my ring.

I came into the office the next day to face a desk piled high with work. Wedged between the piles was a little red box. A coworker explained that it was a gift from several Koreans, visiting while I was out of the office. I smiled but didn't take time to open the box. I was devoting all my energy to preparing for a message I had to give at a big banquet in Dallas, Texas, that weekend. Suddenly I looked down at my bare finger and thought, "Oh bother, I don't want to go on a trip without my wedding ring! What shall I do?"

A couple of days later, as I was about to leave for my trip, I was hurriedly tidying up my desk. I spotted the red box and sensed a strong urge to open it. My friend unwrapped it for me—and I sat stunned. There, glittering in the middle of velvet was a lovely gold ring with a dazzling diamond-like stone. A wedding ring! At just the right time, in a moment of need, a gift was opened, a ring was placed on my finger, and the wattage of God's glory blazed brightly.

How good the Lord is to provide for us at the moment of need. And just as he once provided Abraham with a ram for a sacrifice up on Mount Moriah, so he provided for you and me in our great need, with the sacrifice of the Lamb of God on Mount Calvary.

Heavenly Father, Abraham was right when he named that altar "The Lord Will Provide." In my Lord Jesus, you have provided so richly for me ... through the days of my life and into eternity.

☙

Eyes ... Blind or Open?

"You will not surely die," the serpent said to the woman. "For God knows that when you eat of it your eyes will be opened, and you will be like God, knowing good and evil."

—GENESIS 3:4–5

The devil will promise you one thing but always deliver something opposite. Take the promise he gave Eve that her eyes would be opened. Inferring that she was somehow blind to really great spiritual things, the devil promised he could open her eyes. He promised she would become spiritually wise, knowing the secrets of heaven, and even the loftiest thoughts of God himself. That was the promise. But it was a lie.

The exact opposite happened when Eve believed the devil. Second Corinthians 4:4–5 says, "The god of this age has blinded the minds of unbelievers, so that they cannot see the light of the gospel of the glory of Christ, who is the image of God." People who do not know Christ cannot see his light. The adversary has blinded them.

God is the only one who can spiritually open our eyes. Acts 9:17–18 records the amazing story of Saul's spiritual eye surgery: "Placing his hands on Saul, [Ananias] said, 'Brother Saul, the Lord—Jesus, who appeared to you on the road as you were coming here—has sent me so that you may see again and be filled with the Holy Spirit.' Immediately, something like scales fell from Saul's eyes, and he could see again."

What promise has the devil whispered to you? How has he enticed you to compromise what you believe about God? What command from the Bible has the adversary told you is not necessary? Don't listen to him. "I pray ... that the eyes of your heart may be enlightened in order that you may know the hope to which he has called you" (Ephesians 1:18–19).

Lord God, I choose to listen to you, not the devil. The devil is a liar, but your promises are true. Thank you that Jesus is "the Truth and the Life."

ஒ

What Impresses God

His pleasure is not in the strength of the horse, nor his delight in the legs of a man; the Lord delights in those who fear him, who put their hope in his unfailing love.

—PSALM 147:10–11

Have you ever thought about what impresses God? He is the awesome Creator of our vast, unimaginably wondrous universe, and he has named billions of stars in our galaxy, as though he were naming puppies or kittens. That's just *our* galaxy. Is not God impressed with these accomplishments? In a sense, he is; it says in Genesis that after he created the sun, moon, and stars, he paused and said that it was good. Yet even this is not what strikes him. What about other aspects of his creation? Do lions or tigers make a big impression? The grace and power of a horse? How about human beings, the epitome of all his creative works? After all, he put a lot of thought into developing bones and muscles, the mind, and our nervous systems. But not even these things truly impress God.

So what strikes him? Psalm 147 tells us. It's not kittens, puppies, horses, or even people; rather, the Lord takes pleasure in those who fear him, in those who place their hope in his unfailing love. He is moved when he sees us stand back in awesome respect and worship him. *This* is what touches his heart.

One of my favorite theologians, Dr. John Piper, says that the good news for those who enjoy God simply being God, is that *he* enjoys *them*. He delights in those who depend on his power, and he loves to be the God on the side of the needy. Today you can do—and be—someone who gives God pleasure. (Isn't that amazing? We can actually give Almighty God *pleasure*?!) You don't have to search the universe for a way to move the Almighty ... just place your hope in him.

Purify my heart, Lord God. Refine my motives, sanctify my intentions, and stir within me a deep desire to worship you with a happy heart.

ଡ୬

OCTOBER 28

No Divisions

> God has combined the members of the body and has given greater honor to the parts that lacked it, so that there should be no division in the body, but that its parts should have equal concern for each other
>
> —1 CORINTHIANS 12:24–25

Lon Solomon pastors a large church in Virginia. At one time, his church was lacking direction and vision. Factions and infighting were commonplace. Lon and his elder board were demoralized and at wit's end.

Just when Pastor Lon was considering stepping down, his wife gave birth to a little girl with multiple disabilities. Everyone was shocked and heartbroken. Suddenly, there was no time for divisions. Everyone put their differences aside, the church got focused, and members began rallying around Lon's family. This resulted in an outreach to more families like the pastor's. Today Lon's church is strong and growing and is building a national early-childhood intervention center to minister to parents of special needs children. What a poignant illustration of today's verses (vv. 24–26) for, "God has given greater honor to the parts [of the body] that lacked it, so that there should be no division in the body ... if one part suffers, every part suffers with it."

Galatians 5:19–21 warns, "The acts of the sinful nature are obvious: sexual immorality, impurity and debauchery; idolatry and witchcraft; hatred, *discord, jealousy*, fits of rage, *selfish ambition, dissensions, factions* and *envy*; drunkenness, orgies, and the like. I warn you, as I did before, that those who live like this will not inherit the kingdom of God" [italics mine]. Are there factions in your fellowship? Are you a part of one of them? Put things right *today*. A church that harbors factions cannot live long in God's kingdom.

Spirit of God, show me if I have a spirit of dissension or discord, jealousy or selfish ambition. I confess to you any factions that I may be a part of. Help me to promote unity in my church. Like you, I want no divisions in the body of Christ!

OCTOBER 29

Fighting Fire with Fire

So flee youthful passions and pursue righteousness, faith,
love, and peace, along with those who call on the Lord from
a pure heart.

—2 TIMOTHY 2:22 ESV

Our culture is a pushover when it comes to letting passions prevail.
Especially Christians. It's not at the banquet of the wicked where
we stuff ourselves on evil deeds; we've become voyeurs, sampling what
we've convinced ourselves is a safe, nibbling-at-an-arm's-length distance
from the table of the wicked. It's not pagans who have a problem with the
world, the flesh, and the devil; it's believers.

I'm included. My spiritual battleground is not over a torrid love affair
or the X-rated shelves in the video store. My paralysis prevents me from
reaching for common temptations. My fight of faith is played out on the
field of my thoughts. What my body can't have, my mind will shift into
overdrive to deliver. But daydreams and fantasies only frustrate, bringing
feelings of restlessness and dissatisfaction with the way things are.

The way you fight fire is with fire. To combat powerful passions, you
need something far more powerful in your arsenal. In fact, the fire of
enticing thoughts *must* be fought with the fire of the pleasures God offers.
If you try to fight lust with a bunch of threats and warnings alone, you're
going to fail. The fight of our faith against wrong thinking is the fight to
stay satisfied with God. The battle involves more than rejecting evil; it's
pursuing God. It all comes down to knowing Jesus better. When faith has
the upper hand in your heart, you are satisfied with Christ. He's enough.
He is sufficient. This is what Jesus means when he says, "He who believes
in me shall never thirst."

If you satisfy your thirst for joy and passion by the presence and
the promises of Christ, then the power of sin in your life is broken. That's *real* passion.

*Draw me deeper, Lord, into your presence, and draw me higher into your great
joy. Let the star-bright radiance of your life within me chase away the shadows
of lesser desires.*

෨

In Season ... and Out

Preach the word of God. Be persistent, whether the time is favorable or not.

—2 TIMOTHY 4:2 NLT

xhausted, Judy and I hoped for a minute or two of peace when we arrived at our airport gate. Glancing at the woman a few seats away from me, I noticed that her fingernails were very long ... and dark purple. She seemed absorbed in a thick book, *Real Ghosts ... and Other Haunted Places.*

I really didn't want to get involved, but breathing a quick prayer, I spoke to the ghost reader, "I see from the book you are reading that you must be on a spiritual journey." I was surprised by her response. "Why yes," she replied. She seemed interested in discussing spiritual things. Within minutes, I learned that her name was Jane and that she had left the Mormon Church. She seemed shy but grateful for the chance to talk about her questions. "The spirit world is very real," I said, motioning to her book. "But Jesus Christ is greater than any spirit of deception. And, Jane, this meeting is not by chance. God is concerned that your spiritual journey leads you to Christ." Suddenly, our gate agent called and we had to head for our flight. But not before I got Jane's address to send her follow-up material.

As our plane lifted off for home, the Spirit brought a convicting verse to mind: "Preach the Word; be prepared in season and out of season." I confess that I'd been hoping for some "time off," a few minutes of privacy and retreat, a chance to be "out of season." But in the next moment, God insisted that I be *in* season. My few moments of privacy were nothing compared to the eternal destiny of Jane's restless spirit.

Agree with God today that you will be alert to the Spirit's voice when he says, "Go start a conversation with that person."

Father, I know if I lack courage to speak, you are the Source. Help me to be willing to step into someone's world with the very word that could save them.

෨

The Real Halloween

> But the children of the kingdom shall be cast out into outer
> darkness: there shall be weeping and gnashing of teeth.
>
> —MATTHEW 8:12 KJV

It was the middle of October when an acquaintance passed away—his death was particularly sad because he never embraced Christ as his Savior. Later that month, I went to a friend's home for a Halloween party. Ghosts draped the front door, skeletons dangled from the porch, and plastic spiders wove their webs through the bushes. I stayed at the party only a minute. Witch and goblin costumes weren't cute or funny in light of my friend's demise.

Jesus likens the real Halloween to being "outside"—he described it as outer darkness. There is no shimmering dance of a candle in hell—no promising sunrises. No welcoming glow of Christmas lights through the windows. No sun-washed vistas of ocean or landscape. No lovely or pleasant faces. Eventually, no memory of what a smile ever looked like. In abject darkness, people can do nothing but think—remorse for missed opportunities and memories of friends and family on earth. There will be company in hell, but none of it pleasant. Jesus talked frequently about hell because he wanted to warn us of its real-life horrors. He's left us an example, but how often do we speak about hell, the *real* Halloween?

There's nothing cute about encouraging children to dress up like Harry Potter from the Hogwarts School of Wizardry. Yet October 31 *can* provide a powerful backdrop to an earnest discussion about hell. Jesus' descriptions of it are not figurative. Whenever biblical writers describe the afterlife, you sense they are straining for adequate words—the realities are *greater* than the figures. If hell is not literal fire, it's not because Jesus was exaggerating. It's because hell is worse.

Lord God, I confess I don't like to think—or speak—about hell. But your Son was constantly warning people about the kingdom of darkness. Give me courage to share the light of the gospel with my coworkers and neighbors!

November

NOVEMBER 1

The Devil's Real Weapon

> He forgave us all our sins, having canceled the written
> code, with its regulations, that was against us and that
> stood opposed to us; he took it away, nailing it to the cross.
> And having disarmed the powers and authorities, he made
> a public spectacle of them, triumphing over them by the
> cross.
>
> —COLOSSIANS 2:13–15

A guest on a Christian talk show was telling about an exorcism
he performed. He described frightening displays of demonic
power in the room of the demon-possessed individual. Furniture moved
and the demoniac howled horribly. Several friends heard the same program; they said, "You'll never find me getting into stuff like that!" Fear
gripped their hearts, making them think that demon-possession was the
worst of all evils.

But is it? The devil's most damning weapon is not demon possession,
or even the oppression he forces on weak Christians. His most damning weapon is not evil spirits, ghostly appearances, weird sounds, green
flashing lights, levitation, or chairs scooting around a room. The devil's
most powerful weapon is unforgiven sin. It is the *only* ammunition he has
against us. Sin that we try to shield from the Holy Spirit's scrutiny becomes
a weapon in the devil's hands. With it, he can accuse us, belittle us, strip us
of confidence and, finally, he can rob our joy and peace of mind.

Take heart from today's verse. Jesus took away our sin and nailed it to
the cross. Having done that, he disarmed the powers of darkness—even
making a public spectacle of demonic forces.

Your sin was nailed to the cross, but you nevertheless have the
responsibility of bringing every sin before the throne of God in
confession—God wants you to acknowledge your transgressions
and iniquities. When you do, those sins are no longer weapons
the devil can use to defeat and discourage you. What wrongdoing
can you acknowledge before God today?

*Lord Jesus, thank you for nailing my sin to the cross. Search my heart, Holy
Spirit, and reveal any transgression I need to turn from.*

☙

When in Pain

Remember your word to your servant, for you have given me hope. My comfort in my suffering is this: Your promise preserves my life.

—PSALM 119:49–50

My heart goes out to people who suffer with physical pain. Oh, how hope is needed! Michael wrote, "Two years ago, tumors were pinching my sciatic nerve, and I was forced to my knees in tears. I couldn't stand the pain anymore. I shut myself in a room, lay on the floor, and shouted to the Lord, 'I am not leaving here until you do something. Kill me, heal me, but don't let me suffer like this!!!' It was a little later, and then I heard a still small voice, 'Peace I leave with you; my peace I give you. I do not give to you as the world gives. Do not let your hearts be troubled and do not be afraid'" (John 14:27).

Michael was encouraged by John 14:27 because when God gives peace, he is imparting a sense of the presence of the Prince of Peace, his Son, Jesus. Michael can endure almost anything, as long as he knows Jesus is "laying on the floor" with him. And as Psalm 119:49 assures, God's comfort envelops Michael every time he remembers a promise like that from the Word.

I can identify. For me, when the pain doesn't go away, I'm quick to remember promises like John 14:27. My comfort in my suffering is this: the promise of God's presence *preserves* my life. Just knowing he's "with me," gives me peace, hope, and comfort. It sees me through.

Meditate on today's verse. Think of God's promises you know from Scripture. How do they preserve your life, especially when you are suffering physical or emotional pain?

Lord Jesus, thank you for giving me your peace when I hurt. Bless you for the hope and comfort I always find in you. Every single one of your promises preserves my life—I could not survive without your precious Word sustaining me every moment.

ᏸ

Focus in Service

> But Martha was distracted by all the preparations that had
> to be made.
>
> —LUKE 10:40

Everywhere you look in the Bible, the ministry of service is lauded. Even Jesus said, "The Son of Man did not come to be served, but to serve, and to give his life as a ransom for many" (Matthew 20:28). The heart of humility is found in sacrificial service, and great leaders are made great through their tireless aid on behalf of others. Martha was on the right path, even with her "*much* serving," as the King James Version puts it. We can never do enough in God's kingdom, and Martha is not to be chided for rolling up her sleeves to prepare a meal for such an honored guest as the Lord Jesus.

The problem was Martha's focus. Today's verse tells us she "was *distracted* by all the preparations." It wasn't that she was too busy or planned too many things on the menu; hustle and bustle and vigorous activity weren't the culprit. Martha simply allowed those things to distract her from her focus—the Savior. She lost joy in her labor, gladness in ministering to her Lord, and delight in exercising her gift for the good of the group. A complaining spirit took over as she focused on her sister, Mary, along with all the pots and pans!

It requires great spiritual discipline, as well as a consuming adoration for the Savior to *not* become encumbered by the hard work of energetic service. Great Christians of the past—and many in the present—have worn their fingers to the bone in the advancement of Christ's kingdom while maintaining a tranquil spirit and an unyielding focus on Christ. Don't shrink from serving the Lord today; just be certain to keep Jesus and his glory as your goal.

Lord Jesus, may your Spirit convict me if I become sidetracked by the demands of my Christian service, whether at home, work, or at my church. May you and your glory always be my focus.

NOVEMBER 4

God Repenting?

So the Lord relented.

—AMOS 7:3

God was so exasperated with the rebellion of Israel, that he was just about ready to devastate the nation's crops with a swarm of locusts. When you read the book of Amos, God appears to come across as impatient and hotheaded. But just when you hear the swarming in the distance, he seems to cave in and have a change of heart. How can this be? He's *God*. Did God relent in the sense of deciding one thing yesterday and another today? No, for he knows everything from the beginning, including how he would act in all future situations. Did he have a change of opinion? No, it's almost blasphemous to speak of God having an "opinion" about anything—it implies that the Lord makes judgment calls without knowing all the facts or that his preferences are mere tastes or whims with no reference to what is pure and right. So how can God "relent"?

As humans change, God shows them different "sides" of his character fitting with their behavior. His wrath shows itself when people rebel, his kindness when they turn again—kindness that he had all along. It may appear to *us* that he has repented—and the Bible may use that language so we can grasp the idea—but he has not repented or reconsidered. Professor A. A. Hodge said, "When [God] is said to ... be grieved, or to be jealous, it is only meant that he acts towards us as a man would when agitated by such passions."

God graciously condescends to accommodate himself to our finite and often one-dimensional world. He uses human metaphors so that we might understand as best as we can. How gracious of him! God is bending over backward to give expression to his great love and passion for you. No matter how many mistakes you make, God will never change his mind about your sonship.

Lord God, I thank you that you only "borrow" human metaphors. Thank you for never changing your mind about me.

A Wall of Hostility

> For [Christ] himself is our peace ... and has destroyed the
> barrier, the dividing wall of hostility, by abolishing in his
> flesh the law with its commandments and regulations ... to
> create in himself one new man out of the two, thus mak-
> ing peace, and in this one body to reconcile both of them
> to God through the cross, by which he put to death their
> hostility.
>
> —EPHESIANS 2:14–16

Bosnia is a splintered country, with towns separated by barbwire
and land mines. We had come to offer help to those disabled
from the war. A million-and-a-half Muslims live in Bosnia, and only five
hundred or so Christians. Ministry here was not going to be easy. At a
hospital, Muslim doctors were skeptical but quickly warmed as we dis-
cussed rehabilitation philosophy and laughed over the tactics of politicians.
Departing, we were invited to return with wheelchairs. Walls of hostility
were beginning to come down.

Dario was a young Bosnian-Croat soldier assigned as our driver. He
shared his experiences as a commander during the war ... three years of
killing, carnage, rape, and plunder. Land mines exploded at his feet by day
and in his head at night. His private horror was unspeakable. On the last
day, Dario tucked a letter in the side of my wheelchair. On the plane, I
unfolded it: "I asked a German missionary if God can forgive even so big
sins like mine. He answered that Jesus pays some 2,000 years ago ALL the
sins from this world. That night I fall upon my knees, begging from God
to forgive me and change my life. When I wake up next morning, I felt
very strange deep peace and joy inside me. I wanted to share that joy with
Jesus with others."

Christ is the only solution for the Jew and Gentile, the Muslim,
Arab, and Serb. And for you. What steps can you take to overcome any walls of hostility in your life?

*Lord, may I be an instrument of your peace, gracing every circumstance with
a spirit of unity ... for then your blessing will rest upon me.*

ᘓᘔ

May the Mind of Christ My Savior

Let this mind be in you, which was also in Christ Jesus.
— PHILIPPIANS 2:5 KJV

*I*f ever there was a hymn that served well as a prayer, it's "May the Mind of Christ My Savior." In the dead of night when I cannot sleep, when anxious thoughts erode my peace of mind and keep me awake, I recall the words to this hymn. When I feel far from God and unable to pray, I borrow each stanza of this hymn and make it my prayer. Before I know it, my heart is at rest.

> *May the mind of Christ my Savior live in me from day to day*
> *By his power and love controlling, all I do and say.*
> *May the word of God dwell richly in my heart from hour to hour;*
> *And may all who see I triumph, only in its power.*
> *May the peace of God my Father rule my life in every thing;*
> *That I may be calm to comfort sick and sorrowing.*
>
> *May his beauty rest upon me, as I seek the lost to win;*
> *And may they forget the channel, seeing only him.*
> *May the love of Jesus fill me, as the waters fill the sea;*
> *Him extolling, self abasing—this is victory.*
> *May I run the race before me, strong and brave to face the foe;*
> *Looking only unto Jesus as I onward go.*[1]

The next time you cannot find words to wrap around your circumstances, flip open the hymnal. One of the blessings of memorizing Scripture songs, praise choruses, or beautiful old hymns is that each stanza provides a ready resource of rich and fruitful fodder for prayer. For your prayer time today, choose a favorite hymn you know by heart ... borrow the words and turn them into your personal praise, confession, and intercession to the Father.

May the mind of you, my Savior, live in me from day to day ... by your power and love controlling, all I do and say.

NOVEMBER 7

Send Me

Then I heard the voice of the Lord saying, "Whom shall I send? And who will go for us?" And I said, "Here am I. Send me!"

—ISAIAH 6:8

I'm a big fan of world history. The other day I was reading about the conquests of Alexander the Great. This young general in his twenties led his Greek army across all of North Africa as well as present-day Iran. He marched his troops over the mountains in Afghanistan, forged into Uzbekistan, and even battled his way into India. Amazingly, he did it all in a relatively short time. Alexander the Great's reputation went so far ahead of him, that people in villages simply "got out of his way" when they heard he was coming. When asked how he conquered the known world so quickly, it is said he replied, "Time after time I acted without delay!"

It was the same way with Abraham—God told him to leave his country, and Abraham did so immediately (Genesis 12:4). Then there's Isaiah. When he heard the Lord calling, he jumped up and said happily, "Here am I. Send me!" Too often when we sense God calling us into action, we check and double-check the inward prompting until we've reasoned away the command. Sometimes we rationalize away the call, thinking we didn't quite hear God correctly.

Like Abraham, let's be willing to exchange the known present for the unknown future. When we sense the Spirit pushing us into action or urging us to obey God's command, let's exclaim, "I'm with you, Lord!" Perhaps we would respond more quickly if we understood the blessings that accompany simple obedience. These times call for drastic obedience and for breaking outside our comfort zones. If your get-up-and-go has got up and went, then go get it. Time and again, act without delay. You will end up conquering your world for Christ.

Lord God, I am a foot soldier in the army of Christ. When I hear you give a command today, I purpose to step out and follow you. Give me courage to do this.

NOVEMBER 8

Quality and Quantity

A thief is only there to steal and kill and destroy. I came so
they can have real and eternal life, more and better life than
they ever dreamed of.

—JOHN 10:10 THE MESSAGE

Have you ever wondered why Jesus launched his public ministry by turning water into wine at a wedding party? I once
heard my friend, Bible teacher Kay Arthur, describe this miracle as one of
highest quality *and* quantity. "That," she exclaimed, "is the way Jesus does
things."

Those six stone jars Jesus told the servants to fill with water were
huge, each containing thirty gallons. And those servants filled each jar to
the brim. Surely one—or possibly two—of those containers would have
been plenty. But Jesus did six. And quality? This wasn't the plain label stuff
they sell in a jug. The wine Jesus made was Gold Medallion—probably
ten grades above the best French vintage. The master of the banquet was
astounded after he tasted the wine that only moments before had been
common well water. *"You've saved the best for last!"* That's what Jesus chose
to do. He gave much better than anyone expected.

Quality. Quantity. Not either/or, but both/and. That's what he wants
to do in your life: "I have come that you may have life, and have it to the
full." The life he is talking about, of course, is his very own life, flowing
in and through you. This is life that spills over the brim. As the apostle
says, you are a participator in the divine nature. You can't get any better
than that!

The key to this life is in the counsel the Lord's mother gave to
the servants that day. Mary said, "Do whatever he tells you." Follow that advice, my friend, and be prepared for his abundant
life—lavish with quantity and radiant with quality.

*Great God of grace, you didn't have to fill my life to overflowing ... and yet you
did. You didn't have to share your character, your strength, and your joy with
me ... and yet you have.*

☙

The Interests of Others

> Do nothing out of selfish ambition or vain conceit, but in humility consider others better than yourselves. Each of you should look not only to your own interests, but also to the interests of others. Your attitude should be the same as that of Christ Jesus.
>
> —PHILIPPIANS 2:3–5

Christ is the ultimate example of selfless humility, and we are never more like him than when we demonstrate this godly quality. The quickest and surest path to humility is to follow the advice of today's verse—"Consider others better than yourself."

I have seen my husband, Ken, time and again look out for my interests before his own. It's not the big things like getting up at 3:00 a.m. to turn me; it's the little things. Making sure my wheelchair batteries get charged every night, that the coffee is prepared for the morning, and that I have plenty of soy milk for my special drink each day. When I notice that he's placed a full box of tissue on the counter, I smile. It's that quality of humble service I appreciate most about him (and it's what energizes my love and respect for him).

When does humility happen? When you get in a conversation and do more listening than talking. Humility is cultivated when you push others into the spotlight. When you put a lid on your itchiness to take credit for a positive outcome. When you work behind the scenes to ensure the success of the other, to promote their interests, or to make certain they get recognition for a project (especially if you contributed significantly to that project). A sure path to humility is to not quickly raise your hand in Bible class when you know the answer (especially if you've already given answers). Plan a way to "look out for the interests of others" today.

Jesus, thank you for reminding me to make my neighbor's case my own. Help me not to focus on humility but only on my friend and my Christian service to him.

Crowded to Christ

In this you greatly rejoice, though now for a little while you may have had to suffer grief in all kinds of trials. These have come so that your faith—of greater worth than gold, which perishes even though refined by fire—may be proved genuine and may result in praise, glory and honor when Jesus Christ is revealed.

—1 PETER 1:6–7

*S*oon after a wartime marriage, Margie Hamilton's husband was killed. Then a little later her baby was born with a cruel deformity. After about forty operations, poverty followed. Still she said, 'All this trouble has crowded me to Christ. It's simply mud around the gold.' "

I don't know who Margie Hamilton was, but this little story is as precious as gold. It's easy to run happily and willingly into God's arms, but I praise God for the trials and pain that literally *crowd* me to Christ. It's one reason I'm glad for this wheelchair. If I were on my feet, I'd either be checking out the sales or heading for the tennis court, coffee-klatching with too many girlfriends or flicking through daytime soaps. So I greatly rejoice in the "all kinds of trials" that accompany my wheelchair; it is headaches and hardships that thrust me flat on my face before the throne of grace where I find divine help (Hebrews 4:16). Sometimes the help God gives is an increased measure of faith—I am able to believe God more, as well as act on it. *This* is what makes faith golden!

I may feel weary and tired now, but one day the mud and dirt of my earthly heartaches will be washed away, revealing the gold of refined faith. Thank you for the reminder, Mrs. Hamilton.

What circumstances are crowding you to Christ right now? Can you "rejoice greatly" that these things force you to lean on your Lord? Recognize that the testing of your faith is more precious than refined gold.

Thank you, God, for crowding me into the arms of your Son, Jesus Christ. May I learn to see my troubles as merely "mud around the gold."

Remember Them!

When your people go to war against their enemies, wherever you send them, and when they pray to you toward this city you have chosen and the temple I have built for your Name, then hear from heaven their prayer and their plea, and uphold their cause.

—2 CHRONICLES 6:34–35

I was at an airport once, watching a handsome elderly man who wore a blue jacket with several medals pinned on the lapel. Atop his silver hair was his Veterans of Foreign Wars hat cocked at an angle. He was standing by a red carpet that led to the check-in counter, and he was helping young soldiers arriving at the airport from Iraq. To every young man or woman in uniform he would say, "Hi, there, soldier, where are you heading home today?" He then would take their ticket and direct them to the proper line. "Welcome home, friend," the veteran would say softly, then pat the soldier on the back as he went on his way. "Thanks, sir," the soldiers would often say, sometimes saluting.

That elderly veteran inspired me. That day when I passed through security and encountered several other soldiers, I decided to thank them and welcome them home too. I thought of the many soldiers who had become disabled like me. Their sacrifices mean something—their courage has opened paths for freedom and, with that, paths for the gospel.

Today's verse is part of the prayer Solomon offered before the Lord at the dedication of the new temple in Jerusalem. We can pray the same today. May God hear the pleas of our brave men and women in the Armed Forces, and may he uphold their cause. Today is Veteran's Day. Go out of your way today to encourage a veteran from a foreign war.

Father, I look forward to the day when the people will beat their spears into plowshares. Until then, may your will be accomplished as we fight the war against terrorism. Protect our brave soldiers and encourage their families this day.

☙

November 12

Caribbean Pines

Consider it pure joy, my brothers, whenever you face trials
of many kinds, because you know that the testing of your
faith develops perseverance. Perseverance must finish its
work so that you may be mature and complete, not lacking
anything.

—JAMES 1:2–4

The Tamiami Trail is a long, straight highway across Florida's south
Everglades. When I drove it with a friend, I was struck by the
wild, rugged, oddly beautiful pine trees dotting the landscape. My friend
called them Caribbean Pines; they are stunning against a South Florida
sunset. Unlike tall straight pines, they are wiry, contorted and primitive
looking. Caribbean Pines routinely withstand long periods of drought, fire,
and they hold their own against the fiercest of hurricanes. In fact, these
particular trees seem to love a rugged environment. They cannot tolerate
cultivation. When they are protected, planted in a yard and given water
and fertilizer, they often die. Experts can't pinpoint why Caribbean Pines
do best in the wild, but they know enough to warn landscapers against
using them in a decorative, cultivated setting.

We are like Caribbean Pines. Our souls usually don't thrive during
good times. Our hearts grow complacent, our need of God becomes less
urgent, our hope of heaven dims, and our prayer life often dries up. We
may be planted in a beautiful setting with our needs met and every resource
at our fingertips, but our soul shrivels. It seems we need an occasional blast
of storm or fiery trial, if our faith is to mature.

Are you in a hurricane? Experiencing a drought? A fiery trial? You
certainly don't need to ask God to bring on the hardships, but
you *can* ask Jesus for a closer walk with him in the midst of the
difficulties you *are* experiencing (I would guess there are plenty of
them). As you hold on to Jesus today, your soul will thrive both
in good times and bad.

*Lord Jesus, thank you for creating so many examples in nature that inspire us to
trust you. Help me to see lessons in your beautiful world around me.*

NOVEMBER 13

How'd It Go?

> They got up, drove him out of the town, and took him to
> the brow of the hill on which the town was built, in order
> to throw him down the cliff.
>
> —LUKE 4:29

When I return from a ministry trip, I'm often asked, "How'd it go?" Praying friends want to hear about the lives that were changed, as well as how my flight went. A writer named Steven James once pondered how the Lord would have replied: "If Jesus had returned to Capernaum from an afternoon of preaching and had one of the disciples asked him 'How'd it go?' he probably would have paused and answered, 'Let's see, most of the people didn't understand what I was talking about, and the ones who did called me demon-possessed and a drunk. Half of the people walked out in the middle of my sermon and then a bunch of folks picked up some rocks and tried to drive me out of town. Other than all of that, I'd say it went pretty well.' "[2]

Working in the kingdom has its ups and downs. Things do not often go the way we want, or even *pray.* Perhaps you serve on a deacons' board or a church outreach committee—if plans are going well, volunteers are signing up, and people are responding to Christ's invitation, be *thankful.* But if everything is falling apart, if helpers are few and pagans are throwing tomatoes, be *faithful.* The Father blessed Jesus' ministry, yet consider all the opposition he experienced, the doors he could barely crack open, and the people who signed up in the beginning, then found better things to do. If the Father is in it, the effort *will* be blessed.

> If in your ministry someone asks today, "How's it going?" and you're tempted to give a long litany of all that's gone askew and haywire—don't. Remember Jesus. If you are faithful to that which he's called you, it's going pretty well!

Lord God, may I remain faithful to that which you've called me, no matter what the opposition!

ॐ

And Can It Be?

> He turned to me and heard my cry. He lifted me out of the
> slimy pit, out of the mud and mire; he set my feet on a rock
> and gave me a firm place to stand.
>
> —PSALM 40:1–2

It was November 14, 1964, and I was in Natural Bridge, Virginia, for a Young Life weekend retreat. That morning as I sat on the hardwood floor of the camp meeting hall, I felt my heart open to the soul-stirring hymns they were singing. The words hit their mark. When the speaker asked if any of us wanted to embrace Christ as Savior, I shoved my hands into the pockets of my jeans and stood up. My heart wouldn't allow anything less.

Everything looked different during the meeting that night. Even the hymns. Now they really *meant* something. And none was more striking than "And Can It Be?" Especially the third verse: "Long my imprisoned soul lay fast / bound in sin and nature's night. / Thine eye diffused a quick'ning ray: / I woke — the dungeon flamed with light! / My chains fell off, my heart was free, / I rose, went forth, and followed Thee."

Twenty-four hours earlier, I would have given you a weird look had you told me my "soul lay imprisoned." Bound in sin? No way! But now with the Spirit of Christ residing in me, I knew beyond a shadow of a doubt I had left behind "nature's night." It truly felt as though chains had fallen off. And it was the Lord who had made me alive — absolutely nothing I had done.

Can you recall that moment when you understood the good news for the first time? Can you remember how it felt? There will be people all around you today who have yet to experience that life-transforming, destiny-changing moment. Pray for opportunities to simply tell them what happened to you when you stepped from darkness into light.

Lord, what a moment that was when I opened my heart and invited you inside. Thank you a million times over for drawing me to yourself!

NOVEMBER 15
The Shovel Spoon

> In his heart a man plans his course, but the Lord deter-
> mines his steps.
>
> —PROVERBS 16:9

The other day after work, my friend Judy and I decided to treat ourselves to dinner at a fancy restaurant. When we sat down, she looked in my handbag for my bent spoon. (I feed myself with a special spoon "crooked" at an angle so that it fits into my arm splint.) It wasn't there. Our first thought was to try to bend one of the restaurant spoons, but they were too heavy.

I groaned. I was *so* disappointed. Judy would have to feed me my dinner. Just then she piped up, "There's a kitchen store across the street. After we order, I'll see if they have an easy-to-bend spoon." I wasn't very hopeful.

When she returned, Judy held up the oddest-looking spoon I'd ever seen. It was small with a flattened edge, like a little shovel. After Judy bent it and slipped it into my arm splint—about the time our dinners arrived—I gave my new utensil a try. It was perfect. It worked much better than the old one. I never would have known such a spoon existed had I not lost my "favorite." I thought my old spoon was irreplaceable, but God had a better idea. I only discovered God's idea after I lost "what I couldn't live without."

Often we cannot envision the better "new thing" God has in mind until we lose the old. I had planned to sit glum-faced at the restaurant, be fed, and be disappointed. God, however, was determined to "turn my mourning into dancing," as well as teach me a lesson about his provision. Obviously our great God determines not only our steps, but sometimes ... how we eat dinner.

Lord God, the next time I lose a prized possession, help me not to be discouraged. Enable me to accept my loss and to anticipate the "better thing" you have in mind. And I realize that that "better thing" may well be my attitude.

☙

God's Got Reasons

But let all who take refuge in you be glad; let them ever sing for joy. Spread your protection over them, that those who love your name may rejoice in you.

—Psalm 5:11

In preparation to go to Africa last year, I was stuck with every kind of shot, from yellow fever to hepatitis. I even took malaria pills. When I left the doctor's office, I relaxed, knowing I was under God's protection. While overseas, I was careful with the food and water. I became doubly cautious when, midway through our trip, everyone else was running to the restroom. We all knew that if I became ill, it would be awful—I wouldn't be able to get up and run to a bathroom!

Mealtimes were challenges. To make things worse, I lost my special spoon again (remember yesterday's story?). My friend thought she had cleaned it off after breakfast and put it back in my handbag. But not so. I was demoralized, knowing someone would have to feed me. I asked the Lord to show me where that spoon was, but God was quiet on the subject. At the close of the trip during our last meal, I was struck by a crystal-clear thought: *Joni, you lost your spoon because it was contaminated. Had you used it, you would have become sick.* Immediately I shared this with my friends at the table. One of them gasped, "God just told me that same thing this very instant." God was no longer quiet on the subject. Neither was I. I kept praising him, happy to not only be healthy, but to be able to hear his reasons for hiding my spoon!

We say it all the time. We pray to the Lord, "Deliver us from evil." God answers that prayer with a resounding "I *will*," yet we cannot see the thousands of ways he does it every day.

Lord, I thank you for the countless times you will protect me today. I'll name a few right now...

෨

NOVEMBER 17

A Warm Spot

But I will sing of your strength, in the morning I will sing
of your love; for you are my fortress, my refuge in times of
trouble.

—PSALM 59:16

On an icy morning, it's natural to look for a warm spot. For you,
it may be a steaming hot shower. Or flicking on the space heater
in the bathroom while you brush your teeth. Perhaps you enjoy lighting
the fire in the living room to have devotions while snuggling on the couch
under an afghan. My sister Jay who lives on a farm, greets many a freezing
dawn by turning on the oven and standing by its open door with her hands
wrapped around a cup of tea.

Once I'm dressed and sitting up, once I've finished breakfast and am
ready to head out the door, my friends and I take an important pause. We
head for our favorite warm spot. It's the bedroom bay window seat, which
looks out over my backyard. A tree frames one side of the window while,
beyond the hedges, the distant Santa Susana Mountains complete the view.
With pillows on the window seat, it's one warm spot that invites you to
sit and linger.

In that cozy corner, the three of us always take time to open up our
hymnbook to harmonize together over some beautiful old hymn. "When
morning gilds the skies, / my heart awakening cries: / may Jesus Christ be
praised!" Whatever the hymn, and whatever the weather, this is our warm
spot. Safeguarding a quiet moment, admiring God's creation, and giving
God pleasure each morning with our song—it's something that warms not
only the body, but the soul.

Don't be in such a hurry with life that you rush past those warm,
quiet places where you have met with the Lord and enjoyed each
other's company. The peace and perspective that comes from
those few sweet moments will color the rest of your day.

*Thank you, Lord Jesus, that though you are the One holding the universe together,
you still treasure the time with me in some quiet corner of my morning.*

಄

God's Idea of Good

For the Lord God is a sun and shield; The Lord gives grace
and glory; no good thing does He withhold from those who
walk uprightly. O Lord of hosts, how blessed is the man
who trusts in You!

—PSALM 84:11–12 NASB

I learned those verses from Psalm 84 when I was a teenager. I rel-
ished the thought, *No good thing does he withhold....* The way
I figured it, I just needed to do my homework, finish my chores, keep
myself from spats with my sisters, be nice to Aunt Kitty, go to church, say
my prayers ... and ... and.... I assumed that if I kept my nose clean, God
would give me good grades, good friends, a good college to attend, and
good knees to last me through field hockey season. We think that if we
are obedient, God will give us financial blessings or trials that can be easily
managed. If we do our part, God will dole out the good. Won't he?

I've lived long enough in this wheelchair to know that sometimes our
idea of "good" is very different from God's. So how do we read Psalm 84? If
our walk is blameless, God will not withhold peace. He will not withhold
virtue or faith or courage. He will not withhold grace when we come to
him in need. We will be able to run spiritually and not grow weary; we'll
be able to walk in faith and not faint. He will not withhold opportunities
to sow his seed, to shine his light. He will not withhold patience or endurance or the favor of his nearness and sweetness. He will not withhold the
gift of heaven-sent joy. None of these things will he withhold from those
who walk uprightly.

Some of God's best gifts must be unwrapped in the darkness.
Think of your last major trial. What "good thing" did the Lord
slip into your hands in those difficult days?

*Lord, lift my gaze to see life from your perspective. Help me to understand—and
treasure—every good thing you send from heaven.*

༄

In Everything ... for Everything

> Sing and make music in your heart to the Lord, always giv-
> ing thanks to God the Father for everything, in the name
> of our Lord Jesus Christ.
>
> —EPHESIANS 5:19–20

Once I was discussing the subject of gratitude with a friend who had broken her ankle. For her, being on crutches wasn't fun. There were many appointments and travel plans she had to cancel. "I can accept a verse like 1 Thessalonians 5:18, 'Give thanks *in* all circumstances ...'" she sighed, looking at her leg cast, "but I don't think I could give thanks *for* this clunky thing."

Something about her comment troubled me. People are willing to thank God *in* the midst of their circumstances for his grace, comfort, and sustaining power. But they draw a line when it comes to the circumstances themselves. We segregate God from the suffering he allows, as though a broken ankle merely "happens," and God shows up after the fact. We don't thank God for the problem, just for finding him in it.

But today's verse underscores the supreme sovereignty of God over all suffering. The apostle Paul—who endured his share of tragedies—never considered his circumstances as tragic. He tells all believers we should be "always giving thanks to God the Father *for* everything, in the name of our Lord Jesus Christ" (italics mine).

> I give God thanks for my quadriplegia. It has become the strange friend that helps me know Jesus better. It is the shadowy com-panion that walks with me daily, pulling and pushing me into the arms of the Savior where I find grace and comfort. Your affliction falls well within the overarching decrees of God. It comes from his wise and kind hand, and for that, you can give thanks. In it and for it.

Sovereign God, today I bring my affliction and disappointment before your throne. I thank you in it ... for it ... and ultimately I thank you for bring-ing me through it. Please increase a spirit of gratitude that I might always be thankful.

NOVEMBER 20

Remember

He allowed no one to oppress [his anointed].... The Lord made his people very fruitful.... He brought out Israel, laden with silver and gold.... He spread out a cloud as a covering, and a fire to give light at night.... He ... satisfied them with the bread of heaven. He opened the rock and water gushed out.... He remembered his holy promise given to his servant Abraham.... Praise the Lord.

—PSALM 105:14, 24, 37, 39, 40–42, 45

Emotions are one of the least reliable yet influential forces in our lives. One day, we are hopeful; the next, we hate. Despair at one time; delight, the other. Emotions are the surging, restless tides that keep ebbing and flowing, drawing us up, then pushing us down.

The Psalms are a gyroscope, keeping moving things level, like a ship held steady in turbulent seas. This is why the Psalms often repeat the admonition to "*remember* the wonders he has done, his miracles and the judgments he pronounced" (Psalm 105:5).

My friend used to say, "Never doubt in the darkness what you once believed in the light." When hardship settles in, dark and brooding emotions can surge over us in a tide of doubt and fear. The only sure dike against a flood of glum feelings is to *remember*. We must recall sunnier times when we drove the pilings of God's goodness deep in our hearts. Happier times when we felt our moorings of trust hold ground. When we lived on his blessings, knew his favor, were grateful for his gifts, and felt the flesh and blood of his everlasting arms underneath us. This is what all forty-five verses of Psalm 105 call us to do.

While it is light, write down things you know to be true. When darkness comes, pull out your list and *remember* what your feelings have forgotten!

Lord, you are the Light of the World. Help me to remember your kindness and goodness to me when the horizon on my life begins to darken. Thank you for Psalm 105.

ᕲ

NOVEMBER 21

Sweeter Than the Day Before

Salvation is nearer now than when we first believed.

—ROMANS 13:11

It's true. My salvation is so much dearer, sweeter, and nearer to me than when I first believed as a teenager. I appreciated what Jesus had done when I was new in the faith, but I never considered him ... precious. Only old hymn writers spoke of him as precious! Now *I* am old. And Jesus is my true Friend, my Fortress when I am frightened, my Beloved when I give him praise, my Righteousness when I have sinned, the Shepherd who seeks me when I've gone astray.

How did Jesus become so precious to me? I look at it this way: *today is the first day of the rest of my salvation!* The Christian idea of salvation involves the past, present, and future. Ephesians 2:8 says, "By grace you *have been saved*, through faith" (italics mine). First Corinthians 1:18 explains that the gospel is the power of God "to us who *are being saved*" (italics mine). Romans 13:11 says, "*Salvation is nearer now* than when we first believed" (italics mine). We have been saved. We are being saved. And we will be saved. At every stage we are saved by the death of Christ. In the past, our sins were paid for by Christ on the cross. In the present, the death of Jesus secures the power of God's Spirit to save us from the domination of sin. And in the future, it will be the blood of Christ that saves us from the wrath of God and ushers us in to perfection and joy eternal.

As the old gospel song goes, "Every day with Jesus is sweeter than the day before!" Grasp the sweetness of all that the death of Christ purchased for you in the past, present, and future. Today, get actively engaged in your present salvation, and praise the Lord that you will be saved from the wrath to come.

Precious Jesus, I humbly bow before you, thanking you for all that your death on the cross purchased for me. I want to honor you by obeying you today.

&

NOVEMBER 22

In Weakness, Made Strong

He was crucified in weakness, yet he lives by God's power.
Likewise, we are weak in him, yet by God's power we will
live with him to serve you.

—2 CORINTHIANS 13:4

Back in 1967 missionary Doug Nichols fell ill while serving in India and had to spend several months in a dingy tuberculosis sanitarium. While there, he tried to give gospel tracts to the patients and doctors, but no one would accept them. Understandably, Doug became discouraged. He was sick, weak, lonely, and disappointed no one would listen to him.

One night around 2:00 a.m., Doug woke up coughing. Across the aisle, he noticed an old man trying to get out of bed and get to the bathroom. Too weak to stand, the man fell back into bed crying and exhausted. Although sick himself and as weak as he had ever been, Doug got out of bed and with a smile placed one arm under the patient's neck and the other under his legs. With all his strength he lifted the man and carried him down the hall to the filthy, smelly washroom. Then the missionary carried him back to his bed. The old man smiled and said the Indian word for "thanks."

What happened the next morning was amazing. One of the other patients woke Doug up with a steaming cup of tea, making motions that he wanted a gospel tract. Then other patients asked for the booklets. Even nurses and a doctor asked for one. Over the next few days, several patients and staff gave their lives to Christ. The whole situation changed because of Doug's sacrificial act in the middle of the night.

The power of the good news is released in your life when you allow your weaknesses to showcase the awesome might and love of our Savior. Plan on doing that today.

Father, I confess that I pass by opportunities to help others in the name of Jesus because I just don't want to get involved or don't want to get my hands dirty. Move me, by your Spirit, to reach beyond my own strength.

☙

Thanks but No Thanks

> Give thanks to the Lord, for he is good. His love endures forever.
>
> —PSALM 136:1

*T*learned early on in my disability how important it is to say, "Thank you." So many people do so many things *for* me or *to* me. Someone has to help me into bed, help me out of bed, pour the coffee, get me dressed, brush my hair, brush my teeth, blow my nose ... and I am quick to say, "Thank you for helping me." And I mean it. What's more, I say it a lot. The other day my friend Judy came into my office and asked if she could borrow ten dollars. I was busy and absentmindedly told her to take it out of my wallet, which she did. When I heard my purse snap shut, I automatically said in a cheery voice, "Thank you!" Judy gave me the strangest look and another friend standing nearby said, "What did you thank her for? She's the one who ought to thank you!" It was an odd thing for me to say, but I guess I'm just programmed to express my gratitude to people.

Oh, were it only that way with the Lord Jesus! If only we were better "programmed" to be more grateful to God, to lift prayers countless of times during a day, saying, "Thank you, Lord, for this ..." and "I am so grateful to you, Jesus, for that ..."

The entire Psalm 136 is a litany of thanks to God and a wonderful portion of Scripture to recite on Thanksgiving Day. Plan a special celebration of gratitude with the family after dinner — make copies of Psalm 136 and go around the table, each person reading the first part of a verse, then everyone exclaiming the second part in unison, "His love endures forever!"

I give thanks to you, dear Father, for choosing me to be a part of your eternal family. I give thanks to you, precious Jesus, for rescuing me out of the kingdom of darkness through your death and resurrection. And I give thanks to you, Holy Spirit, for applying to me and all the church, every benefit of salvation.

ᏀᎲ

NOVEMBER 24

She Did What She Could

"Leave her alone," said Jesus. "Why are you bothering her? She has done a beautiful thing to me.... She did what she could. She poured perfume on my body beforehand to prepare for my burial. I tell you the truth, wherever the gospel is preached throughout the world, what she has done will also be told, in memory of her."

—MARK 14:6, 8–9

When it comes to the Christian life, the stakes are high. Things like heaven, hell, and eternal reward. You and I get only one chance on earth to live a life pleasing to our Master. No starting over and no reincarnation. We have been given life and breath to prove our faith and demonstrate what we believe. It's why I sometimes wake up at night, wondering, *Am I doing this thing called "the Christian life" right? Am I making the most of the moments God gives me?*

I found a calming, reassuring answer the other day in Mark 14. When the woman poured expensive perfume on Jesus' head, some people at the banquet thought she did a stupid thing. But Jesus rebuked them harshly and said, "Leave her alone ... she did what she could do ... and I think it's beautiful." I identified with the woman. I feel like I have often done stupid things in my service to the Lord. *Am I doing this right? Is this pleasing to God?* But like the woman in Mark 14, I did what I could. And that's all God asks. We can only do what we are able to do; but inspired by the Spirit, it's always a *beautiful* thing in Jesus' sight.

"She did what she could—Mark 14" is written on the tombstone of Fanny Crosby, the blind composer of over four thousand hymns. Don't have anxious thoughts about the high stakes involved in Christian service. Just ask for the Spirit's help and do what you are able to do. Jesus will think it's beautiful.

Holy Spirit, empower me this day so I can do what I'm able to do in service to my Master.

❧

NOVEMBER 25

For a Song

> O Lord, open my lips, and my mouth will declare your
> praise.
>
> —PSALM 51:15

I have this game. Well ... really, it's more than a game. For me, it's serious fun. In my travels around the world, I will sometimes find myself in a great, cavernous hall or cathedral. If it's empty and no one is around, I will fill the place with music by singing one particular hymn—"Now Thank We All Our God"—as loud as I can. I think it's important to remind these great places of who designed them, who is King of their space, and that they are only great because God gave the ideas to the architects in the first place.

The first big, important place I remember singing this hymn was in a railway station at eleven o'clock at night with a few of my friends from high school choir. "Now thank we all our God, with heart and hands and voices, / Who wondrous things has done, in Whom this world rejoices...." The second place was in the Notre Dame Cathedral in Paris. Then there was the Church of the Holy Sepulcher in Jerusalem, and Westminster Abbey in London. "Who from our mothers' arms, has blessed us on our way, / With countless gifts of love, and still is ours today." And just last fall when I toured the Sydney Opera House, someone said, "Hey, Joni, want to sing something?" I could think of no better song to fill the wide-open spaces of that world-renowned, acoustically perfect concert hall than to sing my signature hymn. Everywhere you and I go, everywhere we visit, every place, every square foot of ground, is territory we can claim for a song for the God of all nations.

Try it! The next time you're in a big empty building—or even the great cathedral out-of-doors, declare his praise out loud ... in a psalm, a chorus, a hymn, or a shout!

Great God and Savior, may your praise be on my lips more and more as the days and weeks of this year slip by.

Genuine Contrition

He who conceals his sins does not prosper, but whoever confesses and renounces them finds mercy.

—PROVERBS 28:13

When Ken and I get into a disagreement, it doesn't often erupt into a torrent of nasty words. Rather, it leads to an icy silence. There have been evenings when he will hide behind his fishing magazine and I will find solace in a book. But the eerie quiet in our home never lasts beyond bedtime and "lights out." Before we say goodnight, one of us will finally break the frozen silence with a "Can we talk?" What a relief! Neither Ken nor I can bear it any longer. We are the perfect picture of Psalm 38:4, 18 where the psalmist confesses, "My guilt has overwhelmed me like a burden too heavy to bear.... I confess my iniquity; I am troubled by my sin."

It's during those times of confession and forgiveness that our love for each other always deepens. He will sit on the side of the bed and confess his selfishness.... I, in turn, will ask him to forgive me for my stiffnecked, stubborn pride. The most powerful moment then comes when we both acknowledge our sin before Almighty God. Psalm 51:4 reminds us, "Against you, you only, have [we] sinned and done what is evil in your sight." *That's* when the love of God overwhelms us with a renewed appreciation for his awesome mercy and majesty! And, finally, when Ken and I turn out the lights and kiss goodnight, we find *our* love for each other is renewed, as well.

Genuine contrition involves two things: honest confession and true repentance. Confession is an acknowledgment of personal wrongdoing before God and those we've injured. Repentance is a change of mind as well as changed behavior. Do you need to make personal amends with anyone today? Remember, genuine contrition will ultimately result in a deeper appreciation for God's mercy, for his love ... *and* an appreciation and love for the one we've hurt.

Jesus, give me a spirit of humility to approach today those I've shunned or injured.

Divine Distastes

And he could bear Israel's misery no longer.

—JUDGES 10:16

God has a strong distaste for suffering. His tenderness is aroused by human anguish. *But what about all of those natural disasters?* you wonder. *If he's so touched by suffering, why does he allow events like that terrible tsunami that swept across the shores of Asia in 2004? The suffering and loss of life were beyond comprehension.*

I can't begin to explain the unexplainable. But I know this: if Adam had never fallen, if the Creator could rewrite the story, he would have never allowed suffering out of the cage. "For he does not willingly bring affliction or grief to the children of men" (Lamentations 3:33). But sin *did* leave the cage, and consequently the curse fell. And ever since man's rebellion in the garden of Eden, our world has groaned under wars, floods, earthquakes, diseases, and much more. Like you, I shake my head at the mysterious plans and purposes of God. Tragedies like these either drive people away from God ... or draw them to him. Calamities either harden people's hearts ... or soften them as they run to the Lord for help and hope.

And beyond all else, I know this about my Father's heart: "God put his love on the line for us by offering his Son in sacrificial death while we were of no use whatever to him." And again, "God didn't hesitate to put everything on the line for us, embracing our condition and exposing himself to the worst by sending his own Son" (Romans 5:8; 8:32 The Message).

No one could ever accuse God of "sitting back and watching" while people suffer. How could anyone look at the cross and say anything like that?

Tragedies, great and small, happen every day in your community! How can you become God's hands and feet, his tender touch and his encouraging voice to those who suffer in your city—and in your world? Ask him to express his compassion toward hurting people through you.

Father, may I simply trust your heart, even today, when I can't trace your path.

NOVEMBER 28
Yours for a Song

Jehoshaphat appointed men to sing to the Lord and to praise him for the splendor of his holiness as they went out at the head of the army, saying: "Give thanks to the Lord, for his love endures forever." As they began to sing and praise, the Lord set ambushes against the men of Ammon and Moab and Mount Seir who were invading Judah, and they were defeated.

— 2 CHRONICLES 20:21 – 22

*P*eople facing fear have often resorted to song. But for God's people, it's not any old song. When King Jehoshaphat was confronted by a great force of allied armies, he had his people fast, pray, and then he assembled the troops ... placing the *choir* out in front of the army! As they marched, the singers lifted up praise to the beauty of God's holiness. And as they sang and praised the Lord, the opposition was thrown into confusion.

Songs and hymns of praise clear the air like nothing else. If you're in any kind of spiritual conflict, the best *defense* is to sing. It's a way of resisting the devil. Singing is also the best *offense*. Songs of praise will confuse the Enemy and send the devil's hoards hightailing. Amy Carmichael, missionary to India, wrote: "I truly believe Satan cannot endure the power of song and so slips out of the room ... when there is a hymn of praise. Prayer rises more easily, more spontaneously, after one has let those wings, words and music, carry one out of oneself into that upper air."

Victory over the Enemy can be yours for a song! Sing a hymn or a worship chorus as you march into your day or wrap up your evening. And if you can't sing, read one of David's praise psalms out loud. To begin and end the day with God's praise will do much to chase away dark thoughts, and open the door to peace.

Lord, you are worthy of endless praise. Help me to make room in my thoughts for the songs that declare your greatness and love before both men and angels.

NOVEMBER 29

Finishing Well

> For I am already being poured out like a drink offering, and the time has come for my departure. I have fought the good fight, I have finished the race, I have kept the faith.... Do your best to come to me quickly, for Demas, because he loved this world, has deserted me and has gone to Thessalonica. Crescens has gone to Galatia, and Titus to Dalmatia. Only Luke is with me.
>
> —2 TIMOTHY 4:6–7, 9–11

The book of Acts records the golden days of Paul's ministry. It seemed no effort for him to be wide awake at midnight in a jail cell, praying despite his biting chains and singing hymns at the top of his lungs. Scripture tells us the jail doors flew open wide and everyone's chains fell off. Prisoners applauded him and the jail keeper, saved instantly, invited him to his house. Things were looking up!

But if you look closer at his last epistle, you see a softer side. Paul was in jail again when he wrote 2 Timothy. But this time there was no miracle, no escape. Winter was approaching and Paul felt old and tired. Deserted by his friends, he struggled against sickness. His friend Trophimus was sick, yet Paul couldn't do a thing to heal his friend. He couldn't even heal himself!

Yet the old apostle didn't allow discouraging circumstances to get him down. Things were different than the "golden days of old," yet he hung on courageously to God.

Some days you feel life is on the upswing, other days it's flat. Sometimes you sense the miracle in your life, other times life seems very ordinary. Are you energized today to meet a challenge head-on? Or do you feel tired and trapped? Life's circumstances can make you feel like a yo-yo, but don't allow the "ups and downs" to get you down. Commit to God to fight the good fight ... finish the race ... keep the faith.

Give me strength, Lord, to finish well and not allow life's disappointments, along with age, aches, and pains to dampen my trust.

༄

NOVEMBER 30

The Real Tragedy

In him we were also chosen, having been predestined according to the plan of him who works out everything in conformity with the purpose of his will.

—EPHESIANS 1:11

It's one thing for God to deliberately let something awful happen for reasons we may not understand, but it would be another for God to wish he could have prevented it but have one hand tied behind his back. Either God rules, or Satan sets your life's agenda and God is limited to only reacting. In which case, the Almighty would become the devil's cleanup boy. Although God would manage to patch things up, your suffering would be meaningless. One Christian writer who believes that God has little to do with the specific circumstances that come your way expressed it like this: "In 1982 someone laced capsules of the pain reliever Tylenol with cyanide and then put them back on store shelves in Chicago. Seven people died after swallowing poisoned pills, the families of those seven people no doubt agonized trying to find some shred of meaning in why God or fate or luck had picked on their loved ones, of all the people in Chicago. We can concoct some answer and perhaps take some small comfort in it, but sadly, *there was no meaning in those deaths. Each was a bizarre, horrible coincidence, nothing more.* Therein lies the tragedy."[3]

No, the real tragedy is that any Christian would settle for such darkness with the light of the Bible shining so clearly. If God didn't control evil, the result would be evil uncontrolled. Our suffering has meaning because "his kingdom rules over all" (Psalm 103:19).

We may not grasp it this side of eternity, but if his kingdom rules over all—and it does—that includes the tiniest details of your life. Praise God that evil has a governor—our great and wise God.

Lord God, I am grateful that you purpose and permit. You give suffering meaning simply because you and you alone are in control!

༖

December

DECEMBER 1

Be of Good Cheer

> These things I have spoken unto you, that in me ye might
> have peace. In the world ye shall have tribulation: but be of
> good cheer; I have overcome the world.
>
> —JOHN 16:33 KJV

Whether it's alarming reports on the nightly news or the bruising pain I experience after a long day in my wheelchair, God tells me to be of good cheer. This world may trouble me, but I can take heart. Why? Christ has overcome the world. Our source of joy is always this: Christ is victorious over the world, the flesh, and the devil. *This* is the fountain of our happiness in this world.

Jesus Christ has done everything, first to last, that is involved in bringing you from death in sin to life in glory. Our Savior planned and achieved redemption, called and is keeping you, has justified and is sanctifying you, and will glorify you when you are finished with this world. What a cause for joy! Colossians 2:13–15 says, "When you were dead in your sins ... God made you alive with Christ. He forgave us all our sins, having canceled the written code, with its regulations, that was against us and that stood opposed to us; he took it away, nailing it to the cross. And having disarmed the powers and authorities, he made a public spectacle of them, triumphing over them by the cross." Did you hear that? Jesus triumphed, conquered, and overcame. He gives you power to do the same. *This* is why you can be joyful!

This world may get you down, you may be constantly wrestling against the devil, and your flesh may feel the crunch of older age, but be encouraged by 1 John 5:4, "For everyone born of God overcomes the world. This is the victory that has overcome the world, even our faith." Take a moment to enjoy all that Christ has done.

Stretch my faith, oh God, to be of good cheer in this dark world. Help me to remember that you are my one and only source of true joy.

ॐ

DECEMBER 2

In Jesus' Name

> I will do whatever you ask in my name.... You may ask me
> for anything in my name, and I will do it.
>
> —JOHN 14:13–14

These are profound words from the lips of Jesus. Let's examine his promise closely. "I will do whatever you ask *in my name*." What does that mean? Surely, more than saying, "In Jesus' name" at the end of a prayer just before saying the amen. To pray in the name of Jesus is to pray admitting that God hears me only because I'm the guest of his Son. It's to pray in the bold but respectful way that Jesus did while on earth.

To pray in Jesus' name is to ask God for the things Jesus taught us to. He summarizes them in the Lord's Prayer: spiritual things, eternal things. "May your kingdom spread.... May your plans be accomplished on this rebellious planet.... Forgive the way I've treated you.... Keep me from falling for the evil that allures me" (Matthew 6:9–13). Only one request in six deals with earthbound matters, and even there he taught us to pray, "Give us this day our daily bread" — not, "Bless the Dow Jones Average and please be with the NASDAQ in the next financial quarter."

Of course it's not *wrong* to pray beyond our basic needs — to pray that Susie will find her lost kitten, that none of us will catch colds this winter, and that Christmas will hurry up and get here. God loves to hear preschoolers pray. But Jesus also invites grown-ups to "cast all your anxiety on him," and "pray about everything" (1 Peter 5:7; Philippians 4:6 NLV). But do we really think Jesus gave us a blank check for an easy life? Do we imagine we can pray our way clear of trials? Think again, and "in your thinking be adults" (1 Corinthians 14:20).

Your name is precious, Jesus, and I want to come before you in prayer and ask for the sorts of things that are on your heart. Give me your ideas in prayer.

෨

Lifesaving Truth

As for you, you were dead in your transgressions and sins.

— EPHESIANS 2:1

I once heard Dr. R. C. Sproul paint a fascinating picture of how "dead in sin" we are. He described the unbeliever as lying "flat-dead-drowned" on the bottom of a pool under six feet of water. The man is so dead he can't possibly hear the "good news" that a lifesaver is on the way. He can't respond. God is the Lifesaver who must reach down, pull the unbeliever out of the water, and breathe life into his dead body. Once quickened, the man happily recognizes his Savior, reaches up, and embraces him. That's the gospel.

There are two different interpretations of the gospel. One makes salvation dependent on the work of God, the other on a work of man. One regards faith as part of God's gift of salvation, the other sees faith as man's own contribution to salvation. One gives all the glory of saving to God; the other divides the praise between God who "built the machinery" of salvation, and man who operated it by believing.

John 1:13 underscores that we are spiritually born "not of natural descent, nor of human decision or a husband's will, but born of God." We are made alive out of the deadness of our sin by the will of God, for Jesus said, "You did not choose me, but I chose you" (John 15:16).

As much as it goes against our natural grain, we are not masters of our own fate or captains of our own souls. Throughout this day, rehearse in your heart that (1) all men are sinners and cannot do anything to save themselves; (2) Jesus Christ, God's Son, is a perfect Savior for sinners, even the worst; and (3) the Father and the Son have promised that all who know themselves to be sinners and place their faith in Christ the Savior shall be received into favor and no one cast away.

Father, I praise you for quickening my spirit and giving me saving faith that I might recognize Jesus as my Savior!

DECEMBER 4
Deliver Us from Evil

And lead us not into temptation, but deliver us from the
evil one.

—MATTHEW 6:13

Some Christians don't think much about the devil. It's "I'm going
to heaven, he's going to hell, and so what's the beef?" They pooh-
pooh him, thinking, *I'm never going to be tempted to smoke or party to 2:00
a.m. That's beneath me.* The truth is, genuinely mature Christians are a *huge*
target for everything and anything—and they know it. They are aware of
the evil of which they are capable.

The closer you draw to the Lord, the greater your degree of humility.
And humility is your most powerful defense against temptation. Humility
recognizes that we are so weak, so inept and powerless in ourselves to stave
off the wiles of the devil, that we must cast ourselves at all times on God
for help. It is then in God's strength—and God's alone—that we become
victorious.

The answer to Question 127 in the Heidelberg Catechism states, "'And
lead us not into temptation, but deliver us from evil.' That is: since we are
so weak that we cannot stand by ourselves for one moment, and besides,
since our sworn enemies, the devil, the world, and our own sin, ceaselessly
assail us, be pleased to preserve and strengthen us through the power of the
Holy Spirit so that we may stand firm against them, and not be defeated in
this spiritual warfare, until at last we obtain complete victory."

When you ask God, "Lead me not into temptation," you are asking him to preserve and strengthen you through the Holy Spirit.
You are asking him for specific guidance as you tiptoe through
the minefield of the world, the flesh, and the devil. You are asking
him to cause you to stand firm against every trap and snare. You
are asking him for victory.

*Lord God, open my eyes today to the subtlety of the devil's strategy when I'm
tempted. Lord, I am weak! In humility, I ask you for strength and help!*

DECEMBER 5

Private Praise

Do those things that are pleasing in his sight.

— 1 JOHN 3:22 KJV

My friend Careen has been blessed with a beautiful voice. When we travel together, whether riding in the van or walking down the hotel hallways, we always harmonize on a hymn. On long trips together, when she has a "night off," she'll usually go back to her hotel room, put on a worship CD, sit on the edge of her bed with hands lifted high, and sing private praises to God for an hour or two. It's just her and her Lord. She absolutely *loves* delighting Jesus with her personal songs of worship offered behind closed doors. Although her musical gift is extraordinary, she'll probably never land a recording contract or be spotlighted on a big stage. But that's okay. Careen has the honor of singing command performances before the most prominent audience in the universe: Jesus Christ.

Careen reminds me of an alpine flower that blooms high in the mountains, far from the eyes of most people. No one but God ever sees those stunning flowers in mountain meadows; he has created them for his sole delight and enjoyment.

God delights in those who meet with him in personal worship. Before you turn the lights out tonight, find a quiet corner in your home and meet with God alone. Recite to him any Scriptures or inspirational poems you have memorized, or sing to him several of your favorite hymns or praise choruses. Enjoy the privilege that you have a private audience with the most important Person in heaven and on earth. Make it your ambition to be pleasing to him … far from the ears and eyes of others.

Lord, I thank you for blessing me with the talents I have. I'm not looking for a spotlight or a stage; I simply want to come before you by myself and bless you with my song. What a privilege and honor it is to consecrate my worship and focus on you and you alone.

ဆ

DECEMBER 6

Worth the Wait

> Wait for the Lord; be strong and take heart and wait for the Lord.
>
> —PSALM 27:14

Waiting for the Lord means putting his desires before our own, believing that he will meet our needs with generosity and love in his good time. But it's difficult sometimes. You may find yourself mightily tempted to do something on the spur of the moment. It may be an important decision. A desire you want gratified. A choice you don't feel like putting off. Or something you just want *now*. Your itchiness to have things your way has you ready to settle for something of lower quality or less value. It could be a special purchase. Or a choice in jobs. Or a relationship. It could be a crossroads in your ministry. And the truth is ... you really don't want to check in with the Lord, discern his mind and his desires, and wait for his green light.

Ah, but while we may regret a hasty decision a million times over, we will never regret waiting for the Lord. You can never go wrong as you wait and pray and still yourself in his presence, seeking his mind and heart. He'll end up giving you something better. He will give you wisdom as well as himself. And when you have apprehended him in a new, fresh way, it will all come clear. The choice will be obvious. The waiting will be worth it.

> What you might provide for yourself by your effort, in your wisdom, and in your timing cannot be compared to what God has for you in his plan and in his timing. Are you at a crossroads of decision in your life? Are you dealing with a desire that's pushing you to hurry? Fight the temptation to run ahead of him. Lay your desires and petitions at his feet, and wait for his peace (Philippians 4:6–7).

Father, how could I not trust you — you who gave your own Son so that I might become your child? I bow before you today, yielding up my hopes, dreams, desires. I know you will give me what is best.

☙

DECEMBER 7

The Bad News

What shall we conclude then? Are we any better? Not at all! . . . As it is written: "There is no one righteous, not even one; there is no one who understands, no one who seeks God. All have turned away, they have together become worthless; there is no one who does good, not even one. Their throats are open graves; their tongues practice deceit. . . . There is no fear of God before their eyes." . . . No one will be declared righteous in his sight by observing the law; rather, through the law we become conscious of sin. But now a righteousness from God, apart from law, has been made known. . . . This righteousness from God comes through faith in Jesus Christ to all who believe.

—ROMANS 3:9–13, 18, 20–22

*S*omeone once asked an evangelist, "Is it hard to get people saved?" He thought for a moment, then replied, "No, but it sure is hard to get them lost!" He's right. It's hard to get people to see how utterly lost they are. Yet before the good news can sound good, a person must hear the bad news—that "all have sinned and come short of the glory of God" (Romans 3:23).

No one is righteous before God—not even the person who tries to consistently do the right thing. It's impossible to *always* live the right way, to always keep the law. The purpose of the law is to show a person how far he misses the mark. But bad news never sounded so good . . . for then, we see the need for a Savior.

Christmas is upon us and our hearts are happy as we celebrate the arrival of Jesus, God's good news! But let's not forget the bad news—that a heart without Christ is full of deceit. Oh, how we need Jesus; and to live rightly is to live daily in his grace. It really *is* all about him!

Father, it's hard to understand how lost I really am without Jesus Christ. Help me to live completely and totally on the grace of Jesus today!

You're a Jewel!

The Lord their God will save them on that day as the flock
of his people. They will sparkle in his land like jewels in a
crown.

—ZECHARIAH 9:16

The Bible gives us this unusual detail about the construction of the
Lord's temple: "In building the temple, only blocks dressed at the
quarry were used, and no hammer, chisel or any other iron tool was heard
at the temple site while it was being built" (1 Kings 6:7). An unbelievable
amount of scraping, hammering, and chiseling had to be done on those
mighty rocks that were used in the construction. But it was all done out of
view and out of earshot of the temple site.

It's a little like the way God "dresses" us, fitting us for heaven. The
apostle Peter reminds us that you and I are living stones, and we are being
mined in the quarry of earth, a place of noise, chiseling, and clouds of
dust. God is using our sufferings and afflictions to hone and shape us so
we might fit perfectly into heaven's landscape, where there is "no hammer,
chisel or any other iron tool." Where there is no suffering. No tears, pain,
sorrow, or death. As polished stones, not only will we fit in heaven, we will
fit as glittering jewels in his crown. Soon we will enter the utter serenity of
heaven—a place of peace and quiet—and God will set us in his diadem
as sparkling and dazzling jewels.

God's quarry is still busy. He is active with his hammer and chisel
in your life, honing you and shaping you for a high and eternal
destiny. The shaping isn't always easy. How well I know! But take
heart today, friend. Bear a bit longer with the noise and hammering. Serve others while you wait. One day all of heaven will be in
awe over what the Master Jeweler has accomplished in your life.

*Lord, even though I am still in process, still being shaped and chiseled, I pray
that your radiant beauty would shine through my life today.*

෨

December 9

Adding Muscle to Our Prayers

When you received the word of God ... you accepted it not
as the word of men, but as it actually is, the word of God,
which is at work in you who believe.

—1 Thessalonians 2:13

Our flight was late, and the seats in the waiting area of gate D7
were full. Judy and Bunny stood beside me to pray—something
we often do before flights. Bunny knew I needed a prayer lift. She knew
I was pretty down over a number of things, including the sad news that a
certain foundation had just turned down our funding request for a project
to help disabled children.

Bunny reached for our hands and after praise and thanksgiving said,
"Lord, send forth the corn and the wine and the oil. Send forth the early
rains, the late rains, and produce a wonderful crop of blessings." Her voice
was soft, yet laced with confidence. I recognized in her prayer strains of
Joel 2:19.

As we prayed, I felt the presence of a fourth and fifth person. A husband and wife, who had crowded close—together they punctuated Bunny's
prayer with amens. When we finished, the husband folded a hundred-dollar
bill into Bunny's hand, and they rushed off to catch their flight. You know
... it didn't really surprise me. When Bunny prays, things happen. "Joni,"
she said, tucking the bill into my coat pocket, "this is the first fruits of
what God *will* supply." Bunny has learned how to pray using God's own
words, from the Bible. It's a way of using God's language when we talk to
him—his dialect, so to speak. The Bible tells us there are two things God
honors and exalts above all else: his name and his Word. Prayer that is
spiced with his Word is exalted prayer. And it is powerful.

As you read the Scriptures, underline portions that speak to your
heart, make them personal, and then pray them back to God.

*Father, teach me to pray in the way that pleases you and touches your great
heart.*

࿇

DECEMBER 10

God Impressions

Live wisely among those who are not Christians, and make the most of every opportunity. Let your conversation be gracious and effective so that you will have the right answer for everyone.

—COLOSSIANS 4:5–6 NLT

Have you ever played with Silly Putty — that pink, squeezable, rubbery clay that comes in a plastic egg? One of the most fun aspects of the putty is the way it will copy color pictures out of a magazine or comic book.

I often think of that property of Silly Putty when I want to leave what I call "God impressions" on people. You squeeze in a moment or stretch out the time to press your love of Christ up against someone. Maybe it's just a smile and a "God bless your day." Or returning a kindness with "Thanks for helping me, and the next time you're near a Bible, look up Hebrews 6:10 ... it's definitely you!" Often, I'm able to leave a God impression on someone by singing a hymn. People see me in this wheelchair, hear me singing praises to God, and wonder, *Where in the world does her joy come from? It has to be God.*

It's a way of pressing my life up against theirs for a brief moment so that when I peel away ... I've left a God impression on that person — however brief or fleeting it might have been. And once you encounter the Lord, you find yourself thirsty for something this world can't offer, hungry for something this world can't satisfy.

Busy as you may be, you still encounter many people during the course of your day. Press your love for Christ up against that friend down the street or that coworker or that woman you regularly greet at the cash register. When you do, you'll leave them with a God impression ... and make them thirsty for more.

Father, may the fragrance of your Son be upon my life, so that even entering or leaving a room, some lingering sense of his presence will draw hearts to seek you.

☙

December 11

Incline My Heart

Incline my heart unto thy testimonies, and not to covetousness.

—Psalm 119:36 KJV

I had wheeled up to my desk with every intention of spending a half hour or so in my Bible. Before I had a chance to open the Word, my eye glanced to a couple of clothing catalogs that had arrived in the mail that morning. A brightly colored blouse on the cover of one grabbed my attention. *Lord, I'll get to the Bible in a minute. . . . I just want to check out the price on that blouse!* Twenty minutes later, I still had my nose in the catalog. I'm ashamed to say, the Word had been pushed aside.

This is why I have learned to pray, "Lord, incline my heart unto thy testimonies, and not to covetousness." There are days when I don't even want to pick up the Bible. But I know if I succumb to a ho-hum attitude toward the Word of God, my spirit will shrivel, my faith will shrink, and my hope will become dull and dim. So I plead, "Lord, don't let me get away with this! Put the 'want to' in my heart ... persuade it ... bring it around ... predispose it ... please, *incline* my heart to your Word and don't let me covet anything in its place!"

Another prayer is from Psalm 86:11, "Give me an undivided heart, that I may fear your name." My heart is fragmented and often I find it going every which way. I'm thinking about laundry to pick up, a project to finish for Sunday school, a birthday card I need to put in the mail, and a "warning" light on my dashboard that needs to get checked out. So many things vie for my heart's undivided attention. So I ask God to gather the fragments, get my heart together, and *unite* it to fear his name.

Ask God to be the Lord of your heart. Give him full rein to rule it. Invite him to sit on the throne of your heart.

Lord Jesus, incline my heart to recognize and respond to your voice ... and your voice alone.

৯৯

Christmas: The Defeat of Darkness

Your eyes are too pure to look on evil; you cannot tolerate wrong.

—HABAKKUK 1:13

God permits all sorts of awful things to happen ... things he doesn't approve of. God allows others to do what he would never do. At the same time, he hates evil. Please don't think that God sits back and nods appreciatively at the peddling of drugs to ninth graders. He's not the one who fired the ovens of Auschwitz and other Nazi death camps. He does not smile when doctors slip up leaving children with crippling defects, or high school linebackers crush the neck of the opposing team's quarterback. He hates these things.

God is truly grieved over evil. He is grieved at how we've ruined the world and abused each other. This grief is partly why he gave the Ten Commandments: Don't murder, he says—I hate unjust killing. Don't commit adultery—I despise seeing families ripped apart. Don't steal—society will crumble if you do. God cannot tolerate wrong ...

This is why he sent Jesus to be born into our dark world. From the day of his birth, the forces of darkness began plotting against the Babe in the manger. Why? Because the adversary and his wicked hoards knew that this was the Child who would ultimately crush Satan and bring an end to wickedness in this world. God is so grieved over evil that he sent his only Son to die in order that righteousness and peace, truth and love would prevail ... in order that *we* might escape the clutches of hell and be welcomed into heaven. God permits what he hates to accomplish that which he loves.

Celebrate the defeat of darkness by singing this verse today from the Christmas carol, "Joy to the World": "No more let sins or sorrows grow, / nor thorns infest the ground; / He comes to make His blessings flow / far as the curse is found!"

"God rest ye merry gentlemen, let nothing you dismay, / remember Christ our Savior was born on Christmas Day; / to save us all from Satan's power when we were gone astray. / O tidings of comfort and joy!"

☙

We Band of Brothers

Therefore, my dear brothers, stand firm. Let nothing move
you. Always give yourselves fully to the work of the Lord,
because you know that your labor in the Lord is not in vain.

— 1 CORINTHIANS 15:58

My husband, Ken, would never think of going into spiritual
battle alone. When the adversary turns up the heat, Ken
reaches out to his brothers in Christ. He has invested years in prayer, Bible
study, and Scripture memorization with a handful of close friends, and he
knows these faithful believers will "cover his back" when the devil's bullets
start flying. He calls these men his "band of brothers."

The line comes from Shakespeare's account of Henry V at Agincourt.
King Henry's army had been reduced to a small band of tired and weary
men. They were outnumbered by the French five to one. But Henry rallies
them with these words of inspiration:

We few, we happy few, we band of brothers;
For he to-day that sheds his blood with me
Shall be my brother; be he ne'er so vile,
This day shall gentle his condition;
And gentlemen in England now-a-bed
Shall think themselves accurs'd they were not here,
And hold their manhoods cheap whiles any speaks
That fought with us ...

Henry took them to victory.

Encourage a weary believer today ... go into prayerful battle on
his or her behalf ... remind your brother or sister in Christ that
victory is assured. This tired and worn down friend needs your
help; the fight against the devil is dark and dangerous. We Christians may be few, but we are a happy few. We are fellow warriors
with each beside the other. And as long as we stand firm and let
nothing move us, our Captain shall take us to victory!

Lord, help me to take my friendships to a deeper level in which prayer, study,
confession of sin, honesty, transparency, and spiritual openness rally us to your
side. Make us aware of the spiritual warfare in which we are engaged today.

DECEMBER 14
Jacob's Ladder

And Jacob went out from Beersheba, and went toward
Haran. And he lighted upon a certain place, and tarried
there all night ... and lay down in that place to sleep. And
he dreamed, and behold a ladder set up on the earth, and
the top of it reached to heaven: and behold the angels of
God ascending and descending on it.

— GENESIS 28:10 – 12 KJV

When I was a girl in Sunday school, we used to sing a popular chorus: "We are climbing Jacob's ladder ... soldiers of the
cross." The song harkened to a story in the Bible about Jacob. He fell asleep
and had a wonderfully mysterious dream — Jacob saw a ladder stretching
from heaven to earth with angels ascending and descending on it. The ladder bridged the yawning gulf between man and God. When he woke up,
Jacob realized it was a divine visitation. It's interesting that Jacob's ladder
is never mentioned again in the Old Testament. That is, until Jesus arrives
on the scene ...

Right after he was baptized, Jesus begins proclaiming his true identity
and divine mission. He announced in John 1:51, "I tell you the truth, you
shall see heaven open, and the angels of God ascending and descending on
the Son of Man." Jesus was pointing to himself as Jacob's ladder! He had
come to close the distance, to bridge the gaping chasm between God and
man. Just as angels were ascending and descending on the ladder in Jacob's
dream, so they were ascending and descending *on* the Son of Man, glorifying the One who stretched the gulf between heaven and earth!

We live in a "spiritual" age with many people searching for meaning. As a believer in Jesus, you have the gospel ... you know the
Way ... you know the Truth: Jesus Christ is man's only "ladder"
to heaven. Look for opportunities today to help nonbelievers find
the first rung on that Ladder. Show them that Jesus has provided
a way — the only way — to heaven.

*Jesus, thank you for being my Bridge to God, my Stairway to the Father, my
Highway to heaven!*

ରୁ

Tidings of Comfort and Joy

> And suddenly there was with the angel a multitude of the
> heavenly host praising God and saying: "Glory to God in
> the highest, and on earth peace, goodwill toward men!"
>
> —Luke 2:13–14 NKJV

I heard the bells on Christmas day,
their old familiar carols play ...

Those "old familiar carols" are becoming harder and harder to find
these days. Our contemporary culture is waging an all-out war against the
true meaning of Christmas. I especially notice it in the music on the radio
and in the stores. I hear plenty of songs about silver bells, jingle bells, and
sleigh bells, but not a whisper about the church bells that announce the
birth of the Babe in the manger. Melodic, rich, and deep, the true carols of
Christmas have spoken for centuries to countless generations, informing
people of the real reason behind this holy day.

I used to sing carols by rote. In seasons past, I would put myself on
automatic pilot and just let the music carry me. At other times, the tune
became the focus, and I would work hard to get the harmony just right. I
admit there were many times when I would gloss over the power-packed
truth in each stanza. Not this year! No more am I taking Christmas carols
for granted. It's because they're becoming so *rare*. I am savoring and trea-
suring each line of every carol I gladly lift to the Lord.

I encourage you on this Christmas Day to do the same. Ask the
Spirit to quicken the words, illumine your understanding of the
Christmas text, and make your worship of him pure and purposeful as you sing. Pray that others around you will sing the same
way! If the media and the malls can bend over backwards to take
Christ out of Christmas, then we who believe in the Lord Jesus
can *more* than match their energy.

Lord, as our world and culture grow darker, I pray that we your people, with
happy hearts, in glad song, and in holy worship, would shine all the brighter
in contrast.

The More Necessary Thing

> For to me, to live is Christ and to die is gain. If I am to go
> on living in the body, this will mean fruitful labor for me.
> Yet what shall I choose? I do not know! I am torn between
> the two: I desire to depart and be with Christ, which is
> better by far; but it is more necessary for you that I remain
> in the body.
>
> —PHILIPPIANS 1:21–24

My grandmother lived to be a ripe old age — so old, in fact, that as a teenager I wondered why God allowed her to linger in so much suffering. Grandmother Landwehr had to leave her cherished home to come live with us. My sister Jay moved out of her bedroom and in with Kathy and me. My siblings and I ran errands, read to her, and took on extra chores so that my mother would be free to tend to all the extra needs. Grandmother Landwehr changed our family dynamics — my sisters and I became *a lot* less self-focused.

As my Lutheran grandmother lay in bed, she probably prayed, "I desire to depart and be with Christ, which is better by far." But it was more necessary for *us* — my sisters and me — that she remain. Sometimes our suffering is mostly for the benefit of others. God did not "take my grandmother home" before he had taught us how to serve selflessly.

Was God only "using" my grandmother's hardship for our benefit? Hardly! Paul explains later in verses 25 and 26, "Convinced of this, I know that I will remain, and I will continue with all of you for your progress and joy in the faith, so that through my being with you again your joy in Christ Jesus will overflow on account of me." God accomplished much in my life through Grandmom ... and it's all to *her* account.

Lord, help me to understand that my suffering can — and does — benefit others. Help me to see that's the more necessary thing.

ᚼ

DECEMBER 17

For Your *Comfort*

> For just as the sufferings of Christ flow over into our lives,
> so also through Christ our comfort overflows. If we are
> distressed, it is for your comfort and salvation; if we are
> comforted, it is for your comfort, which produces in you
> patient endurance of the same sufferings we suffer. And our
> hope for you is firm, because we know that just as you share
> in our sufferings, so also you share in our comfort.
>
> —2 CORINTHIANS 1:5–7

Yesterday we saw how your suffering can benefit *others*. My friend Karla was in and out of hospitals constantly before the Lord finally took her home, releasing her from a very painful disease. Her condition was made more bearable because she was able to witness the impact her testimony had on her nurses and doctors.

There was Christie, the transplant nurse, who was coolheaded in the operating room but coldhearted about spiritual things. Until she met Karla. There was Marge at the nurses' station who constantly whined about the hospital pay scale and new regulations. Her whining ceased when she became friends with Karla. Others going through menopause or midlife crises began to see their problems fade once they spent time with my friend. Eventually she became completely blind and unable to physically do anything. But Karla didn't have to worry about feeling useless or having no purpose for living. Through eyes of faith, she knew her suffering was for the comfort, encouragement, and salvation of others.

If you are distressed, it is for the comfort of others. If you are suffering, it has a bearing on the salvation of those who, even at a distance, witness your perseverance. God invites unbelievers (and a few vacillating believers) to examine the foundations of your faith. Your witness is as bold as the claims upon which your faith rests ... and this makes skeptical people think twice about God.

Father and God of all comfort, help me to live in the way of 2 Corinthians 1:5–7 today.

DECEMBER 18

Salvation Is of the Lord

Here I am! I stand at the door and knock. If anyone hears my voice and opens the door, I will come in and eat with him, and he with me.

— REVELATION 3:20

I love the painting of Jesus standing at a door with a lamp in one hand and gently knocking with the other. When you look closely, you see there is no doorknob. The suggestion is that the door can only be opened from the inside, placing the responsibility of salvation on the person behind the door. It's a lovely painting inspired by Revelation 3:20 (which is actually an invitation of fellowship to believers, not an invitation of salvation to unbelievers).

The true picture of salvation is that we are utterly dead in our sin. We are spiritually deaf and cannot even hear Jesus knocking. A more accurate picture might be Jesus rapping on the door, climbing over it, and then placing our lifeless hand on the inside doorknob! Jesus is the One who gives us the faith to believe (Romans 12:3). He unplugs our ears, opens our eyes, touches our hearts, illumines our thinking, and plants within us saving faith to say, "I believe!"

Ephesians 2:8 – 9 says ,"For it is by grace you have been saved, through faith — and this not from yourselves, it is the gift of God — not by works, so that no one can boast." The spiritual mind would rather speak of conversion in a way that makes plain whose work it really was: "Salvation belongs to our God," says Revelation 7:10.

Jesus says in John 6:44 that "no one can come to me unless the Father who sent me draws him." When we insist "I made up my mind to be a Christian," it indicates a will that believes it has played a major role in salvation. The truth is, "apart from [Jesus] you can do nothing" (John 15:5) — *not even secure* your own eternal life.

Lord, thank you that you awakened me out of complete spiritual lifelessness to give me the gift of salvation.

DECEMBER 19

Anna Leads the Way

> Bless the Lord, O my soul; and all that is within me, bless
> His holy name!
>
> —PSALM 103:1 NKJV

The gospel of Luke tells us that Anna was a prophetess and very old — eighty-four, in fact. Not only that, she was a widow. But not just any old widow. Scripture says that Anna never left the temple but worshiped day and night, fasting and praying. I wonder if people of her day looked askance at her. Perhaps some looked down on her as though she were the temple bag lady. Others surely saw her as a saint of the age. Luke's account tells how Mary and Joseph brought the baby Jesus into the temple, just eight days after his birth. He was there to be consecrated to the Lord, and it was an exciting day for the little family. But when they entered the temple, they had no idea what was about to happen.

The Bible says that Anna came right up to them, gave thanks to God, and spoke about the Child to everybody who was there. She told everyone, "Here's the redemption of Jerusalem." I love to picture it! This saintly old woman wrapped her wrinkled old hands around the infant Jesus, coddled him in her arms, and then pronounced a beautiful blessing upon him. Anna had a chance to celebrate the birthday of Jesus the way it ought to be celebrated.

This Christmas season, we can learn how to celebrate the season from observing Anna. Let's pattern our celebration and worship after what she did in the temple when she saw Jesus. Christmas is a time for pronouncing blessings and praise upon the Lord. It's time for giving thanks and for speaking about the Christ child to all who will listen. It's time to talk about redemption.

Lord, it's just like you to escort a humble, wrinkled old woman to the front of the line to lead us all! Thank you for the story of Anna, her devotion, and her willingness to boldly declare your name to all who would listen.

☙

The Most Unusual Christmas Gift

The Lord will indeed give what is good.

—PSALM 85:12

It was 1968, the Friday before Christmas. Still rather new to my wheelchair, I was feeling sad, frustrated, and tired of being paralyzed. But a few of my friends who dropped by that night knew the best tonic. Singing Christmas carols! On this particular evening, someone suggested we drive down to the old Pennsylvania Railway Station in Baltimore City because "the acoustics would be great!"

We weren't disappointed. The station was nearly empty at that late hour, and our last glorious note of our "Joy to the World" reverberated off the domed ceiling. Suddenly a uniformed guard appeared. "Okay, okay, enough of this now. This isn't a Christmas party or a church," he said gruffly. "You young people need to clear out. Get going! And *you*—" he pointed at me in my wheelchair, "you put that back where you found it! Get out of it, missy, right now!" This was too funny to be true. "Sir," I said, "I wish I *could* get out of it, but I can't. It's mine." The guard was getting angry. "Don't sass me. Now you put it back!"

"Honestly," I said, trying to keep a straight face, "I'm paralyzed. I really am!" All of a sudden he turned red. "Okay, okay, just get out of here. All of you!"

No, I didn't get healed in that Christmas of 1968. But in the eyes of a guard in the railway station, I was just a normal, energetic, mischievous teenager hanging out with her friends. And that, right then, in that place and time, was a wonderful gift.

God gives many, many gifts in the course of our lives that go unnoticed, unthanked, and unappreciated. How different would your days be if you started viewing *all* of the good things of life—down to those small but significant things that bring us pleasure—as love gifts from our Father?

Lord, forgive me for an ungrateful heart, so often blind to your kindnesses. Thank you for your sovereign love revealed even in the little details of my life.

Ꮐ᙮

Apples of Gold

A word aptly spoken is like apples of gold in settings of silver.

—PROVERBS 25:11

My friend Gail MacDonald makes a habit of collecting short sayings of encouragement from saints of old. Whether it's a quote from a missionary or a line from a time-honored hymn, Gail realizes that a few wise words go a long way in lifting one's vision and stretching one's faith. When an envelope arrives in the mail with her familiar handwriting, I know I'm about to be blessed.

Recently when I came home from a long, rigorous trip overseas, I spotted a letter from Gail on my kitchen table. I quickly opened it, read her words of greeting, and then enjoyed several lines from Amy Carmichael, the notable missionary: "There is no need to plead that the love of God shall fill our heart as though he were unwilling to fill us. He is willing as light is willing to flood a room that is opened to its brightness; willing as water is willing to flow into an emptied channel. Love is pressing round us on all sides like air. Cease to resist, and instantly love takes possession."[1]

Those were golden words to me, especially after a long trip. I was tired, weary, and in need of a fresh perspective. Proverbs 20:15 describes Gail perfectly, "Gold there is, and rubies in abundance, but lips that speak knowledge are a rare jewel."

Oh, if only we could more fully appreciate the power of the written word! A new year is just around the corner. Make a commitment to begin collecting favorite Christian verses and quotes. Build a file folder of these, and you'll have plenty of words of encouragement to share with thirsty, hungry sojourners in the months to come.

Lord Jesus, you are the Word and you only have the words of life. Help me to be a spokesperson through which your life-giving words can bless the hearts of friends and family today.

෨

DECEMBER 22

Lo, How a Rose E'er Blooming

A shoot will come up from the stump of Jesse; from his roots a Branch will bear fruit.

—ISAIAH 11:1

or Ken and me, our favorite Christmas tradition is dressing in our finest and treating the rest of the family to a fabulous holiday dinner at Lawry's Prime Rib in Beverly Hills. We drive slowly down Wilshire Boulevard, oohing and aahing at the store window displays, the lampposts trimmed with poinsettias, and the Beverly Wilshire Hotel with its huge Christmas tree out front. With "Silver Bells" echoing down the boulevard, the only thing missing is snow!

Lawry's is an elegant restaurant. Waiters in tuxedos. Crystal and linen, silver and candlelight. While dining, it's fun watching the carolers go from table to table, singing everyone's favorite carol. They're dressed Victorian style, like a quartet straight out of a Dickens novel. When the carolers stop by our table and I give my request, they always look surprised. No one else ever requests "Lo, How a Rose E'er Blooming." But it's no problem; the quartet loves this carol too. The harmony is mystifying and deeply moving. "Lo, how a rose e'er blooming / from tender stem hath sprung, / of Jesse's lineage coming, / as men of old have sung...."

By the time the carolers conclude the last note, I'm coming out of a dream, usually with tears streaming down my face. To me, this song has always been an invitation to know and experience more of what Christmas really means. It's an inkling, a hint, a whisper of an even greater celebration yet to be.

Soon and very soon, the Rose of Sharon will return and, with him, all the fragrance and joy of a longing fulfilled. This year when you ponder his coming as a babe in Bethlehem, remember also that he will come again, putting every wrong to right and reigning as Prince of Peace and King of Kings.

Lord Jesus, you were born a King, but so few acknowledged you. May I never, never be ashamed to own and honor you as my King.

All I Want for Christmas . . .

Delight yourself in the Lord and he will give you the desires
of your heart.

—PSALM 37:4

You've heard the song, "All I Want for Christmas Is My Two
Front Teeth"? When I got out of the hospital back in the late
'60s, my big holiday wish was, "Lord, all I want for Christmas is my body
back!" I'd see a star in the night sky and whisper, "Star light, star bright,
first star I see tonight . . . ," and I'd plead, "Jesus, I know that wishing on a
star and asking for Christmas gifts may not be very 'Christian,' but please
may I have back the use of my hands and legs?" I was spurred on by John
15:7 where Jesus said, "If you remain in me and my words remain in you,
ask whatever you wish, and it will be given you." It sounded like Jesus was
on my side.

I began to follow faithfully the condition of that promise from John
15:7. I sincerely abided in the Lord in prayer, as his Word abided in me. As
I did, I came across Acts 14:22 reminding me I would "go through many
hardships to enter the kingdom of God." Romans 8:17 explained that
I could be a co-heir with Christ if I shared in his sufferings. There were
scores of other verses just like these!

When Christmas rolled around years later, I knew I had received the
best present. I delighted myself in the Lord according to John 15:7, and he
granted me my desire—I had a deeper, more fulfilling relationship with
my wonderful Savior!

Of all the gifts you could receive at Christmas, what would be
your heart's desire? When you see a star appear, for what do you
privately hope? Jesus says that whatever you wish, it will be done
for you *if* his words fill your life and *if* you abide in him. When
you do that, you end up receiving far more than you could ever
hope for—you get the Bright and Morning Star himself.

*Lord Jesus, I want you to be the sole desire of my heart. Grant me this desire,
I pray.*

෬

"Come On In!"

I have told you this so that my joy may be in you and that your joy may be complete.

—JOHN 15:11

One of my favorite moments during the holidays is when the tree is decorated, the cookies are baked, the fire is crackling, music fills the house, and—ta-daaa—you throw open the front door and exclaim to your friends, "Come on in! *Now* the celebration can start!" Suddenly the place comes alive. Welcoming in friends through the front door is pure joy. And it's joy because it's *shared*. Christmas joy is always welcomed with a "Come on in!"

That's the beauty of it. It's appropriate that the Lord Jesus entered the inside of history from the outside. Joy came through a door when he crossed the threshold of this world. Oh, sure, the world had all the "trimmings" of religion, the right props, and all the tinsel, but it was only when Jesus stepped out of eternity into time that our world experienced genuine joy ... perhaps for the first time. Oswald Chambers wrote, "The Lord ... is God incarnate, God coming in to human flesh, coming into it from the outside. Our Lord's birth was an advent, a coming in. And ... so he must come into me from the outside, as well."

So there you are, all dressed up in your Christmas best, waiting to share it with someone special. Well, the room will stay empty (no matter how many people walk through your door) and a little lonely until you invite the Lord of Joy inside. It only happens when he is born in you, a "coming into" much like swinging open the front door to welcome a wonderful guest. Jesus stands outside the door of your holiday season. Don't miss out on the best part of Christmas. Open up and welcome him in.

Lord, as I open my heart to you, I have to admit ... the "house" is not in perfect order. In fact, there is much in disarray. Come in and set things right, Jesus. Come in, come to stay, and fill every corner with your radiant presence.

ॐ

Christmas Day

This will be a sign to you: You will find a baby wrapped in cloths and lying in a manger.

—LUKE 2:12

On Christmas Day of 1959 the snow fell in light, dry flakes, making our barn and springhouse almost disappear. I leaned on my elbow looking out the window of our farmhouse. Our home was busy with a pleasant bustling and Christmas carols from the kitchen radio drifted my way.

During the late afternoon, I pulled on my jacket and boots, stuffed a few carrots in my pockets, and hiked through the snow to the stable. I felt sorry for the horses. Our farmhouse was warm and light; their barn was dark and cold. I didn't want the animals to be left out. I opened the barn door and a blast of icy air whistled down the aisle. As I placed a carrot in one of the mangers, something resonated. I stared at the slats of wood nailed together. *Jesus was born in a wooden manger just like this!*

I knew enough of the Christmas story to understand that being in a stable on a cold evening, surrounded by animals, was somehow appropriate, especially knowing what Mary and Joseph went through and all that baby Jesus had to face. My small heart warmed to know that God chose to enter the world through a barn ... he felt at home in a stable. The Savior of the world was laid in a wooden manger. The Lord of the universe was *that* humble.

God sliced through the veil of time and space and slipped from the body of a woman onto the straw of a damp stable. Jesus entered the world in humility. Perhaps this is why Christmas moments that draw us closest to the Savior are usually the simple ones. Look for down-to-earth and uncomplicated ways to celebrate this glorious day. Jesus is born! God is with us! The Light of the World has entered our darkness!

Oh, joy! You came to earth to rescue sinful man—and I am so blessed to have had my eyes opened to the glorious gift of your salvation! Bless you, Lord Jesus!

The Second Advent

> Look, he is coming with the clouds, and every eye will see
> him, even those who pierced him; and all the peoples of the
> earth will mourn because of him. So shall it be! Amen.
>
> —REVELATION 1:7

The first coming of Jesus attracted very little attention, except for the small group of shepherds who hurried to the manger. Apart from them and a few animals, Jesus' entry into the world was quiet. Not many people noticed. Probably the next morning, it was just another ordinary day in Bethlehem. The Romans set up their census tables and inside the crowded inn—the inn from which Mary and Joseph were turned away—families headed downstairs for breakfast. A few travelers may have headed for the stable. Did any of them hear the cry of the newborn baby in the far stall? I doubt it.

What a contrast it will be when Jesus returns for his second advent—every single eye of every person on earth shall witness his arrival. Those who crucified God's Son will see and mourn. It won't be a quiet entry into the world. It will be loud and thunderous because of man's rejection of salvation. For those who have trusted in Christ's redemptive work, however, the days of mourning will be over, not just beginning. For the Christian, the prospect of Christ's return will be joyous, not terrifying.

Charles Wesley wrote, "Lo! He comes, with clouds descending, / once for our salvation slain; / thousand thousand saints attending, / swell the triumph of His train: / Alleluia! Alleluia! / God appears on earth to reign."[2] The first advent of Christ is inextricably linked to his second. Today, ponder a "Maranatha! Merry Christmas" and say, "Oh, come quickly, alleluia! Come, Lord, come!"

Lord Jesus, I am so grateful that I have a place in your eternal glory. I thank you for coming to earth two thousand years ago to rescue mankind. I look forward to your return. Enable me to share your good news this season with those who don't know you!

☙

Heartbroken Holiday

> Hear my prayer, O Lord, listen to my cry for help; be not
> deaf to my weeping.
>
> —PSALM 39:12

After gathering up torn ribbon and piles of ripped Christmas wrapping, the young mother carried trash out to a back alley. Their traditional Christmas morning had been cut short when her three children said, 'Hurry up, Mom! We have to be at Dad's by 10:00 this morning.' At the beep of his horn, all three raced out the door to repeat the gift-giving scene with their father, his new wife and her two children. They would be there all day and then leave on a trip for the holidays. Suddenly, both house and heart felt alone and desolate. She sat on the warm hearth of the fireplace allowing tears of emotion to run free. Then with an overwhelming sense of loneliness, she cried out to God."[3]

This scene will be repeated countless times during the Christmas season. While the holidays are a happy, festive time when we celebrate the arrival of Immanuel, "God with us," remember our Savior focused so often on the brokenhearted (Psalm 51:17). Jesus proclaimed, "He has sent me to bind up the brokenhearted" (Isaiah 61:1). What a comfort to widows and single parents during Christmas! Psalm 34:18 underscores again, "The Lord is close to the brokenhearted and saves those who are crushed in spirit."

> Loneliness is a state of sadness that comes from feeling cut off from others. If this describes you, join the psalmist in crying out to God, "Turn to me and be gracious to me, for I am lonely and afflicted" (Psalm 25:16). If you are not isolated, ask God to reveal someone in your neighborhood or church to whom you can show his love, compassion, support, and friendship. Find a person who is wounded and hurting. Give the best gift this season, be the hands, heart, and smile of Christ.

Lord, show me someone this Christmas to whom I can be a companion and helper. Reveal to me that one who is wounded. I wait for your answer...

☙

My Savior Leads Me ... and Francie

> The watchman opens the gate for him, and the sheep listen to his voice. He calls his own sheep by name and leads them out. When he has brought out all his own, he goes on ahead of them, and his sheep follow him because they know his voice.
>
> —JOHN 10:3–4

When we arrived in Beijing, China, we knew the next two weeks would be crowded with speaking engagements at churches and rehab clinics. To stave off weariness, my secretary, Francie, and I decided to memorize a hymn as we drove around town. Whenever we piled into our van, we'd start singing "All the Way My Savior Leads Me."

All the way my Savior leads me; What have I to ask beside?
Can I doubt His tender mercy, Who thru life has been my guide?
Heav'nly peace, divinest comfort, Here by faith in Him to dwell!
For I know what'er befall me, Jesus doeth all things well.

Morning, noon, and night, we lightened our journey by singing until we knew by heart all three verses, backward and forward! It helped us to remain focused on Jesus, our Shepherd; we were his sheep, following his lead. Francie and I laughingly labeled ourselves "The Singing Ewes." On the last day, as we drove to the airport, we sang of our wonderful Shepherd one more time—our Chinese pastor-host turned from the front seat and said, "You people back there sing *a lot*!"

James 5:13 says, "Is any one of you in trouble? He should pray. Is anyone happy? Let him sing songs of praise." The words to hymns make excellent prayers—especially when you find it hard to describe your feelings and concerns to God. Consider the last verse of Francie's and my hymn: "All the way my Savior leads me; / Oh, the fullness of His love! / Perfect rest to me is promised / In my Father's house above: / When my spirit, cloth'd immortal, / Wings its flight to realms of day, / This my song thru endless ages: / Jesus led me all the way."[4]

Oh faithful Shepherd, bless you for leading me all the way through this day. I trust you with your rod and staff, guiding and encouraging me all the way.

DECEMBER 29

Come Quickly

The Spirit and the bride say, "Come!" And let him who hears say, "Come!" Whoever is thirsty, let him come; and whoever wishes, let him take the free gift of the water of life.

— REVELATION 22:17

The writers of the New Testament were a bruised and battered bunch. This is why they wrote so much about heaven. The hope of heaven stoked fire in their bones, and their writings were laced with constant references to the second coming of Christ, to the time when their Savior would restore all things and complete the kingdom. Continually they were praying, "Maranatha! Come, Lord Jesus!" They were *eagerly* waiting for Jesus Christ to be revealed (1 Corinthians 1:7).

These suffering saints weren't trying to escape the painful realities of earth; they gladly endured their hardships. They were able to be happy because they knew heaven would reveal the earthshaking significance behind each tear and affliction. They likened themselves to soldiers poised on the watchtower, workers hoeing for the harvest, athletes straining toward the finish line, and virgins waiting wide-eyed in the night, lamps trimmed, hearts afire, and scanning the horizon for the arrival of their beloved. For New Testament writers who suffered — and suffered much — the world was no party. Rather, they were anticipating the coming Party.

We say "Come, Lord Jesus" with one breath, but in the next, we must always pray, "And until you return, give me grace to bear up under my hardship, peace to accept my life circumstances, and courage to tell others about Jesus Christ so that they too can joyously anticipate the Savior's return." So "strengthen the feeble hands, steady the knees that give way; say to those with fearful hearts, 'Be strong, do not fear; your God will come ... he will come to save you'" (Isaiah 35:3–4).

Lord Jesus, I recognize that this earth can never keep its promises; it can never satisfy. Help me to set my heart on heavenly glories above. Help me to make sure I invite others to that heavenly Party!

☙

December 30

Amen

Here is a trustworthy saying: If we died with him, we will also live with him; if we endure, we will also reign with him. If we disown him, he will also disown us; if we are faithless, he will remain faithful, for he cannot disown himself.

— 2 Timothy 2:11 – 13

What a great verse on which to end our year together. For here is a trustworthy saying: it really *is* all about Jesus. We've covered so many promises of God in the last 364 days, and every one of them — every single verse — points in some way to Jesus. He *is* the Word of Life (1 John 1:1). Revelation 22:13 frames Jesus with these timeless words, for the Savior himself proclaims, "I am the Alpha and the Omega, the First and the Last, the Beginning and the End."

What more can we say? Who else would we turn to? There is no one like Jesus. And I think I can hear you say "Amen!" to that. Second Corinthians 1:20 (KJV) says, "For all the promises of God in him are yea, and in him Amen, unto the glory of God by us." Amen signifies "so be it!" Every promise of God that has blessed you this year ultimately finds its conclusion in Christ. Every insight and bit of wisdom you've garnered, every obedience you've learned, every step higher into a more prayerful life, *all of it* finds its center — it's beginning and end — in Jesus Christ.

You are about to turn the corner into a brand new year. It is my prayer that the plans, decisions, and choices you make, the way you will spend your time, the thoughts you entertain and the company you keep, the manner in which you live before others, *all of it* will point to Jesus. May his glory go before you in the new year, friend!

Jesus Christ ... Son of God ... Lord of heaven and earth ... in the year to come, help me to showcase your glory and greatness in fresh new ways. And to this, I say, "Amen! So be it!"

A Final Word

> Then one of the elders said to me, "Do not weep! See, the Lion of the tribe of Judah, the Root of David, has triumphed."
>
> —REVELATION 5:5

On this last day of the year, we look to the future and wonder, *Could this be the year of Christ's return?* If so, you will experience for the first time what it feels like to be pure and blameless. You will see your loved one walk without a limp. You will witness the stroke survivor walk without his cane. You will know family members and friends as God intended them to be all along, their best attributes shining brightly, and their worst traits gone with the wind. No bruises on your daughter, free from the shackles of an abusive marriage. No confused thoughts, no mental illness, no Alzheimer's disease.

You will see what lessons the angels and demons learned about God from observing him at work in your mother, languishing in that nursing home. You will stand amazed at how your perseverance through pain sent repercussions rumbling through the lives of people you never knew were watching. You will be awestruck to see how your endurance through hardship forced others you hardly even knew to make tough decisions about God and suffering. Oh, what a wonderful day that will be!

If you faced deep heartache and disappointment this year, take encouragement that soon the Lamb who sits on the throne—the Lion of the tribe of Judah—will triumph. Every tear will be wiped away. Let this fact encourage you for the weeks and months ahead. Commit afresh and anew to deepen your walk with Jesus Christ in the new year, preserving for yourself "an inheritance that can never perish, spoil or fade—kept in heaven for you" (1 Peter 1:4).

Lord Jesus, I look forward to the day when you will receive endless praise and honor and glory for your amazing grace. Thank you for preserving my life through this year and impart fresh grace in my heart to honor and obey you in the year ahead.

NOTES

January

1. Dr. John Piper, "Brokenhearted Joy," *World Magazine* (December 13, 2003), 51.
2. Quote from David Swartz, pastor of Bethel Baptist Church, Roseville, Michigan.
3. Charles Wesley, "Let All Mortal Flesh Keep Silence" (public domain).
4. Dr. Vishal Mangalwadi, *The Book of the Millennium* (Book of the Millennium International, 1760 N. Gower Street, Hollywood, California 90028), 10.
5. Arthur Bennett, *The Valley of Vision ... A Collection of Puritan Prayers and Devotions* (Philadelphia: Banner of Truth Trust, 1997), preface.

February

1. C. S. Lewis, *Miracles* (New York: Macmillan, 1947), 165–66.

March

1. Quote by Dr. John Piper, pastor of Bethlehem Baptist Church, Minneapolis, Minn.
2. Thomas Merton, *The Word of the Cross*, 94.

April

1. This idea came from a daily devotional entitled "A Willing Captive," *Tabletalk* (Orlando, Fla.: Ligonier Ministries, October 1997), 20.
2. Dr. Dan Allender and Dr. Tremper Longman III, *The Cry of the Soul: How Our Emotions Reveal Our Deepest Questions About God* (Colorado Springs, Colo.: NavPress, 1994), 72.
3. This idea came from Don Kistler, "The Fruit of Assurance," *Tabletalk* (Orlando, Fla.: Ligonier Ministries, October 1997), 15.

4. Dr. John Piper, "Questions and Answers with Dr. John Piper," *Decision Magazine*, (Charlotte, April 2006), 23.

May

1. Paul David Tripp, "You Are Never Alone in the Dark" (Glenside, Pa.: Christian Counseling and Educational Foundation.), 5.
2. Charles Haddon Spurgeon, *Morning and Evening* (Grand Rapids, Mich.: Hendrickson, 1995), 65.
3. Dan Allender and Tremper Longman III, *The Cry of the Soul: How Our Emotions Reveal Our Deepest Questions About God* (Colorado Springs, Colo.: Navpress, 1994), 74.
4. Dan Allender, "Pastor's Pen," *The Epistle* (Calabasas, Calif.: Church in the Canyon, January 2006), 2.
5. C. S. Lewis, *The Weight of Glory* (Grand Rapids, Mich.: Eerdmans, 1949), 14.

June

1. Amy Carmichael, "Let Me Not Shrink," *Mountain Breezes* (Ft. Washington, Pa.: Christian Literature Crusade, 1999), 219.
2. Steve Muzio, "Pastor's Pen," *The Epistle* (Calabasas, Calif.: Church in the Canyon, January 2006), 2.
3. C. J. Mahaney, *Living the Cross Centered Life* (Sisters, Ore.: Multnomah, 2002), 132.

July

1. Steve Muzio, "The Pastor's Pen" *The Epistle* (Calabasas, Calif.: Church in the Canyon, September 2005).
2. Jonathan Edwards, *Heaven: A World of Love* (Amityville, N.Y.: Calvary Press, 1992), 26.

3. This idea came from Tim Stafford, *Knowing the Face of God* (Colorado Springs, Colo.: NavPress, 1996), 16.
4. John Bunyan, *The Acceptable Sacrifice: The Excellency of a Broken Heart,* in *The Works of John Bunyan,* vol. 1, (Philadelphia: Banner of Truth Trust, 1992), 720.
5. Søren Kierkegaard, *Upbuilding Discourses in Various Spirits* (Princeton: Princeton University Press, 1992), 104.
6. Fanny J. Crosby, "He Hideth My Soul."
7. Edythe Draper, *Draper's Book of Quotations for the Christian World* (Wheaton: Tyndale, 1992), 101.
8. Barnes' Notes, Electronic Database Copyright © 1997, 2003 by Biblesoft, Inc. All rights reserved.

August

1. Amy Carmichael, "Not in Vain," *Mountain Breezes* (Ft. Washington, Pa.: Christian Literature Crusade, 1999), 295.
2. Amy Carmichael, *Experience Worketh Hope* (Edinburgh: T. & T. Clark, 1944).

September

1. Frederick Lehman, "The Love of God," copyright ©1917, renewed 1945 by Nazarene Publishing House. Used by permission.

2. James Stockdale, "But Not Through Me," *The Trinity Forum: USA 2002,* viii–ix.
3. Edmund Burke, Irish orator, philosopher, and politician (1729–97).

October

1. E. Margaret Clarkson, "In Pain," *Grace Grows Best in Winter* (Grand Rapids, Mich.: Eerdmans), 54.

November

1. Kate B. Wilkinson, "May the Mind of Christ, My Savior."
2. This story is attributed to Steven James.
3. John Boykin, *Circumstances and the Role of God* (Grand Rapids, Mich.: Zondervan, 1986).

December

1. Amy Carmichael, *Draper's Book of Quotations for the Christian World* (Wheaton, Ill.: Tyndale 1992), 259.
2. Charles Wesley, "Lo! He Comes, with Clouds Descending."
3. June Hunt, "Loneliness ... How to Be Alone but Not Lonely," *Biblical Counseling Keys* (Dallas, Texas: 05.01/4), 1.
4. Fanny Crosby, "All the Way My Savior Leads Me."

INDEX

Old Testament

Genesis 1:28.................June 18
Genesis 3:4–5...............October 26
Genesis 15:6.................February 6
Genesis 15:9–10, 17 .....June 15
Genesis 22:14...............October 25
Genesis 22:17–18 ....January 4
Genesis 28:10–12 (KJV) December 14
Genesis 28:20–21 ....January 24
Genesis 45:7–8.............October 5
Genesis 50:20...............January 6
Exodus 8:32; 10:20.......March 12
Exodus 12:3, 5–6..........March 22
Exodus 15:11 (NASB) ...August 2
Leviticus 19:14.............April 24
Numbers 22:34.............March 20
Deuteronomy 6:5...........August 21
Deuteronomy 21:23.......April 2
Deuteronomy 33:27, 29. April 25
Deuteronomy 33:27.......October 4
Joshua 24:15................January 25
Judges 10:16 ....November 27
Judges 14:3–4 ....March 13
Judges 15:1 (KJV).........August 5
1 Kings 22:23 ....September 16
2 Kings 18:32 ....October 8
2 Chronicles 6:34–35....November 11
2 Chronicles 16:9.........October 24
2 Chronicles 20:21–22..November 28
Ezra 4:3–5...................October 15
Esther 6:1....................January 19
Job 1:8 ....September 27
Job 1:18–20, 22 ....August 13
Job 1:20–21 ....March 7
Job 3:23 ....June 17
Job 14:5 (TLB) ....August 15
Job 39:19–22 ....July 22
Psalm 1:1 ....March 18

Psalm 1:2–3 ....January 14
Psalm 5:3 ....October 1
Psalm 5:8 ....August 8
Psalm 5:11 ....July 26
Psalm 5:11 ....November 16
Psalm 12:6 ....May 17
Psalm 13:2–3 ....May 24
Psalm 16:11 (NKJV)......April 6
Psalm 16:11 ....May 23
Psalm 18:29 (NKJV)......July 15
Psalm 19:1 ....April 11
Psalm 25:16 ....April 30
Psalm 27:4–5 ....July 21
Psalm 27:5 ....February 23
Psalm 27:14 ....December 6
Psalm 31:21 ....June 7
Psalm 32:9 ....September 10
Psalm 34:3 (NKJV)........June 8
Psalm 34:3 ....July 3
Psalm 34:8 ....April 15
Psalm 37:4 ....December 23
Psalm 37:5–6 ....January 2
Psalm 37:18 (NKJV)......June 6
Psalm 38:7–8, 15 ....October 13
Psalm 38:15 ....May 2
Psalm 39:12 ....December 27
Psalm 40:1–2 ....November 14
Psalm 40:3 ....June 19
Psalm 42:8 ....February 22
Psalm 45:8 (NKJV)........May 18
Psalm 46:1 ....May 10
Psalm 51:2 (KJV)..........February 16
Psalm 51:15 ....November 25
Psalm 59:16 ....November 17
Psalm 61:4 ....February 26
Psalm 63:7 (NASB).......January 15
Psalm 63:7 (NASB).......February 27
Psalm 68:20 ....July 29

Psalm 72:19 (NKJV)......September 2
Psalm 73:25–26 ....July 23
Psalm 77:7–9 ....March 14
Psalm 84:5–6 ....January 26
Psalm 84:10 (KJV) ....October 10
Psalm 84:11–12 (NASB) November 18
Psalm 85:12 ....December 20
Psalm 86:17 ....May 4
Psalm 88:6–7, 13–14 ...September 1
Psalm 97:7 ....January 30
Psalm 103:1 (NKJV)......December 19
Psalm 103:1–5 ....July 28
Psalm 103:15–16 (KJV) May 14
Psalm 105:14, 24, 37, 39,
   40–42, 45 ....November 20
Psalm 119:9–10 ....April 17
Psalm 119:35 ....September 20
Psalm 119:36 (KJV).......December 11
Psalm 119:49–50 ....November 2
Psalm 131:1–3 ....October 21
Psalm 136:1 ....November 23
Psalm 139:23–24 ....March 19
Psalm 141:8 ....July 1
Psalm 147:10–11 ....October 27
Proverbs 10:5 ....August 31
Proverbs 12:18 ....May 20
Proverbs 16:4 ....September 24
Proverbs 16:9 ....November 13
Proverbs 18:10 ....May 30
Proverbs 18:16 ....September 15
Proverbs 19:21 ....September 14
Proverbs 20:29 ....March 30
Proverbs 20:30 ....August 4
Proverbs 23:17 ....October 19
Proverbs 25:2 ....February 19
Proverbs 25:11 ....December 21
Proverbs 28:13 ....November 26
Ecclesiastes 3:1, 4 ....July 16
Ecclesiastes 3:14–15 ......September 28
Ecclesiastes 7:10–12 ......March 11
Song of Songs 2:1 ....June 9
Isaiah 6:8......................November 7
Isaiah 11:1....................December 22
Isaiah 30:18...................January 16
Isaiah 30:21...................June 5
Isaiah 30:33...................July 25

Isaiah 37:17...................May 1
Isaiah 43:1–3.................January 21
Isaiah 43:6–7.................August 3
Isaiah 45:3.....................June 2
Isaiah 50:7.....................April 22
Isaiah 53:3 (NASB)........August 27
Isaiah 53:4.....................August 29
Isaiah 53:5.....................August 28
Isaiah 54:1.....................May 6
Isaiah 55:4–6 (NLT) .....May 7
Isaiah 55:9–11 ....March 15
Isaiah 58:2–3, 6–7 ....February 21
Isaiah 58:6–7.................March 5
Isaiah 58:7–8 (TLB)......April 12
Isaiah 59:15–16 ....August 9
Isaiah 64:6.....................August 14
Isaiah 66:2.....................January 11
Jeremiah 1:5...................October 7
Jeremiah 5:22.................July 17
Jeremiah 12:5 (NASB) ...January 5
Jeremiah 29:11...............October 22
Jeremiah 31:3.................February 15
Jeremiah 31:31–33........June 16
Lamentations 3:32–33 ..July 6
Ezekiel 22:30 ....September 12
Ezekiel 43:2 ....January 12
Daniel 2:22 ....February 9
Hosea 2:6–7...................June 4
Hosea 11:2–4.................September 22
Amos 7:3........................November 4
Habakkuk 1:13 ....December 12
Habakkuk 2:20 ....January 13
Habakkuk 3:17–18 ....August 10
Haggai 1:5–7 ....May 22
Zechariah 9:16...............December 8
Zechariah 13:7 ....April 9

New Testament

Matthew 3:16–4:3 ....June 24
Matthew 5:15 ....July 24
Matthew 5:19 ....September 13
Matthew 6:13 ....December 4
Matthew 6:19–21 ....September 23
Matthew 7:5 ....April 7
Matthew 8:2–3 ....September 21

Matthew 8:12 (KJV) ......October 31
Matthew 8:16–17 ....September 7
Matthew 10:8 ....July 20
Matthew 10:24–25 ....March 28
Matthew 11:12 ....October 18
Matthew 13:19 ....January 20
Matthew 14:15–16 ....January 29
Matthew 14:29–31 ....April 8
Matthew 19:29–30 ....March 10
Matthew 25:23 ....July 18
Matthew 26:30 ....January 22
Matthew 26:38 ....May 21
Mark 1:35–38 ....May 11
Mark 3:4–5 ....September 26
Mark 4:31–32 ....June 22
Mark 9:15 ....January 27
Mark 14:6, 8–9 ....November 24
Mark 14:65 ....March 29
Luke 2:12 ....December 25
Luke 2:13–14 (NKJV) ..December 15
Luke 4:29 ....November 15
Luke 4:33–35 ....January 23
Luke 4:38 ....July 13
Luke 7:38 ....March 2
Luke 10:18 ....May 19
Luke 10:40 ....November 3
Luke 11:34 ....July 9
Luke 15:20 (KJV) ....April 5
Luke 15:31 ....January 9
Luke 17:12–18 ....June 3
Luke 17:33 ....March 10
Luke 19:10 ....October 6
Luke 19:17 ....August 12
John 3:16 ....September 3
John 3:16 ....September 4
John 3:16–18 ....August 16
John 3:36 ....March 3
John 5:1–6 ....July 30
John 10:3–4 ....December 28
John 10:10 ....June 12
John 10:10
    (The Message) ....November 8
John 11:35 ....July 7
John 13:5 ....May 15
John 14:13–14 ....December 2
John 14:15, 24 ....February 3

John 15:5 ....July 12
John 15:5, 8 ....June 11
John 15:8 ....September 25
John 15:11 ....February 7
John 15:11 ....December 24
John 15:15 ....July 10
John 16:33 (KJV) ....December 1
John 17:11 ....October 9
John 18:11 ....April 4
John 18:15–17 ....April 18
John 19:17–18 ....March 27
John 20:19–20 ....April 19
John 20:26 ....April 10
John 20:29 ....August 26
Acts 4:29 ....July 31
Acts 8:30–31 ....March 25
Acts 16:25 ....May 25
Acts 17:28 ....March 8
Romans 2:5 ....August 6
Romans 3:9–13, 18,
    20–22 ....December 7
Romans 3:10–12 ....March 17
Romans 5:3 ....April 28
Romans 6:23 ....September 9
Romans 8:28–29 ....February 5
Romans 13:11 ....November 21
Romans 14:7 ....January 28
Romans 15:5 ....February 14
Romans 15:13 ....September 30
1 Corinthians 1:18 ....May 13
1 Corinthians 2:9
    (NKJV) ....January 1
1 Corinthians 2:9 ....February 24
1 Corinthians 3:8 ....May 12
1 Corinthians 8:6 ....August 23
1 Corinthians 9:22
    (NLT) ....August 30
1 Corinthians 10:12 ....April 21
1 Corinthians 10:13 ....January 31
1 Corinthians 10:31 ....March 16
1 Corinthians 12:24–25 October 28
1 Corinthians 12:24–26 January 17
1 Corinthians 12:27 ....June 23
1 Corinthians 13:12
    (NASB) ....February 29
1 Corinthians 14:15–16 May 29

1 Corinthians 15:55–57 June 25
1 Corinthians 15:58.......December 13
2 Corinthians 1:5–7......December 17
2 Corinthians 2:14–15..October 12
2 Corinthians 3:5–6......March 31
2 Corinthians 3:18.........June 10
2 Corinthians 4:7..........August 20
2 Corinthians 4:10–12..April 3
2 Corinthians 4:16.........January 7
2 Corinthians 4:17.........February 1
2 Corinthians 5:9..........April 13
2 Corinthians 5:14.........September 18
2 Corinthians 5:17.........March 1
2 Corinthians 5:21.........August 25
2 Corinthians 6:2..........October 17
2 Corinthians 10:4.........September 8
2 Corinthians 10:12
    (RSV) ....September 6
2 Corinthians 12:7.........May 31
2 Corinthians 12:8–9....February 17
2 Corinthians 12:10.......February 18
2 Corinthians 12:10.......July 11
2 Corinthians 13:4.........November 22
Galatians 2:20...............February 20
Galatians 3:27...............October 20
Galatians 5:22–23.........February 10
Galatians 6:2.................April 26
Ephesians 1:11..............July 19
Ephesians 1:11..............November 30
Ephesians 1:11–12........July 4
Ephesians 2:1................December 3
Ephesians 2:3–5...........March 4
Ephesians 2:14–16.......November 5
Ephesians 3:10..............September 17
Ephesians 3:10–11........June 1
Ephesians 5:2................March 24
Ephesians 5:15–17........July 5
Ephesians 5:19–20........November 19
Ephesians 5:31–33........July 2
Ephesians 6:7–8............August 18
Ephesians 6:16..............September 11
Philippians 1:1–5;
    12–13 ....May 3
Philippians 1:12–14......January 8
Philippians 1:21–24......December 16
Philippians 1:29............March 6

Philippians 2:3–5..........November 9
Philippians 2:5 (KJV).....November 6
Philippians 2:5–9..........October 23
Philippians 2:9–11........September 29
Philippians 2:12–15......February 8
Philippians 2:14–15......May 9
Philippians 3:4–8.........September 5
Philippians 3:12............August 24
Philippians 3:13–14
    (TLB) ....June 30
Philippians 3:17–18......June 26
Philippians 4:1.............July 27
Philippians 4:1–3..........February 2
Philippians 4:4.............May 8
Philippians 4:11............October 3
Philippians 4:11–12......October 16
Colossians 1:4–5..........June 28
Colossians 1:17.............April 1
Colossians 2:13–15.......November 1
Colossians 3:2...............May 5
Colossians 3:5–6..........June 20
Colossians 3:23–24.......July 14
Colossians 4:5–6
    (NASB)....................April 27
Colossians 4:5–6
    (NLT) ....December 10
1 Thessalonians 2:13......December 9
1 Timothy 1:5–6..........August 11
2 Timothy 2:11–13.......December 30
2 Timothy 2:22 (ESV)...October 29
2 Timothy 3:16–17.......April 16
2 Timothy 4:2 (NLT).....October 30
2 Timothy 4:6–7,
    9–11 ....November 29
Titus 2:13–14 (KJV).....August 1
Hebrews 2:10 (KJV)......September 19
Hebrews 2:14.................October 11
Hebrews 3:13.................February 12
Hebrews 4:12–13.........June 21
Hebrews 4:13.................March 23
Hebrews 7:25.................June 27
Hebrews 10:24..............August 19
Hebrews 11:32–34,
    38 ....June 29
Hebrews 12:2–3............March 9
Hebrews 12:10–11........May 16

Hebrews 12:12 – 13 ....May 26
Hebrews 12:15 ....April 20
Hebrews 13:5 – 6 ....February 25
James 1:2 – 4 ....November 12
James 2:5 ....April 29
James 4:10 (NLT) ....May 27
1 Peter 1:1
    (The Message)...........February 4
1 Peter 1:6 – 7 ....August 22
1 Peter 1:6 – 7 ....November 10
1 Peter 1:22 ....January 18
1 Peter 2:4 – 6 ....February 11
1 Peter 2:9 ....May 28
1 Peter 2:11 – 12 ....January 10
1 Peter 2:21 ....June 13
1 Peter 2:24 ....March 21
1 Peter 5:5 ....October 2

2 Peter 1:3 ....March 26
2 Peter 1:5 – 7, 10 ....April 14
2 Peter 3:9 – 11, 15 ....August 7
1 John 3:16 ....June 14
1 John 3:22 (KJV)..........December 5
1 John 4:4 (NASB) ....January 3
1 John 4:16 ....February 13
Jude vv. 22 – 23 ....August 17
Revelation 1:7 ....December 26
Revelation 1:15 ....January 12
Revelation 1:16 – 17 ....October 14
Revelation 3:19 ....February 28
Revelation 3:20 ....December 18
Revelation 5:5 ....December 31
Revelation 5:12 ....July 8
Revelation 11:17 (KJV)...April 23
Revelation 22:17 ....December 29